Advanced Information and Knowledge Processing

Series Editors
Lakhmi C. Jain
University of Canberra and University of South Australia

Xindong Wu
University of Vermont

Information systems and intelligent knowledge processing are playing an increasing role in business, science and technology. Recently, advanced information systems have evolved to facilitate the co-evolution of human and information networks within communities. These advanced information systems use various paradigms including artificial intelligence, knowledge management, and neural science as well as conventional information processing paradigms. The aim of this series is to publish books on new designs and applications of advanced information and knowledge processing paradigms in areas including but not limited to aviation, business, security, education, engineering, health, management, and science. Books in the series should have a strong focus on information processing - preferably combined with, or extended by, new results from adjacent sciences. Proposals for research monographs, reference books, coherently integrated multi-author edited books, and handbooks will be considered for the series and each proposal will be reviewed by the Series Editors, with additional reviews from the editorial board and independent reviewers where appropriate. Titles published within the Advanced Information and Knowledge Processing series are included in Thomson Reuters' Book Citation Index.

More information about this series at http://www.springer.com/series/4738

Peter Lake • Robert Drake

Information Systems Management in the Big Data Era

Peter Lake
Sheffield Hallam University
Sheffield, UK

Robert Drake
Sheffield Hallam University
Sheffield, UK

ISSN 1610-3947
Advanced Information and Knowledge Processing
ISBN 978-3-319-13502-1   ISBN 978-3-319-13503-8 (eBook)
DOI 10.1007/978-3-319-13503-8

Library of Congress Control Number: 2014958029

Springer Cham Heidelberg New York Dordrecht London
© Springer International Publishing Switzerland 2014
This work is subject to copyright. All rights are reserved by the Publisher, whether the whole or part of the material is concerned, specifically the rights of translation, reprinting, reuse of illustrations, recitation, broadcasting, reproduction on microfilms or in any other physical way, and transmission or information storage and retrieval, electronic adaptation, computer software, or by similar or dissimilar methodology now known or hereafter developed.
The use of general descriptive names, registered names, trademarks, service marks, etc. in this publication does not imply, even in the absence of a specific statement, that such names are exempt from the relevant protective laws and regulations and therefore free for general use.
The publisher, the authors and the editors are safe to assume that the advice and information in this book are believed to be true and accurate at the date of publication. Neither the publisher nor the authors or the editors give a warranty, express or implied, with respect to the material contained herein or for any errors or omissions that may have been made.

Printed on acid-free paper

Springer International Publishing AG Switzerland is part of Springer Science+Business Media (www.springer.com)

*For the never ending support and
encouragement from Julia and my Dad,
I am extremely grateful.*
                                        Peter Lake

*For my wife Amelia and daughters Sarah
and Charlotte, thank you for your love,
patience and support.*
                                        Robert Drake

Foreword

You would be forgiven for thinking that Big Data was all about the technology – Databases, NoSQL, Map Reduce, machine learning – but as the hype continues, and application vendors sell their wares, it is innovative leaders who understand that it is about the business rather than just tech.

It is about how we realise value, how we shape our outlook, how we integrate people and systems, and how we can govern our enquiry and operations.

There are some core skills that the emerging role of Data Scientist requires – but as an occupation that needs to bridge the chasm between business and Information Technology, it is more than being conversant with normal distributions and paired-t tests. Data Scientists need to understand the business opportunities afforded by Big Data, but they also have to spot the false-positives. We may have more data at our fingertips then ever before, but if we use the wrong data, our predictions may bring undesirable consequences for our decision-making. In a knowledge economy, this could be disastrous.

Both authors are well-placed to offer their insight into the incorporation of IT into business operations, and this book exemplifies the combination of theory, critical evaluation and real-world experience. Being at the leading-edge of technology is one thing, but it is more likely that prior knowledge of the potential barriers towards implementation will help you succeed in your endeavours.

Organisations often start out with a 'Big Data project', which can rapidly turn into 'another IT project'. Success lies within the people and the systems they interact with, and leadership and management of the necessary change required is a topic that receives its due coverage in this book. This book does not avoid the technology, but it does place it firmly in the context of doing business.

If you are thinking about what Big Data can do for you, planning for the opportunities it can present, or you just need to understand what the fuss is all about, then this book is for you. If your background is business, then you will find sufficient technology-speak to put you significantly ahead of the rest. Similarly, if you understand the technology, but are not sure how to realise the business value, then read on. Good luck on your Big Data journey.

Computing and Mathematics　　　　　　　　　　　　　　　　　　　　　Richard Hill
University of Derby
Derby, UK

Preface

Overview and Goals

This book will explain, using examples, both business and technical issues around the management of information systems in the era of Big Data and beyond. Using examples, this book will explain business and technical issues around the management of information systems in the era of Big Data and beyond. A synthesis of business and technology theory and practice. A synthesis of business and technology theory and practice, the structure is largely built around an enhanced version of the 7-S management model (Waterman et al. 1980).

Designed from the start to support a module on modern information systems, this book is suitable for students with either a management or technology focus, providing a broad discussion of the key elements in modern information systems.

Those coming to Big Data for the first time but not studying on a university course will also find this text of use as it starts from first principles and place Data Science in the context of how it can be used in business.

Key objectives for this book are to:

- Explore the potential use of a variety of Big Data tools and techniques in a business environment whilst explaining how these newer techniques can fit within an organisation's information systems strategy
- Review existing information systems theories and practices and explore their continued relevance in the era of Big Data
- Present an understanding of the key technologies involved in information systems in general and Big Data in particular, and place those technologies in a historic context
- Point out areas for further research in a fast moving domain
- Equip readers with an understanding of the important aspects of a data scientist's job
- Provide some hands-on experience to further assist in the understanding of the technologies involved

Suggested Uses

This book can be used as a solid introduction to the concept of information systems in general, as well as of Big Data in particular. The book is suitable as both a comprehensive introduction as well as a reference text as the reader develops their skills and abilities through application of the ideas. For *University Instructors* we have followed the common 12-week semester pattern, deliberately allowing the tutor to use a chapter per week.

Each chapter concludes with a set of review questions that make specific reference to the content presented in the chapter, plus an additional set of further questions that will require further research. The review questions are designed in such a way that the reader will be able to tackle them based on the chapter contents. They are followed by discussion questions, which often require research, extended reading of other material or discussion and collaboration. These can be used as classroom discussion topics by tutors or used as the basis of summative assignments.

Sheffield, UK
Peter Lake
Robert Drake

Reference

Waterman RH, Peters TJ, Phillips JR (1980) Structure is not organization. Bus Horiz 23(3):14–26

Contents

1 Introducing Big Data 1
   1.1   What the Reader Will Learn 1
   1.2   Big Data: So What Is All the Fuss About? 1
         1.2.1   Defining "Big Data" 2
         1.2.2   Big Data: Behind the Hype 3
         1.2.3   Google and a Case of the Flu 6
   1.3   Big Data: The Backlash Begins 6
         1.3.1   Big Data Catches a Cold 6
         1.3.2   It's My Data – So What's in It for Me? 8
         1.3.3   Bucking the Backlash – The Hype Cycle 9
   1.4   A Model for Big Data 11
         1.4.1   Strategy 12
         1.4.2   Structure 13
         1.4.3   Style 13
         1.4.4   Staff 13
         1.4.5   Statistical Thinking 14
         1.4.6   Synthesis 14
         1.4.7   Systems 15
         1.4.8   Sources 15
         1.4.9   Security 16
   1.5   Summary 16
   1.6   Review Questions 16
   1.7   Group Work/Research Activity 17
         1.7.1   Discussion Topic 1 17
         1.7.2   Discussion Topic 2 17
   References 17

2 Strategy 19
   2.1   What the Reader Will Learn 19
   2.2   Introduction 19
   2.3   What is Strategy? 20
   2.4   Strategy and 'Big Data' 22

	2.5	Strategic Analysis	26
		2.5.1	Analysing the Business Environment	26
		2.5.2	Strategic Capability – The Value Chain	32
		2.5.3	The SWOT 'Analysis'	38
	2.6	Strategic Choice	43
		2.6.1	Introduction	43
		2.6.2	Type, Direction and Criteria of Strategic Development	44
		2.6.3	Aligning Business and IT/IS Strategy	47
	2.7	Summary	51
	2.8	Review Questions	51
	2.9	Group Work Research Activities	51
		2.9.1	Discussion Topic 1	51
		2.9.2	Discussion Topic 2	51
	References	52
3	**Structure**	53
	3.1	What the Reader Will Learn	53
	3.2	Introduction	53
	3.3	What Is 'Structure'?	55
		3.3.1	What Do We Mean by 'Structure'?	55
	3.4	Formal Structures	56
		3.4.1	The "Organisational Chart": What Does It Tell Us?	56
		3.4.2	Structure, Systems and Processes	61
		3.4.3	Formal Structure: What Does This Mean for Big Data?	65
		3.4.4	Information Politics	66
	3.5	Organisational Culture: The Informal Structure	69
		3.5.1	What Do We Mean by 'Culture'?	69
		3.5.2	Culture and Leadership	69
		3.5.3	The "Cultural Web"	71
	3.6	Summary	78
	3.7	Review Questions	78
	3.8	Group Work/Research Activity	78
		3.8.1	Discussion Topic 1	78
		3.8.2	Discussion Topic 2	79
	References	79
4	**Style**	81
	4.1	What the Reader Will Learn	81
	4.2	Introduction	81
	4.3	Management in the Big Data Era	82
		4.3.1	Management or Leadership?	82
		4.3.2	What Is 'Management'?	83
		4.3.3	Styles of Management	86
		4.3.4	Sources of Managerial Power	87

	4.4	The Challenges of Big Data (the Four Ds)	90
		4.4.1 Data Literacy	90
		4.4.2 Domain Knowledge	92
		4.4.3 Decision-Making	93
		4.4.4 Data Scientists	96
		4.4.5 The Leadership Imperative	98
	4.5	Summary	99
	4.6	Review Questions	100
	4.7	Group Work/Research Activity	100
		4.7.1 Discussion Topic 1	100
		4.7.2 Discussion Topic 2	100
	References		100
5	**Staff**		103
	5.1	What the Reader Will Learn	103
	5.2	Introduction	103
	5.3	Data Scientists: The Myth of the 'Super Quant'	104
		5.3.1 What's in a Name?	104
		5.3.2 Data "Science" and Data "Scientists"	105
		5.3.3 We've Been Here Before…	110
	5.4	It Takes a Team…	111
		5.4.1 What Do We Mean by "a Team"?	111
		5.4.2 Building High-Performance Teams	113
	5.5	Team Building as an Organisational Competency	117
	5.6	Summary	121
	5.7	Review Questions	121
	5.8	Group Work/Research Activity	122
		5.8.1 Discussion Topic 1	122
		5.8.2 Discussion Topic 2	122
	References		122
6	**Statistical Thinking**		125
	6.1	What the Reader Will Learn	125
	6.2	Introduction: Statistics Without Mathematics	125
	6.3	Does "Big Data" Mean "Big Knowledge"?	126
		6.3.1 The DIKW Hierarchy	127
		6.3.2 The Agent-in-the-World	128
	6.4	Statistical Thinking – Introducing System 1 and System 2	129
		6.4.1 Short Circuiting Rationality	132
	6.5	Causality, Correlation and Conclusions	133
	6.6	Randomness, Uncertainty and the Search for Meaning	135
		6.6.1 Sampling, Probability and the Law of Small Numbers	137
	6.7	Biases, Heuristics and Their Implications for Judgement	138
		6.7.1 Non-heuristic Biases	142

6.8	Summary		144
6.9	Review Questions		144
6.10	Group Work Research Activities		145
	6.10.1	Discussion Topic 1 – The Linda Problem	145
	6.10.2	Discussion Topic 2 – The Birthday Paradox	145
References			146

7 Synthesis 147
- 7.1 What the Reader Will Learn 147
- 7.2 From Strategy to Successful Information Systems 147
  - 7.2.1 The Role of the Chief Information Officer (CIO) 148
  - 7.2.2 Management of IS Projects 149
- 7.3 Creating Requirements That Lead to Successful Information Systems 151
- 7.4 Stakeholder Buy-In 154
- 7.5 How Do We Measure Success 155
- 7.6 Managing Change 156
- 7.7 Cost Benefits and Total Cost of Ownership 158
  - 7.7.1 Open Source 158
  - 7.7.2 Off the Shelf vs Bespoke 159
  - 7.7.3 Gauging Benefits 160
- 7.8 Insourcing or Outsourcing? 161
- 7.9 The Effect of Cloud 163
- 7.10 Implementing 'Big Data' 164
- 7.11 Summary 165
- 7.12 Review Questions 166
- 7.13 Group Work Research Activities 166
  - 7.13.1 Discussion Topic 1 166
  - 7.13.2 Discussion Topic 2 166
- References 166

8 Systems 169
- 8.1 What the Reader Will Learn 169
- 8.2 What Does Big Data Mean for Information Systems? 169
- 8.3 Data Storage and Database Management Systems 170
  - 8.3.1 Database Management Systems 172
  - 8.3.2 Key-Value Databases 173
  - 8.3.3 Online Transactional Processing (OLTP) 173
  - 8.3.4 Decision Support Systems (DSS) 175
  - 8.3.5 Column-Based Databases 176
  - 8.3.6 In Memory Systems 176
- 8.4 What a DBA Worries About 177
  - 8.4.1 Scalability 177
  - 8.4.2 Performance 178
  - 8.4.3 Availability 179

		8.4.4	Data Migration	179
		8.4.5	Not All Systems Are Data Intensive	182
		8.4.6	And There Is More to Data than Storage	183
	8.5	Open Source	183
	8.6	Application Packages	184
		8.6.1	Open Source vs Vendor Supplied?	186
	8.7	The Cloud and Big Data	187
	8.8	Hadoop and NoSQL	189
	8.9	Summary	190
	8.10	Review Questions	190
	8.11	Group Work Research Activities	191
		8.11.1	Discussion Topic 1	191
		8.11.2	Discussion Topic 2	191
	References	191

9 Sources ... 193

	9.1	What the Reader Will Learn	193
	9.2	Data Sources for Data – Both Big and Small	193
	9.3	The Four Vs – Understanding What Makes Data Big Data	194
	9.4	Categories of Data	196
		9.4.1 Classification by Purpose	196
		9.4.2 Data Type Classification and Serialisation Alternatives	198
	9.5	Data Quality	202
		9.5.1 Extract, Transform and Load (ETL)	205
	9.6	Meta Data	206
		9.6.1 Internet of Things (IoT)	206
	9.7	Data Ownership	209
	9.8	Crowdsourcing	210
	9.9	Summary	212
	9.10	Review Questions	212
	9.11	Group Work Research Activities	212
		9.11.1 Discussion Topic 1	213
		9.11.2 Discussion Topic 2	213
	References		213

10 IS Security ... 215

	10.1	What the Reader Will Learn	215
	10.2	What This Chapter Could Contain but Doesn't	215
	10.3	Understanding the Risks	216
		10.3.1 What Is the Scale of the Problem?	216
	10.4	Privacy, Ethics and Governance	218
		10.4.1 The Ethical Dimension of Security	218
		10.4.2 Data Protection	221

10.5	Securing Systems		224
	10.5.1	Hacking	224
	10.5.2	Denial of Service	225
	10.5.3	Denial of Service Defence Mechanisms	226
	10.5.4	Viruses and Worms and Trojan Horses (Often Collectively Referred to as Malware)	227
	10.5.5	Spyware	228
	10.5.6	Defences Against Malicious Attacks	228
10.6	Securing Data		230
	10.6.1	Application Access Control	233
	10.6.2	Physical Security	234
	10.6.3	Malicious Insiders and Careless Employees	235
10.7	Does Big Data Make for More Vulnerability?		235
10.8	Summary		235
10.9	Review Questions		236
10.10	Group Work Research Activities		236
	10.10.1	Discussion Topic 1	236
	10.10.2	Discussion Topic 2	236
References			237

11	**Technical Insights**			239
	11.1	What the Reader Will Learn		239
	11.2	What You Will Need for This Chapter		239
	11.3	Hands-on with Hadoop		240
		11.3.1	The Sandbox	240
		11.3.2	Hive	248
		11.3.3	Pig	251
		11.3.4	Sharing Your Data with the Outside World	256
		11.3.5	Visualization	258
		11.3.6	Life Is Usually More Complicated!	261
	11.4	Hadoop Is Not the Only NoSQL Game in Town!		262
	11.5	Summary		263
	11.6	Review Questions		263
	11.7	Extending the Tutorial Activities		263
		11.7.1	Extra Question 1	263
		11.7.2	Extra Question 2	264
		11.7.3	Extra Question 3	264
	11.8	Hints for the Extra Questions		264
	11.9	Answer for Extra Questions		264
		11.9.1	Question 1	264
		11.9.2	Question 2	265
		11.9.3	Question 3	265
	Reference			266

12	**The Future of IS in the Era of Big Data**		267
	12.1	What the Reader Will Learn	267
	12.2	The Difficulty of Future Gazing with IT	267
	12.3	The Doubts	268
	12.4	The Future of Information Systems (IS)	269
		12.4.1 Making Decisions About Technology	271
	12.5	So What Will Happen in the Future?	275
		12.5.1 The Future for Big Data	275
		12.5.2 Ethics of Big Data	279
		12.5.3 Big Data and Business Intelligence	280
		12.5.4 The Future for Data Scientists	281
		12.5.5 The Future for IS Management	282
		12.5.6 Keeping Your Eye on the Game	285
	12.6	Summary	286
	12.7	Review Questions	286
	12.8	Group Work Research Activities	287
		12.8.1 Discussion Topic 1	287
		12.8.2 Discussion Topic 2	287
	References		287
Index			**289**

Introducing Big Data

1.1 What the Reader Will Learn

- That the term big data is poorly defined and may mean different things to different people/companies depending upon their viewpoint
- That three of the main technological drivers of big data are cheaper, larger data storage, more efficient data compression and fast computing speeds
- That big data reached the peak of the "hype cycle" towards the end of 2013, carried by overly inflated expectations – followed by a growing sense of disillusionment in 2014 as some early trials ended in highly publicised failure and media interest waned
- That, despite the hype cycle, big data will, ultimately, result in major changes to both social and business life – though this change may takes decades to complete
- That aspects of big data can be represented, and explored, holistically using the 9S-framework

1.2 Big Data: So What Is All the Fuss About?

At what point in time does a concept, a term, a technology move from being a peripheral idea into mainstream thought? And how is that transition noted? For big data that point could have been the year 2012. In that year big data was a featured topic at the World Economic Forum in Davos, Switzerland (World Economic Forum 2012) and the US Federal government announced $200 million research funding for big data projects. That same year The New York Times included headlines such as, "The Age of Big Data" and "Big Data on Campus" and Stamford University informed us, "How Big Data is Going to Change Entrepreneurship". The October issue of the Harvard Business Review was almost completely dedicated to big data with articles such as, "Big Data: The management revolution", "Data Scientist: Thewsexiest job of the twenty-first century", "Making analytics work for you" and "The true measures of success". However, perhaps it is only when techno-geek cartoonist Dilbert puts pen to paper can a technology truly be said to have arrived (http://dilbert.com/strips/comic/2012-07-29/).

1.2.1 Defining "Big Data"

The chances are that, given you are reading this book, you are interested in, and perhaps know something about, "Big Data". So, what do we mean by "Big Data"? How do we define it? Try writing a definition before you progress to the next paragraph. Here's another question to get you thinking: "Why are YOU interested in Big Data?" Perhaps your curiosity has been sparked by one or more of the many headlines in the business and IT press? Perhaps you work for a company that is 'doing' (or is planning to 'do') Big Data and want to know more? Perhaps you are a technical person looking to ride the next technological 'wave', or perhaps you are an executive/manager trying to find out what all the Big Data fuss is about? Whatever your route to Big Data, this book offers a holistic view of the topic encompassing both the business and technological aspects of the subject.

So, what is your definition of Big Data? It might include something about the size of data sets, the structure of data (or lack of it!), the complexity of the data and the speed of data processing. Actually, there is no universally accepted definition. Here are just a few to consider:

- *Big data is high-volume, high-velocity and high-variety information assets that demand cost-effective, innovative forms of information processing for enhanced insight and decision making* (Gartner 2013)
- Big data is the term increasingly used to describe the process of applying serious computing power—the latest in machine learning and artificial intelligence—to seriously massive and often highly complex sets of information. (Microsoft Corp 2013)
- *Big data refers to datasets whose size is beyond the ability of typical database software tools to capture, store, manage, and analyse* (McKinsey Global Institute 2011)
- Big Data refers to digital data volume, velocity and/or variety that enable novel approaches to frontier questions previously inaccessible or impractical using current or conventional methods; and/or exceed the capacity or capability of current or conventional methods and systems (National Institute of Standards and Technology 2013)

Oracle, the database provider, argues that the value of big data arises from the combination of new sources of unstructured data with relational database decision making (Oracle Corp 2013). Their definition is, unsurprisingly, based upon infrastructure and technologies but offers no quantification of what is (or is not) big data. On the contrary, Intel, the microprocessor manufacturer, defines big data based upon the experiences of its business partners who each generate, "a median of 300 terabytes of data per week" (Intel Corp 2012). Perhaps a less commercially-biased, and arguably more interesting, definition is given by the MIKE2.0 open-source project (Method for an Integrated Knowledge Environment), who suggest that, *"A good definition of big data is to describe "big" in terms of the number of useful permutations of sources making useful querying difficult (like the sensors in an aircraft) and complex interrelationships making purging difficult (as in toll road). Big then refers to big complexity rather than big volume. Of course, valuable and complex datasets of this sort naturally tend to grow rapidly and so big data quickly becomes truly massive"* (MIKE2.0 2013).

By synthesising these perspectives of big data, Ward and Barker (2013) developed the following definition which is, increasingly being taken as standard:

> Big data is a term describing the storage and analysis of large and/or complex data sets using a series of techniques including, but not limited to, NoSQL, MapReduce, and machine learning

1.2.2 Big Data: Behind the Hype

So what is driving big data?

- In the retail sector, Wal-Mart manages more than one million customer transactions every hour. These are added to databases that, in 2010, were estimated to hold more than 2.5 petabytes of data (we will examine how data is quantified in the next section of this chapter).
- In science, the Large Synoptic Survey Telescope (LSST), due to come on-line in 2016, is expected to acquire 140 terabytes of data every 5 days. Meanwhile, decoding the human genome requires the analysis of the three billion base-pairs, a task that took 10 years to achieve between 1993 and 2003, can now be done in less than a week.
- In business, IBM, Microsoft, Oracle and SAP have invested heavily (more than $15 billion by 2010) by buying software firms focusing on data handling and analytics. This is just part of global spending on big data initiatives that is forecasted grow at a compound rate of 30 % per year to reach $114.2 billion in 2018.

These examples, and much of the other hype surrounding big data, can be viewed through the lens of the big data three "Vs"; Volume (the amount of data available), Variety (the different types of data available e.g. structured, unstructured) and Velocity (the speed at which data can be collected, analysed and distributed). We will examine these aspects of data in later chapters, but behind these lie three technological trends that from a technical perspective, underpin big data. Namely;

- Data storage
- Data Compression
- Speed of computing

1.2.2.1 Storage

To get some sense of what is driving big data, let's start with some figures:

- As of 2013, the World Wide Web is estimated to have reached 4 zettabytes
- The volume of business data worldwide, across all companies, doubles every 1.2 years
- By 2020, business transactions on the internet will reach 450 billion per day
- Akamai, a provider of Cloud services to companies such as Audi, Nasa, BBC and Boeing, analyses 75 million events per day to better target advertisements
- Walmart, one of the world's leading retailers, handles more than one million customer transactions every hour. These are held in databases estimated to contain more than 2.5 petabytes of data
- YouTube users upload 48 h of new video every minute of the day
- On average 570 new websites are created every minute of every day
- 30 billion pieces of content are shared on Facebook every month, that equates to 100 terabytes of data uploaded every day
- In 2012, Twitter handled roughly 175 million tweets every day, and had more than 465 million accounts
- Finally….**data production will be 44 times greater in 2020 than it was in 2009**

It all sounds impressive, but what does it mean? Let's start by trying to understand the language and magnitude of units (Table 1.1).

Digitised information is stored as discrete "ones" and "zeros" (bits), usually in packs of eight called bytes. Using the binary numbering system an eight-bit byte can represent any number from 0 to 256 i.e. 2^8. Using the American Standard Code for Information Interchange (ASCII) a byte may represents a single character. For example:

- 00110001 – Represents the number 1
- 00110010 – Represents the number 2
- 00110011 – Represents the number 3
- 01000001 – Represents uppercase A
- 01000010 – Represents uppercase B
- 01000011 – Represents uppercase C

Table 1.1 Orders of magnitude of data

Value	Abbreviation	Metric
1,000	kB	kilobytes
$1,000^2$	MB	megabyte
$1,000^3$	GB	gigabyte
$1,000^4$	TB	terabyte
$1,000^5$	PB	petabyte
$1,000^6$	EB	exabyte
$1,000^7$	ZB	zettabyte
$1,000^8$	YB	yottabyte

- 01100001 – Represents lowercase a
- 01100010 – Represents lowercase b
- 01100011 – Represents lowercase c

So how big is a yottabyte compared to a byte? If one byte of information was represented by 1 cm^3 of water, 1 YB would be approximately equivalent to the volume of water contained in all of the seas on the planet. Assuming typical recording rates, digitised music requires, on average, 1.5 MB memory per minute of music recorded and digitised video (high definition movies) approximately 30 MB per minute of film and audio recorded (obviously these will vary depending upon length of song/film, quality of recording etc.) At this recording rate a 1 ZB drive would hold 68 million years of video and, assuming a video camera was able to capture the creation of the universe 13.7 billion years ago, a 1 YB drive would have the capacity to store video from the Big Bang to the present day and still have almost 78 % spare capacity. In 1986 digital storage represented just 1 % of our global technological 'memory' which, at that time, was less than 3 exabytes. By 2007 digital storage accounted for 97 % of that 'memory' which had expanded to 300 exabytes, roughly doubling every 3 years. As Hilbert (2012) notes:

> If we would have liked to store this [global memory] on double printed book paper, we could have covered every square centimetre of the world's landmasses with one sheet of paper in 1986, with one layer of books by 2007, and by 2010 with two layers of books

1.2.2.2 Data Compression

IBM introduced the first disk drive in 1956. This disk was capable of storing 2,000 bits per square inch, a measure known as areal density. Today disks have areal densities of 1 TB bits per square inch and are forecast to reach 1.8 Tb by 2016. Kryder's Law, as it is known, suggests that the density of hard drives increases by a factor of 1,000 every 10.5 years (doubling every 13 months – a rate rather faster than the better known Moore's Law). However, measuring the hardware capacity of technology, rather than actual information content, is only half of the story. Improved compression algorithms have also been a major driver of the growth in informational capacity. Using similar hardware in 2010 than 25 years earlier, Hilbert (2014) found that three times more information could be stored thanks to the increased efficiency of software compression algorithms. We examine data compression in greater detail in Chap. 8.

1.2.2.3 Speed of Computing

Crucially, computing power continues to grow faster than our appetite for data storage – up to three times as fast. Why is this so important? The limits of human cognition mean that without fast computing power the huge volumes of data generated and stored would quickly become unusable. Using computers to sift through the vast amounts of information is, at present, the only viable option we have to make sense of it all. In 1985 the Intel 386 microprocessor was capable of processing 9.9 million instructions per second (MIPS). By 2013, the Intel Core i7 4770k processor, using the Haswell processor architecture, was computing 128,000 MIPS.

1.2.3 Google and a Case of the Flu

So much for the technology, but one might be forgiven for asking, "So what? What does big data mean for me?" In short the answer is, a lot! In November 2008 the journal *Nature* published an article entitled, "Detecting influenza epidemics using search engine query data" by a team of data scientists (Ginsberg et al. 2009) working on the Google Flu Trends (GFT) project. The objective of GFT is to rapidly identify flu outbreaks to allow faster response and thus reduce the impact of a potential pandemic. The article authors concluded that;

> Harnessing the collective intelligence of millions of users, Google web search logs can provide one of the most timely, broad reaching influenza monitoring systems available today. While traditional systems require 1–2 weeks to gather and process surveillance data, our estimates are current each day

In their article the GFT team note that for the period 2007–2008 the correlation between GFT data and that of the U.S. Centres for Disease Control (CDC's) was 97 %. For many, the findings of this report were the ultimate 'proof' of the validity of big data. The results of Google Flu Trends were quickly weaved into the big data selling propositions of software vendors such as; EMC^2, IBM, Microsoft, Oracle, SAP etc. and consultancies such as; McKinsey & Co., PwC, KPMG and Accenture. In their self-styled 'Journal of high-performance business', Accenture note that, "*By externalizing this search insight into Google Flu Trends, the company has been able to change the game regarding disease prevention*" (Banerjee et al. 2011). Meanwhile, media companies such as Bloomberg and O'Reilly were quick to paraphrase Bill Gates' famous prophecy that, "…the internet changes everything" (Gates 1999), by announcing "Big Data changes everything" (Needham 2013; Bloomberg TV 2013). While Bill Gates prediction may have been proved right in the long term, within 18 months of his book being published the dot-com boom became the dot-com bust, something the big data pundits might, in hind-sight, have considered…

1.3 Big Data: The Backlash Begins

1.3.1 Big Data Catches a Cold

Deciding when a bull market turns bearish or a 'hot new thing' becomes yesterday's news is difficult to judge – except in hindsight. For big data the seeds were sown as early as 2009 when GFT completely missed the U.S. non-seasonal H1N1 influenza pandemic (Cook et al. 2011). As a consequence the GFT data scientists updated the algorithm but this didn't stop GFT repeatedly over-estimating the number of cases of flu (by a wide margin) from 2011 to 2013 (Lazer et al. 2014). However, the breaking point was, arguably, an article in the "Science" magazine in March 2014 entitled, "The Parable of Google Flu: Traps in Big data Analysis" (Lazer et al. 2014), where the authors criticised the transparency and replicability of GFT results:

> Even if one had access to all of Google's data, it would be impossible to replicate the analyses of the original paper from the information provided regarding the analysis… Oddly, the few search terms offered in the papers do not seem to be strongly related with either GFT or the CDC data — we surmise that the authors felt an unarticulated need to cloak the actual search terms identified… What is at stake is twofold. First, science is a cumulative endeavour, and to stand on the shoulders of giants requires that scientists be able to continually assess work on which they are building. Second, accumulation of knowledge requires fuel in the form of data… Google is a business, but it also holds in trust data on the desires, thoughts, and the connections of humanity. Making money "without doing evil" (paraphrasing Google's motto) is not enough when it is feasible to do so much good

This assault on, arguably, the most iconic and best known big data application was soon followed by others on the wider concepts of big data. The New York Times (NYT) identified what they described as, "Eight (no nine!) problems with big data" (Marcus and Davis 2014). The NYT article may have exaggerated the issues, but it's clear that big data faced a number of challenges:

- **Correlation versus causality**: In 2013 Mayer-Schonberger and Cukier noted, "*Causality won't be discarded, but it is being knocked off its pedestal as the primary fountain of meaning. Big data turbocharges non-causal analyses, often replacing causal investigations*". However, as we discuss in Chap. 6 (Statistical Thinking), many correlations such as murder rates with market share of Internet Explorer and occurrence of autism with sales of organic food (both genuine correlations) are not necessarily meaningful. In the search for 'quick wins' many data scientists (and big data authors!) believe we should 'let the data speak' and have been quick to sacrifice causality for correlation. Unfortunately, data are, inevitably, biased due to structure and how, when and why it was collected. Data scientists bring their own biases including the intent of the analysis and the suitability of the data to support that intent. This in addition to explicit assumptions such as the population the data set represents (is it a sample or the entire population? is it a random sample? etc.). As Rickert (2013) notes, "*The data never really speak for themselves. At best, they tell a plausible story for which they have been well-rehearsed*"
- **Limited robustness**: Big data results can be less robust than they initially seem. This can be unforeseen and unintentional such as Google Flu Trends where, as we saw earlier, patterns in data collected at one time may not apply to data collected at another. Web data may be consolidated in different ways with different purposes leading to skewed data sets and incorrect conclusions. Furthermore, search engine indexes, a common component of data gathering, can be deliberately manipulated (spamdexing, google bombing) by modifying HTML to increase the chance that a particular website will be placed close to the beginning of search engine results, or to influence the category to which the site is assigned
- **The echo-chamber effect**: In media, the echo chamber effect arises in a situation where information, ideas, or beliefs are amplified or reinforced by transmission and repetition inside an "enclosed" system, often drowning out different or

competing views. Big data sources utilising web data are particularly prone to this effect. People using web forums and communities often surround themselves with voices that echo similar opinions to their own. Dissenting opinions are ignored, marginalised or dismissed as 'trolls'. This has the effect of distorting what is then considered to be the general consensus. This theory of cognitive dissonance, how humans strive for internal consistency, is well-established. When we experience inconsistency (dissonance) we become psychologically distressed and will try to avoid and/or reduce the dissonance and achieve consonance (Festinger 1957). The implications for big data are clear – web data-sets, social media in particular, may be heavily biased and require significant interpretation before conclusions can be drawn

- **Correlations everywhere!**: Given sufficient sample size, a comparison of two random variables will, at some stage, exhibit what appears to be correlation, purely by chance. In Chap. 6 (Statistical thinking) we discuss the nature of randomness and the tendency of human cognition to identify 'patterns' in random data. In these instances correlations may appear to be statistically significant, but have no meaningful connection. For example:
  - Increasing ice cream consumption leads to more murders
  - Reducing the number of pirates increases global warming
  - Living in a poor country (defined by GDP) increases penis size
- **Quantification without qualification**: This could, arguably, be summarised as, "Ask a silly question, get a silly answer…" In the book, "Who's bigger? Where historical figures really rank" (Skiena and Ward 2013), the authors evaluated the 'significance' of historical figures using big data techniques. Their methodology drew upon Wikipedia, using PageRank, number of hits, article length and number of page edits to identify important historical persons. Factor analysis, a statistical method used to describe variability among observed, correlated variables, was used to abstract underlying factors. The authors found two independent factors which they described as 'gravitas', arising from analysis of PageRank and defined as achievement-based recognition, and 'celebrity', arising from analysis of hits, revisions and article length and defined as 'popular notions of reputation'. These factors were then summed to give an overall value of fame, thus:

$$FAME = GRAVITAS + CELEBRITY$$

This value of fame is then 'time-corrected' to give a figure of overall historical significance. Skiena and Ward's work offers a useful insight into the strengths and weaknesses of some big data methodologies. After all, what are we to make of the quantification of the subjective, of methodologies that rank Dr Seuss as the 17th most significant poet of all time?

1.3.2 It's My Data – So What's in It for Me?

Though recent months have seen criticism of the results of big data, the future may hold more important developments. Recent research (Ernst Young LLP 2013) suggests that 78 % of on-line consumers believe companies exploit their personal information to make more money. As a result, 55 % of consumers say they have become less willing to share that data. Ernst Young suggest that, *'Today's organisations are used to a "Golden Age" of anytime, anywhere, free-for-all access to customer data'*. Tomorrow's consumer backlash may mean an end to this Golden Age, as customers begin to ask, "So what's in it for me?" Ironically, as companies become increasingly reliant on customer-generated information as an important source of data for insight programmes, customers are beginning to distance themselves from the data collection process. However, evidence suggests that few businesses are responding to this backlash. In 2013, just 20 % of business leaders polled were concerned that consumers would begin to restrict data and only 16 % said they would consider incentivising consumers to gain access to their personal data (Ernst Young LLP 2013).

Separately, in May 2014 the European Court of Justice upheld a privacy test case against Google brought by Mario Costeja González. Costeja González had tried to secure the deletion of an auction notice of his repossessed home dating from 1998. He argued that the case, in which his house had been auctioned to recover his social security debts, had been resolved and should no longer be linked to him whenever his name was searched on Google. The court ruled that under existing EU data protection laws Google had to erase links to two pages on the website of La Vanguardia, a Catalonian newspaper, from the results found when Costeja González's name is put into the search engine. The judges explicitly stated that, in their view, the existing EU data protection directive already established a "right to be forgotten". Within 24 h, Google had received 12,000 requests to "be forgotten" – an average of seven requests per second. Professor Luciano Floridi, appointed by Google to determine how the company should comply with an EU court ruling, said the era of freely available information is now over in Europe (Harper and Owen 2014).

So, what are we to make of the right to be forgotten and the dilemma that matches freedom of information against the right to privacy? Who decides what information should be made available and what suppressed? Floridi, a professor of philosophy and the ethics of information at Oxford University, notes that:

> People would be screaming if a powerful company suddenly decided what information could be seen by what people, when and where…[but]…that is the consequence of this decision. A private company now has to decide what is in the public interest. (Harper and Owen 2014)

1.3.3 Bucking the Backlash – The Hype Cycle

So, is this the end for "big data"? The answer is both 'yes' and 'no', or, perhaps better stated, it is the end of the beginning of the big data era. Gartner's Hype Cycle, developed in 1995, was designed to give an overview of the relative maturity of technologies in a particular domain (Fenn and Raskino 2008). The hype cycle (Fig. 1.1) describes the typical evolution of an emerging technology from feverish hype, driven by media, technology vendors and consultants, inflated expectations,

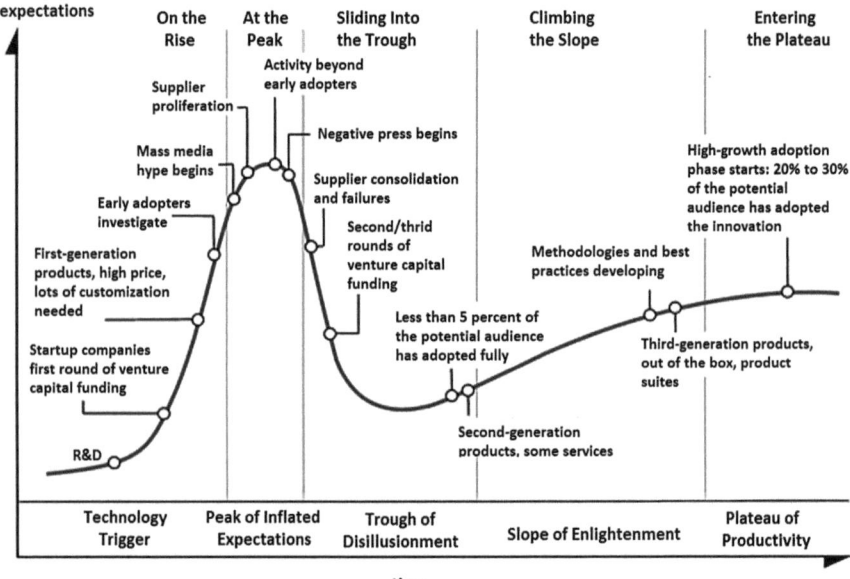

Fig. 1.1 Gartner's hype cycle (Fenn and Raskino 2008)

disillusionment, enlightenment and, finally, a plateau or productivity. Progression through the hype cycle occurs at different speeds for different technologies. Broadly these may be categorised as;

- **Fast-track technologies (2–4 years)**: Adopted with little fanfare, these technologies often bypass the Peak of Inflated Expectations and the Trough of Disillusionment (or pass through them so quickly that, historically it seems like they never occurred). An example might be Short Message Service (SMS). Fast-track technologies are typified by:
  - High value
  - Ease of use
  - Strong vendor support
  - Use of existing infrastructure
  - Fast transition from consumer to corporate use
- **Normal technologies (5–8 years)**:
- **Long-fuse technologies (10–20 years)**: Examples such as e-mail, the internet, biometrics, artificial intelligence, video-on-demand, quantum computing, and nanotechnology typify long-fuse technologies. Indicators include:
  - Science-fiction based expectations of the technology that far out-strips its capabilities in the short- to medium-term
  - Complexity that requires advances in science and engineering
  - Reliance on a new infrastructure (railways, telephones, fibre optics etc.)
  - Dependence upon skills that are unavailable or in short supply
  - Changes to business processes or business models

Only time will tell whether, "The Parable of Google Flu: Traps in Big Data Analysis" (Lazer et al. 2014), was the turning point, the peak of expectations, but much of the subsequent press regarding big data has been negative. However, even big data's detractors are careful to separate their criticisms of big data as hyped, and big data as a potential force for the future. As the Economist notes,

> Behind the big data backlash is the classic hype cycle, in which a technology's early proponents make overly grandiose claims, people sling arrows when those promises fall flat, but the technology eventually transforms the world, though not necessarily in the way that the pundits predicted (The Economist 2014)

What is certain is that never, in the whole of human history, have we had the ability to record so much data, so quickly from so many sources. Thanks to developments in both hardware and software, the technology to store, interrogate and analyse that data is improving rapidly. What remains is a simple question with profound implications; "What are we going to use it for?"

1.4 A Model for Big Data

Big data has many perspectives. Arguably, the two most discussed are the business perspective; how might big data change the way we do business? Is big data an opportunity or a threat? And the technology perspective; what impact will big data have on my IT infrastructure? Will big data require more/different resources than those already deployed? But how about the human resource perspective? What is a data scientist and why is it the sexiest job of the twenty-first century? Or a security perspective; what makes my company a suitable custodian for our customers personal data?

We believe that companies and managers need to view big data simultaneously from a number of closely related perspectives in order to have a holistic understanding of its impact (Fig. 1.2). The 9S-Framework or Big Data "Wheel" includes hard technological standpoints such as Security and Systems, but also softer, more managerial perceptions such as Style and Staff. Conversely, while many business observers have stressed that big data is not about technology. The 9S-framework addresses their concerns by balancing the role of technology with other perspectives of big data. However, we believe that, without technology as an enabler, big data would not be possible. Finally, at the centre of the wheel, at the hub, lies Statistical Thinking and it is this common perspective that permeates all the other aspects of big data.

We have used the 9S-framework to structure most of the chapters of this book, however, it would be a mistake to believe that each topic exists, or can be considered, in isolation. Strategy and structure are tightly related such that how a strategy is developed may be determined by how the organisation is structured and where the power lies. Conversely, most strategies result in some measure of change in organisational structure. Likewise, management styles are inextricably linked to the type of staff employed, as well as the structure and strategy of the organisation. As a result each chapter will refer to other chapters creating a web of interconnectedness.

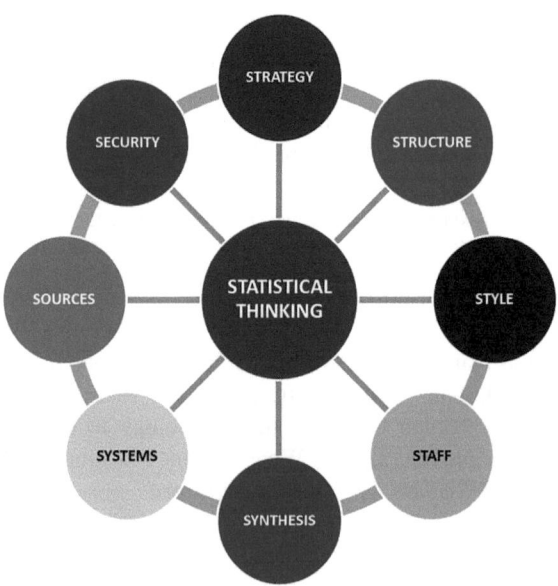

Fig. 1.2 The big data "Wheel"

You may choose to read the book chapter-by-chapter, bearing in mind the relationships between each aspect of the 9S-framework. Alternatively, you may choose to follow your own path by using the chapter 'signposts' which link similar topics.

1.4.1 Strategy

Search any bookstore, online or high street, and you will find a surplus of books on business strategy. Some are 'how to' recipe-style books, others are written by various captains of industry urging you to do it "my way". In this chapter we give an introductory view of strategy but focus primarily on the significance of big data for the traditional strategy development process and its potential to inspire new, information-driven strategies. Earlier we suggested that big data is defined by three attributes; Volume, Velocity and Variety, all of which have consequences for strategic analysis and strategic direction. The promise of detailed data granularity, extensive transparency and rapid information transfer makes innovative business models increasingly viable and offers unique dimensions of competitive advantage. However, integrating big data into cohesive corporate strategy requires a strong technical environment and accomplishing this, while maintaining strategic flexibility, presents a number of dilemmas. Accordingly, this chapter also examines the perennial challenge of aligning IT/IS strategy with business strategy and discuss some of the tools and techniques used to achieve this.

1.4.2 Structure

Structure, much like the 9S's framework we propose, comprises both 'hard' and 'soft' elements. Like an iceberg, the 'hard' elements of structure; the hierarchical chart, the job descriptions and spans of control, are easy to see in that they are explicit and, often, in the public domain. On the contrary, the 'soft' elements, those that make up the organisational culture, are often submerged beneath company routine, rituals, symbols and stories. Often it is these hidden elements of organisational structure that determine how a company 'works' and how it responds to change. Management can be thought of as a blend of five interrelated functions; commanding, controlling, coordinating, organising and planning and of these five functions, four are associated with organisational structure. But how is structure created? How does it evolve? And what are its implications for big data? In this chapter we examine the role of company founders on establishing and developing both formal and informal structure. We investigate how both the internal organisational environment and the wider business environment shape how a company responds to change. Finally, by reflecting on the failed enterprise resource planning (ERP) system implementations of the last 25 years, we examine what lessons can be learned for the roll-out of big data projects.

1.4.3 Style

Style is about *how* things are done. In this chapter we examine the process of management (that is, how management is 'done') and investigate the implications of big data for existing management styles. Today's managers view big data in one of three ways; some have anticipated the impact of big data and have positioned themselves (and their companies) for the opportunities; some recognise the threats that big data brings but have buried their heads in the sand and, finally, some see neither opportunity or threat and believe that the role of the manager in an era of big data will be unchanged. In this chapter we argue that big data disrupts the role of management in four ways; it requires that all staff, including managers, become data-literate, it questions existing notions of experience and expertise, it disrupts how decisions are made (an important lever of management control) and it defines the role and responsibilities of the data Scientist. Big data also affects the balance between 'management' and 'leadership' within an organisation. In this chapter we examine the difference between management and leadership, how the business environment shapes the balance between the two and why, arguably, leadership is more important than management for big data.

1.4.4 Staff

In this chapter we will examine how the demands of big data are changing the roles of staff and the skills required to fulfil those roles. We start by examining "the sexiest job of the twenty-first century", that of the Data Scientist. What, precisely, is a Data Scientists? What do they do? And where do they fit within the organisation? At first sight, the skills needed for Big Data are both broad and deep and individuals with this highly desirable skill set are already in huge demand. But do these 'Data Scientists' actually 'do' science? Does the company really want these employees to be 'scientists'? Perhaps, more importantly, do individuals with this huge set of skills actually exist? Taking a practical view of the big data skill shortage we argue that a more realistic approach may be to build data science teams. Consequently, we examine how teams are created, how they develop and how they are managed. Lastly, we argue that for big data to grow rapidly companies need to recruit and develop data science teams as part of a wider big data strategy.

1.4.5 Statistical Thinking

This chapter is devoted to 'statistical thinking' rather than to the formulae, equations and mathematics of statistics per se. How do we, as individual human beings, interpret data, process information and define knowledge? Why are our instincts, gut-feelings and hunches often irrational, illogical and sometimes lead to poor decision-making? In this chapter we investigate how our internal cognitive and perceptual filters assign data into meaningful categories, mould expectations and condition the characteristics that we adopt towards the world i.e. our knowledge. We will examine why statistical thinking is hard work, often counter-intuitive and requires a clear understanding of randomness, probability and correlation. We also explore our two, quite different, but inextricably linked cognitive systems; the first, a fast, emotional, automatic system, and the second, a slow, rational, lazy system. The first often responds to situations in an irrational or illogical way due to the bias-laden heuristics used to achieve lightening-speed reactions. Statistical thinking requires an acute awareness of these biases. In this chapter we investigate these biases as barriers to statistical thinking and examine how our emotional brain, in seeking to make sense of a complex world, misinterprets information and jumps to incorrect conclusions. That this chapter forms the hub of the 9S-framework should come as no surprise, after all statistical thinking is at the heart of Big Data.

1.4.6 Synthesis

In Chap. 2 (Strategy) we examined the strategy-making process in great detail but said little of how that strategy could be implemented. In this chapter we discuss some of the challenges of implementing strategy, with a particular focus on IS/IT strategy. We investigate the importance of the requirements-gathering process and examine some of the methodologies used to bring additional rigour to this process. We also consider the importance of change management and the role users play in actively promoting or resisting the implementation of a new system. In this chapter we consider some of the main reasons for project failure and what lessons can be learned from earlier project failures. We discuss why effective project management is imperative if the system roll-out is to be a success and what the terms 'success' and 'failure' mean in the context of information systems. For many executives success may be defined as built to specification and delivered on time and on budget. However, the measurement of system benefits is often an after-thought. We close the chapter with a discussion of benefits realisation and the impact of big data and the cloud on the concept of success.

1.4.7 Systems

In this chapter we explore different methods of storing data. While we touch on the ubiquitous Relational Database Management System (RDBMS), we also explore more exotic 'big data' storage systems such as Hadoop, Cassandra and MongoDb. We investigate how different systems support the use of data in different ways and contrast online transactional processing systems, decision support systems and column-based databases. In this chapter we also discuss the practical aspects of designing and maintaining such as scalability, performance, availability and data migration. We also contrast system costing including the open source versus proprietary software dilemma that faces many companies. Cloud computing in particular has transformed the cost of system ownership and increased the viability of open-source solutions, even for many wealthy companies. Consequently, we investigate both cloud computing and open-source tools such as Hadoop and NoSQL.

1.4.8 Sources

In this chapter we look specifically at the 'data' aspect of big data. Regardless of the volume, velocity, variety and veracity of the data (the big data four "V"s), it must be accessed, processed and stored – all of which offer their own unique challenges in a big data environment. Big data often draws upon a wide variety of different sources, usually in different systems and structures but, as we discuss in this chapter, there are some immutable characteristics of data regardless of how it is stored. To this end we explore a number of data classification alternatives. But what happens when the situation is reversed? When an organisation provides data to many individuals or sub-contractors and asks them to process the data? In this chapter we discuss the relatively new concept of Crowdsourcing and ask, "What is actually happening when organisations, in effect, outsource to many?" We also investigate the thorny issue of data quality, arguably data's most important attribute, and the one that, even today, absorbs the time of most data scientists (Kandel 2014). Lastly, this chapter examines the question of data ownership. Who owns your medical records or your bank statements? If you buy something online should the vendor have the right to sell your details to a third party? What about the 'right-to-be-forgotten'?

1.4.9 Security

The subject of IS Security covers a broad spectrum of issues that cannot be covered comprehensively in a single chapter. However, no book on big data would be complete without a recognition of the issues and some of the solutions. In practice, IS security is about balancing the business risks posed by a security failure and the cost of making a system secure. This chapter begins with risk assessment; what constitutes a security threat ? and what is the scale of those threats? We explore different aspects of hacking such as denial-of-service attacks, viruses, worms, Trojan Horses and the use of spyware. We also examine some of the counter-measures that are available to protect systems and data. In this chapter we also highlight the weakest link in the security 'chain'; people… Uncontrolled access to server rooms, unattended workstations left logged-on, lap-tops stolen from cars or left on trains and confidential files transmitted over coffee-shop wireless networks etc. Finally, recent developments such as wiki-leaks and the revelations of Edward Snowden have brought the issues of data privacy, ethics and governance to the public's attention. In this chapter we examine these issues and, more generally, the role of data protection and data protection legislation.

1.5 Summary

In this chapter we have attempted to define big data and to introduce some of the concepts that lie behind the promise that it holds. We have discussed the synthesis of technologies such as data storage, data compression and speed of computing that have led us to this technological and social watershed – and the inevitable media hype and commercial feeding-frenzy that goes with the "next big thing". As this book goes to print many early advocates of big data find themselves either questioning their initial enthusiasm or finding that their voices being drowned-out by the big data critics. In this chapter we have investigated this ebb and flow of over-exuberance and excessive negativity as a consequence of the "hype curve". Yet beyond this immediate boom-bust cycle, we believe that the analytic approach to business, enabled by data (expect the "big" to be a casualty of the hype cycle), will have far-reaching effects in the medium to long term. Consequently, we introduce the 9S-framework for big data. The 9S-framework allows a holistic view of data and analytics that encompasses soft and hard, technological and business-oriented aspects. The subsequent chapters of this book explore each facet of 9S-framework, though it is important to note that all are closely intertwined with subtle, sometimes contradictory relationships.

1.6 Review Questions

- How do Ward and Barker (2013) define big data?
- Big data is built upon three converging technological trends – what are they?

- "As of 2013, the World-Wide Web is estimated to have reached 4 zettabytes" – what is a zettabyte?
- What are the stages of the hype curve?
- What are the elements of the 9S-framework?

1.7 Group Work/Research Activity

1.7.1 Discussion Topic 1

In "The Parable of Google Flu: Traps in Big data Analysis" (Lazer et al. 2014), the authors state:

> What is at stake is twofold. First, science is a cumulative endeavour, and to stand on the shoulders of giants requires that scientists be able to continually assess work on which they are building. Sec3ond, accumulation of knowledge requires fuel in the form of data… Google is a business, but it also holds in trust data on the desires, thoughts, and the connections of humanity. Making money "without doing evil" (paraphrasing Google's motto) is not enough when it is feasible to do so much good

Should big data, as done by Google, be expected to meet the same criteria of the scientific method as other scientific research? How might, "*making money 'without doing evil'*" compromise the scientific credentials of big data?

1.7.2 Discussion Topic 2

Progression through the hype cycle occurs at different speeds; fast track, normal and long-fuse technologies. Which of these best describes big data? What are the main barriers to adoption?

References

Banerjee S, Bolze J, McNamara JM, O'Reilly KT (2011) How big data can fuel bigger growth. Retrieved May 20, 2014, from www.accenture.com/SiteCollectionDocuments/PDF/Accenture-Outlook-How-Big-Data-can-fuel-bigger-growth-Strategy.pdf

Bloomberg TV (2013) How big data changes everything in everyday life. Retrieved June 9, 2014, from www.bloomberg.com/video/how-big-data-changes-everything-in-everyday-life-ri~RvDHQQKKEH9uheW1nVA.html

Cook S, Conrad C, Fowlkes AL, Mohebbi MH (2011) Assessing Google Flu trends performance in the United States during the 2009 influenza virus a (H1N1) pandemic. PLoS One 6(8):e23610

Ernst Young LLP (2013) The big data backlash. Retrieved June 4, 2014, from www.ey.com/Publication/vwLUAssets/EY-The-Big-Data-Backlash/$FILE/EY-The-Big-Data-Backlash.pdf

Fenn J, Raskino M (2008) Mastering the hype cycle. Harvard Business, Cambridge

Festinger L (1957) A theory of cognitive dissonance. Stanford University Press, Stanford

Gartner (2013) IT glossary: big data. Retrieved May 14, 2014, from http://www.gartner.com/it-glossary/big-data/

Gates B (1999) Business @ the speed of thought. Warner Books, New York

Ginsberg J, Mohebbi MH, Patel RS, Brammer L, Smolinski MS, Brilliant L (2009) Detecting influenza epidemics using search engine query data. Nature 457:1012–1014

Harper T, Owen J (2014) Google privacy law 'means total rethink of basic freedoms'. Retrieved June 4, 2014, from www.independent.co.uk/life-style/gadgets-and-tech/news/google-privacy-law-means-total-rethink-of-basic-freedoms-9463694.html

Hilbert M (2012) How much information is there in the "information society"? Significance 9(4):8–12

Hilbert M (2014) What is the content of the world's technologically mediated information and communication capacity: how much text, image, audio, and video? Inf Soc Int J 30(2):127–143

Intel Corp (2012) Intel peer research on big data analysis. Retrieved May 15, 2014, from http://www.intel.com/content/www/us/en/big-data/data-insights-peer-research-report.html

Kandel S (2014) HBR blog network: the sexiest job of the 21st century is tedious, and that needs to change. Retrieved June 7, 2014, from http://blogs.hbr.org/2014/04/the-sexiest-job-of-the-21st-century-is-tedious-and-that-needs-to-change/

Lazer D, Kennedy R, King G, Vespignani A (2014) The parable of Google Flu: traps in big data analysis. Science 343:1203–1205

Marcus G, Davis E (2014) Eight (no nine!) problems with big data. New York Times, April 6

Mayer-Schonberger V, Cukier K (2013) Big data: a revolution that will transform how we live, work and think. John Murray, London

McKinsey Global Institute (2011) Big data: the next frontier for innovation, competition and productivity. McKinsey Global Institute, New York

Microsoft Corp (2013) The big bang: how the big data explosion is changing the world. Retrieved May 14, 2014, from http://www.microsoft.com/en-us/news/features/2013/feb13/02-11bigdata.aspx

MIKE2.0 (2013) Big data definition. Retrieved May 15, 2014, from http://mike2.openmethodology.org/wiki/Big_Data_Definition

National Institute of Standards and Technology (2013) Big data questions from a customer perspective for the NBD-WG and draft answers. Retrieved May 14, 2014, from http://bigdatawg.nist.gov/_uploadfiles/M0079_v1_7313892246.doc

Needham J (2013) Disruptive possibilities: how big data changes everything. O'Reilly Media, Sebastopol

Oracle Corp (2013) Oracle: big data for the enterprise – white paper. Retrieved May 15, 2014, from www.oracle.com/us/products/database/big-data-for-enterprise-519135.pdf

Rickert J (2013) Let the data speak for themselves. Retrieved May 27, 2014, from http://blog.revolutionanalytics.com/2013/03/let-the-data-speak-for-themselves.html

Skiena S, Ward CB (2013) Who's bigger? Where historical figures really rank. Cambridge Books, New York

The Economist (2014) The backlash against big data. Retrieved June 4th, 2014, from www.economist.com/blogs/economist-explains/2014/04/economist-explains-10

Ward JS, Barker A (2013) Undefined by data: a survey of big data definitions. Comput Res Rep (Sept)

World Economic Forum (2012) Big data, big impact: new possibilities for international development. Retrieved June 9, 2014, from www.weforum.org/reports/big-data-big-impact-new-possibilities-international-development

Strategy 2

2.1 What the Reader Will Learn

- That strategy can mean different things to different people; consequently there are several 'schools' of strategy, some of which are highly prescriptive, others that are more organic.
- That the model of strategy most commonly used, the Rational Model, involves three distinct stages; an assessment of the firms strategic position, an evaluation of the strategic directions open to the firm and, lastly, implementation of the chosen strategy
- That big data may impact both the strategic direction the company chooses and the way the company creates its strategy
- That big data has implications for analysis frameworks such as; PESTEL, Porter's 5-forces and the Value Chain
- That aligning business and IT strategy is problematic, though frameworks such as the Applications Portfolio Matrix are useful in establishing which applications are strategic and which are operational

2.2 Introduction

Michael Porter (more of whom later) is fond of saying, "The essence of strategy is choosing what not to do" (Magretta 2012). Taking his advice we will specify at the outset what this chapter is NOT:

- This chapter is not an 'Idiots Guide' to strategy – There are several 'schools' of strategy, each with its own advocates and critics. To understand the full complexities and paradoxes of strategy requires an understanding of these different perspectives, something that is unachievable within the confines of a book chapter.

- This chapter is not an overview of all strategic analysis tools available: Given the focus of this book, this chapter will examine a sample of those tools and frameworks that are particularly influenced by "Big Data".
- This chapter will not discuss organisational expectations, stakeholders or culture – These will be covered, in a big data context, in the chapters on Style and Skills

Strategy is concerned with an organisation's direction for the future; its purpose, its ambitions, its resources and how it interacts with the environment in which it operates. As you will discover, strategy is complicated by the fact that there is considerable disagreement between researchers on the subject. If you work for an organisation that manufactures and/or sells products, you should find it easy to relate the tools and frameworks to your organisation. However, if you work for the public sector, a service organisation or a not-for-profit organisation you may find the language used in the models unfamiliar. That does not mean that these models are of less value to you, simply that you will need to adapt them to fit your own organisation and its environment.

We will investigate the consequences of Big Data for the strategy development process and its potential to inspire new, information-driven strategies. Big Data is often defined by three attributes; Volume, Velocity and Variety, all of which have implications for strategic analysis and strategic direction. The promise of comprehensive data granularity, broad transparency and fast, often real-time, information transfer offers the potential to create innovative business models and create unique competitive advantages. Finally, while many commentators have stressed that big data is not about technology, we believe that, without technology as an enabler, big data would not be possible. For big data to facilitate strategy, a company must have a robust technical environment and achieving this, while maintaining strategic flexibility, is not a trivial accomplishment. In this chapter we will discuss the challenge of aligning IT/IS strategy with business strategy and offer some tools and frameworks for you to investigate.

2.3 What is Strategy?

Since the term was first applied to companies in the late 1970s, books and articles claiming to define strategy and specify how it should be developed have flooded practitioners and students. These definitions have incorporated everything from analytic exercises and five-year strategic plans, to brainstorming sessions and simple vision statements. Consider the following definitions:

> Strategy is the direction and scope of an organisation over the long term, which achieves advantage in a changing environment through its configuration of resources and competences with the aim of fulfilling stakeholder expectations. (Johnson et al. 2007, p. 9)

> Strategy is always, and I mean always, lucky foresight. Strategy is always serendipity. Strategy is always the product of a complex and unexpected interplay between ideas, information, concepts, personalities and desires. (Hamel 1997, p. 70)

2.3 What is Strategy?

Fig. 2.1 The rational model of strategy

> Strategy is not the consequence of planning but the opposite: its starting point. (Mintzberg 1994)
>
> Strategy is about stretching limited resources to fit ambitious aspirations. (C.K. Prahalad)

Clearly there is no universal definition of strategy. Some writers include the purpose of the organisation as part of the strategy while others make firm distinctions between the purpose and the actions that fulfil this purpose. Thus, the concept of strategy means different things to different people. Inevitably, this has led to considerable scepticism of strategy among many managers and executives.

Arguably the most common view of strategy (and the most taught on business courses) is what we will call the rational model of strategy. This can be depicted as follows (Fig. 2.1).

The rational model begins with an assessment of the current position of the company with respect to its business environment and its capabilities. Having determined the strategic position, the management of the company must then decide what they wish to achieve, e.g. what is their ultimate objective (often summarised in a 'vision' or 'mission statement'), and the direction they must take to achieve it. Strategic direction inevitably requires hard choices. Choosing a particular direction often means foregoing some opportunities in favour of others, and sometimes this may require a re-evaluation of the 'vision' or 'mission'. Choosing a particular direction may mean committing resources such as finance, which in turn may require the approval of stakeholders such as banks or external investors, and, again, a re-evaluation of the 'vision' or 'mission'. Finally, as management moves to implement its strategy, it may find resistance from its staff, its customers and/or its suppliers. It may find that the business environment has changed, revealing greater opportunities or exposing serious threats to the business. Thus, the rational view of strategy, as a process that proceeds from Position to Direction to Execution, is overly simplistic. In reality the strategy development process must be data-rich, highly analytical, iterative, dynamic and, most important of all, inclusive. Unfortunately, many 'strategic plans' are announced with a fanfare of publicity, then left to languish in bookcases in the Executive Boardroom. These concepts are discussed later in this chapter.

Given its popularity in both business practice and business education, this chapter will focus on the rational model of strategy and the implications of Big Data – but why do companies need strategies in the first place? Firstly, organisations require strategy to define themselves, to set direction, and to manoeuver through threatening environments. Strategy is also needed to focus effort and to promote coordination of activity. Strategy both directs the attention of the individuals working within an organisation, and gives the organisation meaning for those individuals and for outsiders. Strategy also links the management of the firm's internal resources and its external relationships with its customers, suppliers, competitors and the economic and social environment in which it exists. Consequently, strategy is necessary to reduce uncertainty and provide consistency, which, in turn, gives a sense of being in control. However, some would argue that this 'sense of control' is illusory, that companies are complex systems operating within complex dynamic environments and that the level of complexity, as well as the rate of system change, will be different at different points in time. Put simply, it can be argued that complex systems, such as the competitive environment, require complex mental models of strategy and the use of rational mental models fails to address these complexities. In response to this view of strategy, several approaches have emerged, such as:

- Game theory
- Systems thinking
- Pure Complexity-based approaches; and
- Hybrid complexity-based approaches

Unfortunately these techniques are highly mathematical and require a significant amount of data. Consequently, they have, until now, failed to capture the imagination of executives in the Boardroom but, with the advent of big data, may prove to be the future of strategic thinking. But, or now, we will focus on the rational model of strategy development.

2.4 Strategy and 'Big Data'

Big data impacts both the strategy development process and the actual strategies developed in a number of ways, often called the 3-V's (Table 2.1).

Now, let's look at this in more detail. Clearly, how big data influences strategy, depends, first and foremost, on the strategic objectives it has been employed to achieve, the type of data being used and the stage of the 'big data lifecycle' the company is at.

2.4 Strategy and 'Big Data'

Table 2.1 Implications of the '3-Vs' for strategy and the strategy process

The big data 3-V's	Strategy process	Strategies developed
Volume (the amount of data available)	Allows more detailed analysis of strategic position, possibly identifying underlying strengths and weaknesses	Allows greater optimisation of the supply chain and customer relationships. In some circumstances this may become the source of the firm's competitive advantage
	Allows alternatives to the rational model of strategy?	
Variety (the different types of data available e.g. structured, unstructured)	Allows a wider, more complete, analysis of strategic position, possibly identifying underlying opportunities and threats	Allows greater visibility of business relationships and the business environment previously outside the scope of traditional Management Information Systems (MIS). In some circumstances this may become the source of the firm's competitive advantage
	Allows alternatives to the rational model of strategy?	
Velocity (the speed at which data can be collected, analysed and distributed)	Allows faster, more timely, feedback on experimental strategic initiatives, possibly allowing some aspects of the strategy to be modified on-the-fly	Allows faster interactions with customers, suppliers, employees and other stakeholders. In some circumstances this may become the source of the firm's competitive advantage
	Allows alternatives to the rational model of strategy?	

All companies collect data – customer and supplier information, sales, purchases and other financial data, staff details, marketing information etc. Typically this is structured data suitable for storage on databases – we will call this ***transactional data***. In using this data many firms recognise what they are looking for and why they are looking for it. However, it is important to note that not all organisations can boast having an Enterprise Resource Planning (ERP) system, Customer Relationship Management (CRM) system, Supply Chain Management (SCM) system, Human Resource Information System (HRIS) and/or Management Information System (MIS). In some instances a company may be too small, have insufficient resources (financial or human), or simply not regard IT/IS as an operational or strategic priority. In others a company may have implemented, say an ERP system, poorly and (reluctantly!) be using a small selection of the functionality available. Yet others may have a number of disparate systems or functional silos that make the sharing of data problematic. In environments such as these the benefits of big data are unlikely to mature before the company addresses the more fundamental questions of:

- What data do we collect?
- Why do we collect it?
- How might we use it?
- How might we share it?

The companies that are in the early stages of the big data lifecycle are those that have structured databases that they can interrogate in order to improve operations

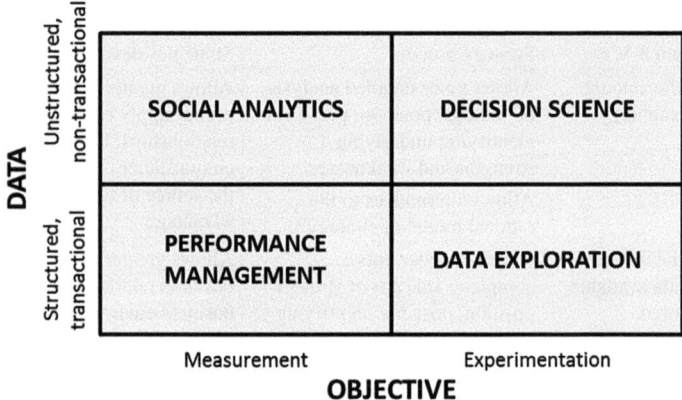

Fig. 2.2 Big Data strategies: What do we want from our data? (Adapted from Parise et al. 2012)

e.g. **Performance Management** (Fig. 1.1). For example, where managers can quickly identify changes in the profitability of customers (or market segments), assisting them to make short-term decisions and help with long-term planning, or systems that allow managers to use pre-determined queries and multi-dimensional analysis, that allow them to drill-down into the data. These systems are increasingly easy to use, have dashboard capabilities and allow multiple reports and graphs to make trends easier to spot.

Companies may then choose to investigate this data further. **Data Exploration** (Fig. 2.2) uses statistical techniques such as:

- A/B testing – to test against a control group to determine whether there has been an improvement based upon the test condition
- Cluster analysis – to group users/customers/suppliers. by similar attributes that may not have been previously apparent
- Data mining – to identify patterns in large data sets
- Predictive modelling – to predict user/customer/supplier behaviour based on previous transactions or preferences

Much of this work is experimental in that it may provide answers to questions that managers may not have considered. It may reveal customised marketing, cross-selling, up-selling or service opportunities to be directed to an important user/customer cluster. Conversely, it may identify groups of users that are unprofitable or groups that required different strategies to ensure retention.

As an alternative to Data Exploration, firms may choose to investigate the non-transactional data available in social media such as Facebook, Twitter and YouTube etc. This data offers scope to measure customer awareness (the exposure of social content, say, number of followers), customer engagement (the level of activity among members, say, amount of user-generated content) and reach (the extent to which content is distributed across other users and other social media platforms, say the number of retweets on Twitter). Social analytics rarely offer direct financial measures and usually need to be correlated with web traffic and/or business data to offer meaningful insight.

Finally, the big data lifecycle reaches maturity as companies begin to use both structured and non-structured data for both measurement and experimentation. Arguably, the most difficult task is that of Decision Science using techniques such as:

- Crowdsourcing – getting services, ideas or content by soliciting contributions from a large group of people (usually and online community)
- Social network analysis (SNA) – viewing social relationships in terms of network theory, consisting of nodes (individuals) and ties (relationships) such as friendship, kinship, organisations etc.
- Sentiment analysis – used to determine the attitude of an individual or group to some topic
- Textual analysis – used to interpret texts (films, television programmes, magazines, advertisements, clothes, graffiti, and so on) in order to try and obtain an impression of the ways in which people make sense of the world around them

The term 'science' is used because much of this work requires the development of hypotheses similar to those required for scientific research. Using crowdsourcing Data Scientists may pose questions to a specific online community and, given community feedback, will determine the value, validity and feasibility of the ideas generated. For example:

> Threadless.com allows their community to submit and score designs. Artists from around the world submit designs, the Threadless community scores each design for seven days and the best designs are printed and sold. New designs are printed each week and the winning artists are paid royalties and cash prizes.
>
> LEGO Mindstorms is an online community that allows users to share and rate robot designs based around the LEGO MindStorms EV3 platform. This community has spawned the First LEGO League (FLL), a robotics programme for teams of 9 to 16 year olds who program an autonomous robot to score points on a thematic playing surface by creating innovative solutions to problems. The FFL currently host more than 20,000 teams in 70 countries.

Equally, using sentiment analysis, firms can quantify topics of interest around a particular product or service, say, changes in pricing, product features or design issues. For example:

> In 2010, shortly after the launch of the iPhone 4, Apple quickly became aware, via monitoring of social media, of a potential design flaw associated with the positioning of the internal aerial. Some users found that calls were being dropped if the handset was held in a particular way or gripped too tightly. Given this early warning, Apple avoided a costly $1.5 billion recall by offering early adopters of the device a free phone case and modifying the manufacturing process to rectify the error on later handsets.

These examples are just a few of the early business models that big data can facilitate, but how might big data impact the strategy process itself?

2.5 Strategic Analysis

To develop a business strategy it is essential to understand the organisation and the relationships that exist between the wider (macro) business environment, the industry-specific (micro) environment and the organisation's resources, capabilities and stakeholder expectations. While the direction of the firm is important to all organisational stakeholders, it is the executives and senior managers who decide upon the organisation's key objectives. Consequently, these are the people with the responsibility for reconciling the objectives with the business environment and the capabilities of the organisation.

2.5.1 Analysing the Business Environment

2.5.1.1 Introduction

The external business environment impacts an organisation at several levels, from the most general, to the most specific, though some factors may occur at all levels (Fig. 2.3). The most general, the macro-environment, may include political, economic, environmental, social, demographic and technological factors. At a more specific level are industry sector factors such as competition, product substitution, customer and supplier power. Finally, at the most intimate level, are the opportunities and threats posed within defined market sectors. In this section we will explore these different levels of business environment and some of the tools, techniques and frameworks used to analyse them.

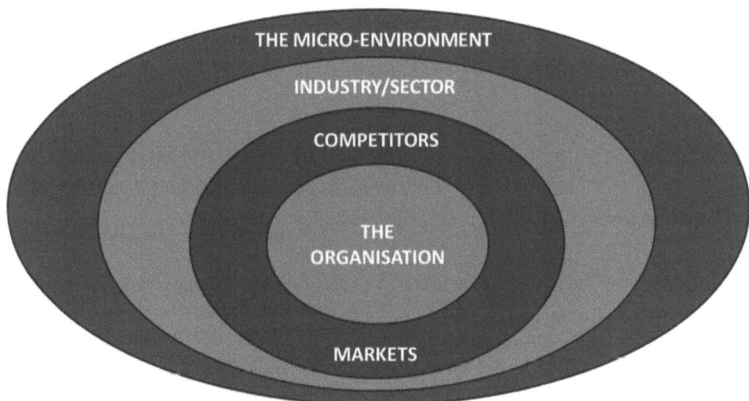

Fig. 2.3 Levels of the business environment

2.5.1.2 Analysing the Macro-environment – The Environmental Audit

No organisation exists in a vacuum, and most are extremely susceptible to influences emanating from external forces, defined by the diversity, the complexity and the speed of change of the environment. Furthermore, how these forces are interpreted is also important. Perceptually, organisations and their employees assist in the "creation" of their own business environment (see Chap. 6) To this end, organisations in the same industry often perceive their environment quite differently from each other, even though the environmental forces may, in fact, be very similar. Indeed, while we will not examine organisational culture in this chapter, it should be noted that companies sometimes use issues in the environment to shape organisational culture. For example, in the early 2000s, Marks & Spencer used the threat of acquisition by Philip Green's Arcadia Group, to create a 'siege mentality' among its staff.

The environmental audit, often called a PEST, PESTEL or PESTLE analysis (for the acronym Political, Economic, Socio-cultural, Technological, Environmental and Legal factors), is used to identify external influences that may impact the organisation (Fig. 2.4).

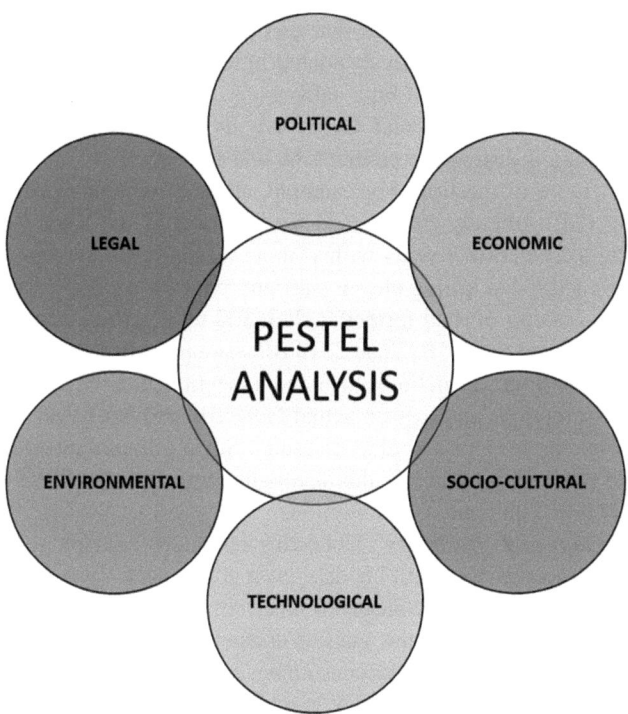

Fig. 2.4 PESTEL analysis

Indicatively, a PESTEL analysis might focus on issues such as:

- Political: Government stability, trade regulations, social welfare policies, attitude to taxation
- Economical: GNP, interest rates, exchange rates, inflation, unemployment, business cycles
- Socio-cultural: Demographics, social mobility, levels of education, disposable income
- Technological: Internet access, mobile phone usage, Government spending on R&D
- Environmental: Environmental legislation, percentage recycling, energy consumption
- Legal: Competition law, employment law, health and safety, intellectual property rights

In some cases, such as environmental legislation or unemployment level, issues span more than one category. Remember, PESTEL is a tool to generate ideas, not a constraint in which everything must be pigeon-holed. So, while widely-used, PESTEL does have its critics who point out that there are problems with:

- *Over-simplification*: It's common for managers and analysts to present a simple list of the environmental factors that can affect the organisation. Unless the underlying factors are critically evaluated in terms of the degree of impact, the findings of the analysis are of little value
- *Signal-to-noise ratio*: External forces are dynamic and sometimes change quickly making it difficult to predict why and how these factors may affect the present or future of the firm. For example, at noon on 20th April 2010 British Petroleum (BP) officials gathered on the platform of the Deepwater Horizon drilling rig to celebrate 7 years with without an injury on the rig. Almost 10 h later the rig exploded killing eleven staff and injuring another eighteen. In less than 7 days leaking oil had formed a slick 100-mile across, 20-miles from the coast of the United States. By June 2010 BP share price had collapsed by 53 %.
- *Invalid assumptions*: Sometimes the factors mentioned in the analysis are based more on assumptions and less on actual facts. An analysis based on unfounded assumptions can lead to planning disasters. So, it's important to device some method to cross-verify whether the factors mentioned in the PEST analysis are not merely based on tenuous assumptions
- *Data collection and 'freshness'*: Collecting enormous amounts of relevant data from the right sources has, until big data, been problematic – especially since most of the revealing data must be collected from external sources. Similarly, maintaining data 'freshness' and keeping the analysis updated has been difficult. Traditionally this has made PEST analysis time consuming, backward looking and costly.
- *Data analysis and presentation*: A good PEST analysis requires volumes of information to be quickly collected, analysed and presented. Historically, when handling too much information users tended to get confused and lose sight of what factors are more critical (see Chap. 6). This ambiguity in prioritizing factors often jeopardised the whole analysis.

However, many of these shortcomings are being addressed by big data. Analytic techniques, utilising big data, are increasingly being used to identify trends. For example, research by Global Pulse (http://www.unglobalpulse.org/) and other groups, has found that analysing Twitter messages can signal spikes in unemployment, price rises and disease. Robert Kirkpatrick, Global Pulse Director, suggests that such "digital smoke signals of distress," usually come months before official statistics. This is particularly important since many developing countries have no access to reliable data. Big data is also facilitating a shift away from assumption-based analysis to data-based analysis. In Chap. 6 we examined how individual and group assumptions can be flawed. By changing the mind-sets of analytic-savvy executives (see Chap. 4), big data demands a more data-centric approach that ensures people question their assumptions and makes evidence a pre-requisite. Ultimately, big data will resolve the issues of data collection, analysis and presentation, transforming the PEST analysis from a technique to initiate discussion to an information-rich intelligence system. But the combination of big data and analytics can do much more in terms of assessing the business environment…

In business environments of high uncertainty, either due to complexity, rapid change or both, it may be impossible to develop a single view of how the environment may impact the company. Scenario Planning allows a company to develop a range of plausible perspectives of how the future might unfold. That is not to say that firms will be able to discern or predict the exact nature of a threat or an opportunity, but they will be better positioned to navigate the eventual outcome if they have considered uncertainty from multiple perspectives. Using big data and big data analytics in the scenario planning process allows for faster, more up-to-date, more accurate visions of the future. In a 2013 survey, the Economist Intelligence Unit asked Chief Financial Officers (CFOs), what strategic aspect of their role had increased data made the biggest positive difference – 40.3 % said scenario planning (http://www.wipro.com/documents/the-data-directive.pdf). Asked where the greatest potential for Big Data laid, 31.8 % of Chief Strategy Officers (CSOs) and 22 % of Chief Information Officers (CIOs) said scenario planning.

How else might Big Data improve scenario planning? Big Data can provide faster, more accurate data, but Big Data can also help quantify the risks associated with a particular scenario. When choosing a strategy from a series of scenarios decision-makers need to understand the probability and consequences of failure; they need to understand risk. Even before Big Data there was a move towards incorporating formal risk assessments into projects, business plans and strategies. Traditionally, risk analysis has involved sensitivity analysis (sometimes called 'what-if' analysis); identifying and challenging the assumptions underlying a particular strategy. For example, what would be the implications (on, say, profitability) if the sales forecast was under-achieved by 5 %? Unfortunately, the term 'sensitivity analysis' like the term 'strategy' has come to mean many things to many people and to some that includes 'brainstorming' and subjective discussion. However, at its most fundamental, sensitivity analysis uses mathematical models to determine how the uncertainty associated with a strategy can be apportioned. Big Data analytics enables the use of Monte Carlo simulations within traditional sensitivity analysis. Monte Carlo Sensitivity Analysis is a simulation tool for exploring the sensitivity of a complex system, such as a strategy, by varying parameters within statistical constraints. These models are simulated in a loop, with probabilistic uncertainty between simulations. The results from the simulation are analysed to determine the characteristics of the system. For example:

A multi-national manufacturer wishes to calculate the risk associated with Asian production plants due to a widespread bird flu pandemic which is currently affecting many workers in the plants. The *primary risk* is the pandemic itself. This leads to the following *influenced risks*:

- High sickness rate and lower productivity in the plants where the pandemic has hit.
- Lower sales of products due to low production rates.

Each influenced risk may have associated with it a series of other influenced risks. Thus, the high sickness rate noted above, results in the following further influenced risks:

- Shipments are not delivered on time.
- This may lead to the further risk of fraud, since if most colleagues are out of the office because of sickness, segregation of duties may be violated.
- This again may lead to a higher impact of the risk if it happens.

By structuring risks in a risk hierarchy and running a Monte Carlo simulation on it, managers can determine more precisely what the final risk will be, in terms of both probability and impact. It is important to note that scenario-planning at this level is highly mathematical and requires the skills of a Data Scientist. We will consider the role of the Data Scientist in Chap. 5.

2.5.1.3 Industry Sector Analysis – The Micro-environment

All businesses operate within a micro-environment determined by the industry structure. Economic models of "perfect competition" and "pure monopoly" tend to be based on somewhat unrealistic assumptions and should be regarded as ideal types of market structure, which establish the boundaries within which genuine markets exist and operate. In practice, oligopoly and monopolistic competition are much nearer to the market structures found in the real world. Since the objective of this chapter is strategy we will not concern ourselves with the detail of economic theories, though you should recognise that models and frameworks that address industry structure are closely aligned with economic theory. Analysing the micro-environment gives rise to a huge range of issues. This analysis can be more easily defined by identifying the key factors influencing the industry and using these to focus the analysis on particularly important matters. Perhaps the best-known framework for this is Michael Porter's five-force framework (Fig. 2.5).

Before we examine the 5-forces we need to briefly visit two core concepts that often get lost in the interpretation of Porter's work, namely, what is meant by the terms; competition and value. Merriam-Webster defines competition in business as "*the effort of two or more parties acting independently to secure the business of a third party by offering the most favourable terms*". However, things are not so simple. Let us assume

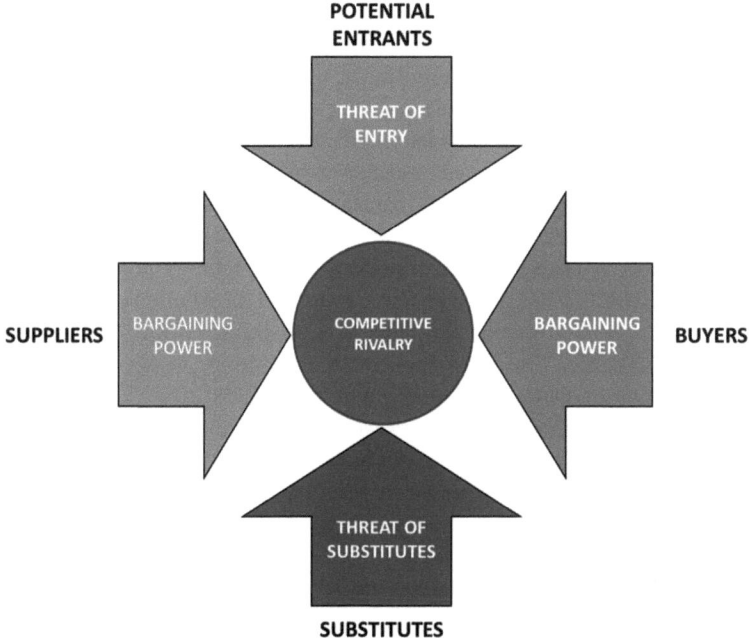

Fig. 2.5 Porter's 5-force framework

that we have two rubber glove suppliers serving a single large customer, say, the British National Health Service (NHS). Both companies offer a product that does a similar job. The product of Company A is slightly cheaper than that of Company B, but Company B's product lasts a little longer. To 'compete', Company A invests in product development to increase the longevity of its gloves. Meanwhile, Company B invests in new machinery to make its product more cost effectively. The resulting 'arms race' drives down the selling price and drives up the durability of both products. Both companies have invested significantly without realising any increase in value – because all of the additional value has been captured by end-user. Consequently, Porter tells us that competition is not about winning a sale, it's not about beating a rival; competition is about capturing value. That means earning profits. Viewed from this perspective Company A and Company B may both be in competition with each other, but they are also in competition with the end-user, in this case the NHS.

Almost without exception, industry structure determines who captures the value (profit!) in any industry sector, and the industry structure is determined by five forces:

- *The bargaining power of suppliers*: Powerful suppliers like, say, the electricity generating companies in the UK, will use that power to impose higher prices or more favourable terms. In either case the profitability of a company (or individual) will be reduced as the supplier captures more of the value for themselves.
- *The bargaining power of buyers*: Powerful customers will use that power to force down prices. They may also demand that more features/benefits be included which, in turn, drive up the cost. In either case the profitability will be reduced as the

customer captures more of the value for themselves. Large multi-national companies such as Monsanto, Tesco and Wal-Mart are renowned for using their buying power to limit the profitability of their suppliers. Monsanto, who have patented seeds for some vegetable and fruit species, monitor seeds sold, used and any seeds arising from the crop itself. All seeds must be returned to Monsanto, who have successfully prosecuted farmers who have tried to grow "unpaid for" seeds.
- *The threat of new entrants*: Entry barriers protect an industry from newcomers that add further capacity to the industry and seek market share (thereby driving down profits). Microsoft, with its operating system, Windows, has created significant barriers to entry due to scale, control of distribution channels and high switching costs. Conversely, the "bed and breakfast (B&B)" accommodation sector has relatively few entry barriers (it is available to anyone with a spare room) and, consequently, profitability is low.
- *The threat of substitute products/services*: Substitute products (or services) meet the same basic need as the industry's product in a different way. For example, in many countries mobile-phones have taken significant market share from both camera manufacturers and watch manufacturers. Substitute products limit the profitability of an industry
- *The rivalry among existing competitors*: As we saw with Company A and Company B above, if rivalry is intense, companies tend to compete away the value they create. They do this by either passing it on the buyers (as discounts or extra features) or by spending it on the costs of competition (higher advertising spend, higher development costs etc.)

Unfortunately, like the PEST analysis earlier, many 5-force analyses are often subjective, heavily bias and devoid of tangible, independent data. Big Data offers the potential to investigate the 5-forces more thoroughly, and at a finer granularity than ever before. What does that does that mean in practice? (Table 2.2).

2.5.2 Strategic Capability – The Value Chain

2.5.2.1 Introduction
The subject of strategy is awash with vocabulary – nowhere more so than describing the internal strengths and weaknesses of a company. Some terms are well-defined while others, like the word 'strategy' itself are used to describe different things at different times by different authors. Consequently we have;

- Threshold strategic capabilities
- Dynamic capabilities
- Threshold and unique resources
- Tangible and intangible resources
- Threshold and core competencies
- Key success factors
- Critical success factors

2.5 Strategic Analysis

Table 2.2 Porters 5-forces and the three 'V's

	Volume	Variety	Velocity	Example
Supplier power	What transactional data is currently collected in your interactions with suppliers? How do you use this data?	What is the potential of integrating third-party unstructured data sources into your supply chain?	What are the implications of faster data flows between you and your supplier?	Supplier capacity risk management: identify/eliminate bottlenecks
	How might more detailed and granular data assist in the prioritisation and evaluation of suppliers?	How might more third party/ unstructured data be used to reduce switching costs?	What are the implications of real-time visibility of product transportation and just-in-time (JIT) delivery?	Demand–supply matching: use intersections of supply/demand curves to optimise stock-turn
	How might more detailed and granular data be used to reduce switching costs?	What would be the impact of, say, adding sensor-generated performance data into your supply chain?	How might faster, real-time data be used to reduce switching costs?	Modelling/scheduling: Simulation and contingency planning within your supply chain
	How might greater transparency affect the power balance within your supply chain?		How might JIT and the use of third party data affect the power balance within your supply chain?	
Competitive rivalry	What data do you have on your competitors? How do you use it? How might you use it better?	What is the potential for using third party unstructured data to enhance your competitive advantage? How might you differentiate yourselves using this data?	What alternative business models are enabled by faster, more accurate data? Are these models an opportunity or a threat?	Cross-media Conversion Attribution Analysis: To examine cross-channel pricing and effectiveness
	What data do they have on you? How do they use it? How might they use it against you in the future?	How might competitors use third party unstructured data against you? How might they differentiate themselves using this data?	How might you (or your competitors) use fast data to improve time-to-market, product performance, after-sales service or reduce costs?	A/B Testing: To identify merchandising messaging and placement
				Analyse social media and mobile data: To identify competitive moves or changes in user trends

(continued)

Table 2.2 (continued)

	Volume	Variety	Velocity	Example
Buyer power	What transactional data is currently collected in your interactions with customers? How do you use this data?	What are your customers saying about you on social media?	What are the implications of faster data flows between you and your customers?	Sentiment analysis: Used to micro-segment your market and identify trends in products, services, pricing and promotion
	How might more detailed and granular data assist in the prioritisation and evaluation of customers?	How might more third party/unstructured data be used to increase switching costs?	How might faster, real-time data be used to increase switching costs?	Real-time targeting of customers: Used to increase on-site revenue-per-customer
	Who are your most profitable customers? Who are the most influential?	What would be the impact of adding sensor-generated performance data into your Customer Relationship Management (CRM) system?	What are the implications of product sensor data analysis for future sales and after-sales service?	Recommendations engines: Used to increase shopping cart revenue-per-customer
	How might more detailed and granular data be used to increase switching costs?		How might fast data, transparency and the use of third party data affect the power balance between you and your customer base?	Product sensor data analysis: Used to understand how, when and where the product was used
	How might greater transparency affect the power balance between you and you're your customers?			
Potential entrants	How might more detailed and granular data be used to construct entry barriers?	How might social media and mobile data be used to identify/ quantify new product, market, customer and competitor developments?	How might faster, real-time data be used to identify/quantify new product, market, customer and competitor developments?	Collection of customer data via the "ClubCard" system allows Tesco to adjust pricing offers to suit client preferences. This provides a strong barrier to entry for other retailers

2.5 Strategic Analysis

(New Entrants)	How might this data be used to identify new entrants earlier?	How might potential entrants use third party unstructured data against you? How might they differentiate themselves using this data?	How might fast, real-time data be used to construct barriers to entry?	Big data may be used to identify hitherto unknown switching costs or economies of scale
		How might social media and mobile data be used to construct barriers to entry?		The costs and skills required to achieve the benefits of big data may itself be a barrier to entry for smaller companies
Substitutes	How might more detailed and granular data be used to identify potential substitute products/services?	How might social media and mobile data be used to identify/quantify the threat of potential substitute products or services?	How might faster, real-time data be used to identify/quantify the threat of potential substitute products or services?	
		How might potential substitutes use third party unstructured data against you? How might they differentiate themselves using this data?		

To avoid confusion we will focus on the use of one framework which encompasses all of these concepts, but adds the benefit of quantification to an often highly subjective discussion, namely, the Value Chain.

2.5.2.2 The Value Chain

Before we go any further it is important to differentiate the Value Chain from the "Analytics Value Chain" that is currently *de rigueur* in consulting circles. While the Analytics Value Chain represents a reinvention of the Data, Information, Knowledge and Wisdom (DIKW) hierarchy discussed in Chap. 6, the original Value Chain (Fig. 2.6), initially proposed by Michael Porter in 1985, is based upon understanding an organisation as a system, made up of activities each with inputs, transformation processes and outputs. These, in turn, involve the acquisition and consumption of resources – money, labour, materials, equipment, buildings, land, administration and management. Thus, how these activities are carried out determines costs and affects profits. What Porter calls 'activities', others variously call 'capabilities' or 'competences'. However, before we immerse ourselves in the Value Chain, lets us first examine another, often misused, term; competitive advantage. Google the term "competitive advantage" and you will get 53 million hits. The top two hits describe competitive advantage as:

- ...*when an organization acquires or develops an attribute or combination of attributes that allows it to outperform its competitors* (Wikipedia); and
- ...*an advantage that a firm has over its competitors, allowing it to generate greater sales or margins and/or retain more customers than its competition* (Investopedia)

Unfortunately, both are rather vague when, actually, the term is both concrete and specific. A company has a 'competitive advantage' when it can command a premium price or operate at lower costs relative to its rivals. Thus, competitive advantage is about creating and maintaining superior value which, as discussed earlier, equates directly to profitability, that is;

Value Created and Captured − Cost of Creating that Value = Profit Margin

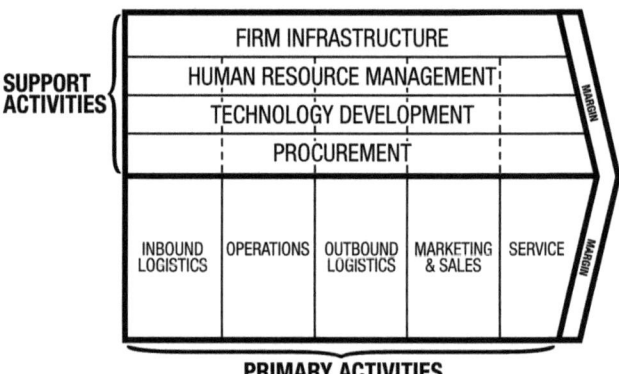

Fig. 2.6 The value chain

2.5 Strategic Analysis

Competitive advantage arises from the myriad of activities (and relationships between activities) that companies perform as they operate and compete. The activities themselves are discrete economic functions or processes, such as managing a supply chain or sales force, developing new products or the delivery of after-sales service. Activities are often multi-faceted, requiring a team of people with different skills, unique technologies, fixed assets and, of course, information. How activities, both individually and as value chains, use, create and distribute information is increasing being seen as an important driver of competitive advantage.

- *Primary Activities*: Primary activities are associated with the physical creation, sale, maintenance and support of a product or service. They are:
  - *Inbound logistics* – The activities associated with the receiving, storing, and distributing inputs internally. Relationships with suppliers and integration into the supplier's value chain are an important factor in creating value here.
  - *Operations* – These are the transformation activities that convert inputs into outputs that are then sold to customers. Here, it is the operational systems that create value.
  - *Outbound logistics* – The activities associated with the delivery of the product or service to the customer, for example: collection, storage, and distribution systems. These may be internal or external to the organization.
  - *Marketing and sales* – The activities uses to persuade buyers to purchase from you rather than your competitors. The benefits offered, and how well those benefits are communicated, are sources of value here.
  - *Service* – The activities associated with maintaining the value of the product or service to the buyer, once it's been purchased.
- *Support Activities*: These activities support the primary activities. The dotted lines in Fig. 2.6 indicate how each support activity may assist each primary activity. For example, procurement may support operations by, say, negotiating lower prices for manufacturing machinery, while supporting marketing and sales by agreeing better terms on company car leasing .
  - *Infrastructure* – These are the functions that allow a firm to maintain daily operations e.g. accounts, legal, administrative, and general management are examples of necessary infrastructure that businesses may use to their advantage.
  - *Human resource management* – This refers to how a company recruits, trains, motivates, rewards, and retains its employees. People are a significant source of value and businesses can create a clear advantage with good HR practices. We will examine this in more details in the Chap. 5
  - *Technological development* – This refers to managing and processing information, as well as protecting a company's knowledge base. Minimizing technology costs, preserving technological advances, and sustaining technical excellence are important foundations of value creation.
  - *Procurement* – These are the functions that allow the firm to get the resources it needs to operate. This includes finding supplier and negotiating best terms and prices.

In many industries one company's value chain forms one part of an overall *value system* which creates value from the extraction of raw materials to the delivery of a finished product to and end-user. In this instance, how that specific company value chain relates to its suppliers and buyers, those downstream or upstream in the value system, can be a major source of competitive advantage. Consider a company producing canned foods for sale in retail supermarkets. *Upstream,* the company must choose whether to make the cans itself or to buy them in. If it chooses to make them, does it buy the raw materials from a supplier or produce them itself? *Downstream*, does the company distribute its own products or does it use a third party logistics company? If it distributes for itself, does the company own the trucks or does it lease them from a supplier? It is important to remember that the profitability of every company within the value system will be determined by how much value that particular company is able to retain. Within a value system Porters 5-forces analysis can help understand who is profitable, and why.

Much of the work on business processes, business process management (BPM), business process re-engineering (BPR), owes a major debt to the value chain. Consequently, many companies, particularly those with established Enterprise Resource Planning (ERP) systems, are overflowing with internal, transactional data. Data-intensive techniques such as Total Quality Management (TQM) and Six-Sigma methodologies collect copious amounts of information and have transformed product quality and reliability in many manufacturing industries, but often the data remains isolated and compartmentalised. If the value chain analysis (and its extension to the wider value system) gives us a framework to determine and define a firm's competitive advantage, then Big Data gives us the tools to enable more detailed analysis and decisions using the transactional date at our disposal (Table 2.3).

2.5.3 The SWOT 'Analysis'

Having determined our strategic position we now have a clear understanding of our business environment and our place in that environment. Through value chain analysis we understand what we are good at (the things that add value) and the areas that we need to improve. In short we have all we need to prepare a SWOT analysis. Another acronym, SWOT stands for;

- Strengths
- Weaknesses
- Opportunities; and
- Threats

It has been argued that the acronym should be written as; TOWS, since analysis of the external environment is usually done first but, in practice, it is the insight that is important, so we will leave that particular debate to the academics.

Despite its name, the SWOT analysis isn't really an analysis. It is a synthesis of all the preceding analyses. The outcome of both the PEST analysis and Porters

Table 2.3 Big data in the value chain

Firm infrastructure		
Performance management		
Predictive real-time dashboards and scorecards (enables companies to see emerging trends and act sooner)		
Cost management		
Activity-based costing (ABC)		
Mergers & acquisitions		
Due diligence to include:		
Cash flow analysis		
Supply chain efficiencies		
Predicted customer reaction		
Impact on costs		
Governance		
Identify insider trading		
Questions:		
Which activities have greatest impact on performance?		
Are we executing against strategy?		
Human resource management		
Innovative talent acquisition	Innovative talent utilisation	Innovative talent retention
How do prospective employees find us?	How are we going to get them their first salary cheque?	How do we identify/ intervene if employees are unhappy and/or under-performing?
How do we hire the best employees?	What are the drivers of strong motivation and performance?	How can we engagement our staff more completely?
How do we get them productive as soon as possible?		

(continued)

Table 2.3 (continued)

Technology development

Sensor-based logistics e.g.	What are the preferences and behaviours of our consumers and market segments?	Sensor-based logistics e.g.	In-memory analytics alerting management regarding merchandising performance changes	Loyalty programmes e.g.
FedEx 'Senseaware'	Innovation and Quality Control through crowdsourcing e.g.	FedEx 'Senseaware'	Sentiment analysis e.g.	Pepsi 'Loot'
	Idea generation e.g.		Gatorade Command Centre	MyCoke Rewards
	Dell Ideastorm		Dell Listening Centre	Samsonite Travel Miles
	My Starbucks Idea		Platform-centred campaigns e.g.	Crowdsourced Feedback
	Co-creation e.g.		Nike Human Race	
	4food		Dewmocracy	
	Threadless.com		Social commerce e.g.	
	Lego Mindstorms		Levi's store	
	Concurrent engineering & Product Lifecycle Management (PLM)			
	Digitally-enabled products & services		Disney F-store	
	Nike++		Twitter support e.g.	
	ecoDrive		Best buy Twelp Force	
	Kraft iFood		Delta Assist	
			Crowdsourced research	

2.5 Strategic Analysis

Procurement

Credit scoring	
Fraud detection	
Supplier pricing	

Inbound logistics	Operations	Outbound logistics	Marketing & sales	Service
			Demand forecasting	
			Use merchandising insights from granular POS data to negotiate superior supplier terms and conditions	
Shelf management systems	Total quality management (TQM)	Optimise scheduling/routine	Bayesian inference techniques to improve monthly & quarterly revenue forecasts	Warranty analysis
Inventory replenishment	Six sigma	Yield management	Conversion Attribution Analysis to optimise ad placement and messaging	Determine drivers of warranty claims
Truck scheduling/routing	Statistical process control (SPC)	Leverage social media and mobile data to uncover merchandising insights to optimise merchandising performance	How can we optimise our price, promotion and merchandising strategies?	Provide personalised content
Optimise supply chain management (SCM)	Process variations	Engagement of distributors	How can we determine most profitable channel partners	Customer loyalty programme
Predict supplier stock levels	Product customisation	JIT distribution	What are the drivers of distribution channel profitability?	Customer retention
Determine drivers of supplier quality and performance	Defect rates		How can we optimise our store locations?	Predict customer defection
Use real-time POS data to identify and notify suppliers of potential out-of-stock situations more quickly	ERP systems		How can we understand consumer price sensitivity?	Optimise use of support channels

(continued)

Table 2.3 (continued)

Engagement of suppliers	Use real-time POS and RFID data to manage markdowns, identify slow and no movers and optimise in-store inventory	What is the best way to target offers and messages to consumers and segments?	% customer testimonials
Transparent sourcing	Sensor data-driven operations analytics	How can we determine most profitable customers?	% goods returned
	"digital factory" for lean manufacturing	How can we determine advertising and promotional effectiveness	CRM
			Combine social media with POS data to identify potential product or service performance problems
			Product sensor data analysis for after-sales service
			Customers experience enhancement
			after-sale experience enhancement

2.6 Strategic Choice

Table 2.4 SWOT analysis of Apple

Strengths	Weaknesses
A combination of horizontal and vertical integration created formidable competitive advantage	Lack of products at different price points limits the market scope
Successful product lines driving the growth	High dependence on iPhone and iPad product lines
Robust growth rates	
Opportunities	**Threats**
Growth opportunity in the enterprise market	Intense price competition in the emerging nations
Emerging nations provide strong growth opportunities	Operating in complex and challenging environment could impact market position
Apple TV to benefit from the growing smart TV market	

5-force analysis should reveal the most pertinent opportunities available to the company and identify the most relevant threats. Likewise, value chain analysis (coupled with other techniques such as marketing audits, product development road maps etc.) should reveal core competences (strengths) and identify possible weaknesses. A SWOT analysis for Apple ™ might look something like this (though in practice these issues would require more quantification to be meaningful).

The SWOT is our starting point for strategy development. For example, from Table 2.4 we can deduce the following about Apple's strategy:

- Emerging markets provide strong growth but low margins: How can Apple either reduce costs to maintain margins or differentiate the products (add value) to maintain margins?
- Current product lines are highly successful and widely adopted but the product range is limited: Should Apple increase their product portfolio or seek more markets (such as the enterprise market) for their existing products?

How might Apple approach questions such as these? Should they focus on cost-effectiveness or product development? Should they seek more markets or more products? These questions require hard choices…

2.6 Strategic Choice

2.6.1 Introduction

Choice is at the centre of strategy formulation, for if there are no choices to be made, there can be little value in thinking about strategy at all. However, even when managers are apparently free to make strategic choices, results may eventually depend as much on chance and opportunity as on the deliberate choices of those managers (see Chap. 6). In an ideal world, any process of choice could be rationally divided into four steps – identify options, evaluate those options against preference criteria, select the best option, and then take action. This suggests that identifying and choosing options can be done purely analytically. In practice, it may be difficult to identify all possible options with equal clarity or at the same time. Unexpected events can create new opportunities, destroy foreseen opportunities, or alter the balance of advantage between opportunities. Identifying and evaluating options is a useful approach but it has limitations – the future may evolve differently from any of the options…

2.6.2 Type, Direction and Criteria of Strategic Development

In Fig. 2.6 we offered a possible SWOT analysis for Apple. From that SWOT we raised a number of questions, namely;

- What kind of strategy do we need? and
- What direction should the company take?

However, these questions are not specific to Apple; these questions are applicable to all companies developing a strategy. In discussing the 'type' of strategy we return, initially, to Michael Porter, and then to later work on 'the value disciplines'.

In his 1980 book, "Competitive Strategy", Michael Porter first postulated his 5-forces framework. In the same book he also suggested that firms had to choose between one of three generic strategies:

- Cost leadership: in which a company competes by offering low *relative* price (that is, to maintain profit margin low prices are match with low operating costs). Example: BMW cars
- Differentiation: in which a company offers a different product or service to a customer base that is prepared to pay a premium for unique design, styling, quality, reliability or other variable. Example: Ferrari sports cars
- Focus: in which a company segments its market into one or more specific niches. Within this niche the company may choose a cost leadership or differentiation strategy but the prime focus remains the needs of the niche. Example: Morgan cars

Choosing one of the generic strategies requires a thorough understanding of the organisations position and its long-term objectives – but Porter argues that it is a choice that must be made. Each of the generic strategies has implications for how the company structures its value chain and the metrics used to measure the success of the strategy. Trying to be 'all things to all customers' some firms are outflanked by cost leaders on one side and differentiators on the other, the common strategic mistake of being caught 'stuck in the middle' (Fig. 2.7).

2.6 Strategic Choice

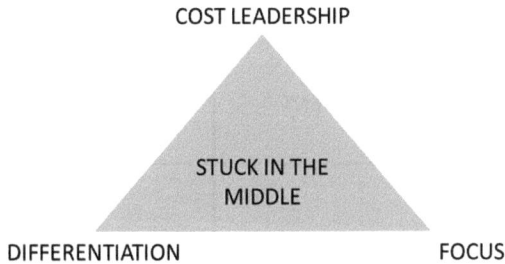

Fig. 2.7 Porter's generic strategies (Porter 1980)

Critics have argued that hybrid strategies, combining two of the generic strategies, can be successful and that companies often need the flexibility to move between strategies. In 1993 Treacy and Wiersema introduced a revised framework, the Value Disciplines, namely;

- *Operational excellence*: The focus of this strategy is on efficiency, cost-effectiveness, supply chain management, quality by systems and volume production. The strategies of most multi-national corporations are an interpretation of this discipline
- *Product leadership*: The focus of this strategy is strong innovation, R&D and brand marketing. Key metrics are based upon time-to-market and high margins in a short time frame.
- *Customer intimacy*: The focus of this strategy is in tailoring products and services to individual or niche customers. These require good CRM systems, on-delivery of products/services, lifetime value concepts, reliability and maintain close personal contact with the customer.

In contrast to Porter, Treacy and Wiersema suggest that while a company must focus on one of the disciplines, it must also aim benchmark itself with its competitors on at least one of the other disciplines. But what are the implications of generic strategies for big data?

Perhaps, most importantly, a firm's choice of generic strategy sets the parameters (particularly funding) for big data initiatives. For an operationally excellent strategy the big data focus will most likely be on optimising internal and supply chain processes, for example, the use of real-time POS, RFID data and sensor-driven operations analytics. A company pursuing a product leadership strategy will, no doubt, focus on big data applications such as product lifecycle management, innovation and idea generation through, say, crowdsourcing and advances in digitally-enabled products/services. Finally, a customer intimate organisation will seek to deploy techniques such as conversion attribution analysis to optimise advertising, Bayesian inference techniques for forecasting, sentiment analysis and crowd-sourced market research. Thus, given the scope of big data techniques, it is imperative that managers and executives clearly understand the firm's generic strategy before they commit to the objectives of a big data initiative.

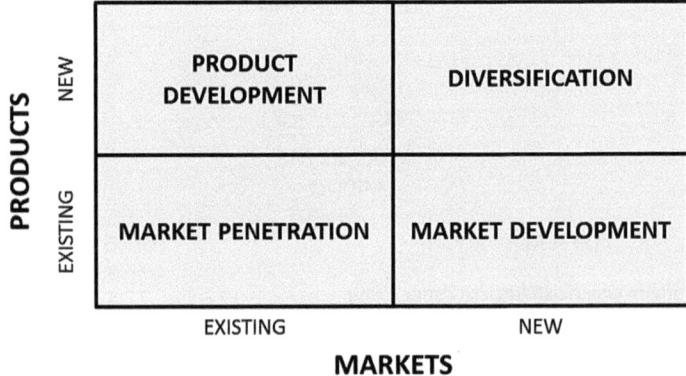

Fig. 2.8 Strategic direction – the Ansoff Matrix (Ansoff 1988)

Given a core business with a distinguishing competitive posture, in terms of differentiation and scope, we now come to the question, "What strategic directions are available to develop that core business?" Furthermore, what impact might the level of risk have on the viability of the strategy? An organisation can develop a business in a number of ways. It can develop its product offerings within that market, it can develop its markets via new segments, new channels, or new geographical areas, or it can simply push the same products more vigorously though the same markets (Fig. 2.8).

This simple framework asks a number of questions, the answers to which help determine strategic direction and accompanying risk. A market penetration strategy focuses on delivering more value to existing customers in existing markets. This is suitable if the market is relatively new, is expanding or if your company is a new entrant to the market. This is considered a low risk strategy. However, assuming the market for your product is getting saturated, the two medium risk alternatives are to design new products for your existing customers or seek new customers for your current products. These two strategies are considered medium risk because:

- *Product development*: The company must be sufficiently innovative to design products acceptable to the existing customer base. This requires investment in staff, time and technology. Risks include; failure to develop new product, poor adoption by customer base, new product cannibalises sales of old product, or lack of adoption of new products damages the brand of the existing product.
- *Market development*: To be successful in new markets the company must understand the market dynamics. Selling a product to the government organisation requires different skills to selling to a private company. A product that meets market requirements in the United Kingdom may be unsuitable for consumers in, say, Japan. Risks include: Wrong market entry strategy, aggressive response by new competitors, product unsuitable for consumers, new competitors respond by attacking your existing market.

The fourth, and most high risk strategy, is that of diversification. Developing new products for unfamiliar markets requires significant resources and is usually considered a last resort.

2.6.3 Aligning Business and IT/IS Strategy

So far we have examined strategic analysis in some detail. We have also touched upon issues associated with strategic direction. Finally, we will investigate one important aspect of strategy implementation, particularly for big data, that of aligning IT/IS strategy with business strategy. A number of commentators have made the point that big data is not about technology. However, it is important to recognise that, without technology as an enabler, big data would be difficult, if not impossible, to achieve. Only companies with a robust technical environment can expect to reap the benefits of big data. Unfortunately, large investments in technology often commit companies to long-term infrastructures that may constrict their strategic flexibility. So, what is the relationship between business and IT/IS strategy and how might these two be aligned?

Alignment can be defined as the extent to which the IT department and business needs, objectives and/or structures are consistent with each other. Particularly, researchers have focused on how four aspects combine to deliver the full potential of information technology, namely; business strategy, IT/IS strategy, business infrastructure and processes and IT/IS infrastructure and processes (Fig. 2.9):

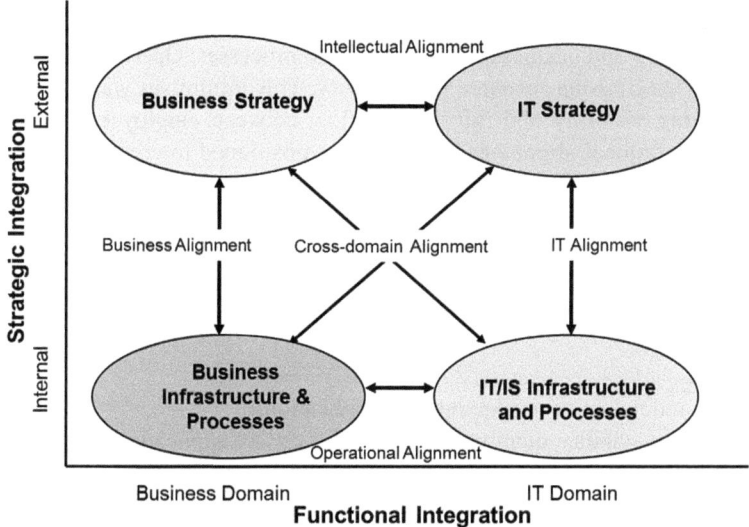

Fig. 2.9 Figure 11: The strategic alignment model (Henderson and Venkatraman 1993)

Alignment at a strategic level (intellectual alignment) and at an operation level (operational alignment) may be considered challenging, but is achieved due to relevant stakeholders holding comparative positions and perspectives within the company. Likewise, domain alignment is possible due to existing hierarchical relationships within the same domain. Where alignment becomes problematic is at hierarchical and domain boundaries. Researchers propose four combinations of these alignment types:

- *Strategy execution*: Business strategy impacts the IT infrastructure but is constrained by the business infrastructure
- *Technology transformation*: IT infrastructure is affected by the business strategy but is constrained by the IT strategy
- *Competitive potential*: Business infrastructure is affected by the IT strategy but is constrained by the business strategy
- *Service level*: IT strategy impacts the business infrastructure but is constrained by the IT infrastructure

Companies pursuing technology transformation and competitive potential focus chiefly on aligning their IT and business strategies (intellectual alignment) to differentiate their firm from competitors. That is, the utilisation of IT is directed towards sustaining the business strategy in the marketplace, with a primary focus on improving customer service and taking value from competitors. Thus, these firms are more likely to have higher levels of profitability and customer satisfaction.

Conversely, companies may focus on cost-effectiveness as a necessary condition to compete. However, since competitors can also purchase similar technologies, it is difficult to differentiate production processes and customer service from the competition. Firms practicing a strategy execution and service level focus on aligning their IT and business infrastructures & processes. Operational alignment focuses on maximising resource productivity. This minimises wasted resources by improving visibility and information flow between employees. Thus, firms pursuing operational alignment will be better positioned to create a competitive advantage through the development of greater operational efficiencies e.g. operational excellence.

Another framework used to manage enterprise IT software applications and software-based services is Applications Portfolio Management (APM). Based around the Growth-Share Matrix, developed by the Boston Consulting Group, APM enables organisations to:

- identify redundant or semi-redundant applications
- quantify the stability, quality, and maintainability of applications
- quantify the relative importance of each application to the business
- allocate resources to applications based upon business priorities

2.6 Strategic Choice

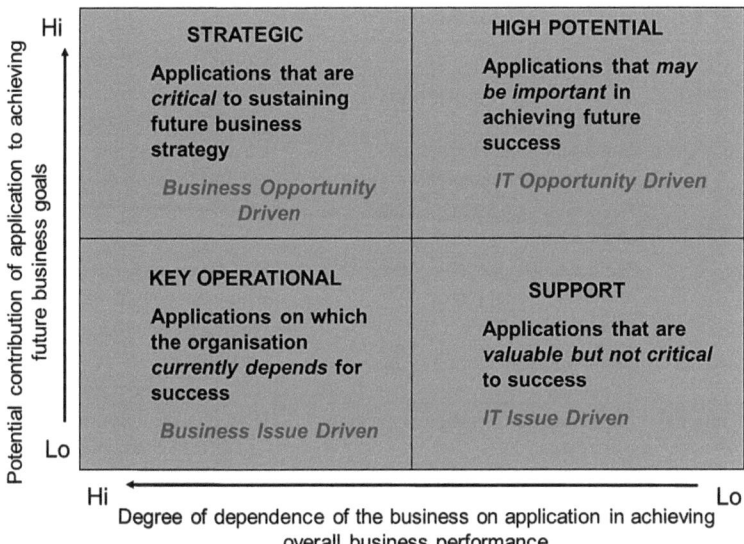

Fig. 2.10 Applications portfolio

APM also allows managers to understand how applications support their business functions. This helps defuse business/IT conflict.

Using their contribution to current and future objectives, the APM matrix (Fig. 2.10) allows applications to be categorised as strategic, key operational, high potential or support. Each application has a lifecycle and, over time, may move from one segment to another. How each application is resourced is determined by where it lies in the APM matrix.

One of the benefits of APM is that it compels both business and IT managers to define the term 'application', to understand where the boundaries between applications lie and to make explicit the business rationale for each application. To be included in the portfolio matrix an application must (Table 2.5):

- be simple for business team members to explain, understand, and apply
- make sense to development, operations, and project management in the IT groups
- have clearly defined boundaries

Figure 2.11 shows how a manufacturing company may view its applications. The matrix can be made more elaborate by, say, using the cost (either purchase price or annual maintenance costs) to signify the diameter of an application 'bubble'. This is a useful way to capture the cost/benefits of each application.

Table 2.5 Key issues in portfolio segments

	Business driver	Critical requirements
High potential	Business idea or technology opportunity	Rapid evaluation to avoid wasting resources on failures
	Individual initiative – owned by a 'product champion'	Clear understanding of potential benefits to business strategy
	Need to demonstrate the value of the idea	Identify best way forward
Strategic	Market requirements, competitive or other external forces	Fast development to meet objectives within window of opportunity
	Business objectives	Flexible system that can be adapted for future use
	Achieving/maintaining competitive advantage	
Key operational	Improving performance of existing activities	High quality, long-life solutions and effective data management
	Integration of data and systems to avoid duplication and inconsistency	Balancing costs with benefits and risks
	Avoid business disadvantage or allowing risk to become critical	
Support	Improved productivity and/or efficiency of specific business tasks	Low-cost, long-term solutions
	Comply with legislation	Compromise the processes to the software available
	Most cost-effective use of IS/IT funds	Objective cost/benefit analysis to reduce financial risk then manage costs carefully

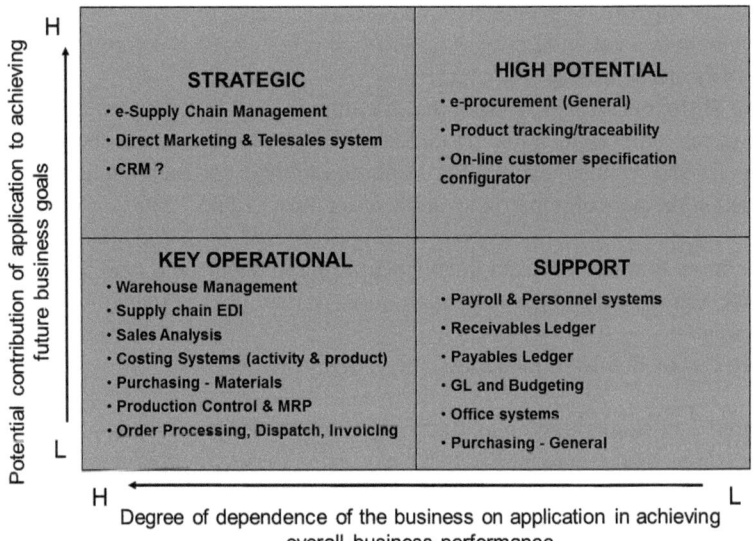

Fig. 2.11 Applications portfolio – an example from manufacturing

2.7 Summary

In this chapter we have examined how big data impacts organisational strategies and how those strategies are developed. We have investigated the strategy process before going on to examine some of the frameworks used to investigate the business environment and evaluate strategic alternatives. Finally, we have looked, briefly, at how business strategy and IT/IS strategy may be aligned.

2.8 Review Questions

The answers to these questions can be found in the text of this chapter.

- what does the acronym PESTEL mean, and what is it used for?
- describe Porter's 5-forces. What can they tell us about the business environment?
- what are the implications of big data on a firms value chain?
- describe the three 'value disciplines'
- what are the advantages and disadvantages of Application Portfolio Management

2.9 Group Work Research Activities

These activities require you to research beyond the contents of the book and can be tackled individually or as a discussion group.

2.9.1 Discussion Topic 1

In this chapter we have discussed scenario planning. In the 1970s Oil giant, Royal Dutch Shell, established a Scenario Planning Division which has become the envy of many multinationals (Cornelius et al. 2005, p. 53). Using a search engine, investigate the phrase, "Three decades of Scenario Planning in Shell". Alternatively, explore the Shell web-site: www.shell.com/global/future-energy/scenarios.html. How does Shell's approach to scenario planning compare to that of the PESTEL analysis discussed? What are the implications of big data for the way Shell prepares its scenarios?

2.9.2 Discussion Topic 2

Choose a company you are familiar with. What is its generic strategy (choose either one of Porters strategies or one of the Value Disciplines)? What sort of applications do you think the company will have in its applications portfolio? Try drawing an application portfolio matrix for the company you have chosen. Are the applications in the 'Strategic' quadrant consistent with the firms generic strategy?

References

Ansoff H (1988) Corporate strategy. Penguin, London
Cornelius P, van de Putte A, Romani M (2005) Three decades of scenario planning in shell. Calif Manage Rev 48(1):92–109
Hamel G (1997) Killer strategies that make shareholders rich. Fortune 135(12):70–84
Henderson J, Venkatraman N (1993) Strategic alignment: leveraging information technology for transforming organisations. IBM Syst J 32(1):4–16
Johnson G, Scholes K, Whittington R (2007) Exploring corporate strategy: text and cases, 8th edn. Financial Times/Prentice Hall, London
Magretta J (2012) Understanding Michael Porter: the essential guide to competition and strategy, 1st edn. Harvard Business Review Press, Boston
Mintzberg H (1994) The rise and fall of strategic planning: reconceiving roles for planning, plans, planners, vol 458. Free Press, New York
Parise S, Iyer B, Vesset D (2012) Four strategies to capture and create value from big data. Ivey Bus J 76(4):1–5
Porter M (1980) Competitive strategy, 1st edn. Free Press, New York
Porter M (1985) Competitive advantage, 1st edn. Free Press, New York
Treacy M, Wiersema F (1993) Customer intimacy and other value disciplines. Harv Bus Rev 71(1):84–93

Structure   3

3.1   What the Reader Will Learn

- Organisational structure is both formal and informal – informal structure is known as organisational culture.
- Formal structure comprises five basic elements and how power is assigned to each of these elements determines how the organisation is structured
- Information politics determines how information is (or is not) shared across the organisation
- The Cultural Web offers a framework with which to investigate organisational culture
- For some organisations an inability to change culture will limit their response to the opportunities promised by big data

3.2   Introduction

Many people, when asked to describe organisational structure, would immediately reach for the firm's hierarchical chart used to identify levels of authority, individual roles and scope of responsibility (Fig. 3.1). But what does this tell us about the company? And, perhaps more interestingly, what *doesn't* it tell us? At first sight we can, conceivably, understand the 'power' structure – who has it and in what measure. We can clearly see demarcations of operational functionality and, arguably, the importance given to a particular function or role. However, things may not always be as they seem. For example, can we assume from this chart that each of the directors has the same amount of influence with the CEO? Are the roles of the Network Administrator, the Sales Ledger Clerk and the truck drivers all considered equally valuable (and rewarded accordingly)?

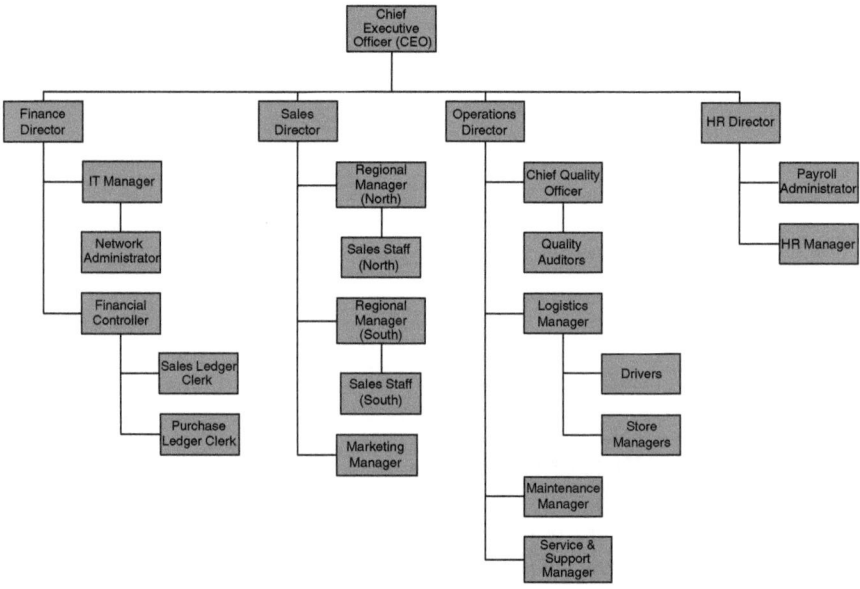

Fig. 3.1 Typical organisational chart

In 1949 Henri Fayol specified the five primary functions of management as:

- **Commanding**: Giving instructions to employees in order to maintain activity towards the organisations objectives
- **Controlling**: Inspection, monitoring and surveillance of work done
- **Coordinating**: Structuring of the resources of the organisation so that, when combined, they work to achieve the organisations goals
- **Organising**: Acquiring/developing the necessary structures and resources to best meet the needs of the organisation
- **Planning**: Looking to the future in order to anticipate the changing needs and circumstances of the organisation.

Of these five functions, four are associated with organisational structure and in this chapter we will discuss the role of formal structures. We will also investigate informal, underlying structure (often called organisational culture) and examine the challenges today's leaders face in introducing Big Data. In order to understand the barriers to Big Data adoption we will start by reviewing established organisational theory. We will then examine how this perceived wisdom is being challenged and how organisations are responding to those challenges. Finally we will look forward and try to visualise what the possible legacy of big data will be for the structure of tomorrow's organisations.

3.3 What Is 'Structure'?

3.3.1 What Do We Mean by 'Structure'?

Beyond very small organisations, those in which the leader makes all key decisions and communication is carried out using one-to-one conversation, most companies have some manner of formal bureaucratic structure (King and Lawley 2013), that is, structure determined by:

- A hierarchy, defining roles and responsibilities, with each level reporting to the level above and directing the level below
- Explicit rules, procedures and policies which control activity across the organisation
- Forms, records and timetables used to codify information about the firms people and processes in an efficient manner
- Rationalisation, the replacement of traditions, values, and emotions as behavioral motivators with rational, calculated ones (targets, bonuses, commissions etc.)

Historically, hierarchy, such as that shown in Fig. 3.1, arose as a response to controlling employees as companies grew larger. In a small company the number of staff an owner/manager can manage (the *span of control*) are usually in the region of 5–7 people (King and Lawley 2013). However, as the company grows and the number of staff increases the ability to maintain a close relationship with each member of staff is diminished. By delegating some control to 'managers' the owner can reduce personal, face-to-face interaction with employees and thus focus on other tasks.

The formalisation of written rules, procedures, and paperwork is an equally important aspect of the bureaucracy, ensuring standardisation of behaviour and activities throughout the organization, without the direct intervention of the owner/manager. These rules and procedures require, and are enabled by, the keeping of records and paperwork. Record keeping serves two purposes in controlling the organization.

- It standardises the information to enable ease of access, retrieval, and use in controlling the policies that it supports
- It provides a record of an employee's activities that can be accessed as required. This allows further control through surveillance and monitoring of employees. For example, in a large organisation an employee's performance or attendance might be 'lost'. However, time and attendance data, time sheets and appraisal records allow management identify and exert control if, for example, there is a problematic absence record.

So, for many, structure is encapsulated within the organisational chart and accompanying rules and paperwork – what we will call the formal structure of the organisation. This structure is often an abstract manifestation of the deep-rooted organisational culture or informal structure. In the same way that hierarchy is an instrument of control, culture is a mechanism of social control, used to manipulate employees into perceiving, thinking and feeling in certain ways. Likewise, in the same way that the formal structure uses rules, so the 'rules' of social order help employees anticipate behaviour in others and find meaning in what they do. Schein (2010) suggests that:

> ...culture is to a group what personality or character is to an individual. We can see the behaviour that results, but we often cannot see the forces underneath that cause certain kinds of behaviour

In the following two sections we will examine both formal and informal structures and how the two are related. We will also consider the role of the leader in shaping organisational structure.

3.4 Formal Structures

3.4.1 The "Organisational Chart": What Does It Tell Us?

Take another look at Fig. 3.1, what do you see?

Each 'box' represents a particular function within the organisation and is (or should be!) accompanied by a title and a job description, let's call this a 'role'. The job description specifies the number and breadth of tasks allocated to the post (horizontal job specialisation) and the role-holders control over these tasks (vertical job specialisation). The job description, along with other rules, procedures and policy manuals define how work will be standardised. Typically, unskilled jobs are much more formalised than skilled jobs.

The roles are arranged at different levels forming a triangle (hierarchy) with a number of roles at a lower level being grouped with a single role at a higher level. This identifies the span of control of the higher level role, thus, in Fig. 3.1 the CEO has a span of control of four. While traditional management thinking suggests that an acceptable span of control is considered to be 5–7 staff, other control mechanisms allow managers to stretch the span of control much wider than this (the span of control for the Vice-President of Engineering at Google is approximately 160). In addition to the horizontal 'tiers' there are also functional groups that run vertically through the hierarchy. We will discuss the advantages and disadvantages of functional groups later in this chapter. Clearly, in larger organisations the organisational chart may be multi-dimensional with groups representing product markets or international regions.

Unfortunately, for large and complex organisations, hierarchical charts quickly outgrow their usefulness and individual roles are lost, only to be replaced with overarching functions or departments. Organisation charts fail to differentiate between

3.4 Formal Structures

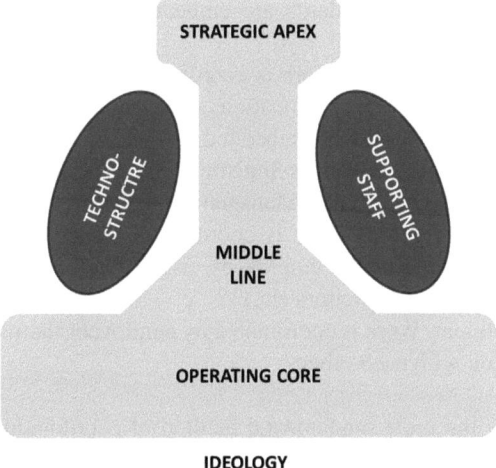

Fig. 3.2 The basic elements of the organisation (Mintzberg 1980)

those who produce the basic product or service and those whose role is the design and maintenance of the structure itself. Finally, organisation charts rarely indicate what is 'important' to the firm, what 'type' of company it is.

Mintzberg (1980) suggests that organisations have five basic elements (Fig. 3.2):

1. **The Strategic Apex**: the senior managers/executives of the organisation
2. **The Operating Core**: the employees who produce the basic products/services or directly support their production
3. **The Middle Line**: the managers that sit in a direct line of formal authority between the strategic apex and the operating core
4. **The Technostructure**: Staff outside of the formal 'production' structure who help design, maintain and adapt to organisation to its environment (accountants, work-schedulers etc.)
5. **Support staff**: Employees that provide indirect support (legal counsel, payroll, catering etc.)

However, far from being a rigid structure, the hierarchy of the firm is malleable and can be shaped by forces exerted by each of the structural elements and contingent factors such as; the age and size of the company, the business environment and the nature of the work being done. As we noted earlier coordination is one of the five key functions of management. If the boxes and job descriptions of the organisation chart are an indication of division of labour, coordination defines how these disparate roles and resources are brought together to achieve the organisational objectives. Coordination can be achieved in a number of ways:

(i) Direct supervision: A manager gives orders to others and in so doing coordinates their work
(ii) Standardisation of work processes: The work is coordinated by the definition of standards regarding the work itself i.e. work orders, rules, regulations etc.

Today many of these standards are embedded within Enterprise Resource Planning (ERP) systems

(iii) Standardisation of outputs: Work is coordinated by the definition of standard performance measures or specifications concerning the outputs of the work. Again these standards may be embedded within ERP systems and are typified in production techniques such as Statistical Process Control (SPC), Six-Sigma manufacturing or Total Quality Management (TQM).
(iv) Standardisation of skills: Work is coordinated by the internalisation of the skills and knowledge of the employees, usually before they begin to do the work (doctors, nurses, solicitors etc.)
(v) Mutual adjustment: Work is coordinated by employees themselves by informal communication with each other.

Unquestionably the most fundamental method of coordination is that of direct supervision. Here the strategic apex, in small companies or start-ups the owner/entrepreneur, retains control over decision-making. This gives rise to the *Simple Structure* (Fig. 3.3).

In this structure coordination is achieved by informal communication as the staff who perform the work constantly interact with each other. Consequently, there is little formalised behaviour and limited division of labour. Consequently, the structure is both flexible and organic. As a result the organisation does not require a Technostructure or Middle Line and many of the support activities are done on an ad hoc basis. Information systems are typically unsophisticated, informal, stand-alone systems, or small networks. Given the organisations size, its information processing needs are limited and financial resources are mainly dedicated to growing the business.

As a company grows in complexity (and headcount) managers are employed in the Middle Line to control the Operating Core. However, this is insufficient to ensure coordination as each individual in the Middle Line may have different norms regarding how the work should be done. Consequently, the Technostructure emerges in response to the need for standardisation of work processes, thus creating the *Machine Bureaucracy* (Fig. 3.5). Initially, the power of the Technostructure comes at the expense of the Operating Core, whose work becomes highly formalised.

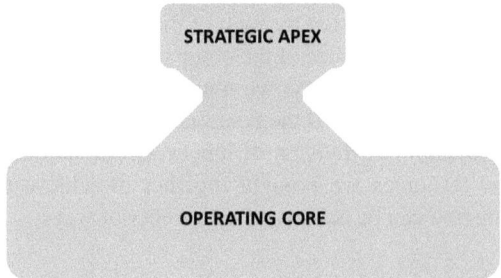

Fig. 3.3 The simple structure

3.4 Formal Structures

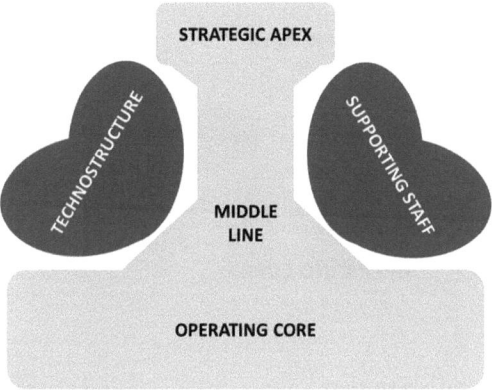

Fig. 3.4 The machine bureaucracy

However, as its influence grows rules, procedures and policies pervade the whole structure, communication becomes increasingly formalised and decision-making follows a formal chain of command. This need for formalisation, standardisation of processes and the subsequent rules and policies can be achieved using comprehensive Management Information Systems (MIS) or Enterprise Resource Planning (ERP) systems (Morton and Hu 2008).

The Machine Bureaucracy is typically found in large, mature companies operating in business environments that are both simple and stable. However, as can be seen in Fig. 3.4, a major disadvantage of this structure is the relative isolation of functions from each other (functional silos). In Machine Bureaucracies functional responsibilities only converge at the strategic apex, often making cross-functional planning and decision-making slow.

The simple structure and the machine bureaucracy both reflect the desire of the strategic apex to centralise power. However, the behaviour of the operating core can be coordinated and decentralised through the standardisation of skills. This *Professional Bureaucracy* (Fig. 3.5) allows the 'professionals' in the operating core to work more autonomously and relatively free from the burdens of administrative hierarchy. This permits the, much leaner, Middle Line to have far larger spans of control.

The Technostructure is limited since the complex work of the professionals cannot be formalised. Conversely, the support function may be relatively large in order to minimise the time professionals spend on less value-added tasks. This structure is found in universities, accounting firms and some craft manufacturing businesses where the environment is complex, thus requiring knowledge and skills accrued through extensive training, but sufficiently stable for those skills to become embedded within the organisation.

Given that many of the professionals work independently one might expect the IT requirements to be high. However, the inherent skill of each person often requires very little task-oriented information processing between individuals (unless a

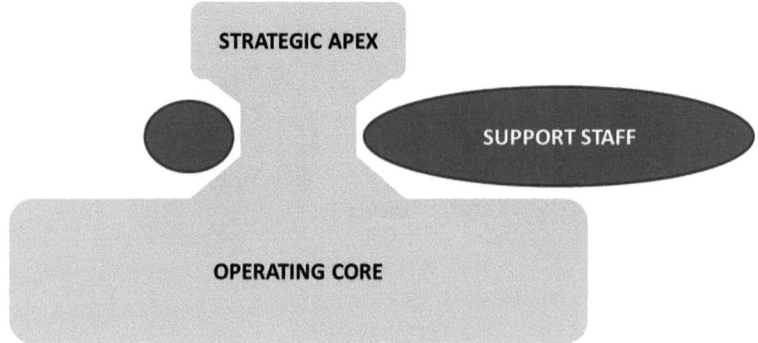

Fig. 3.5 The professional bureaucracy

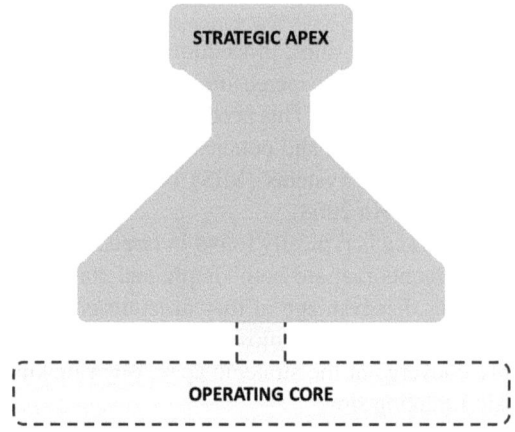

Fig. 3.6 The adhocracy

particular skill set is required from another colleague to resolve a problem). More important is the ease of access to external sources of information such as journal articles, medical case studies, stock market activity or legal briefs. Conversely, the support function may require complex administrative information systems to maintain the skill-based technical core.

Complex innovation requires a structure that allows the rapid assembly of experts from various specialties into efficient project teams. The *Adhocracy* (Fig. 3.6) groups specialists into functional groups for the purpose of housekeeping, but with little formalisation and coordination by mutual adjustment these specialists can be deployed to market- or product-based teams quickly and easily. Adhocracy is suited to complex and dynamic environments such as consultancies, advertising agencies and film companies (Operational Adhocracies) where the innovation is achieved on behalf of the client or, alternatively, where internal project work such as research and development (Administrative Adhocracies) is required.

Adhocracies are built on teamwork and require a high level of information sharing and processing. Frequently these information requirements limit the size of the structure (adhocracies are often transient divisions within a more rigid divisional structure). Consequently, the greatest threat to the adhocratic structure is that of age, as time encourages the shift to bureaucratisation. This can be seen in once-flexible companies such as Microsoft, Oracle and SAP, all of which have evolved from adhocracies to other more rigid, formal structures.

These contingent approaches to organisational structure are regarded by some as a major shift from the one 'ideal type' of bureaucracy advocated by Max Weber in the 1900s. However, these structural designs still use aspects of bureaucracy and rationalisation. For example, to maintain its efficiency levels McDonalds, the fast-food franchise, uses rationalised techniques founded in scientific management, bureaucracy, and the assembly line of a century ago (Ritzer 2011). Furthermore, these organizational techniques are still found in most modern-day organizations, with one difference, they have been automated by technology...

3.4.2 Structure, Systems and Processes

We noted at the start of this chapter that formal bureaucratic structure is determined by:

- A hierarchical structure: used to define roles and responsibilities
- Explicit rules and procedures: used to control activity across the organisation
- Forms and records: used to codify information

Moreover, we noted that one method of coordination was by the standardisation of work processes and that a particular drawback of the traditional hierarchy was the tendency towards functional isolation (functional silos). Consequently, as organisations grew larger and more complex, the efficiency of cross-functional business processes, such as order fulfilment (Fig. 3.7), began to deteriorate. Deliveries were late, wrong goods were shipped or were unavailable from the manufacturing department.

In the 1990s rapid improvements in computer-based manufacturing resource planning (MRP) systems coincided with a shift to restructure organisations around core processes, the business process re-engineering movement. Using the newly designed 'enterprise resource planning systems' (ERPs) a single transaction such as a sales order could "flow through" the entire applications suite, simultaneously updating financial and inventory records without further data entry. The move towards ERP systems was accelerated as companies recognised the implications of the Year 2000 (Y2K) problem and by 1998 almost 40 % of companies with annual revenues of more than $1 billion had implemented ERP systems (Markus et al. 2000). Today the ERP market is worth in excess of $25 bill/annum with leaders SAP having a 25 % market share followed by Oracle with 15 %. So are structural issues are a thing of the past? Not at all...

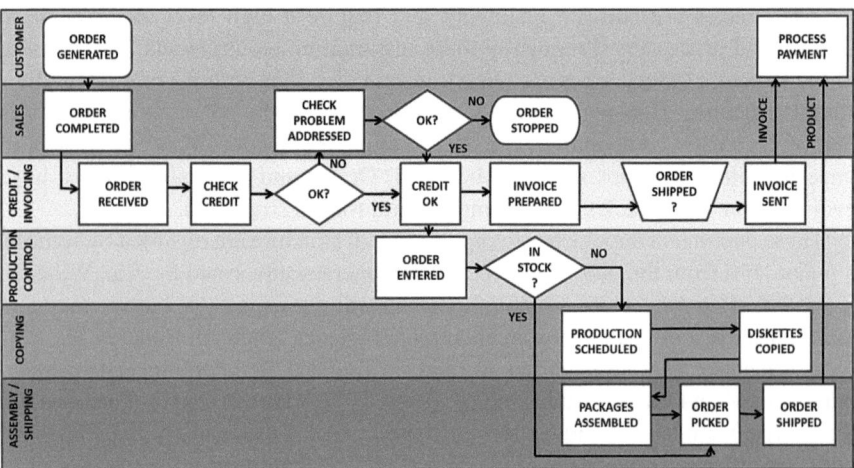

Fig. 3.7 The order fulfilment process

Far from being the much-vaunted 'silver bullet', ERP systems have exposed many of the structural complexities hidden behind the 'Org. Chart'. By 2000 more than half of ERP implementations were judged to be failures (Scheer and Habermann 2000). High profile failures include:

- In 1999, US Confectioner, Hershey, whose ERP implementations problems prevented it from delivering $100 million worth of chocolate 'Kisses' for Halloween and caused the share price to fall 8 %
- In 2000, sports clothing manufacturer Nike, spent $400 million upgrading their ERP systems only to incur $100 million in lost sales, a 20 % fall in share price and a series of legal battles
- In 2004, technology manufacturer, Hewlett Packard, intended to centralise its disparate North American ERP systems onto one system. The project eventually cost HP $160 million in order backlogs and lost revenue — more than five times the project's estimated cost. "We had a series of small problems, none of which individually would have been too much to handle. But together they created a perfect storm" Gilles Bouchard, then-CIO of HP's global operations
- In 2010, the rancorous legal battle between garbage-disposal giant 'Waste Management' and ERP vendor SAP was resolved when SAP finally settled out-of-court. The initial 18 month project started in 2005, but the legal saga began in March 2008, when Waste Management claimed that SAP executives participated in fraudulent selling that resulted in the massive failure ($100 million). Several months later SAP claimed that Waste Management had violated its contractual agreement by "failing to timely and accurately define its business requirements," and not providing "sufficient, knowledgeable, decision-empowered users and managers" to work on the project.

3.4 Formal Structures

- In 2008, when bedding-maker Select Comfort's $20 million multi-module ERP implementation of ERP hit problems shareholder pressure led to the project being shelved. As one shareholder said of the project, it was, "indicative of extremely poor judgment by management"
- In 2012, the United States Air Force scrapped the Oracle ERP project that began in 2005. After 7 years and costs of $1 billion, the Air Force were notified that project delivery slip to 2020 (3 years after the original deadline) and costs would increase by a further $1.1 billion

Contrast these failures with successes such as Motts North America Inc., a large producer of fruit-based products, who claim highly successful implementations and major costs savings. So, why does ERP work for some companies and not for others? Is there some correlation between ERP implementation success and the contingency structures discussed earlier?

In 2008 Morton and Hu compared the contingent organisational structures with ERP implementation success (Table 3.1).

The results suggest that ERP systems are more easily implemented and adopted in formal, centralised organisations, typically those with a machine bureaucracy structure. The biggest challenge in these particular implementations is achieving task interdependence; that is reducing the effect of functional silos. Conversely, experts within professional bureaucracies demand considerable autonomy in their work, while the standards of that work are formalised by the professions themselves, not by procedures. Consequently, imposing formal structures on professionals often leads to political conflicts and resistance. For example Montclair State University (Kanaracus 2011):

> Montclair State University is suing Oracle over an allegedly botched ERP software project, saying a series of missteps and delays could ultimately cost the school some $20 million more than originally planned…The school entered into contracts with Oracle in 2009 for a PeopleSoft suite that was supposed to replace a 25-year-old set of legacy applications. The school and Oracle also agreed on a $15.75 million fixed-fee contract for implementation ser-

Table 3.1 Contingency fit between ERP and organisational types (Adapted from Morton and Hu 2008)

Organisational type	Structural dimensions			Degree of fit and likelihood of ERP success
	Formalisation	Structural differentiation	Centralisation	
Machine bureaucracy	High	Medium	High	High
Professional bureaucracy	Low	High	Low	Low
Professional bureaucracy (support function only)	High	Medium	High	High
Adhocracy	Low	High	Low	Low

vices…the project was supposed to be done over a 25-month period, but Oracle "failed to deliver key implementation services, caused critical deadlines to be missed, refused to make available computer resources that it had promised, failed to deliver properly tested software, and overall, failed to manage properly the project," the complaint alleges. In the end, Montclair suspended the project, fired Oracle and began looking for a replacement systems integrator. Due to the problems, the school's costs will increase by greater than $10 million…After conferring with an Oracle attorney, the [Oracle] workers handed their access keys to Montclair's CIO, "said 'here you go' and 'we're out of here,'" left campus and never returned

Adhocracies are equally problematic for ERP implementation. Organisations with little formalisation and centralisation make process integration difficult. Furthermore, most adhocracies require structural flexibility and are often quite transient (ComputerWeekly.com 2002):

Hewlett-Packard spin-off Agilent Technologies yesterday blamed the company's poor third quarter results on a problem-strewn big-bang ERP rollout. The failure to get the system up and running properly cost the company $70 m (£46 m) in lost operating profits, as manufacturing went offline for a week. Addressing shareholders, Agilent Technologies chief financial officer Adrian Dillon said: "In truth, it was almost impossible to fully anticipate how things would go wrong even with the extraordinary amount of training and testing we did in preparation for the big-bang rollout." Given the size and complexity of the project, Dillon said Agilent expected some teething troubles during the early phases of the implementation. However, the company encountered three major problems: a fundamental software flaw that caused the system to crash each time it handled 50 % or more of Agilent's operations; poor system uptime; and a problem migrating data from its legacy system

So what's actually happening with organisational structure? For decade's management consultants, academics and ERP vendors have urged large companies to flatten or delayer their hierarchies. Flattening, it has been suggested, offers the potential for reducing costs and improving response times while pushing control, decision-making and accountability down the hierarchy to the operating core, the 'front-line workers'. Likewise, the demise of the hierarchy itself has been predicted by pundits and scholars for almost 40 years. Indeed, the emergence of email, social networking and crowdsourcing has increased the perception that hierarchy is becoming less relevant.

Certainly companies have de-layered, leaving CEO's with broader spans of control and with some decision-making authority being pushed down the hierarchy (Wulf 2012). However, far from decentralising control, this de-layering has led to more centralised control and decision-making at the top. CEOs have accrued more functions (note the advent of CFOs, CHROs, CIOs, COOs, CXOs etc.) and paid lower-level managers less, thus increasing the differential salaries of the "top team" versus "everyone else". Furthermore, in interviews CEOs claim to have flattened the structure to "get closer to the business" and become more involved (Wulf 2012). What of hierarchy itself? Its departure has long been forecast, only to be replaced by the matrix structure, adhocracy or other such structure. However, as Pfeffer (2013) observes:

The persistence of hierarchy and the competition for advancement it engenders suggest that the political dynamics and competition that characterize both work organisations and relations among employees are unlikely to have changed in the recent past or to change much in the future.

This is something worth considering given much of the hype surrounding the potential effects of Big Data.

3.4.3 Formal Structure: What Does This Mean for Big Data?

Despite all of the management and academic rhetoric, despite stories of success of Google, Yahoo, Amazon and the other internet businesses, we are left with a much more fundamental question, "How can 20th century organisational structures handle 21st century information business?" Consider the following two quotations (note the dates):

> Today, in fact, the information-based organisation is largely a fantasy. All of the writers on information-based organisations must speak hypothetically, in the abstract, or in the future tense. Despite forty years of the Information revolution in business, most managers tell us that they cannot get the information they need to run their own units or functions (Davenport et al. 1992)

> The biggest reason that investments in big data don't pay off…is that most companies don't do a good job with the information that they have…One reason might be that their management practices haven't caught up with their technology platforms. Companies that installed digital platforms – ERP and CRM systems, real-time data warehouses, and home-grown core information systems – over the past 10 to 15 years have not yet cashed in on the information those platforms make available (Ross et al. 2013)

It seems little has changed in the last 20 years. In 1992 it was widely believed that the use of information technology would allow information to flow freely through the organisation and to quickly eliminate the need for hierarchy. Today, we are told that success in Big Data requires; a single, authorised source of 'the truth' (centralised data), analytical scorecards clarifying an individual's accountability (control) and performance and explicit business rules (Ross et al. 2013). Furthermore, the early-adopters of big data companies appear to be:

(i) The 'Internet-centric' companies: Such as Google, Amazon, LinkedIn etc. These are the companies whose life-blood is the data that they capture; it is in their organisational DNA. Perhaps, for them, the challenge is not how to exploit Big Data, but how to manage organisational growth and the traditional challenge of control versus innovation
(ii) The 'data-ready' companies: These include logistics companies such as UPS, who have evolved a data-rich infrastructure as a consequence of their type of business. Businesses that have a broad use of telematics are already collecting significant volumes of data – big data simply adds value to their current business models
(iii) Science/engineering research organisations: Oil companies (or certainly their geology functions) collect and collate significant amounts of data, similarly pharmaceutical and bio-tech firms are data-rich and have organisational structures that encourage the acquisition of data.

Interestingly, almost without exception, the 'data-ready' companies and, to a lesser extent, the 'research organisations' are more likely to be those that have invested in ERP systems. These companies have thousands of business rules – in some cases the rules embedded in ERP system essentially run the company. Whereas in the past employees had to learn the rules in order to execute their jobs, today they are automated within ERP systems. The advantages of this are that:

- The business rules, developed by the Technostructure, are consistently executed
- The rules are easier to analyse
- They are clearly codified and so provide more opportunity to test, experiment and learn

The downside is:

- Companies have to specify who has responsibility and authority for a given set of rules (who change them), this re-enforces the 'control and command' structure of the company
- Current rules engines are an intrinsic part of the overall ERP system. Consequently, managing and changing rules requires IT expertise (Technostructure) which can be very expensive

It seems that data, be it big or small, presents problems for many organisations. Those with highly bureaucratic, hierarchical structures are able to impose and enforce the use of ERP systems but, as we saw above, "don't do a good job with the information that they have". For other, less rigid structures, ERP systems are considered counter-productive and rigid. Why, in the 'information age' is the way we collect, use and share information so difficult? Perhaps the answer lies in the politics surrounding the information we use.

3.4.4 Information Politics

> As people's jobs and roles become more defined by the unique information they hold, they may be less likely to share that information – viewing it as a source of power and indispensability-rather than more so. When information is the primary unit of currency, we should not expect its owners to give it away. Furthermore...as information becomes the basis for organisational structure and function, politics will increasingly come into play (Davenport et al. 1992)

In 1992 Davenport et al. concluded a two-year study of twenty-five companies. During this time they examined how individuals used and shared (or withheld) data. Their findings suggested that companies (or in some cases departments within companies) could be defined by one of five models of information politics:

- ***Technocratic utopianism***: Driven by technical professionals within the IT department, part of Mintzberg's Technostructure, this model pays less attention to the data and more to the IT infrastructure. This approach stresses the categorisation of all the organisations information assets with a strong focus on emerging technologies. It assumes that data will be shared willingly across the organisational hierarchy

- *Anarchy*: The absence of any form of information management, each individual acquires and maintains their own information
- *Feudalism*: The management of information by business units, functions or groups, which define their own information needs and report a limited amount of this to the organisation as a whole
- *Monarchy*: The information requirements, categories and reporting is determined by the senior management team (strategic apex) who may choose to share it or not after it is collected
- *Federalism*: An approach to information management based on consensus and negotiation regarding the firms key information elements and reporting structures

In considering organisational structure and big data, combining organisational structure and models of information politics is quite interesting:

	Machine Bureaucracy	Professional Bureaucracy	Adhocracy
Technocratic Utopianism	May occur if senior management team does not realise the importance of common information and the CIO is influential. The main big data sponsor is likely to be CIO	May occur if the professionals can see the benefits of big data but delegate the realisation of big data to the IT department and/or the CIO. The main big data sponsor is likely to be CIO	May occur if the various groups can see the benefits of big data but delegate the realisation of big data to the IT department and/or the CIO. The main big data sponsor is likely to be CIO
	Big data initiatives likely to fail due to lack of business strategy/buy-in	*Big data initiatives likely to fail due to lack of business strategy/buy-in*	*Big data initiatives likely to fail due to lack of business strategy/buy-in*
Anarchy	May occur if senior management team does not realise the importance of common information and CIO/IT department lacks influence	Highly likely if professionals have no reason to collaborate and/or do not realise the importance of common information	Unstable. Unlikely to occur for anything but a short period of time as groups within the adhocracy rely on a solid IT infrastructure to collaborate
	Big data initiatives are unlikely	*Big data initiatives are unlikely*	*Big data initiatives are unlikely*

(continued)

	Machine Bureaucracy	Professional Bureaucracy	Adhocracy
Feudalism	Without central coordination, business unit or functional managers attempt to build their own analytic fiefdoms. Hard to break analytics efforts out of institutional silos	Without central coordination, each professional attempts to build their own analytic fiefdoms	Without central coordination, adhocratic groups attempt to build their own analytic fiefdoms
	Big data initiatives possible at department level but insufficient data sharing for enterprise-wide initiative	*Big data initiatives possible by individuals or small groups of professionals but insufficient data sharing for enterprise-wide initiative*	*Big data initiatives possible within groups but insufficient data sharing for enterprise-wide initiative*
Monarchy	**Fully centralized**. The corporate centre takes direct responsibility for identifying and prioritizing initiatives	Requires strong leadership to overcome the tendency for professionals to horde information	Requires strong leadership to manage the inclination of adhocratic groups to focus on their own information requirements
	Netflix is an example of a company that pursues this route	*Big data is achievable but requires major cultures change*	*Big data is achievable but requires strong management, a flexible IT infrastructure and major cultures change*
Federalism	**Business unit led**. When business units have distinct data sets and scale isn't an issue, each business unit can make its own Big Data decisions with limited coordination	**Business unit led with central support.** Professional groups, led with central support. The groups make their own decisions but collaborate on selected initiatives	Some companies establish an independent **Centre of Excellence** (CoE) that over-sees the company's Big Data initiatives and units pursue initiatives under the CoE's guidance and coordination
	AT&T and Zynga are among the companies that rely on this model	*Google and Progressive are examples of this approach*	*Amazon and LinkedIn rely on CoEs*

At present, in those organisations that are 'doing' Big Data, it is typified by one of four organisational structures:

- Fully centralised
- Business unit led
- Business unit led with central support
- Centres of excellence

However, much depends on the extent to which the corporate body, that is the Strategic Apex, wishes to involve itself with big data initiatives. Figure 3.8 indicates the most common areas of involvement of the Strategic Apex:

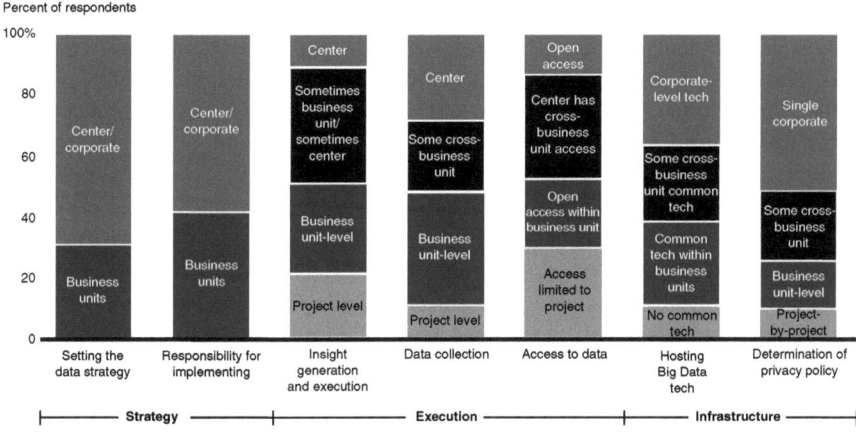

Fig. 3.8 The role of the strategic apex and business units in shaping big data (Pearson and Wegener 2013)

3.5 Organisational Culture: The Informal Structure

3.5.1 What Do We Mean by 'Culture'?

If formal structure is explicit, as inferred by the hierarchical organisation chart, then the informal structure, the organisational culture, is far more implicit and hidden. If an organisation were a person, formal structure might reflect that way that the person looked or dressed, whereas organisational culture would be that person's character or personality. Outwardly we would be able to see how that person behaved but we would have no insight into the forces driving that behaviour. Schein (2010) defines organisational culture as:

> …a pattern of shared basic assumptions learned by a group as it solved its problems of external adaptation and internal integration, which has worked well enough to be considered valid and, therefore, to be taught to new members as the correct way to perceive, think, and feel in relation to those problems

Ultimately, it is organisational culture, crafted by those 'shared basic assumptions' that will determine how far and how fast the phenomena of Big Data grows and which companies are the winners and losers in the era of Big Data.

3.5.2 Culture and Leadership

In Chap. 4 we will discuss management 'style' and leadership. However, it is in the creation, embedding and shaping of organisational culture that leadership plays its most formative role. Imagine a group of people gather to discuss the possibility of working together to start a new company (or society, or club). At this stage there is no leader, no manager and no hierarchy. Each person tables their ideas, concerns and questions which culminate in one or more immediate dilemmas; "What will we sell?", "What kind of product/service will we offer?" and so on. One member of the team puts forward her solution which reflects her own assumptions about what is right or wrong, what will work or not work. Others join in and, ultimately, the group will either, fail to agree and break-up, or accept one or more of the ideas proposed. Those individuals whose ideas are adopted, who have influenced the team to assume a certain approach, may be tacitly identified as possible leaders. At this point the team has no collective knowledge because it has not yet taken any action and whatever has been proposed will be regarded as a test of leadership. Once the group takes action and observes the result, the 'leaders' proposition will either be considered a success, and her credentials for retaining the mantle of leadership re-enforced, or considered a failure and her credentials damaged.

Going forward, assuming what the leader proposes continues to work, what once were only the leader's assumptions gradually become shared throughout the group. This, in turn, defines the personality and distinctiveness of the group and in this way culture is created, embedded, evolved, and manipulated by leaders. Thus, all group learning ultimately reflects the original assumptions, beliefs and values of one or two key founding individuals (for example, Bill Gates, Steve Jobs, Larry Ellison etc.). Consequently, the talents of the founders and leaders of the group may also determine which functions become dominant as the group evolves. For example, engineers establishing firms based on their own discoveries set up very different internal structures than, say, venture capitalists who pull together external technical and marketing skills. So what of more established companies? Even here the legacy of the founder casts a long shadow. Once a culture has been established it influences the criteria for future leadership, thus defining who may or may not be a suitable leader. Consider Apple, founded in 1976 by Steve Jobs and Steve Wozniak, both engineers. Apple was grounded on a technical, individualistic "do your own thing" mind-set. The decision to bring in John Sculley from PepsiCo in 1983 to improve market focus succeeded in growing the company from $800 million to $8 billion but alienated the technical community within Apple who never accepted Sculley. Jobs and Sculley clashed over management styles and priorities, Jobs focusing on future innovation and Sculley more on current product lines and profitability. Scully fired Jobs in 1985 but Apple eventually returned to its roots in bringing him back in 1996. By 2011 Apple had become the world's most valuable publicly traded company.

In this way culture truly evolves. Successful cultures are perpetuated, unsuccessful ones, those that result in failure, die. Likewise, some cultures can adapt to changing environmental conditions and grow those that can't wither. Consider, for example, the search-engine 'eco-system'. In July 1999 The Economist published a special report, "The Net Imperative", in which it examined the rise of the internet. The article discussed a number of fast growing companies including; Alta Vista (est. 1995), Northern Lights (est. 1996) and Yahoo! (est. 1998), all search

3.5 Organisational Culture: The Informal Structure

engine-based companies. In 2002 Northern Lights ceased trading, in 2003 Yahoo! bought Alta Vista and today Google (est. 1998) dominates the web search market. However, it would be wrong to take this metaphor too far. An organisation can rarely be considered a single, indivisible 'organism'. Within the organisation may be one or more sub-groups that do not have the same learning experiences that allow them to evolve a united culture in this sense. There may be a significant turnover of leaders or members or the fundamental task may change. Under these circumstances the company may split into differentiated or fragmented cultures. For example, a company managed by a CEO from a sales background may believe that the culture of the sales team permeates the whole company while being unaware that product development, product support and finance all have quite different cultural norms.

3.5.3 The "Cultural Web"

Perhaps one way to consider organisational culture is as a succession of layers (Fig. 3.9).

In this way the outer layers are the easiest to identify e.g. mission statements, objectives, strategies, work routines etc. but these are artefacts of a much deeper, much more complex 'paradigm', the set of taken-for-granted assumptions based upon the collective experience. Indeed, formal statements of values and beliefs may simply reflect the aspirations of the CEO, while being at odds with the actual

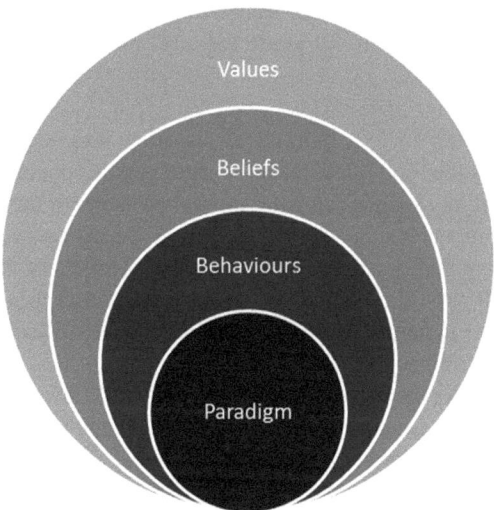

Fig. 3.9 Layers of culture (Schein 2010)

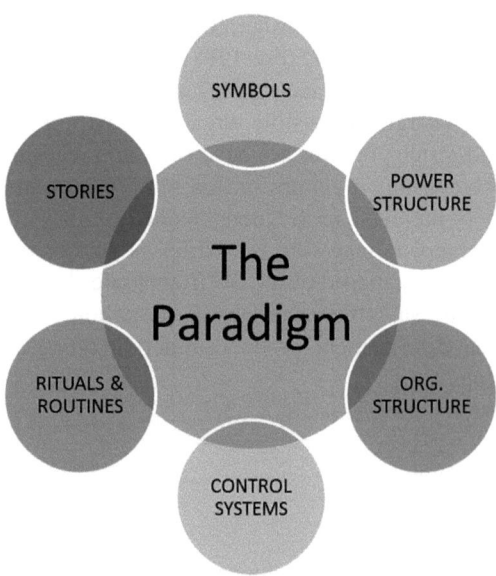

Fig. 3.10 The cultural web (Johnson 1992)

behaviour and paradigm of a company. For instance, a company may explicitly state that its strategy is to, "…attract and retain the very best talent who are valued and a key part of our success and growth", while having a high staff turnover due to lower-than-average salaries and poor staff development policies.

So, if we are to glimpse the paradigm that lies at the heart of organisational culture, it is often more important to see what a company *does*, on a day-to-day basis, rather than what is says. A useful guide for our observations is the cultural web (Fig. 3.10):

- *Symbols*: These may include things such as; office size, location or furnishings; company car models; job titles; business class versus economy class flights, the type of language used when referring to, say, products or customers. For example, in many companies desks by the window or the corner office (with windows on two sides) are highly regarded and are often symbols of the owners place in the hierarchy. It should be noted that many of the other aspects of the cultural web are symbolic in nature. However, symbols can be misleading and it is important not to infer from such artifacts alone.
- *Power structure*: As discussed earlier, power can take different forms within the organisation. The organisational chart is often symbolic of the formal power structure without reflecting where true power lies. For example, in one company we are familiar with a particular individual has a title of "Product Development Director". It is, to all intents and purposes, an honorary title. He continues to do the job of a senior software developer, spending little time in planning or budgetary meetings. However, unlike many of the senior management team, he has been

with the company throughout the development of its most successful products and has overseen many of the products improvements and elaborations. Consequently, he determines how the product will evolve in the future and, by doing so, defines major parameters of the firm's strategy.
- **Organisational structure**: Beyond the formal hierarchy chart it is useful to establish how information flows within the organisation. Are 'orders' sent from the top of the hierarchy and disseminated to the lower ranks of the Middle Line and Operating Core? Is there much two-way communication? Are there specific meetings that seem to determine the short and medium term actions? Who attends these meetings?
- **Control systems**: What metrics are used to measure and reward performance? Reward systems often disclose what is genuinely important to organisations. For example, a company claiming to be employing a "customer intimate" strategy (see Chap. 2) that has a highly structured commission plan for its sales force but an ad hoc reward process for its Service and Support staff is, at best, dysfunctional. Likewise, the way organisations account for, say, out-of-pocket expenses or the purchase of train or air-tickets or hotels, often infers what is considered 'valuable' within the paradigm
- **Rituals & Routines**: Both the day-to-day behaviour of organisational staff and that shown on special occasions often gives insights to the deep-rooted paradigm. Understanding 'the way things are done around here' is important and insightful. How are major decisions communicated? Is information leaked and followed by formal announcement? Is it acceptable to disagree with one's boss? One company we know regularly organises golf tournaments, visits to rugby matches and evenings at a casino. These are always attended by the sales staff (all male) and, sometimes, a handful of other staff. While no-one is obliged to attend, sales staff who fail to attend are considered 'light-weight' and tend to be marginalised within the team. Conversely, the non-sales staff that attend are often regarded as gate-keepers between the sales team and the rest of the company, thus enhancing their status within the organisation
- **Stories**: Tales, anecdotes and narratives shared within the organisation, to outsiders and new employees help contextualise and embed the company as it is at present with its history. These stories often underpin what the organisation defines as success (and failure). Stories are also used to emphasise the heroes and villains, and what differentiates the former from the latter. For example, what do you think the following stories say about the culture at retailer Marks & Spencer?

I remember when I started work at M&S Durham Store in 1964 everyone had to address you by your full name… Mrs Smith or Miss Jones.. no first names were allowed to be used at all. It seems so silly now when I think about it, but it was like this for a great many years

My memory is of the time when my father was Manager of the Swindon store. He came home and expressed concern about what was to happen to his staff after Lord Marks had decided to reduce the amount of paperwork used in ordering. He said he should trust those he employed and not need all this paper!

> In 1986 I started working for M&S as a cleaner, when we had to clean the staircase with a toothbrush. Who would believe that 25 years later and still passionate about working for the business I am now the Store Manager?

So, is there such a thing as a "Big Data culture"? The answer is yes…and no. There can never be a specific 'Big Data culture' simply because each company evolves within its own unique environment and is driven by individuals that have a unique set of experiences. There can however be cultures that are more amenable to big data. In Sect. 3.4 we highlighted the 'Internet-centric' companies: Google, Amazon, LinkedIn. Culturally these companies have a number of things in common;

- They each have an original founder that is still involved with the company, still perpetuating the original values of the company
- They were all formed within an 8 year period spanning the dot-com bubble in 2000, initially employing a small number of young, enthusiastic staff who bought into the internet vision
- LinkedIn and Google are both based in California. Amazon is based in Seattle, Washington
- LinkedIn(3) and Google(9) are both ranked in the top ten best companies to work for (along with Twitter(2) and Facebook(5))

As noted earlier, trying to determine organisational culture at arms-length, using purely publicly-available artefacts, is extremely difficult given the risk of misinterpretation. However, in order to capture facets of a "big data culture", here we attempt to develop a cultural web for Google:

- ***Symbols***:
  - *Terminology* – Full-time staff are known as "Googlers" (this term doesn't extend to contractors who comprise approximately 30 % of staff) and defines employees as intelligent, insightful and committed. To be considered a 'Googler' is, for many, a badge of honour, of being included in a select, elite group. Contractors are less enthusiastic:

    > As someone who has worked for a temp job working for Google, the worst part is the smug attitude of those who work for the REAL Google. They seem to think that anyone who isn't working for the actual Google like they are is somehow mentally and morally inferior (Edwards 2013)

  - *Work environment* – Google initially paid their employees less than many other Silicon Valley firms, but used other perks to attract staff. The headquarters is known as "the Googleplex". The Googleplex was designed as 'a fun place to work'. It is very colourful, decorated with lava lamps and offers daycare facilities for those with young families. Lunch and dinner are free. It has free snack rooms offering Googlers cereals, gummi bears, nuts, fruit juices, soft drinks and cappuccino. It also includes recreational facilities such as gyms, video games, pool tables, table tennis and an area for roller skate hockey. Googlers are also allowed to bring their pets to work. "Having a good work environment helps us recruit and retain good employees" Sergey Brin, co-founders. However, some employees disagree:

> It's not uncommon to see 3-4 employees in a single cube, or several managers sharing an office. With all the open areas for food, games, TV, tech talks, etc. it can be surprisingly hard to find a quiet, private place to think", "In Zurich there is a quiet room where people go to relax, or take a nap. There was a 100+ emails thread about removing the massage chairs from that room because some people allegedly were being kept from sleeping because the massage chairs were too noisy", "It's like never-never land - people never grow up. They drink at all hours, socialize constantly, play games, and do little to no work (Edwards 2013)

- *Recruitment*: "The most important thing for a prospective employee is intelligence. Someone can always learn a skill or gain experience but intelligence is innate. All of Google's employees are talented and skilled in their field. However, more than that, they are smart people who offer intelligent insight or suggestions outside their field of expertise. This has brought many new ideas and business opportunities to the company" Sergey Brin, co-founder. It has also brought problems:

> The worst part of working at Google, for many people, is that they're overqualified for their job. Google has a very high hiring bar due to the strength of the brand name, the pay & perks, and the very positive work culture. As a result, they have their pick of bright candidates, even for the most low-level roles. There are students from top 10 colleges who are providing tech support for Google's ads products, or manually taking down flagged content from YouTube, or writing basic code to A|B test the colour of a button on a site. (Edwards 2013)

- **Power structures**: Googlers are encouraged to communicate across all departments and they have unrestricted access to top executives. Furthermore, there is little formal management. "We had management in engineering and the structure was tending to tell people, 'no, you can't do that", said Wayne Rosing, Vice-President of Engineering. Google eliminated the managers and engineers now work in teams of three with project leadership rotating among the team and each team reporting directly to Rosen. This informal structure has caused friction with financial analysts who question who 'runs' Google, the founders or the CEO. Google insiders suggest that the founders continue to call the shots while the CEO, Eric Schmidt, is merely a figurehead.
- **Organisational structure**: On paper Google's formal structure is similar to many companies (other than a few unique positions such as Chief Culture Officer and Chief Internet Evangelist). Company oversight is by a board of directors, which passes instructions down through an executive management group. This group oversees departments such as Engineering, Products, Legal, Finance and Sales and each department is divided into smaller units. However, executives encourage employees and managers to work directly with each other, instead of through formal channels. The executives work closely with employees and other departments in a form of cross-functional management. However…

Google wasn't a start-up environment by the time I left. The same office politics. It was easy to get promoted if you worked on the right projects and projected your work in the right way. A major drawback to working at Google is, "...the relentless daily mediocre thinking of middle management types who are completely focused on metrics to the exclusion of all other factors. They don't want to rock the boat, they don't know how to inspire their workforce, and they rely far too much on the Google name and reputation to do that for them (Edwards 2013)

- **Control systems**: Rather than setting objectives for staff, Google's management encourage employees meet the objectives that the employees set for themselves. In this way Google controls employee responsibility through a series of checks and balances. All employees set out and evaluate goals on a quarterly basis. While Google's management may make suggestions, employees use metrics that they themselves choose to be measured by. Supervisors act as managers to ensure that the employees meet their own goals, but employees see them as leaders because the employees themselves set the benchmarks.
- **Rituals & routines**:
  - *Don't be evil*: This code functions on two levels; corporate and individual
    At a corporate level many of Google's policies and corporate decisions are based on trying to live up to this motto. While profit is always the final concern, employees report feeling very differently about working at Google as opposed to other companies.
    At an individual level, as Google only holds employees accountable to management to a degree, this code helps to guide employee behaviour
  - *Ten things we know to be true*: This is a long-standing statement of intent regarding how Google perceive the world and the company's role in that world;
    Focus on the user an all else will follow
    It's best to do one thing really, really well
    Fast is better than slow
    Democracy on the web works
    You don't need to be at your desk to need an answer
    You can make money without doing evil
    There's always more information out there
    The need for information crosses all borders
    You can be serious without a suit
    Great just isn't good enough
  - *70-20-10 rule*: All Googlers follow the 70/20/10 rule, under which they devote 70 % of each day to projects are assigned by management, 20 % to new projects related to their core projects, and 10 % to any new ideas they wish to pursue regardless of what they might be. This allows programmers, salespeople and even executives enough space to be creative.
  - *Communication*:
    All Googlers are encouraged to have lunch at the cafeteria so they get a chance to meet other Googlers from various departments.

Every Friday afternoon the founders brief Googlers about new products/features launched, competitors and financial performance

Every Friday Googlers have a 1-hour session discussing new ideas. Every engineer whose idea has been selected has a 10 min slot to present and defend his/her idea. If successful, the idea is developed into a product/feature with the engineer as project manager.

…but things are changing, *"Everybody believes he (males dominate) is better than his neighbour. So it is really hard to discuss any issue unless it is your friend you are talking to. Objective discussions are pretty rare, since everybody's territorial and not interested in opinions of other people…"*, *"I worked at Google for 3 years and it was very difficult to leave but there was one major factor that helped me make the decision – the impact I could ever have on the business as an individual was minimal. Unless you are an amazingly talented engineer who gets to create something new, chances are you're simply a guy/girl with an oil can greasing the cogs of that machine"* (Edwards 2013)

- **Stories**:
  - *"We try to provide an environment where people are going to be happy. I think that's a much better use of money than, say, hundred-million-dollar marketing campaigns or outrageously inflated salaries"* Sergey Brin, Co-founder, 2003
  - During the dotcom boom in the late 1990s Google was the only company that did not experience any employee turnover (at other major technical companies the rate was typically between 20 and 25 %)
  - When trying to get funding for the initial start-up the co-founders were refused by the owners of many internet portals. The CEO of one portal told them, "As long as we are 80 % as good as our competitors that's good enough. Our users don't really care about search"
  - The name 'Google' chosen by accident (their first investment cheque was made out to 'Google Inc' before the entity existed) indicated the company's mission to sort and organise the vast data available on the web
  - An engineer posted a new feature (Google news) on the Google intranet for testing by fellow Googlers. The service immediately attracted the attention of lots of Googlers and was quickly developed and launched. Within three weeks of beta launch Google News attracted 70,000 users per day
  - Commenting on meetings with Googlers, one business partner said, *"Typically half the people turn up 20 min late, so you have to repeat your presentation; another couple leave 10 min early. Most of the time they're not paying attention anyway, but messaging each other and their friends…"*. In reply Sergey Brin suggested that, *"If people aren't prepared in meetings, it's not because they think they're too good for them, but because they're working around the clock"*. Googlers regularly work 12 h per day.

In 2010 Google CEO, Larry Page, was asked what he thought the greatest threat to Google was, "Google" he replied. In less than 12 years Google became Silicon Valley's unwieldy incumbent with some of its best engineers chafing under the growing bureaucracy. Former CEO Eric Schmidt notes, "There was a time when three people at Google could build a world-class product and deliver it, and it is gone. That's probably our biggest strategic issue."

3.6 Summary

The foundations of formal and informal structures are laid by the entrepreneurs that began the company and are shaped by the internal and external environment over time. Data-based companies, those founded in the hot-bed of the dot-com revolution of the late 1990s, have inherent advantages over their more 'bricks and mortar' cousins, for whom data has simply been a by-product of business-as-usual. Firstly, they have access to large volumes of data, secondly, from inception, data has been the *de facto* currency of the organisation and thirdly they are relatively young companies, still full of missionary zeal embedded by the founders. However, as our analysis of Google has shown, the pull towards machine bureaucracy from adhocracy is almost inexorable.

Perhaps we can learn lessons from the implementations of ERP systems. Bain & Co. (2013) note that "big data isn't a technology initiative at all; it's a business programme that requires technical savvy". Much the same could have been said about ERP. In Big Data, as was seen in ERP, changing organisational structure and culture may prove to be the biggest challenge of all.

3.7 Review Questions

- According to Mintzberg, what are the five basic elements of organisational structure?
- What are the advantages and disadvantages of an ERP system?
- Define organisational culture
- What are the seven elements of the cultural web
- Define what is meant by the term 'paradigm'

3.8 Group Work/Research Activity

3.8.1 Discussion Topic 1

Choose an organisation you are familiar with, it could be somewhere you have worked or possibly the college or university in which you are studying. Try to draw the formal organisational chart. What does it tell you about the organisation? What *doesn't* it tell you about the organisation? What might the formal structure of an organisation tell you about its ability to adapt to big data?

3.8.2 Discussion Topic 2

Earlier we examine the cultural web for Google. The information used spanned a time period from 2002 to 2010 during which time the organisation grew rapidly and the culture began to shift. Using information available on the web, draw a cultural web for Google in 2002. Repeat this for the company in 2010. How has the culture changed? What was the paradigm in 2002? What was it in 2010? How might the change in cultural paradigm affect Google's ability to maximise the opportunities of big data?

References

ComputerWeekly.com (2002) ERP errors cost Agilent $70m [online]. Last accessed 14 Feb 2014 at: http://www.computerweekly.com/news/2240047109/ERP-errors-cost-Agilent-70m
Davenport TH, Eccles RG, Prusak L (1992) Information politics. Sloan Manag Rev 34(1):53–65
Edwards J (2013) Business insider [online]. Last accessed 8 Mar 2014 at: http://www.businessinsider.com/google-employees-confess-the-worst-things-about-working-at-google-2013-11
Fayol H (1949) General and industrial management. Pitman, London
Johnson G (1992) Managing strategic change: strategy, culture and action. Long Range Plann 25(1):28–36
Kanaracus (2011) Oracle sued by university for alleged ERP failure [online]. Last accessed 14 Feb 2014 at: http://www.computerworld.com/s/article/9216940/Oracle_sued_by_university_for_alleged_ERP_failure
King D, Lawley S (2013) Organizational behaviour. Oxford University Press, Oxford
Markus ML, Tanis C, van Fenema PC (2000) Enterprise resource planning: multisite ERP implementations. Commun ACM 43(4):42–46
Mintzberg H (1980) Structure in 5'S: a synthesis of the research on organization design. Manag Sci 26(3):322–341
Morton NA, Hu Q (2008) Implications of the fit between organizational structure and ERP: a structural contingency theory perspective. Int J Inf Manag 28:391–402
Pearson T, Wegener R (2013) Big data: the organisational challenge. Bain & Company, Atlanta
Pfeffer J (2013) You're still the same: why theories of power hold over time and across contexts. Acad Manag Perspect 27(4):269–280
Scheer AW, Habermann F (2000) Making ERP a success. Commun ACM 43(4):57–61
Schein EH (2010) Organisational culture and leadership, 4th edn. Jossey-Bass, San Francisco
Wulf J (2012) The flattened firm: not as advertised. Calif Manage Rev 55(1):5–23

Style

4.1 What the Reader Will Learn

- That 'management' and 'leadership' are quite different and, in an era of Big Data, leadership may be a more valuable asset than management
- That the shift to analytical decision-making will transform many of the interpersonal, informational and decisional roles of the manager
- That big data creates four major challenges for management at all levels, the 'four Ds':
  - Data literacy
  - Domain knowledge
  - Decision-making
  - Data Scientists
- That, as demand for data-literate, business-savvy Data Scientists grows, the power balance between managers of the 'old school' variety and the "data leaders" of tomorrow may shift
- That in order to create a 'culture of inquiry', executives themselves need to become more data-literate, to make decisions based upon data and to ask analytics-based questions

4.2 Introduction

What do we mean by 'style'? Definitions of the word 'style' include (Oxford Dictionary of English 2010):

- a particular procedure by which something is done; a manner or way (noun)

- a distinctive appearance, typically determined by the principles according to which something is designed (noun)
- to design or make in a particular form:(verb)

Style, then, is about how things are done, how they are designed and how they manifest themselves. Consequently, we will examine the process of management (that is, how it is 'done') and investigate the implications of big data for management styles. Today there are three types of manager; those who anticipate the impact big data will have and have positioned themselves for the opportunities, those who recognise the threats that big data brings and have buried their heads in the sand and, finally, those who see neither opportunity or threat and believe that the role of the manager in an era of big data will be unchanged. Subsequently, many executives and managers are anxious about the changes big data will bring, and perhaps those that aren't should be.

We start this chapter with a little management theory, a precise of management thinking in a pre-analytics, pre-big data world. We then introduce what we believe to be the four major challenges to management in an era of big data; decision-making, data literacy, domain 'knowledge' and the data scientist, the four Ds. We will discuss these challenges and how companies and management teams are currently responding to them. Finally, we will look to the future and investigate what the legacy of big data era will be for management.

4.3 Management in the Big Data Era

4.3.1 Management or Leadership?

In business literature few terms get more confused than 'management' and 'leadership'. The two words are often used synonymously but are quite different. Martin Luther King, Winston Churchill, and Ghandi are all regarded as great leaders – does this mean that they were also great managers? No it does not. This confusion occurs because:

- The terms "management" and "leadership" are used interchangeably without distinguishing the fundamental difference between the two and the vital functions that each role plays
- The term "leader" in some instances refers to the person at the top of hierarchies, while people in the layers immediately below him/her in the organization are called "management." Everyone else are; workers, specialists, and individual contributors. This is both wrong and misleading
- "Leadership" is usually discussed in terms of personality characteristics, such as charisma. Assuming only a few people have great charisma leads to the conclusion that few people can provide leadership, which is not the case

In short, 'management' is a series of established processes, such as planning, budgeting, structuring jobs, measuring performance and problem-solving. The objective of management is to facilitate an organization in doing what it does, better. This means ensuring that the company produces the products and services as promised, of consistent quality, on budget, day after day, week after week. In all but the smallest and simplest of companies this is an enormously difficult task. We will examine the different roles of management in more detail shortly.

In contrast, leadership is about aligning people to a vision, and that means buy-in and communication, motivation and inspiration. Leadership is not about personal characteristics, it's about behaviour. In truth, while managers must be capable of leadership, leaders don't necessarily have to be managers. Indeed, today the notion that a few extraordinary people at the top can provide all the leadership needed is both outdated and unrealistic and has led to many companies being over-managed and under-led. So, should we replace management with leadership?

How an organisation balances management and leadership depends on the business environment in which it operates. In a stable environment management is essential in mobilising people to do what they've always done and to continue to do it well. Conversely, leadership is about change. When the environment is dynamic and fast-changing, good leadership may be more important than good management. Big data, and the consequential move to analytics, require good management and company-wide leadership. In the next two sections we will examine the *role* of management (what management does) and different *styles* of management (how it does it). In both role and style leadership is an important aspect of management, as you will see.

4.3.2 What Is 'Management'?

What do you think of when you hear the term 'manager' or 'management'?
What do you think are the key functions that define the term 'manager'?
In 1949 French Industrialist, Henri Fayol (1949) defined these functions as:

- *Planning*: Looking to the future, trying to calculate and predict future circumstances (such as demand, competitors, etc.), and acting so as to be able to respond to this
- *Organising*: Building up the required structures, resources, and people to best meet the needs and goals of the organisation
- *Coordinating*: Bringing together the structure, human, and resource elements of the organization to act in harmony and towards the goals of the organisation
- *Commanding*: Giving orders and directions to people within the organisation to maintain activity towards achieving the organisation's goals
- *Controlling*: Checking and inspecting work–monitoring and surveillance of work done rather than direct command

Table 4.1 Roles of management (Mintzberg 1989)

Category	Role	Description
Interpersonal	Figurehead	Perform social and legal duties, act as symbolic leader
	Leader	Direct and motivate subordinates, select and train employees
	Liaison	Establish and maintain contacts within and outside the organization
Informational	Monitor	Seek and acquire work-related information
	Disseminator	Communicate/disseminate information to others within the organization
	Spokesperson	Communicate/transmit information to outsiders
Decisional	Entrepreneur	Identify new ideas and initiate improvement projects
	Disturbance Handler	Deals with disputes or problems and takes corrective action
	Resource Allocator	Decide where to apply resources
	Negotiator	Defends business interests

Do you think much has changed in the last 60 years?

As we saw in Chap. 3 organisational structures are designed in such a way to facilitate these management responsibilities. Bureaucracy and hierarchy are used to execute coordination and control, while 'commanding' and communication is frequently (but not always) a top-down process. If we accept Fayol's definition of management functions, then management 'style' is less about what the responsibilities are but how they are accomplished by each manager.

Beyond Foyol's basic responsibilities, management is a multi-faceted task requiring the individual to assume a number of roles, sometimes simultaneously. These roles may be categorised as (Table 4.1).

Furthermore, much of a manager's work is, inherently, at the boundary of their company, department or team. Consequently these categories have both an internal component (within their span of control) and an external component (outside their span of control). Different roles plus the different perspectives of those roles ensure that management is highly complex. In trying to reconcile these roles, the manager is faced with a number of fundamental challenges (Table 4.2).

Clearly, the role of a manager is diverse and often contradictory. In short, managers need to be both generalists and specialists simultaneously due to:

1. Frustration (including operational imperfections and environmental pressures)
2. Power struggles (which disturb even basic routines)
3. Fallibility (yes, managers are human!)

4.3 Management in the Big Data Era

Table 4.2 Internal & external roles of management

	Internal role	External role	Challenges
Interpersonal	Leading	Linking	How to bring order to the work of others when the work of managing is itself so disorderly?
	Figurehead (internal)	Figurehead (external)	How to maintain the necessary state of controlled disorder when one's own manager is imposing order?
	Motivating individuals	Networking (liaison)	How to maintain a sufficient level of confidence without crossing over into arrogance?
	Developing individuals	Convincing/Conveying	
	Building teams	Transmitting	
	Adjudicating	Buffering	
Informational	Communicating (internally)	Communicating (externally)	How to keep informed when managing removes the manager from the very things being managed?
	Monitoring	Spokesperson	How to delegate when so much of the relevant information is personal, oral and, often, privileged?
	Nerve centre	Disseminating	How to manage it when you can't rely on measuring it?
	Controlling: (See 2.5.3 Decision-making)		
	Designing		
	Delegating		
	Designating		
	Distributing		
	Deeming		
Decisional	Doing	Dealing	How to act decisively in a complicated, nuanced world?
	Resource allocator	Negotiator	How to manage change when there is a need to maintain continuity?
	Disturbance handler	Building coalitions	
	Managing projects	Mobilising support	

The bad news is that these perspectives of management, plus the challenges and limitations they represent, were all recognised before big data. Big data complicates the situation in four distinct ways; we call these the four Ds:

(i) Data literacy
(ii) Domain knowledge
(iii) Decision-making
(iv) Data science

However, not only do the four Ds impact on *what* a manager does, but also on the *way* that he/she does it, their management *style*. As we have seen the role of management is complex and contradictory, so how do managers cope? What strategies do they employ to make sense of, and meet the demands of, the job? Firstly we will look at management style before examining the challenges posed by the four Ds.

4.3.3 Styles of Management

How would you describe 'management'? As a science; using systematic evidence to analyse and solve problems? Or, possibly as an art; using creative insight to develop innovative strategies? Or maybe as a craft; drawing upon experience and practical learning to move the company forward? Mintzberg suggests that, in practice, management is all of these things (Fig. 4.1).

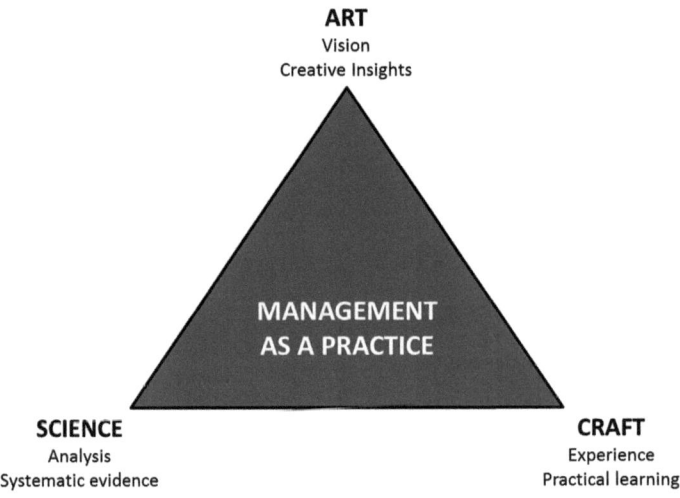

Fig. 4.1 Managing as art, craft and science (Mintzberg 2011)

Consequently, Mintzberg concludes that;

- The manager who practices all craft with no science or art may be absorbing (usually with lots of anecdotes and 'war stories') but, ultimately, tedious
- The manager who is all vision and creativity may provide insight but, without experience or analysis may prove narcissistic
- The manager who applies scientific technique without vision or experience may be cerebral, logical and intellectual but may also be calculating and manipulative
- The manager who leads with experience and vision but without analysis may be disorganized
- The manager who leads with experience and analysis but without vision may be dispirited
- The manager who leads with analysis and vision but without experience may be disconnected

Many established managers have cultivated a balance between the art, craft and science of management. Unfortunately big data will require re-thinking that balance, in fact the search for balance may be less important than the flexibility of being able to select and use a management style appropriate to the circumstances at hand.

Using the three categories that define the role of management; interpersonal, informational and decisional, we can establish a number of different management styles (Table 4.3).

Having examined the roles and styles of management we now have a grasp of what it is a manager does and how he or she chooses to do it. Or do we? Perhaps a manager has less choice regarding his/her management style than they believe.

We said earlier that managers *must* be capable of leadership, but leaders don't have to be managers, why? Because managers, by virtue of their position in the organisational hierarchy, supervise other people. Managers have power!

4.3.4 Sources of Managerial Power

Managerial power is the ability of managers to control subordinates using implied or explicit threats to career advancement opportunities, required resources, access to information and, ultimately, the loss of employment itself (Clarke and Newman 1995). Managerial power arises from:

(i) The individuals place in the organisational hierarchy (*Structural power*): This is the most common form of managerial authority and if often formalised in the organisation chart. Structural power can take the direct form of "pulling rank" during disputes. Alternatively, the influence can be indirect, such as a manager having access to more information (or other resources) than those available to subordinates. The greater the manager's structural power, the greater the control over subordinates' actions.

88 4 Style

Table 4.3 Management styles versus management roles

Management Style	Interpersonal	Informational	Decisional	Pros/Cons
Autocratic	No regard for subordinates and their opinions	Need to know basis	Made unilaterally	May help complete urgent tasks that need doing quickly
				Can project an image of a confident, well-managed business
			Reflect opinions & personality of manager	Leads to over-dependence upon manager
				May lead to lack of creativity or resistance if subordinates have no input
Consultative/ paternalistic	Consultative/ paternalistic approach to subordinates (manager 'knows best')	Feedback encouraged (but for maintenance of morale only)	Made unilaterally	Works well when it creates loyalty, thus reducing staff turnover
			Take into account interests of subordinates to a certain extent	Without loyalty it suffers the same issues as Autocratic management
Persuasive	Aware of subordinates and engages with them	Active discussion encouraged (but for maintenance of morale and buy-in only)	Made unilaterally	Used when buy-in is required from subordinates
			Take into account interests of subordinates but is still not inclusive	Often the stance taken by IT professionals when rolling-out systems
Democratic	Extensive engagement between manager and subordinate	Extensive communications between manager and subordinate	Subordinates involved and everything agreed by majority	Used when complex decisions require a range of specialist skills and/or the manager is less skilled than the subordinate
				Often results in job satisfaction, quality of work and the contribution by subordinates improving
				May make decision-making process slow and less optimal for the business
Laissez-faire	Leadership emerges organically from the group	Extensive communications between group members	Group members make decisions	Often results in job satisfaction, quality of work and the contribution by group members improving
			Little guidance from managers	Can result in low productivity from group members

(ii) The individual's relationships within the organisation (*Ownership power*): Senior executives accrue their power in their capacity as representatives of the shareholders. Indeed, many senior executive are significant shareholders in the companies they manage and this shareholding helps strengthen their power base. Managers who are founders of the firm, or who are related to the founders, gain power through their long-term interactions with the board. Thus, managers with ownership power can often gain some measure of control over board members.
(iii) The individuals' expertise, and therefore value, to the organisation (*Expert power*): The operational environment creates uncertainty and risk for the company. Managers with contacts and relationships that limit this uncertainty and increase the organisations ability to cope have significant power. Similarly, managers with relevant expertise are often sought out for their advice – a form of expert power. However, most power accrues to the manager that has expertise in an area that is critical to the organisation performance or survival
(iv) The individuals' status with stakeholders (*Prestige power*): A manager's reputation in the business environment and/or among stakeholders influences others' perception of their influence. An individual considered to be one of the 'managerial elite' garners power from external contacts which may provide valuable information to an organisation. Prestige also confers power by implication; that the manager is highly qualified and has powerful friends. In some instances a company's reputation depends upon the prestige of its managers.

In examining management styles we saw that styles are distributed over a continuum from autocratic to laissez faire. However, it is important to recognise that management style is often determined by the balance of power between the manager and the subordinates. So, what of big data?

Big data requires a major shift in the managerial mind-set. The move to more statistical and analytical decision-making may transform many of the traditional roles of the manager as the equilibrium between interpersonal, informational and decisional categories shifts. Indeed, management as art, craft and science may be brought into question as the intuitive role of experience gives way to data-driven decision-making. Finally, as the demand for data-literate, technologically-minded, hypothesis-developers grows so will the power balance between managers of the 'old school' variety and the "data scientists" and "data leaders" of tomorrow. The effects of big data on management will, potentially, be both long-lasting and profound. This shift won't happen overnight, but, perhaps, the next generation of managers will view their predecessors much as we view the Neanderthals, under-informed, slow to react and extinct.

4.4 The Challenges of Big Data (the Four Ds)

As we have seen, the role of management is about using established skills and prior experience to make decisions. But what if the skill-set required to do your job changes, leaving you feeling uncertain, isolated and vulnerable? What if the significance of your experience is undermined, leaving you feeling under-valued and at risk? What if your ability to make decisions is continually questioned as colleagues, superiors and subordinates ask, "Where's your evidence?" What if, like the Emperor in his new clothes, everyone knows more than you..?

4.4.1 Data Literacy

In February 2010 Accenture, a major consultancy firm, surveyed 600 companies in the US, UK and Ireland and found that more than 50 % of organisations surveyed were "structured in a way that prevents data and analytical talent from generating enterprise-wide insight" (Hatter and Pilarz 2010). Moreover, only 5 % of manufacturers used analytics to support supply chain and resource planning. As we enter the big data era the focus of most management literature is on the potential benefits to the company bottom line. However, this overlooks the fact that, for many executives and managers, mathematics and statistics classes are a distant, long-forgotten memory. Most will be proficient with spreadsheets but beyond the terms; 'mean', 'mode' and 'median', many will feel quantitatively challenged. In time this will change, as the effects of big data are trickle through society the importance of statistical thinking and analytics will permeate through secondary and tertiary education. Schools and universities will reinforce the role of statistics in their courses and, given the increasing relevance to employment, students will immerse themselves in practical analytical problems. Today's need for "data-literacy" will seem as archaic as yesterday's demand for "computer literacy", but what of today?

Unfortunately, todays executives and managers are faced with a stark choice; learn statistical techniques or work closely with those who already understand them. However, while a number of companies are beginning to up-skill their staff in basic analytical techniques, many managers are choosing to (or being advised to) partner with the 'quants' in their company. Regrettably, for the manager, this can mean significant sharing of information and with it a loss of managerial power. Conversely, Davenport (2013) urges managers to consider themselves as "consumers of analytics" and notes that:

> …highly analytical people are not always known for their social skills, so this [forming relationships] can be hard work. As one wag jokingly advised, "Look for the quants who stare at your shoes, instead of their own, when you engage them in conversation.

The demarcation is unlikely to be so easy. Davenport's stereotype of the "stats geek" is not something many highly numerate employees such as researchers,

4.4 The Challenges of Big Data (the Four Ds)

engineers and scientists are likely to relate to. Furthermore, in defining the segregation of duties between the 'manager' and the 'quant', Davenport suggests that the role of the manager is to ask "tough questions":

> Producers [analytical staff] are, of course, good at gathering the available data and making predictions about the future. But most lack sufficient knowledge to identify hypotheses and relevant variables and to know when the ground beneath an organization is shifting. Your job as a data consumer [manager] – to generate hypotheses and determine whether results and recommendations make sense in a changing business environment—is therefore critically important

Clearly, asking the right question is 'critically important'. However, to imply that a data-illiterate manager is more able to construct a working hypothesis than, say, a data-savvy employee is to value domain-knowledge higher than an instinct and understanding for the data. When Jonathan Goldman, a PhD from Stamford, joined LinkedIn in 2006 he did so with a wealth of analytics knowledge and experience but very little domain-knowledge. Looking at the data he began to formulate theories and hypotheses that eventually led to the "People You May Know" product and algorithm responsible for getting millions of users connected and engaged with LinkedIn. LinkedIn's engineering team, for all of their domain knowledge, had failed to join the dots and actually opposed Goldman's idea.

Ultimately there will be no substitute for learning quantitative techniques and the managers who embrace the shift from hunch to hypothesis will flourish. Those managers that increasingly rely upon the support of a team of quants will see their power slowly, but inexorably, slip away along with their perceived control over information. Perhaps the last bastion of the data-illiterate manager will be the informational role of communication:

> If you're a non-quant, you should focus on the final step in the process—presenting and communicating results to other executives—because it's one that many quants discount or overlook... Davenport (2013)

Unfortunately, even here the analytically-challenged manager may find no place to hide. Davenport suggests that analytics is all about 'telling a story with data'. That perhaps the manager should spend time considering the language and tone to be used, deciding whether the presentation should be narrative or visual. But who decides what the 'story' is? Indeed, what if there is no 'story'? The narrative fallacy (see Chap. 6, Statistical Thinking) arises from a human need to ascribe sequences of facts with an explanation or force a logical link, an arrow of relationship upon them. Where this inherent desire is mistaken is when it increases the impression that we understand what the data is telling us (Taleb 2008). Alternatively, what if there are multiple 'stories', multiple interpretations of the data? In this instance the manager becomes an informational gate-keeper with the story chosen owing as much to the managers implicit and explicit biases as the data available. This is the antithesis of big data analytics.

4.4.2 Domain Knowledge

What do we mean by 'domain-knowledge'? The word 'domain' refers to (a) what one is master of or has dominion over and (b) the scope or range of any subject or sphere of knowledge (The Chambers Dictionary 2011). By this measure the term 'domain knowledge' may be highly subjective. Among his peers, an Englishman may be considered to have gained significant domain knowledge of India from the writings of Rudyard Kipling but to have never travelled there. Conversely, a foundry worker may have a spent a lifetime working on a single stage of the steel-making process. He may be able to gauge the precise temperature at which the steel should be poured based upon subtle changes of colour, but have no knowledge of why or how this is so. Thus, in discussing domain knowledge we must be very careful to differentiate between expertise and experience. In some jobs the two may appear to be the same thing, in others however there is a world of difference. Contrast the following Oxford English Dictionary definitions:

Experience: practical contact with and observation of facts or events
Expertise: expert skill or knowledge in a particular field

What's the difference? According to Kahneman and Klein (2009) true expertise requires the individual to acquire a skill and this, in turn, demands:

- An environment that is sufficiently regular to be predictable
- An opportunity to learn these regularities through prolonged practice

The game of chess provides a regular, if complex, environment (as does that of, say, physicians, nurses and firefighters) and it is possible to build expertise over time by a constant cycle of recognition and repetition. In contrast, share-dealers, wine aficionados, political pundits and, all too often, managers operate in a non-regular, complex environment. In these instances what we may consider experience lacks the legitimacy of expertise. True intuition, the ability to understand something instinctively, without the need for conscious reasoning, arises from expertise, due to subconscious recognition of the circumstances and parameters of a situation. On the contrary, much of what is considered to be 'management intuition' stems from the validity heuristic (see Chap. 6, Statistical Thinking). Consider that the most common way business schools teach management is to identify successful businesses, isolate "best practices" and train their students to replicate these practices (classic examples of this are the books "Good to Great" (Collins 2001), and "In Search of Excellence" (Peters and Waterman 1982). This all seems pretty intuitive doesn't it? However, as we will see, in non-regular environments performance depends on both ability and chance. Thus, a particular strategy will only succeed for a time and with that strategy some companies will be succeed (the lucky) and others will fail (the unlucky). Ascribing an organisation's success to that strategy may be wrong if you sample only the winners (the Survivorship bias). The real question should be, "How many of the companies that tried the strategy actually succeeded?"

In 2005 Philip Tetlock published a twenty-year study based upon interviews with 284 political/economic 'experts'. Tetlock asked these specialists to assess the probabilities of events likely to occur in the near future. For example; would the status quo be maintained? Would there be more of a particular variable (political freedom, economic growth etc.)? or less of that variable? He also asked how they reached their conclusions and how they evaluated evidence that didn't support their opinions. In all Tetlock collected 80,000 predictions and his findings were overwhelming. The experts' opinions were less reliable than if they had simply allocated similar probabilities to each of the three outcomes. He also observed that those with most 'knowledge' tended to perform worse due to an illusion of skill which bred overconfidence. As Kahneman (2012) notes:

> Claims for correct intuition in an unpredictable situation are self-delusional at best

Perhaps this is only to be expected. In low-data environments, where information was scarce, expensive or non-existent, individuals with 'experience' (based upon perceived patterns and relationships seen and adopted over a long period of time) were highly esteemed. These were the executives, managers and experts whose opinions of the future were sought, respected and used for planning. But, in the same way that medicine-men and faith-healing has given way to scientific, evidence-based medicine, so hunches, opinions and intuitively-based management decisions will give way to evidence-based decision-making. Conversely, as big data separates authentic experts from their pseudo-expert counterparts, the value of those authentic domain experts will rise and their roles will change. These domain experts are likely to be prized more for the nature of the questions they ask and their interpretation of analytical results than for their opinions.

4.4.3 Decision-Making

As we have seen earlier in this chapter, decision-making is a fundamental aspect of management. Consequently, big data is of little value to the organisation unless it informs employees and facilitates better, more evidence-based decisions. However, decision-making is rather more than cerebral consideration, and choice, from a series of alternative. Decision-making is, for many managers, the tacit mode of control (Fig. 4.2).

Today all of the key "design features", the infrastructure of the company, are determined by the executives and managers. Managers define the purpose of the organisation in order to control employee behaviour (Chap. 2, Strategy), how work divided and allocated to control employee actions (Chap. 3, Structure) and the plans, objectives, budgets and processes in order to control performance (systems).

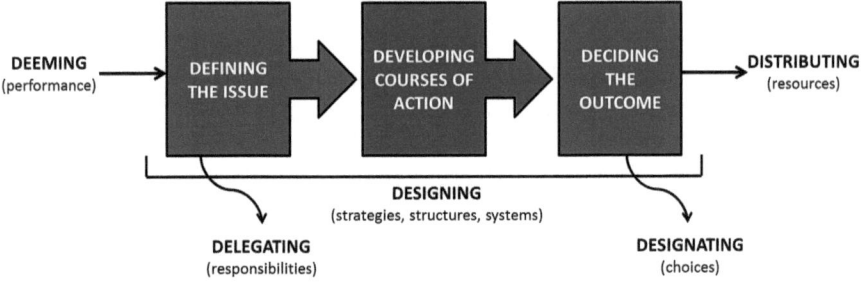

Fig. 4.2 Controlling through decision making (Mintzberg 2011)

Table 4.4 Decision-making tools (Adapted from Courtney et al. 2013)

	Decision outcome knowable (Single)	Decision outcome knowable (Possibilities)	Decision outcome unknowable
Causal model known	Conventional capital-budgeting tools	Information aggregation tools + Quantitative multiple scenario tools	Qualitative scenario analysis + Case-based decision analysis
Causal model unknown	Case-based decision analysis	Information aggregation tools + Case-based decision analysis	Case-based decision analysis

When an issue arises, the manager may decide to delegate the responsibility for resolving the problem to a subordinate. Alternatively, he or she may decide on the final outcome unilaterally. Having decided, through delegation or designation, what the outcome is to be, the manager then chooses how to (formally and informally) resource that outcome. A more hands-off approach may require the manager to set targets for an individual or a team and allow them to perform accordingly (deeming). This is often described as Management by Objective (MBO).

Unfortunately, when making decisions, many senior managers underrate the levels of uncertainty they face. Furthermore, they may unaware of the decision-making tools available to them, when to use those tools to analyse a decision, or when to delay a decision until it can be framed better. Choosing suitable decision-making tools depends on the executive's interpretation of the challenge being faced and the possible outcomes. Where the executive has a strong causal model, that is an understanding of the critical success factors, the required economic conditions and the desired metrics to be successful and the decision outcome is knowable then conventional budgeting tools are acceptable. However, if there is less certainty regarding the issue and/or there are multiple outcomes (or the outcome is completely unknown) other decision-making techniques are more suitable (Table 4.4):

- Capital-budgeting tools: Use estimated cash flows from potential investments to establish whether a project is worth being funded. They include discounted cash flow, expected rate of return, and net present value models.

- Quantitative multiple scenario tools: Analyse decisions by fully specifying possible outcomes and their probabilities. They use mathematical, statistical, and simulation methods to identify the risk/return properties of possible choices. They include Monte Carlo simulations, decision analysis and, real options,
- Qualitative scenario analysis tools: Develop a series of qualitative scenarios concerning how the present may evolve into the future and then identify the possible consequences of the decision being evaluated
- Case-based decision analysis: A systematic approach to synthesising information from similar past experiences – those experiences that are most similar to the decision being considered are given more weight in shaping the final choice
- Information aggregation tools: Used to collect information from diverse sources. They include the Delphi method, Crowdsourcing, Similarity-based forecasting etc.

Of course, things are never that simple... These techniques all assume that an executive can accurately determine the level of ambiguity and uncertainty they face. But like all human beings executives and managers are subject to cognitive biases (see Chap. 6), particularly overconfidence in their ability to forecast uncertain outcomes. As Donald Rumsfeld, the then United States Defence Secretary, at a press briefing during the Iraq war:

> ...there are known knowns; there are things we know that we know
> There are known unknowns; that is to say, there are things that we now know we don't know.
> But there are also unknown unknowns – there are things that we do not know we don't know

While the comment earned Rumsfeld the 2003 "Foot in the Mouth" Award by the Plain English Campaign for "a baffling comment by a public figure", it underlines the point that, in essence, executives don't know what they don't know, but they're generally happy to assume that they do!

Furthermore, as a result of organisational hierarchy, more and more crucial decisions are being made far removed from the source of information. These decisions, based on managerial intuition and gut-feel, are subsequently justified by carefully chosen data that support the decision. As Gary Hamel (2011) argues, "... [Often] the most powerful managers are the ones furthest from frontline realities" and, in the search for control, managers frequently obstruct decision-making rather than facilitate it. Furthermore, in a typical hierarchy the power to spoil or destroy a new idea regularly rests with one individual, whose personal biases and agenda may distort the decision-making process. The outcome is a hierarchy that disempowers lower level employees, limits their scope of authority and narrows the incentive to contribute.

So, what of big data? Re-visiting his work on leadership in (2013) Gary Hamel wrote:

> ...instead of moving decisions up to where people have expertise, you move expertise down to the people close to the front lines

As we have seen, in an era of big data the expertise is *already with* the people close to the front lines. If those people have the information they require and the business skills to use it, all they need is the authority to act, accountability for those actions and a short feedback cycle between the decisions made and rewards received. This is the basis of leadership and at that point the role of many managers becomes defunct.

Finally then, one challenge to executives is to commit the company to training existing employees to increase their data-literacy. Managers should be given the opportunity to up-skill and, as part of the appraisal process, have analytical proficiency targets that have to be met. A second challenge is the recruitment of new staff. Companies need to hire the best and brightest they can afford. At present statistically-savvy Masters and Doctorate students will be difficult to find and, if a company lacks an analytics-based culture, even more difficult to recruit and keep. However, as the hype behind big data fades and analytics become embedded within the core education curriculum, more and more highly numerate graduates will be available. Until then the sector will be dominated by a few highly sought-after, highly paid Data Scientists.

4.4.4 Data Scientists

Davenport and Patil (2012) famously defined the role of Data Scientist as, "The sexiest job of the twenty-first century", a job that requires a skill set incorporating mathematics, machine learning, artificial intelligence, statistics, databases, and optimisation, plus an ability to formulate problems and engineer solutions. We will examine the role of, and the skills required by, Data Scientists in much more detail in Chap. 5. In this section we will focus on the relationship between managers and Data Scientists. Though, before we proceed we need to deconstruct what we mean by 'manager'. So far we have used the terms 'executives' and 'managers' rather loosely, the inference being that 'executives' are at the top of the organisational hierarchy and the 'managers' in the middle (we discussed different types of hierarchies in Chap. 3). However, the advent of the Data Scientist brings with it different (though closely related) managerial challenges depending upon ones position in the hierarchy. Let's start with the relationship between a mid-level manager, say, the Marketing Manager and the Data Scientist.

For the Marketing Manager whose company is about to move into the era of big data life has suddenly become rather more uncertain. In addition to the greater scrutiny of her numbers she has also been told that she will be working with a 'data scientist', but what does that mean? As we have seen earlier, the stereotypical view of a data scientist implies someone who is extremely intelligent but lacks social skills and finds communication difficult (a stereotype that Davenport 2013, reinforces). In this case the Marketing Manager may be forgiven for considering her role as that of 'Data Consumer' supported by the Data Scientist as 'Data Producers'. She recognises that she will need some basic analytics training (her last statistics course was on her Marketing degree). That said, her role will be to frame the questions (naturally, this is where her experience and intuition are most important), assess the results and present the findings to the board. Obviously she will need to ask lots of questions during the process to keep the data scientist focused but the hierarchy, the decision-making power and the control remains unchanged – so why does she feel uncomfortable?

What happens if she can't frame the 'right' initial questions? After all when Jonathan Goldman joined LinkedIn he did so with lots of analytics knowledge but very little domain-knowledge. Indeed, one of the strengths of data scientists, one of the reason they can demand such high salaries, is that they can develop novel, innovative hypotheses. How can she intervene in the process? How can she ask any 'smart' questions if she doesn't understand the process and techniques? How can she evaluate the outcome of the project if she hasn't understood the initial hypothesis, never mind the ultimate outcome? Finally, despite the stereotype, the job description for the data scientist includes presentation, graphics and communications skills, so what does she have to offer? Where will the data scientist fit in the overall organisational structure? Will he work for her, or vice-versa? Will he be in her team? If so, given the salary advertised, how will the rest of the team react? The CEO has said that the data scientist role has a 'high level of autonomy', what does that mean for her interactions with the higher levels of management?

Perhaps our Marketing Manager is right to be uncomfortable, but so should our executive. Many of the questions raised by the Marketing Manager have yet to be addressed at a senior level. As yet there is no consensus on where the data scientist role fits in an organization, how they can add the most value, and how their performance should be measured. Davenport and Patil (2012) note;

> Data scientists don't do well on a short leash. They should have the freedom to experiment and explore possibilities. That said they need close relationships with the rest of the business

The challenge for senior management is how to develop the necessary culture, processes, behaviour, and skills in order for a data scientist to operate without undermining the business at the same time. Mid-level management can, indeed must, be able to partner with data scientists in order for the company investment to yield better strategic and tactical decisions but this relies on them forming strong relationships that allow them to exchange information and ideas easily. Davenport (2013) urges managers to, "align yourself with the right kind of quant!" but 'alignment' can mean many things. Likewise, how can a manager decide what the 'right kind if quant' looks like?

In some companies the move to big data is starting from the bottom-up with some business unit managers trying to push analytics through their departments and on to the rest of the business. Often it starts when a manager somewhere in the organization gets frustrated and decides that "there has to be a better way." The manager introduces a small-scale big data initiative and gets interesting results. However, what motivation or authority does that manager have to push beyond his or her department? In the end, the company is left with good analytics in a few areas and poor ones everywhere else. Rising above that plateau takes the commitment of senior leadership. For big data, and data scientists in particular, leadership must begin at the top, with the principal sponsor, the CEO.

4.4.5 The Leadership Imperative

Earlier we examined the difference between management and leadership and much of this chapter has focused on management. We now consider the function of leadership. The role of leadership in the creation and maintenance of organisational culture, the 'rules' and 'structure' imposed by a leader, is discussed in more detail in Chap. 3. Here we will consider the leader as advocate and role model in the drive for big data.

As with all major organisational transitions, big data needs the sponsorship, support and passion of the senior management team. However, from a leadership perspective, traditional hierarchical structures often demand much of the few at the top and, arguably, not enough of everyone else, despite the fact that more and more value is being created at the periphery of the organisation. Consequently, many organisations concentrate an excessive amount of power and authority at the top, but perhaps this is inevitable when remuneration is correlated with ones position in that hierarchy. Nonetheless, as big data permeates business it will be clear that senior executives simply don't have the intellectual diversity or time to make all the critical decisions. At that point structures, compensation, and decision-making will begin to catch up with the reality of the big data era and organisations will need to evolve to meet this new economic reality. In the meantime, how might today's senior executives create a "culture of inquiry, not advocacy" (Davenport 2013)?

The first is to 'walk the walk'. Executives themselves need to become more data-literate, to make decisions based upon data and to ask analytics-based questions; "What do the data say?" "Where did the data come from?" "What kind of analyses we conducted?" "What is the confidence level of these results?" They need to create an environment where people can develop new leadership skills that enable them to exercise leadership, even when they lack formal, positional authority. At Protection One, a security company, senior executives have made training one of the key responsibilities of all managers. From the outset, the CEO coaches senior executives intensively, explaining and re-explaining why big data is important, what each manager's big data responsibilities are and how to read, understand and act upon scorecard data. At Seven-Eleven an 'open all hours' grocery chain in Japan, Senior Managerial "Counsellors" visit each of the company's 16,000 stores twice a week, teaching sales staff how to use data effectively. The Counsellors compare each person's previous 'hypotheses' about what would sell during the prior week and what actually sold. They then discuss how that individual might improve his or her performance in the coming week.

Executives need to recognise that big data is not simply about handing managerial decisions to automated algorithms but determining how data can inform, enhance or transform user experiences. Big data is neither servant nor master; it is a new medium for shaping how people and their technologies interact. Consequently, autocratic executives may increasingly find their companies (and themselves!) getting left behind in the search for big data talent. These 'Captains of Industry' may have to give way for highly effective "corporate diplomats", leaders who can use the tools of diplomacy—negotiation, persuasion, conflict management, and alliance building.

However, before we get carried away with dreams of big data heralding in a more egalitarian management era, let's not forget how enduring formal hierarchy is as a social structure. As Pfeffer (2013) says;

> The emphasis on new and different organizational arrangements and new theory often reflects wishful thinking that has beset organizational scholars for a long time... In short, a just world would be more like the one the leadership literature mostly talks about and less like the actual world that exists today

For many academics and business gurus, the downfall of organisational hierarchy has been eagerly anticipated for several decades. The microprocessor, business process re-engineering, Total Quality Management and the advent of email have all been accompanied by dire forecasts for the future of the company hierarchy, and the invasive manipulation that accompanies it. However, as we saw in Chap. 3, hierarchy delivers deep-seated practical and psychological benefits by fulfilling human needs for order and security. Consequently, even in an era of big data, the motivation to climb hierarchies for money and status, despite the inevitable organisational politics, is likely to remain important. Evidence from those firms that have 'flattened' their hierarchies suggests that, far from delegating more decision-making powers, the senior group, led by the CEO actually draws more powers to it. So, will big data help facilitate real organisational change? Will the Data Scientist be big data's ongoing advocate within the senior management team? Or does the future lie with those Senior Managers who, like Davenport, view analytically-savvy employees as a socially-inept resource whose skills can be nurtured, exploited and controlled without major changes to the organisational hierarchy and culture?

4.5 Summary

In this chapter we have introduced the concept of 'style', both managerial and leadership. In many instances the difference between the two depends upon the individual and the constraints of organisational structure and culture. However, management and leadership are not the same. Management relies on the legitimacy of the organisational hierarchy for its authority whereas leadership requires a compelling vision to unite and enthuse. Big data disrupts the role of management in four ways; it demands that all staff, including managers, become data-literate, it brings into question existing notions of experience and expertise, it disrupts how decisions are made (an important lever of management control) and it defines the role and responsibilities of the data Scientist.

4.6 Review Questions

- What are Fayol's five functions of management?
- The roles of a manager can be summarised in three categories, what are they?
- Describe the five major styles of management?
- Compare and contrast the four main sources of managerial power?
- What are the four major management challenges posed by Big Data?

4.7 Group Work/Research Activity

4.7.1 Discussion Topic 1

In "Keep up with your quants", Davenport (2013) suggests that non-analytical managers should consider themselves 'consumers of analytics' who will draw upon the analyses and models prepared by data scientist "producers" and integrate these findings with their business experience and intuition to make decisions. How viable do you think this model is? What difficulties do you perceive with the 'consumer/producer' relationship? How might those difficulties be resolved?

4.7.2 Discussion Topic 2

Which do you believe is easier; for a manager to learn analytical techniques and research methods, or for a numeric scientist/engineer to learn management? Explain your reasoning.

References

Clarke J, Newman J (1995) The managerial state: power, politics and ideology in the remaking of social welfare. Sage, London/Thousands Oaks
Collins J (2001) Good to great: why some companies make the leap and others don't. Random House, London
Courtney H, Lovallo D, Clarke C (2013) Deciding how to decide. Harv Bus Rev 91(12):62–70
Davenport TH (2013) Keep up with your quants. Harv Bus Rev 91(7/8):120–123
Davenport TH, Patil DJ (2012) Data scientist: the sexiest job of the 21st century. Harv Bus Rev 90(10):70–76
Fayol H (1949) General and industrial management. Pitman, London
Hamel G (2011) First, let's fire all the managers. Harv Bus Rev 89(12):48–60

References

Hamel G (2013) Leaders everywhere – a conversation with Gary Hamel, on http://www.mckinsey.com/insights/organization/leaders_everywhere_a_conversation_with_gary_hamel. Last accessed 17 Dec 2014

Hatter A, Pilarz M (2010) Weak analytics capabilities hindering companies' and governments' decision-making abilities. Accenture Research Reveals on http://newsroom.accenture.com/article_display.cfm?article_id=4935. Last accessed 16 Dec 2014

Kahneman D (2012) Thinking, fast and slow. Penguin, London

Kahneman D, Klein G (2009) Conditions for intuitive expertise: a failure to disagree. Am Psychol 64(6):515–526

Mintzberg H (1989) Mintzberg on management: inside our strange world of organisations. Free Press, New York

Mintzberg H (2011) Managing. Financial Times/Prentice Hall, London

Peters TJ, Waterman RH (1982) In search of excellence: lessons from America's best-run companies. Harper, New York

Pfeffer J (2013) You're still the same: why theories of power hold over time and across contexts. Acad Manag Perspect 27(4):269–280

Taleb NN (2008) The black swan: the impact of the highly improbable. Penguin, London

The Chambers Dictionary (12th edn) (2011) Chambers, London

The Oxford Dictionary of English (3rd edn) (2010) Oxford University Press, Oxford

Staff 5

5.1 What the Reader Will Learn

- That much of the current publicity surrounding the role of the "Data Scientist" is driven by the 'hype curve'
- That, in the short-term at least, "Data Science Teams" are more viable than the all-encompassing role of the individual "Data Scientist" as described in the media
- The relevance, and importance, of 'science' in the realm of big data
- That achieving big data success requires the traditional skills of team working and team development
- That quickly building fast, productive teams is an essential organisational competency that may offer competitive advantage

5.2 Introduction

While the increase in volume and variety of data has given rise to the phenomenon of "Big Data" then, arguably, the lack of requisite skills is, currently, a major brake on its growth and adoption. In this chapter we will examine how the demands of big data are changing the roles of staff and the skills required to fulfil those roles. As we discovered in Chap. 3, existing "big data" companies such as Google, Yahoo and LinkedIn have evolved with these things embedded within their organisational culture. For other, older, more bureaucratic, more hierarchical companies, these changes are likely to be painfully hard. The challenge of big data to organisational culture is covered comprehensively in Chap. 3, but to divorce culture from staff and skills is, quite simply, unrealistic. Consequently, where necessary, we will again discuss aspects of culture.

Consulting group, Accenture noted in 2013, *"The U.S. is expected to create around 400,000 new data science jobs between 2010 and 2015, but is likely to produce only about 140,000 qualified graduates to fill them"* (Harris et al. 2013). This followed shortly after Thomas Davenport famously announced that the role of the Data Scientist would be, "The sexiest job of the 21st century" (Davenport and Patil 2012). That's quite a claim, but what, precisely, is a Data Scientists? What do they do? And where do they fit within the organisation? How does the role of Data Scientist compare with that, say, of a Business Intelligence (BI) Analyst or a Business Analyst? In this chapter we will address these questions but we will, however, leave you to decide whether the role of Data Scientist is everything that Davenport claims.

5.3 Data Scientists: The Myth of the 'Super Quant'

Before 2010 the term "Data Scientist" was already well-used. Indeed, both the name and role specification were published as early as 2005 (National Science Foundation 2005). However, Google Trends suggests that from 2010 interest in the Data Scientist role grew exponentially (Fig. 5.1).

So what is "data science"? What makes a "Data Scientist"? and why is it important? To address these questions we will start by reviewing the origin of what we call, "the myth of the 'Super Quant'" and in doing so we will also deconstruct the term 'Data Science' and examine its validity. Finally, we will contrast different perspectives of the data scientist role offered by various authors and compare the hype surrounding Data Scientist with that associated with a similarly publicised role in the 1990s; the Hybrid Manager.

5.3.1 What's in a Name?

According to D.J. Patil, former Head of Analytics and Data Teams at LinkedIn, *data science* as a distinct professional specialisation began in 2008 when he met with Jeff Hammerbacher, then Data Manager at Facebook, to compare notes on building data and analytics groups (Patil 2011). In deciding what to call their teams Patil notes:

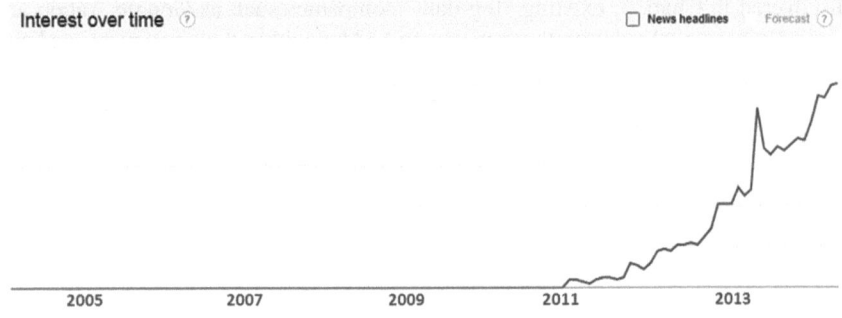

Fig. 5.1 Growth in the number of web searches for "Data Scientist" (Google Trends)

'Business analyst' seemed too limiting. "Data analyst" was a contender, but we felt that title might limit what people could do. After all, many of the people on our teams had deep engineering expertise. "Research scientist" was a reasonable job title used by companies like Sun, HP, Xerox, Yahoo, and IBM. However, we felt that most research scientists worked on projects that were futuristic and abstract, and the work was done in labs that were isolated from the product development teams. It might take years for lab research to affect key products, if it ever did. Instead, the focus of our teams was to work on data applications that would have an immediate and massive impact on the business. The term that seemed to fit best was data scientist: those who use both data and science to create something new. (Patil 2011)

In fact, the term *data science* was in use more than a decade before Patil and Hammerbacher met and even then was being used to describe a wide range of topics associated with data gathering, clustering and multivariate data analysis and knowledge discovery (Hayashi et al. 1997). So what's changed? The answer is: Big Data! With the advent of big data the manipulation of data and the application of statistical hypotheses have become "sexy" (Davenport and Patil 2012) – this is the age of… "the Super Quant Manager"! OK, perhaps that's a bit of a mouthful, but 4 years before Patil and Hammerbacher's meeting, New York University announced a new dual-degree program that "develops the Super-Quant Manager for today's Wall Street". The course promised to:

"…give tomorrow's "quant jocks" both depth in quantitative skills and breadth in management perspective to effectively manage risk, sophisticated trading models and people in today's computation-driven financial markets. "The field of financial mathematics draws on tools from applied mathematics, computer science, statistics, and economics"" said Leslie Greengard, Director of the Courant Institute.

Does this sound a little familiar?

5.3.2 Data "Science" and Data "Scientists"

But why 'science'? According to Davenport and Patil (2012) it is, "…*clear why the word "scientist" fits this emerging role. Experimental physicists, for example, also have to design equipment, gather data, conduct multiple experiments, and communicate their results*". However, there are three other characteristics of scientific discoveries that may make managers rather more cautious;

- Many scientific discoveries are just plain lucky;
  - *Penicillin*: Alexander Fleming received a Nobel Prize when he noticed that a mould had contaminated his flu cultures, but the area around the mould was clear of infection
  - *Viagra*: Designed to help patients with Angina, a painful heart condition, the drug failed to treat the disease but was found to improve blood circulation elsewhere… Test patients mentioned the findings and Viagra was rebranded as a treatment for erectile dysfunction
  - *Big Bang Theory*: In 1968 Arno Penzias and Robert Wilson were trying to use a supersensitive horn antenna to detect radio waves being bounced off the

Project Echo Balloon Satellites. Unfortunately, try as they might, they couldn't eliminate a constant background hum. This hum was actually the residual radiation from the Big Bang and won the two researchers a Nobel Prize
- As Patil notes in the quote above, scientific research takes time and money – with no guarantee of success. For example, in pharmaceuticals most research never leads to a marketed drug and of those that do, 80 % fail to recoup their R&D investment. Ultimately, the cost of developing and commercialising a new drug is estimated at $1 billion. In some instances, a particular break-through, such as the sequencing of the genome, can lead to a series of rapid discoveries, after which scientists resume the long grind of pushing back the boundaries of science step-by-step
- Often the fruits of scientific labour fall, not to the company that makes the initial breakthrough, but to the company that sees the relevance or context. For example, Graphene, discovered in 2004 at Manchester University by Nobel-prize winning scientists Andre Geim and Kostya Novoselov is forecast be worth £300bn by 2022. Yet only four organisations from the UK feature in the 200 most prolific patent owners, compared with 63 in the US, 54 in China, 21 in South Korea and 23 in Japan (Stevens 2012). Likewise, in 1947 John Bardeen, Walter Brattain, and William Shockley of Bell Labs, USA, invented the transistor, a fundamental element of today's microprocessors, but it was the Japanese company, Sony, that commercialised the first 'transistor' radio

Perhaps 'data science' may be called such through its utilisation of the 'scientific method'? The Oxford English Dictionary defines the scientific method as: *"a method or procedure that has characterized natural science since the 17th century, consisting in systematic observation, measurement, and experiment, and the formulation, testing, and modification of hypotheses"*. It may be considered a series of techniques for objectively investigating phenomena, acquiring new knowledge, or correcting and integrating previous knowledge (Goldhaber and Nieto 2010). Specifically, the scientific method follows a number of steps:

1. Formulation of a research question or problem statement: This requires evaluating evidence from previous experiments, scientific observations or assertions, and/or the work of other scientists. This is the purpose of the literature review. Often, determining a good question can be very difficult and may prove to be an iterative process that needs to revisited regularly
2. Generate a hypothesis: A hypothesis is an unproven proposition, arising from knowledge found while developing the research question. It may be very specific, say, "DNA makes RNA makes protein", or it might be broad, "Water molecules can be found in the polar regions of Mars". Importantly, any hypothesis must be falsifiable, that is a possible outcome of an experiment may conflict with predictions deduced from the hypothesis; without this the hypothesis cannot be tested
3. Prediction: If the hypothesis is correct, what are the implications, what is likely to be the outcome of testing? One or more predictions are then selected for testing. Any prediction must distinguish the hypothesis from likely alternatives

4. Test hypothesis through experimentation: Does the 'real world' behave as predicted by the hypothesis? If it does, confidence in the hypothesis increases; if not, it decreases. However, agreement cannot assure that the hypothesis is true; future experiments may reveal contradictions. In the seventeenth century Europeans believed all swans were white based upon all evidence available to them and the term 'black swan' was used to signify something exceedingly rare or non-existent. Explorer Willem de Vlamingh discovered black swans in Western Australia in 1697... Consequently, scientists are loathe consider any hypothesis 'proven'. This perspective is often at odds with that of the general public who are often led to believe that if something is considered a 'theory' then there must remain considerable doubt about its validity, for example; climate change and evolution.
5. Analysis and conclusions: What do the results of the experiment show? What is the next step? If the evidence has falsified the hypothesis, a new hypothesis is required. If the evidence strongly supports the hypothesis a new question can be asked to provide further insight. Depending on the complexity of the experiment, many iterations may be required to gather sufficient evidence to answer a question with confidence
6. Peer review: While not necessarily an integral part of the scientific method, peer review is, nevertheless, an important element in the validation of experimental outcomes. Peer review is the evaluation of work by one or more people of similar competence to those doing the original work. It is a form of self-regulation by qualified scientists within the relevant field. Peer review methods are employed to maintain standards of quality, improve performance, and provide credibility. For example: Cold fusion is a hypothetical type of nuclear reaction that would occur at, or near, room temperature. In 1989 electro-chemists Stanley Pons and Martin Fleischmann, announced that, using a small tabletop experiment, they had created nuclear fusion. These results received world-wide media attention, raising hopes of a cheap and abundant source of energy. However, when other scientists tried to replicate the experiment they were unable to duplicate the original findings, only discovering flaws and sources of experimental error in the original experiment. By late 1989, most scientists considered the cold fusion claims dead

Unfortunately, at present, there is little evidence to suggest that data scientists apply the full rigour of the scientific method to their art. Far from being objective, data and data sets are abstract creations, often chosen with a specific purpose in mind. In this way implicit and explicit biases occur in the collection and analysis of data. Moreover, any inferences and meaning drawn from the data are done so by human interpretation. In this way 'data science' is more akin to a 'social science', but one that, so far, pays little attention to its inherently biased nature. For example, in 2012 Hurricane Sandy generated more than 20 million tweets between October 27 and November 1. A study of the data showed, unsurprisingly, that grocery shopping peaked the night before the storm and nightlife picked up the day after. However, most of the tweets came from Manhattan, not the more severely affected areas of Breezy Point, Coney Island and Rockaway. This creates the illusion that Manhattan was the hub of the disaster, rather than simply being a reflection of higher cell-phone ownership and Twitter use. Indeed, little Twitter traffic came from the most severely affected areas due to power blackouts and limited cellular access (Crawford 2013).

Science and 'Data Science' differ in another major philosophical way; the objective of the process. The Latin origin of the word science, namely *scientia*, means knowledge but has, in modern times, come to mean knowledge of the physical world. Using the scientific method, scientists set up experiments, often with the objective of determining causality in the physical world. As correlation does not necessarily imply causation, it is necessary to use inductive reasoning from observations to strengthen or disprove hypotheses about causal relationships. Consequently, the contrast between hard and soft science arises from the increased uncertainty and vagueness connected to the inductive proofs of causal links in "softer" sciences. In data science the role of causality has yet to be confirmed. While some practitioners believe that to be of real, long-term value to business, Big Data needs to be about understanding the causal links among the variables (Hayes 2014), other do not:

> As humans we have been conditioned to look for causes, even though searching for causality is often difficult and may lead us down the wrong paths. In a big-data world, by contrast, we won't have to be fixated on causality; instead we can discover patterns and correlations in the data that offer us novel and invaluable insights. The correlations may not tell us precisely why something is happening, but they may alert us that it is happening. (Mayer-Schonberger and Cukier 2013)

So, perhaps not everything that is called 'science' is 'science'. Companies that pursue big data initiatives, and fight to recruit the cream of data scientists, must either recognise the traits of science and plan accordingly, or accept that their objectives are more immediate, more specific and require a greater probability of success. If 'Data' Science simply infers a focus on data and, by extension, statistics, then it could be argued that Data Science is simply a 'rebranding' of the term statistics, in which case the cumbersome 'Super Quant Manager' may be a rather more accurate title than Data Scientist' and data science no more 'scientific' than alchemy or astrology.

Conversely, some would argue that statistics is simply one of many skills required by a data scientist. Indeed, that it is the very scope of the data scientists skill-set that make the role so valuable. So what skills does a data scientist need? Based upon a review of eleven articles that included lists of various skills (Hayes 2014) it is suggested that the data scientist requires the following (Fig. 5.2).

It's not hard to see why Data Scientists are so rare! However, could it be that, behind the hype, the Data Scientist is a chimera, that reality is rather more mundane (and less sensational). The disciplines suggested all require quite different education and training with very little overlap. In addition, as we will see, the role of the Data Scientist may include practical domains such as;

- Decision science/business intelligence
- Product/Marketing analytics
- Fraud, abuse, risk and security

5.3 Data Scientists: The Myth of the 'Super Quant'

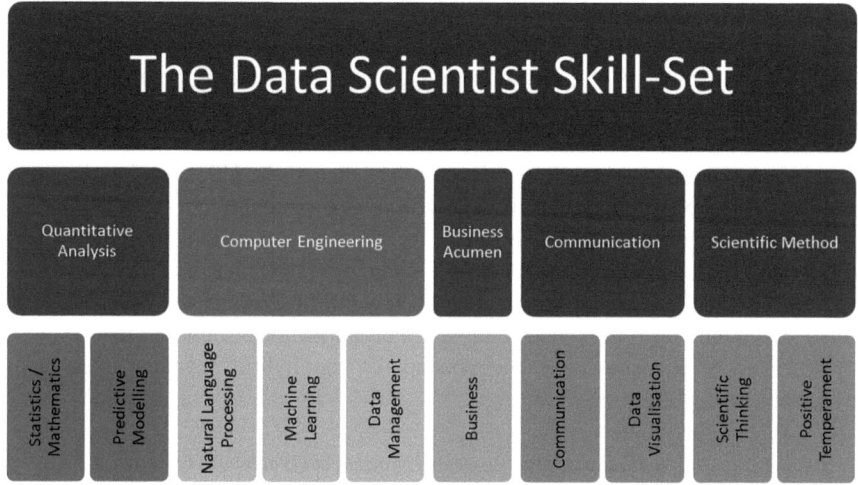

Fig. 5.2 The Data Scientist Skill-set (Adapted from Hayes 2014)

- Data services, engineering and infrastructure
- …plus a thorough understanding of business, organisational politics and 'domain' knowledge

Suppose a company wished to analyse the outliers in millions of insurance claims to identify potential cases of fraud, they would require expertise in sampling and multivariate statistical analysis. When advertising to fill the post, is it likely that they would advertise for an individual capable of doing the sophisticated data analysis, but with equal expertise in finding, cleaning and manipulating large data sets and designing/building the requisite, highly sophisticated, system? This would be tantamount to advertising for a "Rocket Scientist" and expecting to recruit someone who could design the engine and the guidance system, manufacture and assemble the parts, manage mission control and fly the rocket! In practice, such individuals, like unicorns, are rare and expensive. Consequently, in recruiting for Data Scientists, companies will find that they are interviewing individuals who are either the proverbial 'Jack-of-all-trades' or have expertise in one, possibly, two areas and have re-invented themselves a Data Scientists. The business networking site, LinkedIn, contains almost 12,500 data scientists, many with expertise in data mining, software development *or* statistical process control – but no unicorns.

One solution would be to have data scientist specialties, say;

- Statistical Data Scientists
- Software Data Scientists
- Database Data Scientists

Alternatively, we could accept that Big Data requires a *team* approach (call it a Data Science team, if you must!) and revert to more appropriate roles such as statistician, software engineer and database manager.

5.3.3 We've Been Here Before...

Beginning in the late 1980s, one of the biggest challenges facing organisations was how best to utilise the potential of information systems. However, despite huge investments by firms, many systems failed to deliver promised benefits (or simply failed altogether!). The belief, certainly in the UK and the US, was that the problems were neither technical nor fiscal, but organizational and managerial. As early as 1989 Meiklejohn identified the need for "hybrid managers"; individuals who could combine business understanding, technical competence, and organizational knowledge and skills, in order to integrate IT with business better. These 'hybrid managers' would need to be endowed with a broad skill-set (Table 5.1).

However, within a decade the concept of the hybrid manager was being criticised:

> A lot of so-called 'hybrid managers' know very little about IT, particularly the latest client-server systems. Many of them have programmed in COBOL and have knowledge of legacy systems, but not the latest IT such as client server, networking and databases…Having said that, they know all the buzz-words and can bluff their way out of a problem. But I'm not surprised that a lot of poor decisions get taken about IT. (Currie and Glover 1999)

Many hybrid managers found themselves as 'pseudo-managers' with little more than a basic grasp of technical knowledge, struggling for acceptance in either the business or the IT camp. In chasing the hybrid management fad they found that they had conceded specialist skills that were critical in the development of their organisations. As Currie and Glover (1999) note:

> …there is a worrying sort of affinity between the lack of attention to history and the seemingly popular managerialist appeal of the hybrid manager concept (to generalists and specialists alike)

Table 5.1 The traits of the 'hybrid manager' (Earl and Skyrme 1992)

Competence	Comprising	Critical
Business knowledge	Business fundamentals	Business instinct to spot opportunities
	Functional knowledge	
	Understanding specific firm's business	
Organisation-specific knowledge	Familiarity with organisation's culture, structure and processes	Knowing how things are done
	Knowing key people and their motivations	
IT knowledge and experience	Project management awareness	Confidence to ask and challenge
	Awareness of applications portfolio	
	IT fundamentals	
	Methods and providers	
Management	Motivation and communication skills	Ability to get things done
	Interpersonal and group skills	
	Change management skills	
	Cognitive skills	

In demanding such a wide breadth of skills from data scientists it is possible that we create a tier of generalists with a broad 'big data' vocabulary but, at best, superficial practical expertise.

5.4 It Takes a Team…

If we accept that, as described in much of today's popular press, the skill-set the data scientist is too broad, we are left with the alternative of building a data science team. However, while being a more practical approach, team building has its own difficulties e.g.

- Defining complimentary roles and recruiting for those roles
- Assigning team and individual goals and objectives
- Team formation and the establishment of team norms
- Dealing with inter- and intra-team conflict and personality clashes
- Monitoring of team performance
- Restructuring teams as challenges evolve

In this section we will look at teams and team-building, initially from a general perspective, then from the perspective of big data.

5.4.1 What Do We Mean by "a Team"?

An immediate response might be, say, 'a number of people that work together'. A CEO friend of ours regularly sends emails to all 400 of the company's employees, in five different time-zones, in which he addresses everyone as 'the team' – is that a team? The same company has; a Sales team, a Marketing team, a Pre-sales team, a Product team, a Support team and many more – are these teams? In practice the terms 'team' and 'group' are often used interchangeably but in academic literature they have quite specific meanings. The term 'group' tends to cover a wider range of situations and, while maintaining some commonality, the group rarely requires its members to work together towards some common purpose. To this extent, accountability lies with the individual, not the team. Conversely, the origin of the word 'team' is a set of animals yoked together, usually to pull a cart. This emphasises two fundamental aspects of teamwork; common purpose and mutual interdependence. Thus, a team may be defined as,

> …a collection of individuals who are interdependent in their tasks, who share responsibility for outcomes, who see themselves and who are seen by others as an intact social entity embedded in one or more larger social systems. (Cohen and Bailey 1997)

The nature of the task itself also has implications for the type of team required. Many teams are required to *do things*, such as make a product or provide a service. Here it is important to differentiate between teams of manual workers and teams of knowledge workers. Manual teams are often perceived by management as a cost to be minimised (often using technology). Alternatively, teams of knowledge workers are seen as assets who need to be nurtured to deliver the maximum productivity – an asset that must *want* to work for the organisation in preference to other opportunities (Drucker 1999). Other teams *run things* – managers who develop strategies and business plans, teams of directors etc. Finally, some teams *recommend things* e.g. problem solving teams, quality teams etc.

Research suggests that the optimal team size is between four to nine members (Belbin 2004). Below this number they lack resources, are unstable or more likely to split into factions. Above this number members get insufficient individual attention to maintain relationships. This is made even more difficult if they are virtual teams. There is, however, no hard and fast rule since teams are often quite different depending upon;

- *The interdependence the task*: A Sales team often comprises individuals who each have their own geographical 'patch' and/or product range and their own sales forecast and commission plan. Conversely, an engineering team designing a new product have to work closely together to ensure that the individual components of the product can be assembled and/or interfaced together
- *The formality of the task*: The executive board of a company, meeting officially, has particular tasks and responsibilities. However, the same individuals could meet later for a round of golf, thereby fulfilling their need for friendship and mutual support
- *The temporality of the team*: At an executive level the faces might change but the roles and responsibilities of, say, the CEO, COO, CFO & CIO are likely to remain stable. Conversely, project teams are, by nature, quite transitory and often involve roles for which a specialist is brought in for a short period of time. After which, both the individual, and the role, is no longer required by the team
- *The spatiality of the team*: Traditionally teams have met in an office environment where conversation and rapport allow significant informal information transfer. Increasingly, however, team members never physically meet due to geographical spread. In this instance technology such as email and video-conferencing replace face-to-face information transfer

Effective teams are a repository for the sharing and retention of knowledge. As each team member brings with them a range of knowledge, knowhow and experience, the overall scope of knowledge of the team is increased and problems can be perceived from different perspectives. Furthermore, a key advantage of teams is that, should a member leave, the company still retains most of the knowledge within the remaining team. Other benefits include (Table 5.2).

However, these benefits do not come without challenges. Many teams perform poorly due to internal conflict (or the fear of conflict), insufficient commitment, accountability avoidance and/or the inability of individuals to influence the group (to 'have their say'). It is common for teams to appear to function well at a superficial level as they suppress conflict. Unfortunately, this results in compromised decision-making, politicking, personal resentment and, usually, withdrawal from the team.

Table 5.2 The benefits of teamwork (Adapted from King and Lawley 2013)

Benefits of teamwork to team members	Benefits of teamwork to organisations
More meaningful work	Better, faster quality decision-making and problem-solving
Shared responsibilities	Transfer of skills and expertise
Learning from others	Reduced dependency on specific individuals
Job enrichment and rotation	Better utilisation of time
Feeling of belonging	Task responsibility
Increased autonomy within team	Delegation of authority
Emotional/psychological support	Increased commitment

Table 5.3 Recognising high-performing and poor performing teams (Adapted from Kets De Vries 1999)

High performing teams have staff that:	Poor performing teams have staff that:
Respect and trust each other	Have no clear sense of direction
Support each other	Have unequal commitment to the group
Communicate honestly with each other	Lack skills in key areas
Share a strong goal	Are (tacitly or explicitly) hostile to each other
Share strong values and beliefs	
Compromise their own objectives for those of the team	Lack effective leadership
Support 'distributed' leadership	

5.4.2 Building High-Performance Teams

Most of us will have, at some time, worked in a dysfunctional team. At universities, during group-work assignments, it's quite common to see individuals who fail to turn up for meetings, never contribute to group discussions but still expect to see their name on the work submitted. Clearly a group of individuals cannot be simply assembled and expected to perform as a team (though many companies seem to believe this to be the case), so what differentiates a high-performing team from a group of people simply working together (Table 5.3)?

So, where do we begin in building high performing teams?:

- *Create a genuine sense of urgency*: Team members need to be convinced that the team has a legitimate, urgent and meaningful purpose. 'Fake' urgency is difficult to maintain and even harder to replicate once individuals realise that they've been fooled
- *Choose team members for their skills, not their personality*: A team cannot succeed if it lacks the skills needed to achieve its purpose and performance goals. Often teams are assembled based upon 'who will work best together' only to find later that they lack the skills required for the task. Furthermore, teams comprising those that 'work well together' may seek to maintain team harmony at all costs, suppressing conflict and punishing relevant team members if it occurs (Schein 2010)

- *First impressions matter*: The cultural assumptions and norms of the team are determined at the first few meeting (see Chap. 3). Consequently, special attention needs to be paid to these meetings. At the outset each individual observes the signals given by others in order to reinforce or reject their own assumptions and concerns. Particular attention is paid to those in authority, what they do, as much as what they say. Are they late to arrive? Do they leave early? Are they easily distracted by external events after the session has begun? During our work in one company we were 10 min into a kick-off presentation for a major change management project when the Chief Operating Officer's mobile phone rang. He took the call, made his apologies and left the room never to return. Everyone else at the meeting got the message; '…this is a project that I can support verbally, but I don't consider it a priority'
- *Establish clear rules of behaviour*: This doesn't have to be the ten commandments or the Magna Carta but it does have to cover some crucial areas;
  - **Attendance**: Each member must accept that they are vital to the team and that any failure to attend will impair overall team performance. In this instance 'attendance' means physical *and* mental. What are the team rules for answering non-related phone calls, emails or other distractions? What are the consequences for non-attendance?
  - **Contribution**: Teams often break up due to one or more members actually (or being perceived as) shirking or free-riding (Schnake 1991). In setting rules members must decide what it means for each individual to, 'pull their own weight' and what the consequences are for those who fail to do so. Are all members assigned to the team equally? Or does the team comprise some individuals whose time is completely dedicated to the team and others who maintain other responsibilities within the organisation? Does the Team Leader do 'real' work or act in a purely supervisory role?
  - **Goal orientation**: Every team member understands the team's *raison d'etre*, its reason for existence and what it exists to achieve. They also understand their own role in achieving the end goal. In this way everyone signs up for assignments and does them. To develop a high performing team, each team member must understand the context of the team's work as much possible. This means replacing information sharing on a "need to know" basis with sharing on a "right to know" basis. It means each team member understanding the relevance of their job and how it impacts the effectiveness of others and the overall team effort. Thus, to increase collaboration, commitment and contribution members should have a clear understanding of the "big picture" and the role they play in painting it
  - **Discussion**: What can (or can't) be discussed? Are there any 'sacred cows'? Things considered beyond question or criticism? The team may comprise individuals from different hierarchical levels of the organisation and some members may require 'permission' before speaking frankly. Similarly in a team comprising long-serving employees and new recruits

- **Constructive confrontation**: The setting of team and individual expectations is a prerequisite of constructive confrontation. As discussed above each member should understand what is expected of them regarding attendance and contribution (arguably the two most common sources of conflict). Likewise with rules established enabling honest communication any confrontation must be expressed in terms of deviation away from the expectations and/or objectives of the team. Confrontation must not be personal, there should be no 'finger pointing'
- **Confidentiality**: This may refer to the objectives of the team, how the work is being done or things said within the team etc. Trust is a vital component of team performance. It takes a long time to establish and is easily broken. A simple rule could be, "…the only information to leave this room are what we agree on"
- **Performance monitoring and feedback**: How are the performance of the team and individual to be measured? What metrics will be used, how often will they be measured, what forms will feedback to team members take? High performing teams have mutually agreed goals that are simple, measurable and unambiguously relevant to the team's task. Each goal must include quantifiable metrics (available to everyone on the team) that can be used to verify the team effectiveness. Understanding and working toward these goals as a unit is essential to the team's effectiveness and future development

- *Start with a few urgent performance-orientated tasks and goals*: Successful teams track their progress to early key performance-orientated events. A number of early 'quick-wins' helps team formation and builds morale.
- *Stretch the team regularly with new information*: New information challenges a team to redefine and improve its understanding of the task. This helps to shape a common purpose, set clearer goals and improve its approach.
- *Spend lots of time together*: To develop the strong, trusting relationships required in high performing teams, it is important that members spend a significant amount of scheduled and unscheduled time together. This is particularly important in the early stages of team formation as group assumptions, norms and values are being established, for example:

"Some of the most impactful decisions at Gore get made by small teams. Within any team you'll find people with very different perspectives; they don't all think alike, and we encourage this. We encourage teams to take a lot of time to come together, to build trust, to build relationships because we know that if you throw them in a room and they don't have a foundation of trust, it will be chaotic, it will be political and people will feel as if they're being attacked" Terri Gore, CEO W.L. Gore & Associates, makers of Goretex™ (Hamel 2012)

It has been suggested that we each have two identities, one individual and one collective, and that any member of the team must be 'de-individualised' to the point that they consider their fate psychologically entwined with that of the team (Abrams and Hogg 2001). In this way the individual's attitude moves from that of 'my task' to that of 'our task', and this is the objective of many of the team-building initiatives that companies undertake.

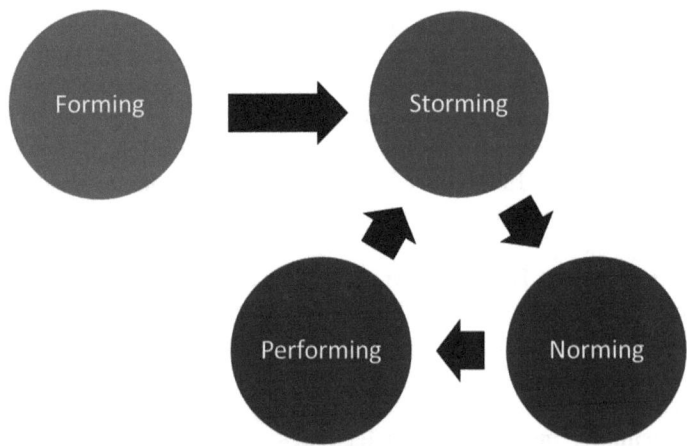

Fig. 5.3 Stages of team formation (Adapted from Tuckman 1965)

How individuals actually behave within a team, the group dynamics, are often determined by two factors; relationships within the group and the level of focus on the job in hand (task-orientation). These dynamic factors determine how the team handles the challenges of communication, conflict, leadership and trust (Tuckman and Jensen 1977), an iterative process of discovery, conflict, reflection and resolution (Fig. 5.3);

- *Forming*: As group members meet for the first time each is apprehensive. The group has no established rules and often no confirmed leader. Conversation tends to be superficial, irrelevant and well-mannered as each individual seeks to avoid offence and conflict
- *Storming*: As the group begins to work together interpersonal issues rise to the surface, bringing with them conflict, polarisation and strong emotional feelings. Members may seek to maintain their individuality and refuse to prioritise group goals above their individual goals, becoming defensive, negative and aggressive. At this stage the group may fracture as individuals refuse to work with each other and withdraw
- *Norming*: As the initial resistance is overcome the group starts to become more unified, standards of behaviour begin to develop and roles are accepted. The group may still be quite volatile but norms and values emerge tentatively. Members begin to accept the characteristics of other group members but may fall back to the 'storming' stage several times before progressing to the next stage
- *Performing*: As the norms and values of the team become established and the structure accepted more and more energy is directed towards the task in hand. Members are prepared to support each other and roles become more flexible and functional

Long-established, Tuckman's model has been criticised as being too linear, that teams move from moderate to optimal performance to dysfunctionality with relatively minor changes in task, members or circumstances. Others have suggested that staff from modern organisations come from such diverse backgrounds that models such as this are no longer relevant. However, we believe that the model still provides a useful lens through which to interpret the formation and development of organisational teams. What it does not do, however, is to explain how performing teams can make the leap to high-performing teams.

In practice high-performance teams are rare. These teams have;

> ...a deeper sense of purpose, more ambitious performance goals, more complete approaches, fuller mutual accountability and interchangeable as well as complementary skills. (Katzenbach and Smith 1993)

In 1942 Brigadier General Leslie R. Groves began assembling what he later described as, "The largest group of prima donnas ever assembled in one place". Many thought his choice for Project Director, the rather undistinguished Julius Robert Oppenheimer, was bizarre. There was nothing in Oppenheimer's background to suggest that he had the skills to lead, what was then, the biggest scientific project in history. Hot-tempered, he was considered patronising, inept in social relations, and thoroughly impractical. However, at Los Alamos, the epicenter of the Manhattan Project, where the first nuclear bomb was designed and constructed, Oppenheimer brought together and led a team of the greatest physicists in the world. Despite massive egos, these highly individualistic scientists amazed everyone (especially the military) with their teamwork and organisation in pursuit of their goal: ensuring that Germany did not develop the bomb first.

5.5 Team Building as an Organisational Competency

Increasingly, an essential competency for any size organisation is the ability to quickly build and empower high performing teams. This requires open communication, close collaboration, flexibility and versatility. In order to facilitate this, companies must provide the initial support and structure for the team. This by employing the team-oriented people, that is, individuals with specific knowledge, skills, and attitudes (Table 5.4).

It is important to note that these KSAs are all individual as opposed to team-level competencies. That is, team members bring these KSAs to the team; the competencies are not unique to the task or the team itself. As members work together these competencies are refined and additional competencies emerge, such a greater understanding of teammates personalities.

In building teams, companies have three basic strategies:

- Select staff that currently have the required knowledge, skills and attitudes
- Modify tasks, workflow and/or organisational structure to facilitate teamwork
- Develop individual team member competencies by training

The first requires precise recruitment, selection and measurement of an individual's team working competencies plus a careful balancing of task-oriented and

Table 5.4 Team knowledge, skills & attitudes (KSA) – (Adapted from Baker et al. 2006)

Teamwork	Definition	Behavioral Examples
Team Leadership (a skill *all* team members must have)	The ability to:	Facilitate team problem solving
	Direct and coordinate the activities of other team members	Provide performance expectations and acceptable interaction patterns
	Assess team performance	
	Assign tasks	
	Develop team knowledge, skills, and attitudes (KSAs)	Synchronize and combine individual team member contributions
	Motivate other team members	
	Plan and organise	Seek and evaluate information that impacts team functioning
	Establish a positive atmosphere	Clarify team member roles
		Engage in preparatory meetings and feedback sessions with the team
Mutual performance monitoring	The ability to:	Identifying mistakes and lapses in other team members actions
	Develop common understandings of the team environment	
	Apply appropriate task strategies in order to accurately monitor teammate performance	Providing feedback regarding team member actions in order to facilitate self-correction
Mutual Support Behaviour	The ability to:	Recognition by potential backup providers that there is a workload distribution problem in their team
	Anticipate a team-member's needs through accurate knowledge about their responsibilities	
	The ability to:	Shifting of work responsibilities to under-utilized team members
	Shift workload among members to achieve balance during high periods of workload or pressure	Completion of the whole task or parts of tasks by other team members
Adaptability	The ability to:	Identify cues that a change has occurred, assign meaning to that change, and develop a new plan to deal with the changes
	Modify strategies based on information gathered from the environment	
	Alter a course of action or team repertoire in response to changing conditions (internal or external)	Identify opportunities for improvement and innovation for habitual or routine practices
		Remain vigilant to changes in the internal and external environment of the team

(continued)

5.5 Team Building as an Organisational Competency

Table 5.4 (continued)

Teamwork	Definition	Behavioral Examples
Shared mental models and communication	Deep knowledge of the relationships between the task the team is engaged in and how the team members will interact	Anticipating and predicting each other's needs Identify changes in the team, task, or teammates, and implicitly adjusting strategies as needed
	Exchange of information between a sender and a receiver irrespective of the medium	Following up with team members to ensure message was received
		Acknowledging that a message was received
		Clarifying with the sender of the message that the message received is the same as the intended message sent
Team/collective orientation	An ability to:	Taking into account alternative solutions provided by teammates and appraising that input to determine what is most correct
	Take another's behavior into account during group interaction and the belief in the importance of team goal's over individual member's goals	Increased task involvement, information sharing, strategising, and participatory goal setting
Mutual trust	The shared belief that team members will perform their roles and protect the interests of their teammates	Information sharing
		Willingness to admit mistakes and accept feedback

team-oriented KSAs among team members. The second requires companies investigate what organisational/environmental conditions are required for team-based work to flourish and reengineer these conditions accordingly. The third, and most common, is the training and development of staff in order to improve team performance. Consequently, a significant amount of research has been done regarding the most effective strategies and techniques for training team KSAs. This includes a wide collection of principles and guidelines, such as, assertiveness training, cross-training, stress management training and team self-correction (Baker et al. 2006). In the aviation industry crew resource management (CRM) programs have been used for over 30 years in an effort to constantly improve safety. Research suggests that CRM training improved communication, coordination, and decision-making behaviors; and enhanced error-management skills.

Thus, team members should, initially, be selected based upon their natural skills and where skills are absent, the team must have the time, resources and training required to develop these skills. Ideally, this will include some elements of 'cross-training' to encourage members to pick up skills from other members. This creates flexibility; when one member is unavailable, others can contribute and ensure the progress of the project. It can also create a unit that is more resistant to attrition. Once the team is functioning, on-going learning and development is highly dependent on the timeliness of performance-related feedback. A key role of the team leader is to ensure that feedback regarding the team's goals and performance metrics reaches the team fast enough for them to make adjustments and corrections. Late feedback has little practical value and can often be perceived as criticism. Team members need to be encouraged to view feedback as constructive communication, not criticism. In this way mistakes can be viewed as opportunities to learn rather than something for which they are penalised; a major step towards the creation of an effective problem-solving team.

Unfortunately in many companies formal (and informal) structures are rigid and ossified. Bureaucracy and hierarchy make team building a slow, highly political venture but, as Hamel notes, *"Structures need to appear and disappear based on the forces that are acting on the organisation. When people are freer to act, they're more able to sense these forces and act in ways that fit best with the external reality"* (2012). Consequently, the ability to build teams that coalesce rapidly and contribute effectively is a key competence required by many businesses. However, an organisations ability to create and manage teams would seem more straightforward to develop than the search for the mythical 'Super Quant'.

Beyond the "Data Scientist" rhetoric many companies such as LinkedIn, Monster Worldwide, the employment website, and American International Group (AIG), one of the world's biggest insurance companies are quietly building Data Science Teams. These teams vary from a handful of people working on pilots projects, to twenty or more for larger projects and open-ended work. A small pilot team might include one or more software engineers and/or quantitative analysts who know Hadoop and can write scripts to prepare, integrate, clean, run and analyze Big Data. The team might also have a systems architect to maintain the data systems and ensure the systems are able to communicate with one another. Bigger projects may require specialists to complement these roles, such as quantitative analysts who can dig deeper into the data and visualization specialists who can convert findings into easy-to-understand graphics and visual stories. The team may also include business analysts who can identify the value of the findings to the business, communicate with operational managers in language they understand and serve as the team's liaison officer with different departments. At Monster, each business function is given a 'navigator', an expert communicator, who reveals the team's findings using simple language and graphics.

Thus, the foundation of a 'Big Data' team lies in three complimentary roles:

- ***The Business Analyst***: Many companies are familiar with the traditional role of business analyst, but within a Big Data team the analyst must do more than understand the structure, policies, and operations of an organisation. He/she must have good technical skills with front-end tools such as spreadsheets and visualisation applications. The best candidates will also have an understanding of databases technologies such as SQL and NoSQL plus experience of Business Intelligence applications.

- **The Machine-Learning Statistician**: Again, companies may be comfortable with developing the job specification for a statistician, but, as with the business analyst, it is the individuals other skills that make him/her suited to a Big Data team. Beyond statistical number-crunching, this role requires individuals capable of building data models and developing algorithms that can be used to predict trends, identify 'meaning' (in, say, YouTube videos) or estimate the influence of a particular individual or event.
- **The Data Engineer**: This role may be considered an enhance version of the traditional Database Administrator. In this instance the individual will need a skill-set that incorporates Hadoop, MapReduce, Hbase and Cassandra etc. These are the people responsible for capturing, structuring, storing and processing of data from multiple sources in a variety of forms. The data engineers provide the raw material for the machine-Learning statisticians to work with.

5.6 Summary

At first sight, the skills needed for Big Data are both broad and deep and individuals with this highly desirable skill set are already in huge demand. The idealised 'Data Scientist' has a potent mix of business and technical acumen, with the added bonus of statistical, communication and visualisation skills. However, in this chapter we have questioned the relevance of the term 'science' in this instance. Do these 'Data Scientists' actually 'do' science? From the perspective of the company, do they really want these employees to be 'scientists'? More pragmatically, do individuals with this huge set of skills actually exist? Taking a practical view of the big data skill shortage we have argued that, for many companies, a more realistic approach is not to seek the illusory, all-encompassing "Data Scientist" but to build data science teams. Consequently, we have examined how teams are created, how they develop and how they are managed. Ultimately, many companies have significant experience in building and managing teams, indeed in companies such as LinkedIn and Google it is, arguably, a core competency of the company. We argue that for big data to grow rapidly companies need to develop data science teams as part of a wider big data strategy.

5.7 Review Questions

The answers to these questions can be found in the text of this chapter

1. Why did Patil and Hammerbacher feel that the term "Data Scientist" best suited staff working on big data projects?
2. Why might the term 'science' be inappropriate for the work done by big data teams?
3. What is the scientific method?
4. According to Hayes (2014) the Data scientist requires ten key skills, what are they?

5. What are the main challenges arising from team-work?
6. When establishing a team, what are the main rules of behaviour that need to be agreed at the outset?
7. Describe Tuckman's model of team formation

5.8 Group Work/Research Activity

These activities require you to research beyond the contents of the book and can be tackled individually or as a discussion group.

5.8.1 Discussion Topic 1

Davenport and Patil famously announced that the role of the Data Scientist would be, "The sexiest job of the 21st century" (2012). Since their article was originally printed in 2012 there has, to some extent, been a backlash (not least of all from practitioners advising a more team-oriented approach). What do you think?

5.8.2 Discussion Topic 2

What's in a name? Would you prefer to be known as a Statistical Data Scientist or a Statistician, a Software Data Scientist or a Software Engineer, a Database Data Scientist or a Database Manager? Do you think the title matters? Justify your answer.

References

Abrams D, Hogg MA (2001) Collective identity: group membership and self-conception. In: Hogg MA, Tindale S (eds) Blackwell handbook of social psychology: group processes. Blackwell Publishers, Oxford, pp 425–461
Baker DP, Day R, Salas E (2006) Teamwork as an essential component of high-reliability organisations. Health Serv Res 41(4 pt 2):1576–1598
Belbin M (2004) Management teams: why they succeed and fail, 2nd edn. Elsevier Butterworth-Heinmann, Oxford
Cohen SG, Bailey DE (1997) What makes teams work: group effectiveness research from the shop floor to the executive suite. J Manag 23(3):239–290
Crawford K (2013) The hidden biases in big data. https://hbr.org/2013/04/the-hidden-biases-in-big-data. Last accessed 16 Dec 2014
Currie WL, Glover IA (1999) Hybrid managers: an example of tunnel vision and regression in management research. In: Currie WL, Galliers B (eds) Rethinking management information systems, 1st edn. Oxford University Press, Oxford, pp 417–443
Davenport TH, Patil DJ (2012) Data scientist: the sexiest job of the 21st century. Harv Bus Rev (Oct):70–76
Drucker PF (1999) Knowledge-worker productivity: the biggest challenge. The knowledge management yearbook 2000–2001
Earl MJ, Skyrme DJ (1992) Hybrid managers – what do we know about them? J Inf Syst 2:169–187

References

Goldhaber AS, Nieto NN (2010) Photon and graviton mass limits. Am Phys Soc 82:939–979

Hamel G (2012) What matters now: how to win in a world of relentless change, ferocious competition and unstoppable innovation. Jossey-Bass, San Francisco

Harris JG et al (2013) The team solution to the data science shortage. Accenture Technology Labs. http://www.accenture.com/sitecollectiondocuments/pdf/accenture-team-solution-data-scientist-shortage.pdf

Hayashi C et al (1997) Data science, classification and related methods. Springer, New York

Hayes B (2014) The one hidden skill you need to unlock the value of your data. [online]. Last Accessed Mar 18 2014 at: HYPERLINK http://businessoverbroadway.com/the-one-hidden-skill-you-need-to-unlock-the-value-of-your-data http://businessoverbroadway.com/the-one-hidden-skill-you-need-to-unlock-the-value-of-your-data

Katzenbach JR, Smith DK (1993) The wisdom of teams: creating the high performance organisation. Harvard Business School Press, Boston

Kets De Vries M (1999) High-performance teams: lessons from the Pygmies. Organ Dyn 27(3):66–77

King D, Lawley S (2013) Organizational behaviour, 1st edn. Oxford University Press, Oxford

Mayer-Schonberger V, Cukier K (2013) Big data: a revolution that will transform how we live, work and think. John Murray, London

Meiklejohn I (1989) A new hybrid breed for IT. Manage Today 13:143–146

National Science Foundation (2005) Long-lived digital data collections: enabling research and education into the 21st century, National Science Foundation, http://www.nsf.gov/pubs/2005/nsb0540/start.htm. Last accessed 17 Dec 2014

Patil DJ (2011) Building data science teams. O'Reilly, Sebastopol

Schein EH (2010) Organizational culture and leadership, 4th edn, The Jossey-Bass business & management series. Wiley, San Francisco

Schnake ME (1991) Organisational citizenship: a review, proposed model, and research agenda. Hum Relat 44(7):735–759

Stevens P (2012) Graphene: invented in the UK, largely being developed elsewhere. Financial Times, 14 June, http://www.ft.com/cms/s/0/d902e60e-b07d-11e1-8b36-00144feabdc0.html#axzz3M4VtDDxE. Last accessed 16 Dec 2014

Tuckman BW (1965) Developmental sequence in small groups. Psychol Bull 63(6):384–399

Tuckman B, Jensen M (1977) Stages of small-group development revisited. Group Organ Manage 2(4):419–427

Statistical Thinking   6

6.1   What the Reader Will Learn

- That the terms 'data', 'information' and 'knowledge' have subtly different meanings though they are often used synonymously. This can be the source of considerable confusion
- That the human cognitive systems (namely the limbic system and the neo-cortical system) operate in quite different, often contradictory ways
- The importance of causality and its relationship with correlation
- That there are inherent difficulties associated with the cognitive processing of randomness
- The nature of cognitive biases and their implications for judgement and decision-making

6.2   Introduction: Statistics Without Mathematics

Prior to publishing his best-selling book, "A Brief History of Time", physicist Stephen Hawking was told by his editor that, "...*each equation I included in the book would halve the sales. I therefore resolved not to have any equations at all*" (Hawking 1988). Likewise, in this chapter we will investigate statistical *thinking* without recourse to formulae and equations. That this chapter forms the hub of the nine-'S' model should come as no surprise, after all, what we call 'statistical thinking' is at the heart of Big Data.

In this chapter we will examine how we, as individuals, interpret data, process information and define knowledge. In the book, "Blink" Malcolm Gladwell (2006) examined how instinctive judgements can, sometimes, be more effective than a considered decision. In this chapter we investigate how those same instincts, gut-feelings and hunches are often irrational, illogical and lead to poor decision-making.

Conversely, statistical thinking is both rational and logical. However, it is also hard work, often counter-intuitive and requires a genuine understanding of randomness, probability and correlation. Unfortunately the human brain, honed as it was on the plains of Africa 150,000 years ago, is ill-equipped to handle such abstractions. Consequently, we assign meaning to random patterns, confuse causality to correlation and overestimate the chances of winning the lottery. In this chapter we will examine some of the inherent barriers to statistical thinking, how our emotional brain, in seeking to make sense of a complex world, misinterprets information and jumps to incorrect conclusions.

Finally, Big Data literature is littered with terminology that, at first glance, looks uncomplicated. Hence, words such as 'statistics' and 'analytics' are used interchangeably, while differences between 'data', 'information' and 'knowledge' are often neglected or confused. Furthermore, if we consider statistics as the study of the analysis, interpretation and presentation of data, and analytics as the discovery and communication of meaningful patterns in data, what precisely do we mean by 'interpretation' and 'meaningful patterns' of data? Perhaps we need to start at the beginning…

6.3 Does "Big Data" Mean "Big Knowledge"?

The truth is "Big Data" isn't about data at all; it's about information and knowledge. Simply put, Big Data gives managers the opportunity to measure, and therefore 'know', radically more about their businesses. Alternatively, as McAfee and Brynjolfsson (2012) suggest, Big Data allows companies to exploit vast new flows of information to radically improve their performance. So what are we to make of the terms, "data", "information" and "knowledge" and the relationships between them?

Let's start with an example. Cryptography is widely used to protect private and sensitive information as it flows around the globe. Algorithms encrypt information deep within data, so while the data may be available publicly, only those with the encryption 'keys' are able to extract the 'information'. Thus cryptography exploits the differences between data and information. Using the same example, let's assume that you receive an encrypted message for which you possess the 'key'. On opening the message you read, "The bird has flown the coop". This could mean one of our feathered friends has escaped its cage but, with different context, it could also mean that a suspect under police surveillance has sped away from a suspicious rendezvous. While you may understand the sentence, "The bird has flown the coop", you may not understand the message. In this case, prior knowledge enables a contextual understanding of the message, and the message, in turn, carries information that modifies that knowledge. Consequently, information and knowledge must be differentiated from each other.

6.3.1 The DIKW Hierarchy

The data–information–knowledge–wisdom hierarchy (DIKW), alternatively referred to as the 'Knowledge Hierarchy', the 'Information Hierarchy' or the 'Knowledge Pyramid' is an important, if contentious, model in the information and knowledge literature (for our purpose we will ignore the role of "wisdom" which, for all of its philosophical merits, has little relevance to our current discussion). The hierarchy (Fig. 6.1) is often used to help define the relationship between data, information, and knowledge and to identify and describe the processes involved in transforming an entity at a lower level in the hierarchy (e.g. data) to an entity at a higher level in the hierarchy (e.g. information).

Ackoff (1989) defines data as *symbols* that represent properties of objects, events and their environments i.e. products of observation. However, most definitions of data are described in terms of what is *absent* in data e.g. it is unorganised, unprocessed and has no inherent meaning or value because it is without context and interpretation.

So, what of information? Information may be considered relevant, usable, meaningful or processed data. Ask a question beginning with, 'who', 'what', 'where', 'when', or 'how many'; and data is processed into an answer to that enquiry - the data is transformed into 'information'. Prior to this transformation the data is of little intrinsic value. Furthermore, information can also be *inferred* from data – it does not have to be immediately available. For example, were you asked, 'What are the average sales for the last three months?', there may be individual monthly sales figures explicitly recorded as data, but perhaps not the average quarterly figure; however, the average sales figure can easily be inferred from the data about individual monthly figures (Fricke 2009).

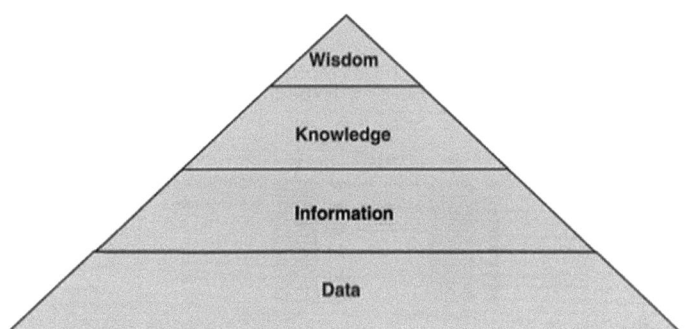

Fig. 6.1 The DIKW Hierarchy (Fricke 2009)

In the DIKW hierarchy knowledge is often construed as know-how, or skill (being able to ride a bike), rather than knowledge in the sense of the "know-that" of propositional knowledge. For example, Paris is the capital of France. Thus, know-how elevates information to a controlling role by transforming it into instructions. For example, the temperature of a room (data) might become information when you ask, 'What is the temperature?' Subsequently, that information can become instructions to turn the air conditioner on (assuming you appreciate the way the temperature of the room is controlled), the information, in this case, evolves into knowledge of how to cool a room (Fricke 2009).

However, the DIKW Hierarchy is not without its critics. As Fricke (2009) notes, "…either DIKW does not permit inductive, or similar, inference, in which case statements like 'most rattlesnakes are dangerous' cannot be information or DIKW does permit inductive inference in which case it abandons its core faith that data and information have to be rock solid true". Note also that, in defining information, we carefully avoided information-seeking questions beginning with 'Why'. To answer a why-question requires digging beneath the surface, to go beyond the 'data'; and that is forbidden within the DIKW hierarchy. Yet it is completely natural for inspectors of a train crash, for example, to search for the information telling why the accident occurred.

6.3.2 The Agent-in-the-World

An alternative way to consider the relationship between data, information and knowledge, is to examine how we, as human beings, interact and interpret the world (Fig. 6.2).

Every moment of our lives our senses are bombarded with stimuli, only some of which are discernible to our sensory organs. Our hearing faculties are limited to a range of sounds between 20 Hz and 20,000 Hz., our vision restricted to the visible range of

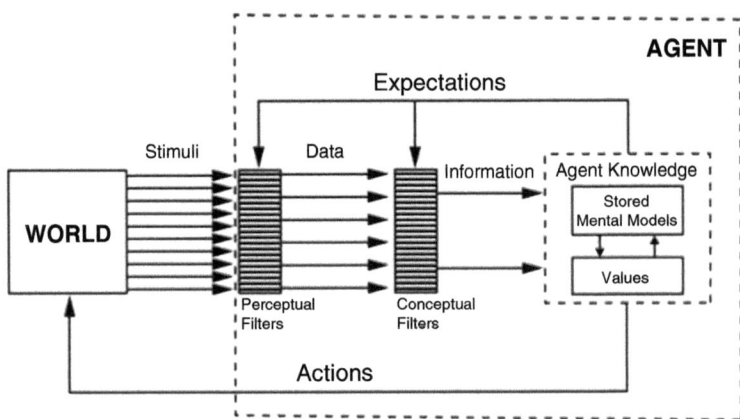

Fig. 6.2 The Agent-in-the-World (Boisot and Canals 2004)

wavelengths within the electro-magnetic spectrum (390–700 nm). In mammals, smells are sensed by olfactory sensory neurons in the olfactory epithelium. An animal's olfactory sensitivity, its ability to "smell", is determined by the surface area of the olfactory epithelium and the density of sensory neurons. A dog's olfactory epithelium is approximately seventeen times the size of a human being's and with a hundred times more receptors per square centimetre. Clearly, a dog "smells" the world in a very different way to a human being.

The signals that can be discerned by our sensory apparatus are processed and filtered. The perceptual filter 'focuses' the senses to certain types of stimuli and only stimuli passing through this initial filter are registered as "data". Thus, a tired mother that doses in a chair, despite the noises of the day going on around her, is suddenly roused into action by the cry of her new born. Failure to filter stimuli in this way may lead to sensory overload and clinical conditions such as; Chronic Fatigue Syndrome and Post Traumatic Stress Disorder. Likewise, conceptual filters extract information-bearing data from what has been registered. Both perceptual and conceptual filters are constantly being tuned by expectations and prior knowledge, to act selectively on both stimuli and data. Thus, the act of extracting information from data represents selective interpretation of the data. However, while you may believe that this interpretation of data is done in a logical, rational manner – reality is rather more complex.

6.4 Statistical Thinking – Introducing System 1 and System 2

Consider the following:

"Peter tends to be rather shy and withdrawn. He's always helpful but shows little interest in people or what is going on in the world. A quiet, tidy soul, he strives for order and structure, and a passion for details". Is Peter more likely to be a librarian or a truck driver?

For most people, the description of Peter's personality is immediately recognisable as that of a stereotypical librarian. However, did it occur to you that there are significantly more truck drivers than librarians? Also, 80 % of all librarians are female. This would imply that there are far more "quiet, tidy souls" behind the steering wheels of trucks than behind the desks of libraries. Thus, the fast-responding "System 1" answers the question and statistical considerations, handled by slow-responding "System 2", are ignored (Kahneman 2012).

Now look at the following two words for a second or two:

BANANAS **VOMIT**

In the brief time it took you to consider these two words you've been busy. Mentally you may have experienced unpleasant images or memories. It's possible that your face briefly registered an expression of mild disgust, that your heart rate increased and your sweat glands were triggered. Fundamentally, you responded to the words on the page in precisely the same way, albeit tempered, as you would have done to the real event. Your brain automatically constructed a causal connection between *bananas* and *vomit* that had both physical, emotional and mental repercussions – and all of this was done automatically and beyond your control (Kahneman 2012).

For this next experiment you will need five pieces of paper or card, something about the size of a business card or Post-IT. On each write a sequence of four digits and place a blank card on the top of the stack. For the test it would be useful to have a metronome (set at one beat per sec), but you could do this by simply tapping out a similar beat. Now here's the task:

> Beating a steady rhythm (or using the metronome), remove the blank card and read the first sequence aloud. Wait two beats then, speaking aloud, say the sequence in which each of the original digits is incremented by one. For example: if the sequence on the card is 6935, the response would be 7046. Maintaining the rhythm is important.

This is hard mental work! During the task, a video camera recording your eye movement would have seen your pupil dilate as your brain strained to achieve the result within the allotted time, then contract as the period of mental stress receded. Focused on this task, your brain may have been 'blind' to other stimuli as you reached a state of mental overload. Your brain has a finite capacity for this type of mental challenge (Kahneman 2012).

In the first task we were able to read three sentences that described a person and immediately make a judgement as to the type of employment that person had. In the second task we found that we could instantly elicit a physical 'disgust' response by simply reading words on a page. In the third task we discovered that we could limit the brain's capacity to perceive further stimuli by performing a relatively straightforward arithmetic task. So what is going on? For good evolutionary reasons the human brain handles different tasks in different ways. The first two tasks are associated with lower-order brain functions within the limbic system, the system that includes to 'fight-or-flight' response – Nobel Prize Winner Daniel Kahneman calls this System 1 (2012). The third task employs higher order analytical functions in the cerebral neocortex – this is System 2 (Fig. 6.3).

System 1 operates quickly and automatically, with little or no effort and no sense of voluntary control. When we refer to our 'instincts', 'intuitions', 'hunches' or 'gut-feelings' or when we "did something on auto-pilot" we are usually referring to System 1;

> "The capabilities of System 1 include innate skills we share with other animals. We are born prepared to perceive the world around us, recognise objects, orient attention, avoid losses and fear spiders. Other mental activities become fast and automatic through prolonged practice. System 1 has learned associations between ideas (the capital of France?); it has also learned skills such as reading and understanding nuances of social situations... Detecting the similarity of a personality sketch to an occupational stereotype requires broad knowledge of the language and culture, which most of us possess."
> "Thinking, Fast and Slow", Daniel Kahneman (2012)

Conversely, System 2 operates much more slowly than System 1 and requires conscious effort and attention. When we talk about 'focussing' or 'concentrating'

	SYSTEM 1	**SYSTEM 2**
CHARACTERISTICS	- Fast, effortless, unconscious - Triggers emotions - Looks for patterns, associations and causation - Creates stories to explain events	- Slow, conscious and requires effort - Logical and deliberate - Can handle abstract concepts
DISADVANTAGES	- Jumps to conclusions - Emotional responses may be unhelpful - Can make errors that are not detected and corrected	- Slow response time - Requires effort and energy, leading to decision fatigue
ADVANTAGES	- Speed of response in a crisis - Easy completion of routine/repetitive tasks - Creativity through associations	- Allows for reflection, consideration and evaluation of consequences - Allows reductive thinking - Can handle logic, maths and statistics

Fig. 6.3 Comparing the Limbic (System 1) and Neo-cortical (System 2) information processing systems

on a task or using willpower or self-control, we are referring to System 2. System 2 handles tasks that require analytical, computational, rational thinking - this is what we will call "Statistical Thinking". Statistical Thinking is, literally, hard work. When you take on a challenging cognitive task or an activity that requires self-control, your blood sugar level falls and, eventually, you will lose concentration (or control) unless the glucose is replenished. Moreover, System 2 has limited capacity and in conditions of cognitive overload protects the most important activity by limiting attention to other tasks. In this way, a good magician may draw your attention away from the mechanics of an illusion, leaving you to see the 'magic' of the end product. Finally, System 2 is lazy. In most instances, unless called upon, System 2 will leave decisions to the ever-accommodating System 1. Do you remember the last time you had some 'thinking' work to do, perhaps an assignment, a sales forecast or a budget? Did you get a sudden urge to tidy your desk/room/house, make a cup of coffee or clean some of the spam from your emails? System 2 is the master of procrastination…

The rest of this chapter will discuss the interaction of System 1 and System 2 and how our instincts, intuitions and hunches often triumph over our willpower, self-control and rationality. We will examine why we overestimate what we think we 'know', underestimate the role of uncertainty and why these things often make statistical thinking difficult.

6.4.1 Short Circuiting Rationality

In April 2013 James Bradley and his family were on holiday in Cornwall. Driving near St. Blazey, their Audi was involved in a minor collision with a Ford Focus belonging to a plaster, Mr Timothy Dunn. Both parties felt that the other was responsible for the accident, but, as the two cars pulled over, it was Dunn who appeared 'angry and furious'. Dunn stormed to the Audi, banging on the car and attempting to force open the driver's door. Clearly shaken, Bradley refused to open the door and chose to drive off. There followed a 30 min chase during which Dunn repeatedly rammed his Ford into the Audi. During this time the terrified Bradleys made five call to police begging for help. The chase ended when the Bradleys found refuge in a car park where they were met by police. In court judge Christopher Harvey Clark said, *"This is one of the worst cases of road rage that I have ever encountered. The extent and nature of the course of conduct that you undertook must have terrified Mr and Mrs Bradley and their young daughters. You were frothing at the mouth in a way reminiscent of a dog suffering from rabies."* Barry Hilliard, for the defence, said Dunn did not know why he had been so angry for so long… (www.thisiscornwall.co.uk 2013)

Timothy Dunn is not alone. A 2013 YouGov survey of 3,000 drivers found that almost a half of UK motorists admitted to feeling 'road rage' (Admiral Insurance 2013). Dunn had experienced what Daniel Goleman, author of "Emotional Intelligence" calls an 'emotional hijacking' (1995).

A key component of System 1 is the amygdala, a pair of almond-shaped structures, one on each side of the brain. Evolutionarily, the amygdala is an ancient brain structure that pre-dates both the cortex and the neo-cortex of modern humans and specialises in emotional memory and responses. The amygdala serves the role of emotional gate-keeper, monitoring every situation, every personal interaction, for signs of potential threat. Given a perceived threat, the amygdala has the neural connections to capture and control much of the brain before the rational mind, System 2, has time to prepare a more reasoned response – thus an emotional hijacking. This is not to say that emotions are not required for rational thinking, indeed they are indispensable. Emotional learning, arising from prior experiences, sets the boundaries of positive and negative motivation, thereby highlighting certain alternatives over others when faced with an array of choices. Thus, emotional intelligence may be defined as, "the ability to perceive emotions, use them to facilitate thought and to understand and control them to promote personal growth" (Goleman 1995). Let's take a look at this definition:

Emotional perception allows us to detect and decode emotions in faces, voices, body language and artefacts such as pictures, and to identify and reflect upon our own emotions. *Emotional utilisation* enables us to harness emotions within various cognitive activities, such as thinking and problem solving, allowing us to fully capitalise on our changing moods to best fit the task at hand. *Emotional empathy* allows us to interpret emotional signals and to understand complicated relationships among emotions. Finally, *emotional control* enables us to regulate emotions in both ourselves and in others.

6.5 Causality, Correlation and Conclusions

As Mlodinow (2008) notes, *"...we all create our own view of the world and then employ it to filter and process our perceptions, extracting meaning from the ocean of data that washes over us in daily life."* Consequently, one of the primary functions of System 1 is to review and revise the evolving mental model of your own personal world and to determine what is considered 'normal' in it. To that extent you are, in every sense, the creator of your own universe. Your unique mental model is created and enriched by linking ideas of situations, incidents, events, and consequences that occur regularly - sometimes simultaneously, sometimes within a relatively short interval. Established and reinforced, these connections become the *norms* used to characterise the structure of events in your life. Thus, System 1 helps shapes your interpretation of the present and your expectations of the future. For example: Quickly write or say aloud how many animals of each kind did Moses take into the ark?

Now, think carefully... Was it Moses or Noah who built the ark? The thought of animals marching into the ark sets up a biblical context and, while incorrect, the name 'Moses' is not abnormal in that context, so System 1 quickly answers the question and moves on to the next task, with no recourse to System 2. How about this, imagine that you are reviewing the appraisals of two employees, Alan and Bob. Alan's appraisal describes him as *intelligent, industrious, impulsive, critical, stubborn* and *envious*. On the contrary, Bob's appraisal says that he is *envious, stubborn, critical, impulsive, industrious* and *intelligent*. What do you think of Alan and Bob?

Most people view Alan much more positively than Bob, not just because the initial traits are more influential but also because the initial traits shape the meaning of the later ones. Given that Alan is originally described as *intelligent* and *industrious* then *stubbornness* may be interpreted as tenacious and single-minded. Conversely, since Bob is initially described as *envious*, a strong negative trait, being *industrious* and *intelligent* may only serve to make him appear deceitful and, possibly, dangerous (Kahneman 2012). Many of the associations made by System 1 occur subconsciously and are interpreted as causal relationships. Causality is defined by the relationship between one event (the cause) and another (the effect), where the second event is believed to be a consequence of the first. For example, I may notice that if I work fewer hours, I earn less money. There is a direct relationship between the number of hours I work and the amount I get paid. So, when you read the words *bananas* and *vomit* earlier, your mind inferred a causal association in which bananas triggered sickness. Reading that Alan was *intelligent* and *industrious* led you to believe he was a reliable, hardworking employee – regardless of later evidence. One way in which System 1 makes sense of the world is by assigning causal relationships to events and actions, but what happens if, in fact, those events are not causally related?

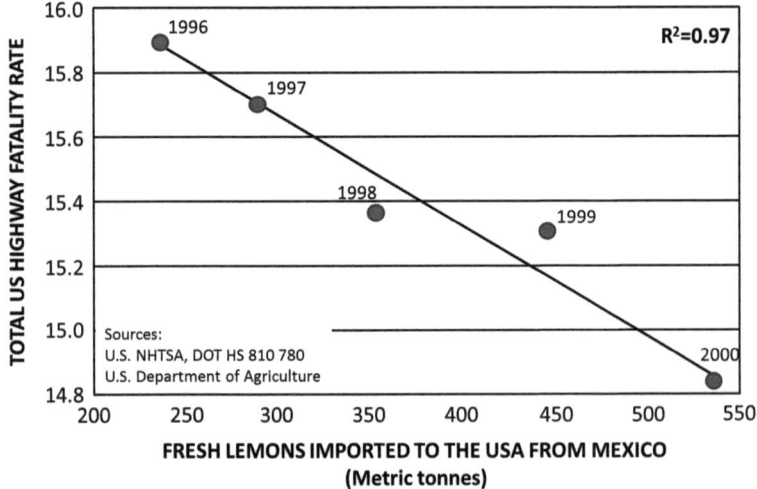

Fig. 6.4 Correlation between imported lemons and highway deaths

Correlation can be described as a mathematical relationship between two (or more) variables and refers to how closely two sets of data are related. From the graph above (Fig. 6.4) we can examine the relationship between the metric tonnes of lemons imported into the USA from Mexico and the fatality rate on the highways of the USA. Can we infer from this graph that by importing more lemons the United States government can reduce the number of deaths on America's roads?

We can see that the volume of lemons imported from Mexico is closely correlated to the number of US highway deaths but is this relationship causal? Intuitively it seems highly unlikely that stopping lemon imports will eliminate highway deaths on US road so it is doubtful that there is a causal relationship between these two variables. The following are examples of variables that, in some instances, are closely correlated. Are these likely to be causal relationships?

1. Increasing ice cream consumption leads to more murders
2. Reducing the number of pirates increases global warming
3. Living in a poor country (defined by GDP) increases penis size
4. Eating organic food causes autism (www.buzzfeed.com/kjh2110/the-10-most-bizarre-correlations)

Another aspect of causality is the direction of the cause and the subsequent effect. If we accept that there is a causal relationship between smoking and lung cancer e.g. smoking causes lung cancer, can we also assume that having lung cancer induces people to smoke? No, causal relationships are, on the whole, unidirectional. If I hit a golf ball, the ball moves, if you hit an egg with a hammer, the egg breaks. However, proving causation can be a major challenge. In some instances the 'cause' may be a composite of many 'sub-causes', some of them too difficult (or impossible) to measure. In general, however, the more data available, the more robust the correlation and the greater the likelihood of causation but, as we will see, Big Data identifies correlation not causation. Unfortunately, System 1 is finely tuned to automatically assign causal connections between events, even when that connection is false. For example:

> After spending a day exploring beautiful sights in the crowded streets of New York, Jane discovered that her wallet was missing

Kahneman (2012) notes that when people who read this sentence were later given an unexpected recall test, the association of the word *pickpocket* was higher than that of *sights*, despite *pickpocket* not having been mentioned in the sentence.

6.6 Randomness, Uncertainty and the Search for Meaning

In addition to identifying, causal links, System 1 is also a highly developed pattern-recognition system capable of identifying as many as 10,000 faces. In experiments, 35 years after leaving school, people have proved able to distinguish 90 % of their classmates. Unfortunately we also have a tendency to see patterns where they don't exist. Pareidolia, the ability to see 'faces' in random patterns (Fig. 6.5) is a well-documented phenomenon, as illustrated by the 'Man-in-the-Moon' and the Turin Shroud (for more examples see http://stuffthatlookslikejesus.com/).

Furthermore, detecting patterns or connections in random data, is equally common. For example, consider the sex of six babies born sequentially in a hospital. Which of the following sequences are most likely, (a), (b) or (c)?

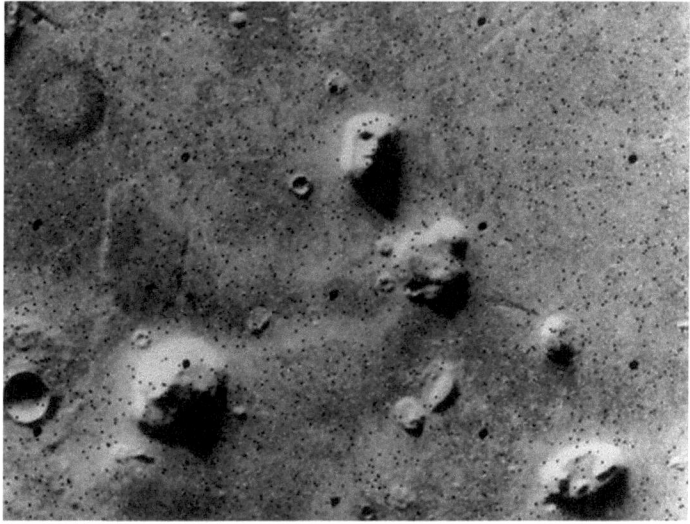

Fig. 6.5 A face on Mars? A photograph by the NASA Viking 1 Orbiter

- BBBGGG
- GGGGGG
- BGBGGB

Given that each birth is independent of another and that the number of boys and girls born previously has no effect on the sex of the next baby, then any possible sequence is as likely as another. Alternatively, suppose you are given the constant pi to a million decimal places and asked to find a possible pattern. You find the sequence: 012345. You look elsewhere and find it again, 012345, and again, and again… Are the numbers trying to tell you something? Unfortunately, unlike the heroine in Carl Sagan's novel "Contact", there is no secret code; all you have found are similar arbitrary sequences amid the noise that is randomness. By chance the same million digits also contain the sequences; 222222, 333333, 555555, 777777 and both my mother and father's birth dates. Moreover, while Apophenia, the tendency to seek meaningful patterns or connections in random data, is a powerful trait of System 1; we can, at the same time, be blind to actual randomness. In 2005 the press reported complaints that the random shuffle function on the Apple iPod wasn't actually random when users observed instances where the same song played twice consecutively. To resolve this Apple re-programmed the function to avoid this, effectively making the programme less random! (Bialik 2006)

Thus evolution has shaped System 1 to identify patterns, contiguity of time (events that happen simultaneously or close together) and causality. It is designed for speed (sometimes at the expense of accuracy) and to prioritise potential threats over possible opportunities. Unfortunately, such a system has a hard time accepting the influence of unrelated, uncertain or random factors. For example, suppose you investigated two similar firms but the CEO of one was 'better' than the other. You then repeat the exercise for, say, 1,000 pairs of firms – again each pair has a 'strong' CEO and a 'weak' CEO. How often do you expect to find the firm with the stronger CEO to be the most successful of the pair? Assuming that the success of the firm (however that may be defined) is determined by the action of the CEO, you would expect the strong CEO to lead the more successful company in each of the pairs – a 100 % correlation between 'strong' CEO and successful company. If, however, a firm's success is determined by factors completely beyond the control of the CEO, you would expect, on average, for 50 % of the firms to be led by a 'strong' CEO and 50 % by a 'weak' CEO. In practice, 60 % of firms led by strong CEOs perform best, an increase of just 10 % above the average flip of a coin (Mlodinow 2008). Similar results have been observed in soccer managers, stock traders and baseball coaches. Interestingly, in his best-selling book, "Moneyball", Michael Lewis gives an account of how the Oakland Athletics competed successfully against wealthier competitors in Major League Baseball by selecting players based upon their performance analytics in the minor Leagues. In contrast, the coaches at other clubs recruited players based upon subjective analysis of 'build' and 'look' (Lewis 2003).

In "Trading is hazardous to your wealth", Odean and Barber (2002) showed that the most active stock traders (those that did most deals), achieved, on average, the poorest results, while those that traded least were the most successful. However, there remains the perception that leaders influence the performance of their firm, their team or even the market in a disproportionate way, leading to high salaries and hero-worship. Richard Fuld, former CEO of Lehman Brothers, received a salary of $34 million in 2007 and $40.5 million in 2006. In March 2008, 6 months before the his bank failed, Fuld was dubbed "Mr Wall Street" and appeared in Barron's list of the 30 best CEOs (Sorkin 2010). For those perceived not to have 'performed' the results are equally stark. The average tenure of a manager in the English 'Premier League' is 415 days, in the Italian 'Serie A' 480 days and in Spain's 'La Liga' 488 days (LMA 2010).

6.6.1 Sampling, Probability and the Law of Small Numbers

As any secondary school statistician can tell you, sample size matters – but why sample in the first place? Indeed, some authors believe that, with the advent of 'Big Data' we no longer need to sample data, that we can now use complete populations (Mayer-Schonberger and Cukier 2013). However, consider the following: The government brings out legislation requiring all car-makers in the UK to demonstrate that their cars can survive certain destructive crash tests. Without sampling the car-manufacturer would need to crash every individual car produced to check that it could survive the test… Similarly, the Lord Mayor of London requests that the air quality of the capital be measured. Assuming for a second that it would be practical to enclose London in a glass dome and measure every air molecule, the task would be prohibitively expensive and time-consuming. So, regardless of 'Big Data', sampling remains important - but why is the actual size of the sample so critical?

Consider a CEO working for the one hundred companies comprising the FT100 index. Let's assume that, given their skills, each CEO has a certain probability of success each year and that for each CEO successful years occur 60 % of the time. Does that mean that, within a particular 5-year time frame, each CEO will have three good years? Unfortunately, the answer is no. Random events often come like chocolate chips in a cookie – in clusters. In sports or business we might call it 'a run of bad luck' or 'a winning streak'. Over a long period of time, say a 1,000 year, for an *average* 5-year period, the CEOs would indeed deliver something approaching three successful years. However, over a short timeframe, a small number of lucky CEOs, by chance alone, will have a run of success and their companies will be successful for the full 5-year period. A similar number will have run of bad years during the same period. The likelihood that a CEO will deliver three successful years within a specific 5-year period is one-in-three. This means that for the same 5-year period sixty-six of the CEOs performed above or below their 'ability'. Kahneman and Tversky (1971) coined this, the Law of Small Numbers.

System 1 deploys strategies to reduce the complexity of decision-making tasks, and an intuitive assessment of probabilities is an essential part of that process. As a result, chance events are often interpreted as accomplishments or failures. In December 1993 a 28 year-old woman took her 6-month old daughter, a suitcase full of papers and fled her home, leaving an abusive husband. Despite describing herself as "the biggest failure I know", and being diagnosed with clinical depression, Joanne Rowling continued to write. The manuscript for "Harry Potter and the Philosophers Stone", conceived during a 4-h train delay, was finished in 1995. The manuscript was submitted to twelve publishing houses, all of which rejected it. The chairman of Bloomsbury, a London publisher, asked his 8-year-old daughter, Alice, for her comments on the first chapter and Alice hurriedly demanded the next. Bloomsbury published the book in 1997.

Consider the role of chance in J.K. Rowling's story. Had her train not been delayed, had she not taken the first three chapters in her suitcase, had she given in to depression or the knock-backs from publishers, Harry Potter might never have been 'born'. Had the chairman of Bloomsbury not had an 8-year-old-daughter or if Alice had not found the time to read the chapter, Joanne Rowling might have completed her teacher training course and be currently working in a school in Edinburgh. Rowling is not alone. "The Diary of a Young Girl" by Anne Frank was rejected by publishers as "very dull" and "a dreary record of typical family bickering". George Orwell was told of Animal Farm, "it's impossible to sell animal stories in the United States" and Dr Seuss's first book was rejected by twenty-seven publishers. Equally, Wall Street traditions of heroic analysts and the reputations of trading superstars have been shown to be based upon no significant evidence of stock-picking ability (Odean and Barber 2002). Despite horoscopes, astrologers (Former US President, Ronald Reagan, was famous for his habit of consulting astrologers before making major policy decisions), lucky charms and superstitions, much of what happens to us, in our careers and our personal lives, is as much a result of randomness as it is a result of skill, expertise and hard work.

6.7 Biases, Heuristics and Their Implications for Judgement

Throughout our lives we make decisions by evaluating the advantages of a particular course of action against its disadvantages, weighing up the pros and cons. This evaluation process we call 'judgement'. Decisions may be 'against ones better judgement' or one may 'reserve judgement' until more information is available, but we all make 'judgement calls'. Moreover, the role of management is synonymous with decision-making and forecasting, both of which require individual and collective judgement. Even where decisions and forecast employ advanced statistical methods, those methods will, inherently, be dependent upon judgement. For example, judgement will be required in choosing, say, a forecasting method, in the selection of variables used for the model and, perhaps, the choice of model structure (will a linear approximation be sufficient?). What data will be used for the model and what data will be used to test the model? Judgement is also necessary to determine the balance between project cost, time, complexity and accuracy (Clements and Hendry 2011).

Unfortunately, far from being reasoned and logical, judgement is nearly always tainted by bias. These biases may be cognitive, motivational or a combination of

6.7 Biases, Heuristics and Their Implications for Judgement

both and can give rise to irrational inferences about other people or situations, often leading to impaired judgement. Sixty years of research has revealed more than a hundred such biases, including:

Bias	Description
Attention bias	The inclination to pay attention to dominant stimuli in one's environment while neglecting other, possibly more relevant, data
Availability heuristic	The tendency to overestimate the likelihood of events with greater cognitive 'availability' due to their recent occurrence or emotional impact
Anchoring bias	The tendency to rely too heavily on one trait, value or piece of information when making estimates
Confirmation bias	The search for information and evidence that confirms ones previously held ideas/beliefs
Endowment effect	The tendency of an individual to demand more to give up an object than he/she would be willing to pay to acquire it
Gambler's fallacy	The inclination to believe that future probabilities are altered by past events when, in reality, they are unchanged.
Halo effect	The perception of a positive or negative trait being 'carried over' into other personality traits – the 'first impressions' fallacy.
Hindsight bias	"I-knew-it-all-along" – the belief that past events were predictable
'Hot-hand' fallacy	The tendency to believe that a person who has experienced success has a greater chance of success in subsequent attempts
Illusion of control	The inclination to overestimate one's degree of influence over external events
Overconfidence	Excessive confidence in one's answers skills etc. (93 % of US students believe they are above average drivers – Svenson 1981)
Pareidolia	A random stimulus (an image or sound) is perceived as significant e.g. seeing images/faces in cloud formations, the man-in-the-moon
Representativeness heuristic (Stereotyping)	Expecting a member of a group to conform to specific traits or characteristics without having information about the individual

Motivational biases affecting judgement are, arguably, the most perceptible and often arise from personal, organisational or political circumstances. Those motivations might include; attracting clients, publicity or prestige, enhancing one's reputation or, simply, satisfying ones immediate boss. Some judgements are motivated by the desire to convince other stakeholders of the decision-makers power and/or influence. Phenomena such as 'groupthink', the need for conformity within the group leading to poor decision-making, or 'herding' in which large numbers of people act in the same, often irrational, way, are extreme examples of motivational bias.

Predictably, herding has been implicated as a fundamental cause of stock market bubbles, booms and busts:

> The fact that stock prices can vary so widely over relatively short durations shows that valuations of stocks is inherently a subjective process, controlled more by herd behaviour than by rational economic analysis. (Rapp 2009)

The idea of cognitive biases was pioneered by Amos Tversky and Daniel Kahneman in 1972. Tversky and Kahneman went on to explain differences in judgement and decision making in terms of "heuristics". Cognitive heuristics are simple, efficient rules used by System 1 to form judgments, make decisions and solve problems when faced with complexity and/or incomplete information. These mental shortcuts usually involve focusing on one aspect of a complex problem and ignoring others. Fine-tuned by evolution, heuristics work well under most circumstances, but in circumstances introduce "severe and systematic errors" (Tversky and Kahneman 1974, p. 1125).

In their seminal paper, "Judgement Under Uncertainty: Heuristics and Biases", Tversky and Kahneman (1974) highlight three heuristics that System 1 employs to simplify the judgement process and maintain cognitive ease:

(i) Representativeness
(ii) Availability; and
(iii) Anchoring

One aspect of the representative heuristic is used when one has to assess the probability that people or objects belong to particular classes, an extension of stereotyping. For example, who is most likely to be an Investment Banker, the smart young man stepping out of a bright red Ferrari in a West London street or the middle-aged woman with two children on the nearby bus? Is the student who sits attentively listening and engages with academic activities more likely to get good grades than the one that always arrives late and messages his friends during lectures? Using representativeness, System 1 develops a simple cause-and-effect relationship without the need to refer to System 2. Often these relationships are valid, but sometimes they're not…

> In August 2013, Oprah Winfrey, one of the world's richest women, was shopping in Switzerland. *"I was in Zurich the other day, in a store whose name I will not mention. I didn't have my eyelashes on, but I was in full Oprah Winfrey gear. I had my little Donna Karan skirt and my little sandals. But obviously 'The Oprah Winfrey Show' is not shown in Zurich. I go into the store and I say to the woman, 'Excuse me, could I see the bag right above your head?' and she says to me, 'No. It's too expensive.' One more time, I tried. I said, 'But I really do just want to see that one,' and the shopkeeper said, 'Oh, I don't want to hurt your feelings,' and I said, 'Okay, thank you so much. You're probably right, I can't afford it.' And I walked out of the store"* Miss Winfrey recounted. (Malkin 2013)

Representativeness is also the heuristic used to estimate the probability that events originate from a particular process, to establish cause-and-effect relationships. Unfortunately, as we have seen, people are pre-programmed for Apophenia, the tendency to see patterns in random events and data. Another aspect of the representative heuristic can be seen in the measurement of performance. Consider Alan and Bill, two sales-staff of similar skills, abilities and track records. In a particular financial quarter, Alan performs exceptionally well and Bill performs poorly. Alan is praised highly and wins the 'Employee of the Quarter' award. Bill is criticised for failing to meet target and warned to avoid future poor performance. The following quarter, Alan has failed to match his previous performance but Bill has improved considerably. What conclusion are we to draw from this?

A common conclusion is that praise serves to make an employee complacent, while criticism and threats provide a major motivator. However, this is an example of a phenomenon known as 'regression to the mean' (Tversky and Kahneman 1973). The same phenomenon can be seen in the height of individuals, the size of dogs, the efficacy of pharmaceutical drugs and the performance of stock traders in trading rooms. In the UK each of the professional football leagues awards a trophy and a bottle of champagne to the team manager whose team have performed best during a particular month. Invariably, the team loses on the Saturday that the trophy is awarded.

Thus, the representativeness heuristic does not consider several factors that should affect judgements of probability, namely

- It is insensitive to prior probabilities of outcomes (such as the base rate frequency)
- It is insensitive to sample size
- It allows misconceptions of chance
- It is insensitive to predictability
- It gives rise to the illusion of validity
- It allows misconceptions of regression

The Availability heuristic involves the anticipated probability of event occurring given the ease with which a similar event comes to mind. For example, if you buy a yellow car, you are then surprised to see how many other yellow cars there are on the road. Newspapers, television and on-line press often fuel availability bias, for example: is it safe to go out into the street?

> It is often suggested [by police and criminologists] that crime, although frequent, is a relatively minor irritant, given the range of problems with which the city dweller has to contend. The public, it is argued, suffer from hysteria about crime fanned up by the newspapers and television. Moral panic abounds, particularly about mugging, sexual assault and violence which are out of touch with reality. People lock themselves in their homes because of their own irrational fears and the fear of crime becomes more of a problem than crime itself. Such an argument is backed up by evidence from sources such as the British Crime Survey, which shows that the 'average' person can expect "a robbery once every five centuries, an assault resulting in injury (even if slight) once every century and a burglary every 40 years … " (Hough and Mayhew 1983, p. 15)

Thus, we tend to overestimate the probability of events if similar events have occurred recently or have received significant media attention. Dramatic natural disasters such as earthquakes, tsunamis, hurricanes and volcanic eruptions are easily recalled and their probabilities overestimated. Furthermore, people pay specific attention to highly desirable events (winning the lottery) or highly undesirable events (getting injured/killed in a terrorist attack), whose occurrence is rare, while neglecting higher probabilistic risks such as road accidents and cancer. Consequently, availability leads to biases due to:

(i) the retrievability of instances
(ii) the effectiveness of a search set
(iii) illusory correlation

> Anchoring often occurs when we are making estimates. Consider the question:
> Was Elvis Presley more than 70 years old when he died?

Now write down the age at which you believe Elvis died. It is likely that your estimate is much higher than it would have been if the question had referred to Elvis' death at, say, 30 years of age. Thus we have a tendency to select a reference point as an anchor (regardless of how this point is chosen) and then make adjustments from it. The suggestion of '70 years old' primed System 1 to seek compatible evidence in order to determine the adjustment around this anchor. Anchoring effects are commonplace in the selling and buying of goods and services. The 'estimate' in fine-art auctions is an anchor meant to influence the first bid, while the initial sale price of a house or a car is meant to anchor the buyers close to the price desired by the seller. The guy offering you a fake Rolex for £30 in Jakarta, Kuala Lumpur or Bangkok isn't expecting to get £30, and if you believe you've got a good deal by offering £10, his anchoring strategy has worked fine…

6.7.1 Non-heuristic Biases

A number of other psychological biases have been identified in addition to those from heuristics. Arguably the most significant is over-confidence. That exaggerated confidence that we, as individuals, have in our knowledge and understanding of the world and its workings. In *'The Black Swan'*, Nassim Taleb (2007) introduces the notion of the *narrative fallacy*, the stories we create to make sense of the world. In these stories events are simple, sequential and causal. We praise talent and intuition rather than accept the role of luck and focus on exceptional events that have occurred rather than the countless ones that have not. Consequently, to read accounts of successful companies such as Google, Facebook and Amazon is to fall prey to the illusion of inevitability. That through superior strategy, excellent leadership or cutting-edge technology, success was assured at the outset. This *hind-sight bias*, accounts for those Wall Street analysts that *knew* the 2008 financial crisis was inevitable and those literary critics that *knew* Harry Potter would be a huge success.

Furthermore, hindsight bias has insidious implications for decision-makers as history defines the quality of the decision based upon the result, not the process undertaken. Seventy-five years after the Munich Agreement, the name of Neville Chamberlain, British Prime Minister from 1937 to 1940, remains synonymous with weakness and appeasement:

We regard the agreement signed last night and the Anglo-German Naval Agreement as symbolic of the desire of our two peoples never to go to war with one another again. My good friends, for the second time in our history, a British Prime Minister has returned from Germany bringing peace with honour. I believe it is peace for our time…

However, on 30th September 1938, a war-weary British public greeted Chamberlain's returned in triumph. Crowds mobbed his plane and the streets were so packed with cheering people that it took him an hour and a half to journey the nine miles from Heston to Buckingham Palace. King George issued a statement to his people, "*After the magnificent efforts of the Prime Minister in the cause of peace, it is my fervent hope that a new era of friendship and prosperity may be dawning among the peoples of the world.*" In truth, we understand the past less well that we believe we do, and of the future we know nothing at all…

Further emphasising the tendency to overconfidence is the illusion of validity. Evolution has designed System 1 to jump to conclusions, often based upon scant evidence. Consequently, the conviction we have in our opinions is derived from the apparent rationality of the story created by System 1, not in the amount of evidence available.

Examine carefully Fig. 6.6, which of the two lines is longer? If you have never seen this before it is likely that you will choose the bottom line. This is the famous Muller-Lyer illusion. However, if you have seen it before you will know that the two lines are actually the same length (you can verify this by measurement). Interestingly, although System 2 *knows* that the lines are the same length, System 1 still interprets the bottom line as being longer. How you perceive the lines hasn't changed but your behaviour has. In the same way, data, statistics and analysis can inform us but these are often helpless in influencing a judgement built upon subjective confidence.

Perhaps the final and often most pernicious illusion that reinforces overconfidence is that of perceived skill. Few would argue that chess is a game of skill, requiring significant practice to rise to a high level of expertise. Likewise, most would concede that roulette is a game of chance. What, however, if the difference between skill and chance was more difficult to define? Is wine-tasting a skill? Consider these two reviews of a red wine, 2010 El Palomar Zarate, Rias Baixas, Galicia, Spain (Decanter.com 2012)

> "Floral, citrus, vanilla aroma. Punchy acidity underneath broad mineral palate; style majors on texture rather than fruit. Long, complex" Score: 88/100 (Sarah Jane Evans)

> "Warm, ripe, mature, some soft oaky notes. Rich fruit, warm oak, nicely balanced, rich fruit finish" Score: 95/100 (John Radford)

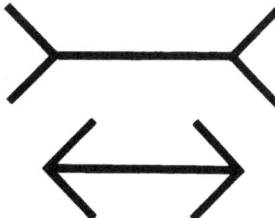

Fig. 6.6 The Muller-Lyer Illusion

Note that the perceived taste of wine arises from a mix of 800 volatile organic compounds on the tongue and the nose. Unfortunately even 'flavour-trained' professionals can only recognise three or four components of a mixture (Mlodinow 2008). Wine 'experts' have been fooled into believing white wine is red by the simple addition of food colouring. Furthermore, brain scans showed greater activity in the areas of the brain responsible for the experience of pleasure when subjects drank 'expensive' wine, despite experimenters having substituted a much cheaper wine. But wine experts are not alone. Experienced radiologists who evaluate chest x-rays as "normal" or "abnormal" contradict themselves 20 % of the time when they see the same image on separate occasions (Hoffman et al. 1968). Similar results have been found in studies of judgement reliability vis-à-vis auditors, pathologists, psychologists and business managers (Kahneman 2012).

6.8 Summary

Much of the hype surrounding "Big Data" focuses on the magnitude of the data sets and the technologies available for interrogating these sets. However, at an individual level, internal cognitive and perceptual filters assign data into meaningful categories which, in turn, mould expectation within the filters. In this way extraction of information from data also represents interpretation of that data and those co-evolving filters condition the characteristics that we adopt towards the world i.e. our knowledge. However, as we have seen in this chapter, we are endowed with two, quite different, but inextricably linked cognitive systems; a fast, emotional, automatic system (System 1) and a slow, rational, lazy system (System 2). System 1 sometimes responds to situations in an irrational or illogical way, often before System 2 is activated. The heuristics that System 1 employs to solve problems quickly are base-laden. Statistical thinking requires an acute awareness of these biases. Statistical thinking is about understanding data, the awareness of data variability, and an appreciation of probability and recognition of bias in data interpretation.

6.9 Review Questions

The answers to these questions can be found in the text of this chapter

- What is meant by the terms; "data", "information" and "knowledge"?
- How important is System 1 in responding to problems/situations? What are its limitations when faced with complex or probabilistic challenges?
- Why is "Statistical Thinking" so difficult? What is an 'emotional hijacking'?
- What is the difference between correlation and causality? Why is this important?
- What is 'Apophenia'? What are its implications for Big Data?
- What are 'cognitive heuristics'? Name three cognitive heuristics and their implications for statistical thinking

- What are:
  - Hind-sight bias?
  - The illusion of validity?
  - The illusion of perceived skill?

6.10 Group Work Research Activities

These activities require you to research beyond the contents of the book and can be tackled individually or as a discussion group.

6.10.1 Discussion Topic 1 – The Linda Problem

The "Linda Problem", devised by Kahneman and Tversky in 1983, is one of the most celebrated puzzles in psychological research. Some of the terms used may appear a little dated but its relevance remains strong.

Linda is 31 years old, single, outspoken, and very bright. She majored in philosophy. As a student, she was deeply concerned with issues of discrimination and social justice, and also participated in anti-nuclear demonstrations.

Which of the following alternatives is more probable?

- Linda is a teacher in primary school
- Linda is a psychiatric social worker
- Linda works in a bookstore and takes yoga classes
- Linda is a bank teller
- Linda is an insurance salesperson
- Linda is a bank teller and active in the feminist movement

Discuss how you decided on this alternative?

Search for references to "The Linda Problem" on the internet – were your assumptions correct?

6.10.2 Discussion Topic 2 – The Birthday Paradox

The "Birthday Paradox" is a famous probability puzzle.

In a room of thirty people, what is the probability that two people in the group share the same birthday?

Discuss how you might calculate the probability?

Had the question been rephrased as, *In a room of thirty people, is the probability that two people in the group share the same birthday about 1 in 360?* Would this have made the question easier or harder?

Search for references to "The Birthday Paradox" on the internet – were your assumptions correct?

References

Ackoff RL (1989) From data to wisdom. J Appl Syst Anal 16:3–9
Admiral Insurance (2013) Motorists see red behind the wheel. [online]. Last accessed 27 Nov 2013 at: http://www.admiral.com/press-releases/16072013/motorists-see-red-behind-the-wheel/
Bialik C (2006) How random is the iPod shuffle? [online]. Last accessed 28 Dec 2013 at: http://online.wsj.com/news/articles/SB115876952162469003
Boisot M, Canals A (2004) Data, information and knowledge: have we got it right? J Evol Econ 14:43–67
Clements MP, Hendry DF (2011) The Oxford handbook of economic forecasting, 1st edn. OUP, New York
Decanter.com (2012) [online]. Last accessed 3 Dec 2013 at: http://www.decanter.com/wine/reviews/el-palomar/584082
Fricke M (2009) The knowledge pyramid: a critique of the DIKW hierarchy. J Inf Sci 35(2):131–142
Gladwell M (2006) Blink: the power of thinking without thinking. Penguin, New York
Goleman D (1995) Emotional intelligence: why it can matter more than IQ, 1st edn. Bloomsbury, London
Hawking S (1988) A brief history of time. 1st ed., Bantam Dell Publishing Group, New York
Hoffman PJ, Slovic P, Rorer LG (1968) An analysis-of-variance model for the assessment of configural cue utilisation in clinical judgment. Psychol Bull 69:338–339
Hough M, Mayhew P (1983) The British crime survey: first report. Home Office Research Study, London
Kahneman D (2012) Thinking, fast and slow. Penguin, London.
Lewis M (2003) Moneyball: the art of winning an unfair game. Norton, New York
LMA (2010) LMA end of season statistics 2010. League Managers Association, London.
Malkin B (2013) Oprah Winfrey victim of 'racism' in Switzerland. The Telegraph, http://www.telegraph.co.uk/news/celebritynews/10232461/Oprah-Winfrey-victim-of-racism-in-Switzerland.html. Last accessed 16 Dec 2014
Mayer-Schonberger V, Cukier K (2013) Big data: a revolution that will transform how we live, work and think. John Murray, London
McAfee A, Brynjolfsson E (2012) Big data: the management revolution. Harv Bus Rev 90(10):60–68
Mlodinow L (2008) The drunkards walk: how randomness rules our lives. Penguin, London
Odean T, Barber BM (2002) Trading is hazardous to your wealth: the common stock investment performance of individual investors. J Financ 55:773–806
Rapp D (2009) Bubbles, booms and busts: the rise and fall of financial assets. Copernicus, New York
Svenson O (1981) Are we all less risky and more skillful than our fellow drivers? Acta Psychol 47(2):143–148
Sorkin AR (2010) Too big to fail: inside the battle to save Wall Street. Penguin, London
Taleb NN (2007) Fooled by randomness: the hidden role of chance in life and the markets, 2nd edn. Penguin, London
Tversky A, Kahneman D (1971) Belief in the law of small numbers. Psychol Bull 76(2):105–110
Tversky A, Kahneman D (1973) On the psychology of prediction. Psychol Rev 80:237–251
Tversky A, Kahneman D (1974) Judgement under uncertainty: heuristics and biases. Sciences 185:1124–1131
www.thisiscornwall.co.uk (2013) 'Rabid' St Austell driver chased family in road rage incident. [online]. Last accessed 27 Dec 2013 at: http://www.thisiscornwall.co.uk/Rabid-St-Austell-driver-chased-family-road-rage/story-20034922-detail/story.html#axzz2lvy4VfIl

Synthesis 7

7.1 What the Reader Will Learn

- that strategies need implementing and therein often lies the downfall of even the best strategic decisions
- that requirements analysis is a vital element of the implementation of successful systems
- that managing change is another important aspect of successful implementation
- that there are a variety of techniques available to help measure the relative success of elements of strategy implementation
- that Big Data and the Cloud do change business models and measures and maybe even the concept of success

7.2 From Strategy to Successful Information Systems

There are some who argue that we have been through a period when Business Strategists were overly venerated. Their ability to envision new futures for their organisations set them apart and a lot of hope was pinned on their visions. However, the world has a way of disturbing the process of turning the vision into reality. As Longman and Mullins (2004) say:

> … strategy was promoted as big-picture thinking: the "vision thing," in Lou Gerstner's words. But as organizations did away with strategic planning departments and put the onus for strategy on line management, and as frustration mounted with "visioning" exercises that wound up in desk drawers, the interest in strategy has moved to the question: How can we get strategy to drive operations? The belief now is that the big picture is important, but it will remain just a vision unless it is implemented.

They go on to make a convincing case for good Project Management being the key element in the successful implementation of a strategy. Whilst they were not talking specifically about Information Systems (IS) Strategy, the truths arguably still hold for IS and IT strategies. It is unfortunately the case that many good strategic IS ideas fail to deliver what was promised, and this is often to do with failures in delivery as opposed to the idea itself being poor. Change management is one area all too frequently mismanaged during information systems implementation. You can write the most wonderful, technically perfect new application, but if the users of the system have not bought into the process the system is likely to fail.

7.2.1 The Role of the Chief Information Officer (CIO)

Many larger organisations, especially those which rely heavily on IT, now employ board level executives to oversee their IT and IS. The common title is the CIO. Most report directly to the Chief Executive or Finance Director. If one exists, then the CIO is most likely to have responsibility for strategy implementation. Their remit is not standard, and varies according to the type and culture of the employing organisation.

That said, their role will typically include:

- Reporting on all IT/IS matters to the Board of Directors
- Managing the IT/IS teams
- Sponsoring internal IT projects
- Responsibility for and IT service outsourcing
- Creating and managing IT/IS related Service Level Agreements (SLAs) across the organisation
- Supporting innovative IS/IT projects
- Being Budget holder for IT/IS

Skills required to carry this out may include: Leadership; Business and Financial understanding and an eye for new opportunities for IT/IS to assist the business. In-depth skills in any particular technical ability are not necessary since the portfolio of responsibilities will be far too broad for them to be expected to wield a screw-driver.

A well known contributor to Computerworld, Paul Strassmann said in a talk in 2003:

> The primary focus of a CIO is not to program, not to operate computers, not to make technical choices. The primary job is power politics – to play several different roles simultaneously. The job is to manage conflict, to oversee the re-distribution of power and to re-allocate money so that information technologies may support the success of an organization…It is not for amateurs, visionaries and certainly not for people whose sole expertise is in computers.

His thoughtful discussion goes on to suggest three propositions about CIO power politics:

1. Installing information technology is the continuation of bureaucratic conflicts by other means

2. Information technology corrodes bureaucracy and therefore will be always opposed.
3. All great ideas about information technologies degrade into budgets.

Whilst not every organisation will have a CIO, it is likely that someone will take the lead in terms of the strategic use of IT/IS. Sometimes this may be the Finance Director and in smaller companies it may even be the Chief Executive. It is undoubtedly true that such a leader is needed to ensure that IT/IS is used effectively since decisions by committee are famously poor. Indeed, in the cut-throat world of board level decision making outlined by Straussmann the lack of a strong leader can clearly be identified as one of the key reasons for IT/IS project failures.

7.2.2 Management of IS Projects

Whilst leadership from someone with vision may well be a requirement for any successful IT/IS project, that does not mean that they can succeed on their own. Implementation of IS systems is notoriously tricky. In a 2007 paper McManus and Wood-Harper point to research showing that:

> … only one in eight information technology projects can be considered truly successful (failure being described as those projects that do not meet the original time, cost and quality requirements criteria). Despite such failures, huge sums continue to be invested in information systems projects and written off.

A success rate of 12.5 % could, one would imagine, be enough for all but the most risk-seeking decision makers to refuse to consider investing in any new IS/IT systems. And yet there is no sign of any such decline in our society's interest in information systems. Why is this so?

One reason may be the ever changing landscape of Information Systems. Big Data is one example of such a change. Only a few years ago organisations typically stored their own data and occasionally used data warehouses and BI techniques to analyse that data. Now, as we see in the chapter on Systems, we can gain access to data from many sources very quickly. Big Data holds out the possibility, at least in the first few years of its evolution, for early adopters to gain some competitive advantage over less forward thinking competitors. Because Big Data is new, and some of the techniques are still unproven, mistakes will be made and failures will happen. However, on balance, the CIO may decide that the potential benefit outweighs the dangers.

Once enough good news stories are heard then competitors will also want to take advantage. No long term competitive advantage can come from IS/IT projects since, if the new technique works, others can copy it. However, not adopting a useful new technique is to run the risk of stagnation, and falling behind the competition. Indeed, with today's more IT-aware customers, to fail to update may cause customers to go elsewhere. IT/IS is, in effect, like a treadmill. You can jump on and get a good position but you will never reach the end and once on board you have to keep running to keep going.

Failure once a technology is mature, is less likely to be about the technology itself, and more likely to be about implementation since the technology will be new for the organisation adopting it. Of course one way of countering this "new to us" problem is to buy in appropriately experienced expertise as part of the project – but consultants are expensive! The same McManus and Wood-Harper paper (2007) mentioned above went on to say, after surveying 51 companies, that reasons for project termination (surely the most severe form of project failure?) were:

Business reasons (N = 10) 19.6 %
Management reasons (N = 27) 53.0 %
Technical reasons (N = 14) 27.4 %

So it seems the management of IS/IT projects is where the problems primarily lie. The research also suggested some more specific reasons for failure:

Business process alignment;
Poor requirements management;
Business benefits overstated;
Differences between management and client;
Lack of management judgement (leadership);
Insufficient domain knowledge;
Loss of key personnel;
Poor communication with stakeholders;
Poor systems integration;
Poor change management procedures

We look at a few of these in more detail below, but in recognising the potential problems associated with complex projects we should also recognise that there have been some extremely successful implementations of IS systems. One report, sponsored by the British Computing Society (Lancaster University and BCS 2007), provides examples of such successes explicitly to:

> ... serve as an antidote to the many, well publicised examples of high profile IT project failures in the private sector and in UK Government.

It goes on to provide some lessons to be learned from the successes:

1. Selective use of outsourcing in the right circumstances is good
2. Do not take for granted that outsourcing companies know more than you do
3. Continuity must be maintained when switching between consultants and outsourcing providers
4. Employ the right project management methodology from the start and rigorously follow it
5. Planning for change should encompass the entire aspect of the organisation
6. Do not change absolutely everything at the same time
7. Relevant preparations should be carried out inside the organisation, thereby laying the foundation for change.

7.3 Creating Requirements That Lead to Successful Information Systems

One influence on success often quoted is that of the suitability of the requirements analysis that begins most IS/IT projects. It seems so obvious that there should be a clear set of requirements for any project to succeed. Imagine instructing engineers to span a river without saying what needs to cross it. If they put a rope bridge across it the project would be deemed a failure if it was intended that large lorries should cross by the bridge. Technically the rope bridge might be superb, but through no fault of the engineers, it will be seen as a failed project.

This is clearly a silly example, but to some degree a failure to fully capture all a system's needs at the outset is a regular cause of project teams underachieving. IT/IS systems are typically complex, with many inter-related elements. This means that fixing the missing requirement after the project has got under way may not be easy, or may even be impossible. So, if it is essential to capture requirements, what do we need to do to ensure we are successful in the gathering and defining processes?

Most IT projects start off as vague and often informal collections of ideas bandied around by a few people who are looking to improve the way things are currently done. The process of turning that good idea into a delivered system starts by more formally defining what the proposed system should do. With projects of any size the end product will be the result of many different sets of input from a variety of people with a mix of skills. For this reason the definitions made at this point need to be clear and unambiguous. Many methods have been devised to assist with this step. They range from mathematically based requirements specification language called "Z" through to the softer, conceptual model-based Soft Systems. The scientific approach believes that requirements are definable and therefore able to be mathematically modelled, whereas Soft Systems recognises that stakeholder perceptions, which are liable to differ between stakeholders, require more flexible approaches to modelling.

Approaches like "Z" start from the premise that one can exactly capture the system requirements and that this allows the verification of the requirements as "true" before continuing with the next phases in the project. Practitioners argue that this saves time since the "true" requirements can be tested in the final output. Softer approaches, such as Soft Systems and, to a lesser degree the currently popular Unified Modelling Language (UML), recognise that no single source of truth may be available at the outset and that the first step is to engage stakeholders and lead them to a shared understanding of what is needed.

Whatever the initial approach there will be tremendous pressure to agree a set of defined requirements, especially if elements of the project are to be outsourced, since these requirements may well turn into elements of a contractual document. Whether this is a sensible approach is another matter. There are arguments that say that the difficulty that exists in capturing all the requirements in a complex system make such an early contractual commitment counter-productive. As refinements, or additions, to the requirements are uncovered during the design and build process, there is no room in the contracted schedule to make any changes. This can result in the delivery of *requested requirements* as opposed to *actual needs*, and the two may be significantly different.

A variety of prototyping techniques exist to allow for the gradual incremental building of a system and thus allowing changes to requirements as the project continues. The developers go through a number of iterations with the system build, asking the customer if they have delivered what was required between each. The downside to this is that the number of iterations that will be required cannot be known upfront, thus making such projects very hard to cost. It is a very hard sell to persuade a customer to trust you to do just enough iterations, even if you argue strongly they will get what they actually need at the end of the process. Sponsors tend to like certainty in costs. In addition many companies focus on pricing when buying systems. Consequently, vendors take more and more non-specified items out of the bid as the process becomes more and more competitive. At the time of purchase service and support hours have often been reduced drastically, thus setting the scene for a problematic implementation.

The traditional software development life-cycle was prescriptive in approach and really did come from the scientific school, believing that clearly established requirements at the very start were an important element in the success of the overall process. Several methodologies exist that fall into this category, perhaps the most commonly used one is Structured Systems Analysis and Design (SSADM).

All tended to use a standard Systems Development Life-Cycle (SDLC) in which a number of steps are followed in the delivery of the system:

- Requirement Gathering
- Analysis
- System Design
- Implementation and Testing
- Deployment
- Maintenance

This list of stages has been modified many times. Perhaps the most sensible addition has been the addition of an Obsolescence phase in recognition that even the best systems eventually become dated and of need of renewal.

Today's "in" terminology in terms of SDLC approaches is "Agile". If you are reading this in 2020 this may no longer be the case as it seems likely there will always be people to look at improving methods. Agile builds on some RAD methods, including the idea of iterative development. This extract from *User-Centered Agile Methods* (Beyer 2010) describes the core of the method:

> short, well-defined iterations that deliver real user value; tight team processes for efficient development; minimal documentation of specifications; and continual feedback from stakeholders to validate progress.

It is worth observing that many of today's new Big Data projects start off as agile projects, with someone, or a small team, with the right skillset and interest in the data to start asking non-traditional questions about it.

7.3 Creating Requirements That Lead to Successful Information Systems

The Beyer monograph goes on to make clear the difference between key people in the project:

[...] **user or end-user** for the person who interacts directly with the product or system to produce a desired result. Indirect users depend on the results of the system even if they do not use it directly.

Customers are the people who derive value from the system: users' management, the purchaser, possibly the IT department that has to maintain the system, and anyone else who has a say in adopting the system. (Watch out. The Agile community sometimes uses "customer" to mean "user"—but this is an important distinction to maintain.)

Stakeholders are people in the development organization who depend on the system being correct. Management of the development team, the product owner, and the marketing team are all potential stakeholders.

This is not too dissimilar to Checkland's CATWOE list in his Systems Thinking, Systems practice book (1981)

Clients – The beneficiaries
Actors – Implementers
Transformation – What transformation does this system bring about?
Worldview – What point(s) of view makes this system useful?
Owner – Who has the authority stop the project?
Environmental constraints – What external constraints does this system have?

Whatever the approach, there are risks with requirements specification. Mathiassen and Tuunanen (2011) established a list of risks (see Fig. 7.1). If you have been involved in the specification phase of a project in the past you may well recognise some of the issues they describe.

The first question in the list is "who are the users". This is a very sensible, but often forgotten first question. Stakeholders are key to the success of projects as we see in the next section. Systems designers can fall into the trap of thinking they know better what a system should do than would a user – particularly a user who does not understand the technology to be used.

As the Mathiassen list shows, there are many other factors that can influence the success of the requirements capture. The size of the project is certainly likely to be another influence. If there are many stakeholders some of them can be difficult to engage in the process. A project that is so large that it will take several years to complete is also very susceptible to requirements creep – the requirements actually change as time goes by and either the needs, the users, or the technology changes.

For IT/IS projects the actually delivery technology is also an influence. If the team is experienced with the methodological approach being used and understands well the technology and how to use it to meet the requirements they will be far more likely to succeed than a team getting to grips with a new technology at the same time as they are designing the system.

Risk type	Questions	Low risk	High risk
Requirements identity	Who are the users?	You know the users and have previously worked with them.	You don't know the users; they're difficult to characterize.
	How are users connected?	You have easy access to users.	Users are difficult to reach.
	What is the system context?	You understand the context and the users' mental models of it.	You're unfamiliar with the context, and it could change radically.
	What are users' needs?	You appreciate users' needs and have experience with similar systems.	You don't know the users' needs and have no experience with similar systems.
Requirements volatility	How experienced are users?	Users are familiar with this type of system.	Users have no experience with this type of system.
	How do users behave?	You know the users' behavior; it's relatively stable.	You have no experience with similar users, and their behavior varies considerably.
	How dynamic is the context?	The context is relatively stable with only a few foreseeable changes.	The context is volatile, and future developments are difficult to forecast.
	When do requirements change?	Requirements remain stable over the project life cycle.	Requirements change over the project life cycle.
Requirements complexity	How large is the project?	The project is small with few stakeholders.	The project is large with multiple stakeholders.
	What technology is involved?	The technology is well known within your organization.	The technology hasn't been often used or is new to your organization.
	How diverse are users' needs?	Users have relatively similar needs.	Users have diverse needs that can be difficult to prioritize.
	What is the nature of the requirements?	Requirements are easy to specify and communicate to stakeholders.	Requirements are difficult to specify and communicate to stakeholders.

Fig. 7.1 Risks in requirements capture (Mathiassen and Tuunanen 2011)

7.4 Stakeholder Buy-In

In their discussion of early warning signs of IT project failure, Kappelman et al. (2006) make it very clear that the involvement of stakeholders is of vital importance. As they put it:

> Any project of significance has a number of stakeholders. These stakeholders have to contribute resources if the project is going to succeed and often have to take away resources from lower priority activities to do so. There are always more demands for resources than there are resources available. If all relevant stakeholders are not engaged and committed to project success, it is just about guaranteed the project will not get the resources and attention required to deliver the promised project scope on time and on budget. If key project stakeholders do not participate in major review meetings, it signals they are not engaged in the project and therefore the project is not a high priority for them. Other stakeholders soon begin to disengage too. The project manager then finds it harder to get the participation and resources necessary for project success, especially from those who are not full-time members of the project team. Often such project team members get reassigned to other projects that are perceived to be more important. However, the project scope and due date remain fixed. The project falls into a death spiral. Important projects have and keep the attention of major stakeholders.

Ensuring that the relevant stakeholders are involved requires some form of Stakeholder Analysis to identify all those legitimately touched by the project and make sure they are taken into account. The sorts of people involved can include end users, managers, technical teams, support teams and recipients of outputs from the proposed system. Of course merely identifying the roles is not enough. There are likely to be competing needs amongst the stakeholders but only limited resources. This may mean that the needs of certain stakeholders have to be given some priority over the others. Analysis beyond merely listing stakeholders will assist with this process. For each one there is a need to recognise:

- their ability to influence the success of the project
- how much they are themselves impacted by the project
- how much they support the aims of the project
- how aware they are of the project.

7.5 How Do We Measure Success

Is an IT/IS project successful just because it is perceived to be successful by stakeholders? After all, perceptions are influenced by individual preconceptions and expectations which may be unrealistic. It seems more appropriate to set out more objective tests for success. And those tests should be more subtle than simply saying "*Success/No Success*" since there are levels of success: Surely one would be happier with "*quite successful*" rather than "*does not quite do what we hoped*", for example. This also demonstrates the need for some sort of pre-defined scale, so that we all know what we mean by "*quite successful*".

Karlsen et al. (2005) tell us that the five most important success criteria for an IT project are:

- the IT system works as expected and solves the problems
- satisfied users
- high reliability
- the solution contributes to improved efficiency
- the IT system realizes strategic, tactical and operational objectives.

In their paper **Success in IT projects** (2008) Fernadez and Thomas sought to report how organisations define success for their IT projects. The results of this Australian study are laid out in the table below:

Success criteria	Category		
	Project management	Technical	Business
On-time	X		
On-budget	X		
Sponsor satisfaction	X		
Steering group satisfaction	X		
Project team satisfaction	X		
Customer/user satisfaction	X	X	
Stakeholder satisfaction	X	X	
System implementation		X	
Met requirements		X	

(continued)

Success criteria	Category		
	Project management	Technical	Business
System quality		X	
System use		X	
Business continuity			X
Met business objectives			X
Delivery of benefits			X

It is clear, then, that measuring success is no simple task. Indeed each stakeholder group, or even individual stakeholder, may have their own ideas on how successful a project has been. The problem is that implementing systems is more than merely a technical task – it is a social task too. Even the completed system that meets all the business objectives, meets extremely high technical quality criteria, is delivered on time and within budget, may be a waste of investment if the users dislike it and that results in low system use.

As opinions about the relative success of a project can be subjective, other human factors can also impact the final judgement. The culture of the organisation will be one such influence, as can the track record of IT project implementation within the organisation. Previous failures can make today's partial success seem wonderful, as this note from the McManus and Wood-Harper (2007) paper we discussed earlier shows:

> On completion of the project both the client and project managers regarded the project as a success. There were, however, a number of design and implementation problems that, with hindsight, could have been avoided. The client and senior management felt that the project was a success, although it was 20 weeks late and was 56 % over budget. **This was a good result based on client's previous track record in information systems delivery**.

7.6 Managing Change

Because, as we have established, implementing systems is far more than getting the technical aspects correct, we need to call on the management discipline of Change Management. Information Systems are often agents of significant organisational change and managers therefore need to carefully manage the effects of those changes.

When looking at an implementation project probably the first question that needs clearly addressing is: **why?** Especially given the failure rates alluded to earlier, there has to be some important reason for starting the project. It could be, for example, a need to bring efficiencies into the organisation's internal bureaucracy; or to attempt to keep up with what the competitors are doing; or simply that the existing systems are crumbling and cannot cope with today's demands. Whatever the rationale, it is important that it is articulated well to the stakeholders to help gain buy-in. There is no greater turn-off for a user than to have to learn a whole new way of doing things if they think the old way worked and cannot see a reason for the change.

As well as business driven rationale, there are often technical drivers too. You may establish that your single server system is not performing adequately and that current multi-core servers solve that performance problem. Expectations of technology can also be involved: If your workforce is all used to using Windows 8 at home, they will not be very happy if the organisation forces them to work with Windows 98, for example.

Literature abounds with books about the management of change. Perhaps one of the most influential early authors in the field was Kurt Lewin who described "planned change" as a way of distinguishing deliberate change effects from changes which are unintended. Amongst other concepts he talked of a three stage model where change happens by unfreezing, then changing, and then refreezing. Many have built on his theories.

Change frequently disrupts because people often prefer stability. If stakeholders see the rationale for change as weak they will probably prefer status quo to adopting the change. Indeed this could lead them to outright resistance, adding to the likelihood of the implementation failing. Many argue that resistance to change is inevitable. The steps that individuals go through are often quite predictable:

- Denial – stunned recognition that something may happen and then refusal to believe that it will happen
- Defence – the "it wasn't my fault the old system doesn't work" response
- Letting Go – accepting that the change will happen
- Adaptation – coming to terms with, and working with the changes
- Acceptance – maybe grudgingly at first, but the changed system becomes the norm

Knowing that people may resist the change that any system implementation will bring about means that the project team also know they need to watch out for resistance and work to reduce it.

The implementation itself can take one of many forms, and the need to help stakeholders understand and adapt may be a driver for the selection of the method chosen. Amongst the alternatives that are available there are:

Big Bang: Implement the entire system all at once.
Pilot: choose a part of the business to try the system out on. Future implementation depends upon how well the pilot goes.
Phased roll out (by Function or by geographic site): Implement in one place or across one department at a time, building to an organisation-wide adoption over time.

Each approach has its benefits and its disadvantages. The Big Bang approach, especially on larger projects, is potentially both the most expensive and the most risky. The resources, particularly in terms of technical skills, needed to cover a large scale implementation will often be extensive, and as the project completes some of those resources become redundant, making short term outsourcing almost unavoidable (see section later in this chapter). The risk comes from the fact that if the original requirements, or subsequent design, were flawed, they may result in large re-writes or even complete system rejection. Project managers seldom start off on a project expecting it to fail. They "know" they will look after their baby well. But researching similar projects elsewhere will result in the sorts of worrying statistics about failure we saw earlier – the reality is that things do go wrong. If they go wrong after a Big Bang that can mean catastrophe rather than the less dramatic problem of a small scale pilot failing. Pilots, on the other hand, slow the adoption process down, as does the phased approach. If change is urgently needed then Big Bang may be the only option.

7.7 Cost Benefits and Total Cost of Ownership

As we have seen there are many ways to judge the success of a IS implementation. Happy users are a nice outcome, but the Finance Director may well be more interested in the effect the project has had on the company's bottom line.

Being able to quantify the financial benefits of any IS project is far from easy. You may be able to add up all the man-time involved, cost all the hardware and software involved, and give a figure for how much has been spent on a project. But how do you factor in the efficiencies the system has brought about? Or how do you measure the cost that would have accrued to the firm if you hadn't replaced that broken old system?

We shall see later in this chapter that Cloud and Big Data change standard models, but as Hill et al. (2013) put it:

> The traditional on-premise approach as we know it, has been costly. It is important to note that the key cost element for the users has been tied in, not in purchasing hardware and software licences, but the required consulting, change management, education, maintenance and enhancements
> and significant management overheads to ensure service availability, security, and performance. At the heart of this there is the cost of labour and expertise.
>
> Taking into account this potentially massive cost to the user organisation topped with opportunity-loss due to up-front capital expenditure, vendor lock-in, inflexibility and operational costs, the overall cost impact is incredibly high. This has changed the attitude towards IT decisions and budgets to become more strategic, giving rise to a whole new discipline of IS/IT strategic planning and benefits realisation to ensure that IT budgets are effective.

7.7.1 Open Source

As we see later there are two fundamentally different approaches to software acquisition. Open Source software is freely available to download for use or modification under a licence agreement that states that the source code is in the public domain. The more traditional approach is to purchase software directly from vendors.

Let's take an example: If your organisation needs a database to store its data you have many possible solutions to choose from. At the premium end of the Vendor market are products like Oracle, IBM and Microsoft SQLServer. All of these companies would charge you for both purchasing and maintaining the products. On the other hand, there are products that are available as Open Source, such as MySQL. You can simply download them and use them immediately for no fee.

Decades ago large corporations would generally choose the vendor solution. The assumption was that large companies like Oracle, with their team of hundreds of skilled developers, would only sell robust products and that, on the odd occasion when something did go wrong, they would have a skilled support team available around the clock. Banks, for example, would typically feel far more secure using premium software delivered by a world leader than they would if they paid an in-house team to develop using Open Source. Indeed, in an era when IBM were market leaders, there used to be a saying: *Nobody ever got fired for buying IBM* !

Since the early 1990s, when Linus Torvalds gave the world the open source Linux operating system (OS) which has competed with other vendor supplied OSs like Microsoft's Windows, the Open Source approach has grown in stature and repute. Of late we have seen an even greater acceptance by businesses of the Open Source approach since the de facto way of handling Big Data has become Hadoop, which is an Open Source product.

7.7.2 Off the Shelf vs Bespoke

As organisations look to automate their business functions one question often comes up: *Do we build this system in-house using our own developers, or do we buy a system that has already been written "off the shelf"?* The former means the system can be built exactly to our requirements, whereas the latter means we may have to amend some, or even all, of our working practices to make them fit around the software we purchase. Balancing that, however, it is almost a certainty that an in-house solution will be more expensive to develop and maintain.

Again, looking at history, in the 1980s the norm was for bespoke systems to be built in-house (or built on their behalf by commissioned specialist consultancies). Historically these systems were also built for specific functions. In a large organisation it was not unusual to have dozens of different systems working in different departments, often not able to communicate with each other. Those unhelpful "siloed" systems doubtless helped with the demand for more integrated, holistic systems. Enterprise resource planning (ERP) came to the fore in the 1990s. They consist of a suite of integrated sub-applications, often called modules, which help the management of a business's functions. Modules will often include:

- Manufacturing and inventory
- Product planning
- Costing
- Finances
- Marketing
- Sales
- Logistics

Whilst it is possible to build your own ERP system businesses began to adopt off-the-shelf solutions from vendors such as SAP and Oracle. There is some "tailorability" in these products to allow them to work within the organisation's working practices, but there is still often the need to adapt practices to suit the software. Since these vendors often have reputations built on implementations in particular market sectors (SAP has specialist extensions for the Oil and Gas trade for example) organisations often see this need to amend their own methods of working as a way of bringing in best practice.

It is interesting to see the history of the use of Information Technology in organisations as a slow move towards it becoming a ubiquitous utility, rather than anything likely to provide any sort of competitive advantage. Information Systems that run on that IT however are slightly less utilitarian. Some organisations will be able to use an off-the-shelf solution for all their business needs, but larger, more complex organisations are likely to need to at least amend standard packages, and many will still see the advantage of writing their own in-house solutions.

7.7.3 Gauging Benefits

Implementation costs are not the only significant cost. Assuming the system is used it will have ongoing maintenance, user training, and system upgrades before it becomes obsolescent. These ongoing costs need to be factored in from the beginning. It can be a false economy if the developers decide to use Open Source software because it costs the company nothing to buy if the ongoing maintenance of that system is a lot higher because of the need to employ technically proficient staff to carry out that maintenance. These ongoing costs, as opposed merely to the upfront costs, are often refereed to as Total Cost of Ownership.

Nor is the decision necessarily only about least cost. The Open Source approach has undoubtedly become far more acceptable to business, but there are some occasions when organisations will pay for guaranteed service. It is not that Open Source is necessarily less reliable than a proprietary package; it is just that with the latter there is a level of certainty that any problems uncovered will be fixed very quickly.

Cost–benefit analysis is a way for organizations to appraise the desirability of a particular project or implementation. In broad terms the expected benefits, both financial and others, are compared with the costs of the project. This balance can be then used to compare with other potential projects or maintaining the status quo. The difficulty, of course, is that not all costs, and many benefits of new systems are non-financial and therefore hard to convert into a sensible measure.

Probably the most infamous alleged misuse of cost benefit analysis is in the field of automobiles. In the 1970s Ford in the US were desperately trying to catch up with the influx of foreign "compact" cars and hurriedly created the Ford Pinto. Unfortunately the design process left the car, according to the law suits that followed, with a dangerous fuel tank which was liable to rupture and cause potentially fatal conflagrations within the vehicle. According to many papers Ford decided not to correct this defect when it was discovered as a result of a cost-benefit analysis which compared the cost of the change and any recall policy with the probable payment that would be made to Pinto owners killed or maimed by a fuel tank related claim. Whilst the cost-benefit went into quite some detail, the fact that was often highlighted was that, as part of the analysis, Ford valued a human life at $200,000. When the sums were added up it appeared that Ford had decided that the cost of paying a few claims was to be preferred to the costs of putting the design right.

There is little doubt that today's Ford, or many other organisations come to that, would never countenance such a cynical approach again. And readers who are disgusted by this story must bear in mind the cultural change that has happened over the past four decades. That said, there was a significant measure missing from the cost-benefit analysis in this case – how much would the negative press in this case cost them in lost sales? This highlights the difficulty of establishing all the important measurements for factors that may not materialise for some time in the future, making cost-benefit a difficult exercise.

That said, to not carry out some sort of analysis would be to make poorly grounded decisions. In IS projects it is important that the users easily come to terms with the new system. For example, to the cost efficiency seeking accountant, training users may seem like an area where costs can be shaved. But to do so may result in less skilled users who do not use the system optimally and therefore not generate longer term savings. Add to those financial costs the human cost of having a potentially disgruntled workforce and those cost savings may seem very short term.

This book is not the place to provide extensive tuition on cost-benefit analysis. There are specialist organisations who can help in this area. The Carnegie Mellon University Software Engineering Institute (SEI) is a good place to start when investigating the process of reviewing the validity of an architectural project: http://www.sei.cmu.edu/architecture/tools/evaluate/cbam.cfm.

7.8   Insourcing or Outsourcing?

Having established the need for some Information System developments an organisation needs to decide who will be responsible for delivery of this systems and their ongoing support and maintenance. For small organisations the system's design and development will often be carried out by the same person who established the business need in the first place. This is potentially a very efficient way of developing systems since there is no likelihood of misunderstanding throughout the development life-cycle. In addition small firms can often be more agile in terms of changing organisational structures to accommodate systems changes, especially if, as if often the case, the CEO has given their support to the system. The downside, however, is that the skills available to that small company are of necessity limited. If their IS specialist is a Java programmer then all problems may be solved using Java, even when that may not be the most appropriate tool. Moreover, the lack of prior experience of similar projects will mean that the inevitable implementation problems will seem almost insurmountable to them and may take a lot of time to solve.

To get around the problem of limited experience the company could choose to buy-in expertise. They might, for example, put the IS implementation out for tender and allow a firm of IS specialists to complete the project on their behalf. The position is slightly different for larger companies. They may well have an internal pool of IT and IS specialists they can call on for a project. However, employing such people permanently is expensive. And although they are closer to the company's needs because they work there, there is still a danger that they will address those needs using only the tools they are comfortable with, rather than the ones that might be of more benefit to the project. For a large project involving new, or at least new to the company, IT/IS tools there will be a need to carry out a skills gap analysis to see what extra skills need to be gained. The options include retraining existing staff (which costs, and slows the project down) or buying-in the skills from elsewhere.

These projects may involve both hardware and software, and once such systems are built there will be a need to train staff, fix bugs, fill in with last minute additions to the requirements that appear once the system is being used, and generally maintain all the elements. The decision for this phase is the same as with the development phase: do we look after it, does an outside company look after it, or do we have a mix of both?

Looking to use external expertise for whatever phase is generally described as Outsourcing. This is defined as when a significant contribution is made to an IS/IT project by an external provider of human resources with particular skills or specialist products. Over time this process has become more and more popular. Starting from an era prior to 1989 nearly all companies looked after their own IT/IS needs, although there was always the fallback of buying in consultants to fill any particular knowledge or skill gap. In 1989 Kodak signed a deal with IBM that has since been seen as the turning point and the first real "outsourcing" deal. What Kodak were looking for was an ability to cut costs and concentrate on their core business, leaving the management of none-core IT, such as running the data centre, to specialists.

Although many people thought Kodak was crazy for giving away control of a part of their business, the idea certainly caught on. Many large companies will now outsource some or all of their IT/IS needs. There has, however, in more recent times, been a slight turning of the tide and some companies are thinking again in terms of regaining some internal control of IS/IT. This trend has been christened Insourcing. As Qu et al. (2010) describe:

> Notwithstanding the much-publicized popularity of IT outsourcing, many firms continue to rely on IT insourcing, which is defined as the organizational arrangement that a firm relies on internal IT department to obtain IT services (Dibbern et al. 2004). Moreover, a considerable number of firms have decided to terminate their outsourcing contracts and bring their outsourced IT functions back in-house (Veltri et al. 2008 and Whitten and Leidner 2006). For instance, JP Morgan Chase announced the early termination of its seven-year $5 billion contract with IBM to consolidate the company's data center and improve distributed computing capabilities (Forelle 2004). Similarly, Sainsbury's, the second largest supermarket chain in the UK, ended its 10-year, £3 billion outsourcing contract with Accenture three years early because the contract had failed to produce the anticipated increase in productivity (Rohde 2004). Various reasons (e.g., poor service quality and high cost) have been

offered for early contract terminations, and companies with early terminations often elect to switch to IT insourcing and develop their own IT capabilities rather than seek another outsourcing arrangement with a different service provider

There are clearly good and bad points for each sourcing method and every company will make its own decision about what is right for it. Losing control of what can be a strategically important resource like IT/IS may well be a step too far for some organisations. They would not be reassured by the Service Level Agreements (SLA) that would "guarantee" certain levels of performance from the supplier. For others, perhaps with a tendency to see IT as a utility which is unlikely to provide any competitive advantage, the costs and other overheads involved with employing IT/IS specialists is something they would rather not take on.

7.9 The Effect of Cloud

One of the significant impacts of the recent arrival of the cloud computing as a way of providing IT/IS solutions is that companies can react quickly to a change in needs by avoiding the time consuming, and potentially expensive task of provisioning for a new project. The idea of being tied into expenditure on hardware and software you may not need if the project fails is often a stumbling block for IS/IT projects so the ability to just use what is needed, when it is needed, can seem appealing. As Hill et al. (2013) put it:

> One of the attractions of cloud computing is the rapid provisioning of new compute resources without capital expenditure. If the marketing director makes claims about a new market niche, then it is much more cost-effective to experiment with new products and services, since cloud computing removes traditional barriers such as raising capital funds, lengthy procurement procedures and human resource investment. Also, if cloud computing is already part of the organisation's IT infrastructure, then new requests merely become additional demands upon the systems, rather than designing and specifying new systems from scratch. Business agility is therefore one key driver for the adoption of cloud computing.
>
> The other key business driver is the potential reduction in ongoing capital expenditure costs afforded by cloud computing. As the use of IT becomes more sophisticated, greater demands are placed upon IT fundamentals such as data storage, and if the requirements fluctuate significantly, the pay-per-use model of cloud computing can realise operational savings beyond the costs of the potential extra hardware requirement.

In that other people are looking after some or all of the company's IS/IT needs, cloud computing is clearly a form of outsourcing. Its recent success, in a period marked by an economic recession in the West, is no doubt partially driven by the way that it moves IT/IS costs from capital expenditure into revenue costs. This means that the old problem of high start-up costs for innovators looking to try new IS systems out has disappeared (or, to be more accurate, been spread over a number of years).

Developing a cloud strategy is not easy, especially since this is a relatively new approach. Some businesses will see the risk of losing control of the IS/IT functions as such a high risk that they do not think benefits of cloud computing are worth taking those risks for. Some will grab the opportunity to spread their costs across longer periods.

7.10 Implementing 'Big Data'

Cloud computing is still a new concept to many organisations, but we do now have many case studies and books on the topic published to act as a resource in any decision whether to adopt cloud or not. This is not quite the case with Big Data. It is true that handling large amounts of data is not new in its own right, but the other the 4 V's together (Volume, Velocity, Variety and Veracity – see Chap. 9 for more on these and the use of big data sources) are what makes Big Data different. There are growing numbers of case studies being published about Big Data projects, but there are still, at the time of writing, few widely accepted standards or guidelines for potential implementers to call upon in their research. As with all new areas of IT/IS, it is often the vendors who are first to publish. There is no paucity of material on Big Data from IBM, SAP, SAS and the like. But independent, academically rigorous reports are still relatively few.

This means that any significant project to implement a new Big Data approach within an organisation is, of necessity, risky. However, the few stories that are available point towards some tremendous successes with using Big Data approaches in all sorts of fields, so the risk may be worthwhile! As we saw in the Strategy chapter, Big Data may impact both the strategic direction the company chooses and the way the company creates its strategy.

Elsewhere, too, we have seen that external factors also heavily influence decisions. The low cost and high availability of storage is probably one of the key drivers in the upsurge in Big Data. As Lake and Crowther (2013) say:

> If the cost/Gbyte were currently the same now as it was in 1990 there can be little doubt that much of this generated data would be discarded as "not worth keeping".

What, then, do implementers of Big Data need to do? Well, the good news is that all the steps outlined earlier in the chapter remain the same: clearly identify the requirements, design with all stakeholders engaged in the process, manage the risks and identify the benefits.

As with other projects which use new technologies there may well be a skills gap within the organisation which will need to be addressed before any such project gets significantly started. We talked about Data Scientists in the Staff chapter. Whilst people with the technical skills can be bought-in (if they can be found), the ideal mix would be for people who understand the business to be involved and perhaps trained so they can fill the skills gap themselves. Large organisations will already have Business Analysts and Business Intelligence Specialist who may be willing to move into these new roles.

One of the key problems such a team faces is in selecting data which might produce useful results after analysis. In a commercial organisation this question is likely to be framed as "can we contribute to the bottom line as a result of this research?" This is where the cost benefit analysis phase we discussed earlier in this chapter will become more tricky since the process is to a degree experimental, and as such the answer is hard to guess. If a supermarket spends 2 months research combining two big datasets and using three highly paid data scientists and only discovers that they sell more ice-cream when the weather is sunny, the project will be deemed a failure. And yet, not to do the research could result in £millions of lost potential revenue. As McKinsey (Breuer et al. 2013) say:

> Recent research by McKinsey and the Massachusetts Institute of Technology shows that companies that inject big data and analytics into their operations outperform their peers by 5 % in productivity and 6 % in profitability. Our experience suggests that for retail and CPG companies, the upside is at least as great, if not greater.
>
> Tesco, for one, attributes its success in part to insights generated through big data and advanced analytics. The European grocery retailer introduced a loyalty card in the late 1990s, using it as a vehicle for the systematic collection and analysis of shopper data. The company has since mined online and social-media information as well. It has developed a full set of advanced analytics— encompassing more than 20 analytical tools in its commercial functions — to support day-to-day decision making. Its insight-driven commercial strategy has contributed to sustained profitability: since 2000, Tesco has improved its profitability every year, more than tripling its profits between 2000 and 2012.

Reviewing some of the papers that do talk about Big Data projects it seems that implementing a Big Data strategy has three key phases:

- Identify useful data sources
  Do not limit yourselves to internally sourced data. Stop throwing data away since historic trend can be useful.
- Ensure you have the tools and people to analyse and probe that data
  Employ or retrain where you have a skills gap. Many open source tools exist for analysis but the duration of the research cycle will probably be reduced using vendor supplied specialist tools
- Allow room for uncertainty. Provide the data scientists with the time they need to experiment
  Treat data scientists as if they are part of your R&D team!

All this said, this disruption to the normal architectural landscape is itself nothing new. Just imagine what changes to the standard IS planning process occurred when it became apparent that Windows had won the battle to be the preferred user interface. With Big Data it is also happening coincidentally with, and to an extent driven by, another trend in IT which is the use of mobile technologies, such as phones and tablets, in the workplace. In short, modern users expect to be able to manipulate large amounts of a variety of data wherever they are, and at whatever time they choose.

7.11 Summary

In this chapter we discussed how IT/IS is implemented and suggested that the journey from strategic vision to implemented systems can be fraught with difficulty. We talked about establishing needs, involving stakeholders, and measuring benefits. We finished by discussing two special cases; Cloud and Big Data.

7.12 Review Questions

The answers to these questions can be found in the text of this chapter.

- What tasks will befall a typical CIO?
- List the stages of a SDLC life-cycle
- Checkland had an acronym to help people remember the key stakeholders; it was CATWOE. What does this stand for?
- New IS systems often meet resistance from users. In managing the change involved in implementing a new system, list the steps that individual users often go through
- What are the three key stages in a successful Big Data implementation?

7.13 Group Work Research Activities

These activities require you to research beyond the contents of the book and can be tackled individually or as a discussion group.

7.13.1 Discussion Topic 1

With any project involving new technology there may be a shortage of appropriate skills within the organisation. In two groups, and in the format of a formal debate, discuss the assertion: *"This house believes that all IS projects should be run using solely in-house staff"*.

7.13.2 Discussion Topic 2

As always with books, there will have been many papers published since the authors wrote this chapter. Do some research to find papers which discuss examples of successful Big Data implementations. How do the papers' authors deal with risk and benefits? If these papers are by commercial organisations, are you able to see any bias in the content?

References

Beyer H (2010) User-centered agile methods. Morgan & Claypool Publishers, San Rafael

Breuer P, Forina L, Moulton J (2013) Beyond the hype: capturing value from big data and advanced analytics. 2014. McKinsey. http://www.mckinsey.com/client_service/marketing_and_sales/latest_thinking/beyond_the_hype

Checkland P (1981) Systems thinking, systems practice. Wiley, Chichester

Fernández W, Thomas G (2008) Success in IT projects: a matter of definition? Int J Proj Manag 26(7):733–742

References

Hill R, (OC, Hirsch L, Lake,Peter (Lecturer in Information Technology), Moshiri S (2013) Guide to cloud computing: principles and practice. Springer, London

Kappelman LA, Robert M, Lixuan Zhang (2006) Early warning signs of IT project failure: the dominant dozen. Inf Syst Manag 23(4):31–36

Karlsen JT, Andersen J, Birkely LS, Ødegård E (2005) What characterizes successful IT projects. Int J Inf Technol Decis Mak 4(4):525–540

Lake P, Crowther P (2013) Concise guide to databases. Springer, London

Lancaster University, BCS (2007)-last update, Case study of successful complex IT projects. Available: http://bcs.org/upload/pdf/casestudy.pdf. 3 Mar 2014

Longman A, Mullins J (2004) Project management: key tool for implementing strategy. J Bus Strateg 25(5):54–60

Mathiassen L, Tuunanen T (2011) Managing requirements risks in IT projects. IT Prof 13(6):40–47

Mcmanus J, Wood-Harper T (2007) Understanding the sources of information systems project failure. Manag Serv 51(3):38–43

Qu WG, Oh W, Pinsonneault A (2010) The strategic value of IT insourcing: an IT-enabled business process perspective. J Strateg Inf Syst 19(2):96–108

Strassmann PA (2003)-last update, Power politics of the CIO. Available: http://www.strassmann.com/pubs/fed/AFCEA-2003.html. 3 Mar 2014

Systems

8

8.1 What the Reader Will Learn

- that Big Data brings challenges to existing Information System platforms.
- that Big Data does not change the basic concerns for a Database Administrator
- that new tools like Hadoop can be used explore large data collections and generate information from data
- that the structured data traditionally stored in a RDBMS is not the only form of data that needs to be handled today
- that the Cloud has changed the way organisations manage their data

8.2 What Does Big Data Mean for Information Systems?

There are those who argue that there is nothing new in Big Data except the badge. And to a degree this is true. Worrying about how to handle large quantities of data has been a Database Administrator's (DBA) task for decades. It really is just the definition of "large quantities" that has changed recently. To evidence this claim, Volume One of the Journal of Very Large Databases, which is a Springer journal, was published in 1992! (http://link.springer.com/journal/volumesAndIssues/778)

As we see in this chapter, although Big Data brings its own challenges, a DBA is still answerable to his organisation about key Information Systems issues like Performance, Availability and Scalability.

8.3   Data Storage and Database Management Systems

Say the word database and many people instantly think of Relational Databases. They may even think of examples they have encountered: Oracle, MySQL, Access. Indeed, for all but the databases savvy, the phrase Relational Database Management Systems (RDBMS) is synonymous with "databases". It's a bit like people calling a vacuum cleaner a Hoover, even when it isn't made by Hoover, but by some other company. Hoover has become synonymous with vacuum cleaner.

In this chapter we will discover that there are indeed many different methods of storing data, other than an RDBMS. Amongst others, we will discuss Hadoop – a distributed data storage system; Cassandra – a column store; MongoDb – a document storage system. But we must not lose sight of the fact that any database system is simply a means for permanently storing information in binary fashion. As Lake and Crowther (2013) say:

> ... a modern computer-based database system's primary purpose is to store and retrieve binary digits (bits). All the data in even the most highly encrypted critical systems, resolves itself into a series of 1s and 0s, or Ons and Offs.

The ons and offs are called bits. Since you can only store binary values (such as true/false) these are not much use on their own, so systems have been designed to use a series of consecutive bits, referred to as bytes, to store data. With 8 bits and some sort of mapping system it is possible to represent 256 different characters – more than enough for most western alphabets. One of the best known such mapping systems is ASCII (American Standard Code for Information Interchange). In this system, for example, **1000001** (decimal 65) represents A.

Thankfully users do not need to worry about the translation between binary and data – that is what a database management system does. Abstract ideas such as data, records, columns, are what the user sees, whereas, behind the scenes, these all get stored in binary form.

If the bytes stored on hard drives are at the physical end of the Information Systems spectrum, then the software used to store the data, and then turn it into useful business information are at the other end. In this book we are more concerned with how Information Systems impact business and although it is always a good idea to understand the way systems work, we do not need to concern ourselves with the Physical architectures here.

Having said that, there are some business driven decisions to make about storage – not least just what are we going to store! Storing data which is never used is just a waste of disk (and a needless expense). Another question to ask is *where should we store the data*? The most frequent answer to this question in commercial systems is *in a central database server*. Often the Database Server will be one part of the overall server picture, with Application Servers and Home Servers, Mail Servers and others forming the "Server" part of a Client/Server architecture. A typical Client/Server solution is illustrated in Fig. 8.1.

8.3 Data Storage and Database Management Systems

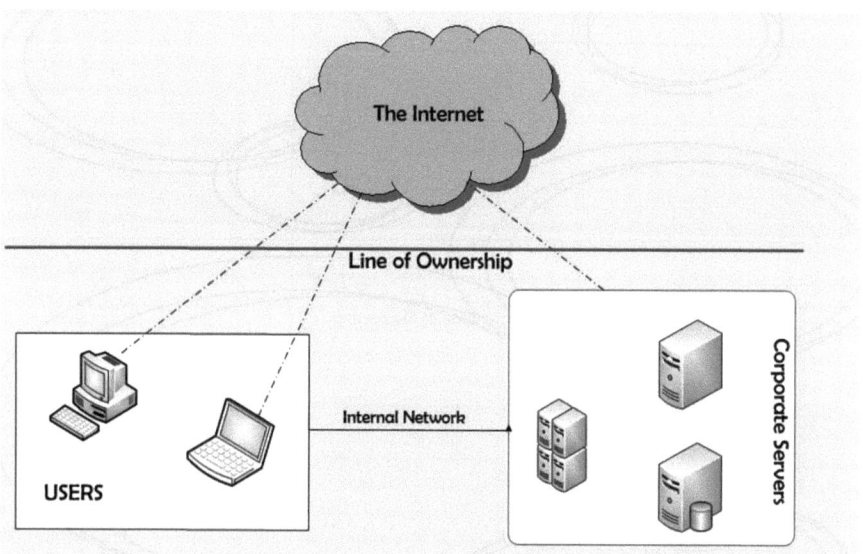

Fig. 8.1 A typical Client/Sever architecture pre-Cloud

The Cloud – the idea of service providers offering access to their Database Servers, and other services on a rental basis – offers a new set of options for architectural decisions. We discuss this in more detail later on in this chapter, but just for now, let us say that the architectural approach is depicted in Fig. 8.2, and note that the key difference is who owns the hardware.

The database system solutions available in the Cloud are known as distributed systems – the data can be stored on any server owned by the service provider in one of many geographical locations. Distributed systems are not new and exclusive to the Cloud, however. Imagine that we work in an organisation with three offices: one in Bangalore (India), one in Sydney (Australia), and one in Oslo (Norway). Each collects data about its customers in their part of the world. The company happens to be Norwegian, so the head office is in Oslo.

One solution in this case would be to have a single Server running in Oslo and for the other offices to connect into that server in the normal client/server fashion. But what if the people in Bangalore want to collect slightly different information about their customers from people in the other offices? In that case, with a single server system the schema would have to be made flexible enough to cope with the differences. And what if the office in Sydney wants to add a column to one of the tables? Changing schemas can cause problems, but the people in Sydney may think it worth the risk, whereas the others may not.

Distributed databases can get around these problems of data ownership by allowing each local office to maintain its own database using a local version of the DBMS, whilst also running a Distributed DBMS (DDBMS) which, at a meta level (that is, at a higher level of abstractness), allows some users to see the database as the sum of all three.

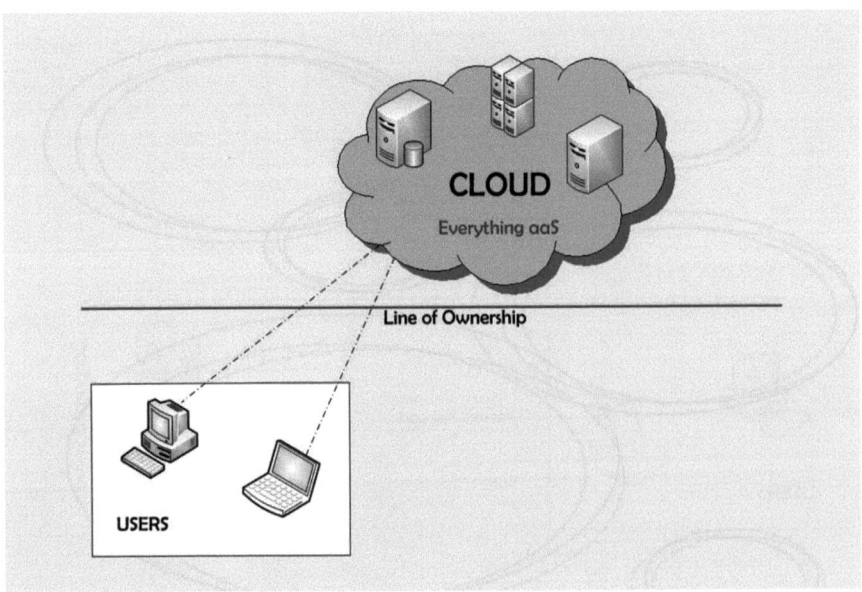

Fig. 8.2 Possible post-Cloud architecture (aaS is As A Service)

For clarity, we will here define a distributed database as:

More than one logically interrelated database elements which are connected by a computer network, and are typically in different geographic locations. (Lake and Crowther 2013)

As well as allowing local flexibility a distributed system can bring its own set of problems in terms of IT Strategy. Does the organisation standardise the application and database architecture to ease maintenance and the internal portability of data? Who should have access to which parts of which databases? How are Disaster Recovery solutions managed when the loss of one server could, in theory, jeopardise the entire database?

8.3.1 Database Management Systems

Database Management Systems are responsible for managing the interface between the logical objects, like records, that users deal with, and actual storage, usually on a magnetic medium of some type such as a hard drive, or Storage Area Network. At their crudest, in the early days of databases, they were simply a repository for data. Functionality mushroomed as these systems grew in importance to businesses. They now manage security, performance related data access processes, reporting, backups and disaster recovery, amongst much else.

Regardless of the type of database the four tasks they all have to perform regularly on the data they store are known in DBA circles as CRUD tasks. They are:

Create
Read
Update
Delete

Database systems can be sub-divided by type according to which business needs they are addressing. Many organisations will simply use one vendor's database products, such as Oracle or SQL Server, and use them for all their data needs. The benefit of this is that you only need recruit people with one set of special skills – SQL and database administration – making the CIO's staff costs smaller than if they were obliged to have a range of skills in their team.

Each of the data needs discussed below has products aimed specifically at that need. As opposed to taking the one-database-fits-all approach, some organisations will use a range of tools to ensure they get optimum use of one of their most important resources: data.

8.3.2 Key-Value Databases

The idea of a **KEY** is central to most database solutions. It is something that uniquely identifies some data. In RDBMS terms, it might be the EMPLOYEE_ID that uniquely identifies the record for each employee, for example.

The simplest form of database is one where one KEY identifies one value. These databases are called Key-value databases. Probably the longest standing example is BerkeleyDB, now part of the Oracle portfolio: http://www.oracle.com/technetwork/products/berkeleydb/overview/index.html.

The benefit of it being simple is that processing overheads are small and performance can be very fast since everything will only revolve around the retrieval of one value, whereas, for example, SQL will often need to return many columns, potentially from several "joined" tables. The small footprint means that these databases can be embedded in Mobile solutions, where processing power is limited.

8.3.3 Online Transactional Processing (OLTP)

By far and away the most frequent use for a business database is to permanently store information about the organisation's transactions with its stakeholders: customers; suppliers; employees. Walk into any large supermarket and it is likely that the till you use to check out will be connected to a relational database somewhere. That database will store information about what you have bought, how much you spent, how you paid. If you paid by cash, it will not store information about you, but if you used a loyalty card it can also record the goods against your ID. These sorts of databases are referred to as Online Transactional Processing (OLTP) databases and they are characterised by the rapid movement of many small packets of data sent to, and from, a server.

Sometimes the server will be centralised, or sometimes the client will communicate with a local server which is a further part of a distributed system. The decisions here will be business driven – a local store which allows no local management of stock and which is part of a chain that has a centralised purchasing department will be less likely to need access to locally stored data.

Most of the major RDBMS database vendors' core products are designed to support OLTP systems. Oracle, Microsoft and IBM are big players in this arena and all their products have been developed over 20 years or more into high performance, robust and secure systems.

Whilst there will be circumstances where this is not the case, most OLTP systems are tuned to allow small packets of data to be written into permanent storage. Once at the database end some processing may take place on that data, and then some message sent back to the user about the success or failure of the process. This series of separate tasks that makes up a complete operation is called a Transaction – hence the T in OLTP. It is vital for a transaction to work fully or else fail – there can be no middle ground of partial success.

Take, for example, the case where you move some money from your account to pay John back for a loan he made to you. Amongst other things the data sent will contain information about your account, John's account and the amount to transfer. The key steps once the server receives this can be thought of as:

- Reduce your account by Amount A
- Increase John's account by Amount A
- Commit the changes (write them permanently down)

When nothing goes wrong, this externally seamless set of tasks produces the required transaction. However, should the server break just after Step 1 and before Step 2 completes the situation looks a lot worse – you are light by the Amount A, but John still thinks you owe him the money and may well be on his way round with a heavy! To prevent this sort of problem, if the entire job doesn't succeed all the tasks are "rolled-back" - that is, put back to the way things were before. This ability to roll-back is a vital part of any OLTP system and requires the storage of what is often called **undo** data. In the transaction above, for example, the value in your account before Step 1 is stored before ny task starts. If the transaction fails, the **undo** is used to put your account back to the way it was. If the transaction succeeds the undo will eventually be discarded. This ability to guarantee that transactions are reliably processed is encapsulated in the ACID model which describes four properties any OLTP system requires to be reliable (see Fig. 8.3).

There are obvious implications for systems that allow multiple concurrent users to access the same data. Databases manage such conflicts by issuing a virtual "lock" on the data when it is being used by a user. In our scenario above, for example, when the system accesses your account in order to reduce your balance, it will acquire a lock until the transaction has successfully completed so that no other transaction can alter the data at the same time.

8.3 Data Storage and Database Management Systems

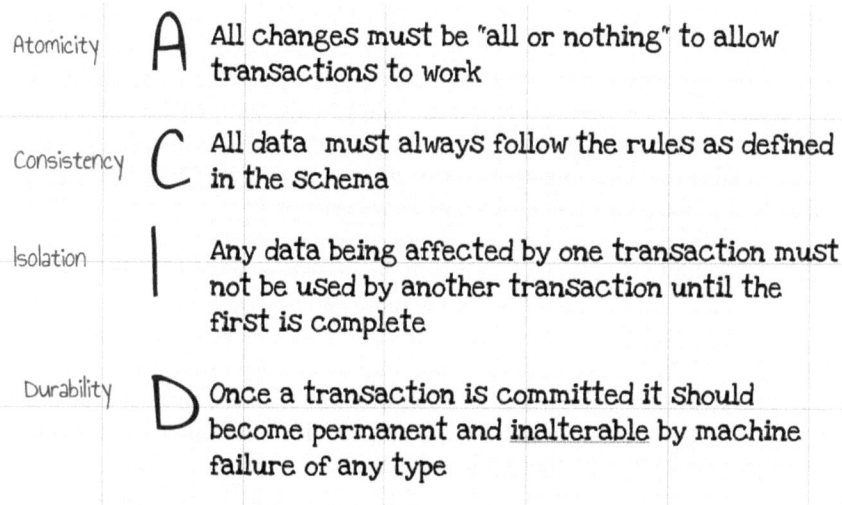

Fig. 8.3 The ACID model

This locking adds to the processing overhead, thus slowing the database down. However, even with locking there are alternative approaches, depending upon the usage the system is put to. It is possible to have optimistic locking which assumes that there will be no conflicts and does not issue locks, but then, at the Commit stage, checks if there have been any other users who have attempted to change the same data and if they have, issues a roll-back. This roll-back intensive approach is speedier (because of the lessening of the locking load) as long as the number of conflicts is low, but for systems where users are regularly changing data that others may be changing, the pessimistic approach of blocking all access to any other users for the duration of the process may be safer and quicker.

8.3.4 Decision Support Systems (DSS)

Once the OLTP data is collected it may well be the focus of considerable analysis: did that promotion of Baked Beans generate extra sales? How many extra people came into the newly decorated store? Are sales on an upward trend overall? And how do they compare with last month? Or this month last year?

Many of these questions will be formalised in a standardised set of regular reports – perhaps weekly, or monthly, or annually. Occasionally however there will be *ad hoc* queries. Data analysts, typically with strong SQL skills will be responsible for making sure the reports give accurate answers and that any instant queries are run against the data.

These sorts of queries have different characteristics than the Insert-heavy OLTP systems mentioned above. Whereas an index slows down the creation of records (because the index needs to be written to and maintained at the same time as the actual data) and will therefore be avoided where possible on OLTP systems, the relatively static nature of DSS data means that indexes are essential to help find particular data items. Moreover, for a variety of reasons, the heavy duty number-crunching that typically takes place in the analysis of the data could be really slow. This could be because much of the data it is trying to access may be the subject of current updates or inserts and the number of locks being issued (see OLTP section) against that data might significantly slow the entire system down as a consequence.

Data warehouses are a central repository of data which is created from the integration of multiple data sources, primarily an organisation's OLTP data. Some of the data loaded will be summaries of the more detailed OLTP system. The differences between OLTP and DSS means that the databases containing the data are often designed differently from the bottom up. DSS systems are write-once read-many and so are very query focused. Tools like views, cubes, and star schemas are used to speed the search and retrieval process for the user. Naturally the quality of the analysis depends upon the quality of data in the warehouse. Transfers from an OLTP system, including any summarising, need to be timely and accurate.

8.3.5 Column-Based Databases

Both Column-based and Document-based databases are relative new alternatives to the RDBMS approach. In data warehousing there is a frequent need to do analysis on one column in a table. The way that the data is stored in an RDBMS is row-based. In a typical relational HR system the data for my salary will be in a column called salary, but it will be stored directly adjacent to data about my age, place of birth, address, and so on. This means that if we have a need to establish what the average salary for our company is, we need to tell the database to open every row, access the salary value for each row, and then keep a running total until it has done this for every row. RDBMS systems have mechanisms in place to speed this process up as much as possible.

However, had we stored all the salaries together, next to one another, the process would be much quicker. This, in essence, is what a Column-based database offers, and they can help the performance of a data warehouse because of this. The downside is that it is not easy to reconstitute a row of data for a particular ID, so you would choose this approach with caution if that sort of record-based query was the norm. Column-based is one of the newer NoSQL database approaches and we look at NoSQL later this chapter.

8.3.6 In Memory Systems

Most Information Systems suffer from physical bottlenecks. It is a natural consequence of the computer architecture that has been used for decades. At one time the bottleneck was a card-reader. You could only insert data as quickly as you could scan the physical punch cards. In today's information systems the bottleneck is around the permanent storage of data. The mechanical aspects of reading data from a Hard Disk Drive (HDD) slow down data retrieval and storage considerably.

One way to deal with this would be to not store data on a HDD and to always keep data in memory. However, until recently this approach was so expensive as to be used only in situations where speed of retrieval was paramount, such as in the Deutsche Börse case study shown on the Oracle TimesTen website: http://www.oracle.com/technetwork/products/timesten/overview/deutsche-borse-db-snapshot-130682.pdf (Unknown 2009).

Oracle TimesTen was an early mover in the In Memory area. As with other such approaches, they naturally allow some form of permanency too, to make sure that power outages would not lose the current state of the database.

Another important player in this area is SAP with their HANA in memory solutions. Hana implementations can be on a specially designed motherboard, known as a blade. They are still very new, and relatively expensive, but are likely to be an important part of the enterprise scale IS arena in the future. We talk about them in more detail in Chap. 12 when we look to the future.

8.4 What a DBA Worries About

Lake and Crowther (2013) identify four key concerns that any DBA will have about their database. One of them – Security – is important enough to warrant a whole chapter in this book (Chap. 10). The other three are Scalability, Performance and Availability. Using the Lake and Crowther(ibid) definitions we have:

Scalability: *The ability of a database system to continue to function well when more users or data are added.*
Performance: *Performance is about ensuring you use all the system resources optimally in the process of meeting the application's requirements, at the least cost.*
Availability: *Ensuring that the database is open and accessible for as long as possible, by planning for as many eventualities as is reasonable, given the constraint of cost.*

We briefly look at these three aspects of database administration below, concentrating on why they matter to the business. This section ends by exploring issues around data movement.

8.4.1 Scalability

If you have ever used Microsoft Access you will probably have come to the conclusion that it is a relatively easy to use tool that allows you to store data. However, it does have limitations. If you were building a system for which you expected there to be many concurrent users you would not use Access since the maximum number of users allowed is 255. But even this maximum can be misleading since Access was designed to be a single-user system and opening it up to many users slows the processing down.

At the time of writing the maximum database size for Access is 2 Gigabytes. Databases like Oracle or SQL Server are able to hold millions of times more data than Access. In addition they were written from the start to be multi-user systems.

As with most IS decisions there are pluses and minuses for all database solutions. If your application holds relative small amounts of data and will be used by only a few people, and you know this will not change in the foreseeable future, then you may well feel that the extra expense involved in using a product like Oracle is not worthwhile. We also need to remember that the costs are not simply the one-off purchase and/or licence fees, but also the costs involved in employing appropriately skilled professionals. An Access programmer will probably be far cheaper to employ than a certified Oracle DBA, for example.

8.4.2 Performance

A DBA dreads the phone call from the Boss's office saying "Report A is running very slowly today". For a start, without previous measurements, they may well not be able to quantify any problem – if indeed there is a problem (users have been known to "feel" it is taking longer just because they are watching the screen this time they run the report whereas every other time they went to make a coffee).

Accepting there is a problem, the next stage is to identify where it might be. Is the user also running other programmes on their PC that are slowing the client? Is the network jammed with other traffic? Or is it actually something to do with the Database Server or the Application itself?

Most database performance problems end up being SQL related. People without an understanding of how the underlying database works can easily build SQL Queries using drag and drop tools that aim to make life easier for the user. Unfortunately these tools do not always write optimised SQL, and this can be a real problem for the DBA.

One of the better paid consultancy jobs in the database arena is that of SQL Tuning specialist. Tuning SQL in a complex database environment is indeed a tricky job requiring many skills. However, the best way to avoid these costs is to ensure that the database is designed well in the first place. Ideal development teams, for example, would include a DBA who can ensure that sensible design decisions are made and thus optimise performance.

The easy way out is the lazy DBA approach – buy more RAM or upgrade your system. Hardware does have a significant impact upon performance but just adding RAM can have knock-on effects elsewhere, such as at the CPU. Because most problems are SQL related, it makes sense to review the application's queries first, before spending on hardware.

8.4.3 Availability

According to IncomeDiary.com (http://www.incomediary.com/20-websites-making-the-most-money#How_Much_Does_Amazon_Google_and_Facebook_Make, Dunlop 2011) Amazon make over $1,000 per second! Imagine what it would cost them in lost income if their servers all went down for a few minutes!

For organisations like Amazon, therefore, having the database always open for business is their goal. However, no database can guarantee to be permanently available. The industry high-end target is often referred to as Five Nines availability. That is 99.999% available in a year. Why not use a calculator to see what that would mean in terms of lost sales for Amazon!

As usual there are conflicting drivers in the decisions you take about availability. Generally speaking the nearer to Five Nines you go the more it will cost, as the higher quality hardware and back-up servers required add to your IT costs. You therefore need to work out if the lost income and good will you may suffer from your system going down is worth paying many thousands of pounds to avoid.

The sorts of things that prevent 100% availability include needing to bring a database down to upgrade the version number, or apply an essential patch to correct some of the software. Things also go wrong with hardware – Hard disks (HDD) get corrupt, for example. Back-up copies of data are taken regularly to allow a DBA to install a new HDD when this happens and then restore the data from the back-up. The problem with this approach is that it is slow – especially if the back-up medium is tape.

Perhaps the easiest way to maintain high availability is to duplicate the database on different servers. Mirroring software allows these multiple systems to hold identical data once they are "synchronised". However, for this to work seamlessly both (or all) servers would need to have equal levels of performance, meaning this could be a very expensive approach.

The final availability consideration for a DBA is what to do when a disaster strikes? Even having back-ups in off-site fire-proof safes will not help if your entire data centre is wiped out by a flood, for example. Keeping exact replica sites at different geographical locations is one alternative. Again, this is a very expensive solution, but the risk for a bank of not being able to service its customers' needs is so enormous that they will pay these costs, and more. The Cloud has helped since off-site, instantly accessible back-up stores can be rented in many different locations, and data replications can be built in to any contract with the service provider.

8.4.4 Data Migration

There are many reasons that a DBA may need to move data around. When we discussed data warehouses earlier this chapter we mentioned that data would be ported to a warehouse from a number of sources, either as raw data, or else having been summarised, or joined with other data.

Moving data internally tends to be the easiest form of transfer since the DBA is often in control of both source and target. Some organisations which are more stovepiped, with discrete pools of data being used only by one department, may have more difficulty, especially if departments have been given the freedom to source their own databases in the past. This freedom can result in organisations running a mixture of Mainframe, Client/Server and stand-alone systems and this makes the data analyst's job far more difficult.

The movement of data, then, has potentially two great hurdles: People (data belonging to someone else) and Systems (data from another type of database). The former problem can be a major headache and can prevent even the most technically able project team succeeding. Strong persuasive powers may be needed to ensure that data owners are happy to release their precious resource. Executive information systems which pull data from across the organisation will need to explain how senior decision making will improve if cross-departmental data is shared. We discussed information politics in the 'STYLE' chapter (Chap. 4).

On the technical front the easiest form of moving data is between databases from the same vendor. All the leading products have Import and Export facilities built into them; typically these use internal compression techniques to create a file that only another database of the same type will recognise and import.

Moving data between different databases, say an Oracle Payroll system and an SQL Server HR System, needs the use of some intermediary format. There are several to choose from. Perhaps the most common now is Extensible Mark-up Language (XML) which is normally a human-readable text file containing a data item descriptor, and the data item's value. A more recent addition is that of JavaScript Object Notation (JSON), again a text file which includes data descriptors. The traditional data transmission technique was either Comma Separated Values (CSV) file, or a Fixed Length file, both of which are text files. They had the advantage, in terms of succinctness, in that they did not repeat the data item descriptor for every record.

Examples of what some of these standards look like are shown in Figs. 8.4 and 8.5 which show the same data in XML format and in CSV format.

Electronic Data Interchange (EDI) has been around for decades. It is a standard which two or more organisations agree on and acts as common interface between their applications. It is frequently used in e-commerce for sending/receiving orders and the like. Parties agree on what the data will look like, and where it will appear in an electronically transmitted document. Sometimes this sort of agreement is industry-wide, as with the TRADACOMS which is used by the retail trade, largely in the UK. Because of the inbuilt complexity of EDI standards, and the fact that they are particular to certain businesses or collections of organisations, EDI is beginning to lose popularity and XML, or XML-like interchanges are now much more the norm.

Common alternative methods for moving data between systems are shown in Fig. 8.6, shown in ascending order of complexity, with the simplest way of moving data being a Create As Select SQL statement within the same database which needs no programming aside from the single line of SQL.

```
      - <Cell>
          <Data ss:Type="String">AURIGNYAIRSERVICES</Data>
        </Cell>
      - <Cell>
          <Data ss:Type="Number">193</Data>
        </Cell>
      - <Cell>
          <Data ss:Type="Number">1388</Data>
        </Cell>
      - <Cell>
          <Data ss:Type="Number">887</Data>
        </Cell>
      - <Cell>
          <Data ss:Type="Number">26585</Data>
        </Cell>
    </Row>
    <Row ss:Height="12.2457">
      - <Cell>
          <Data ss:Type="String">BACITYFLYERLTD</Data>
        </Cell>
      - <Cell>
          <Data ss:Type="Number">300</Data>
        </Cell>
```

Fig. 8.4 XML data

```
domDataOnly (1).csv  ×
AURIGNYAIRSERVICES,193,1388,887,26585
BACITYFLYERLTD,300,545,686.1,30031
BLUEISLANDSLIMITED,168,991,520.8,15308
BMIGROUP,1067,2435,2922.7,142804
BRITISHAIRWAYSPLC,1510,3327,4116.6,307849
BRITISHINTERNATIONALHELICOPTERSERVICESLTD,10,162,57.9,2169
EASTERNAIRWAYS,496,1406,1353,23074
EASYJETAIRLINECOMPANYLTD,1826,3922,4297.2,399308
FLYBELTD,2505,6755,5635.4,297435
ISLESOFSCILLYSKYBUS,12,176,55.3,1200
JET2.COMLTD,22,71,65,4059
LOGANAIR,504,2440,1958.7,32994
|
```

Fig. 8.5 CSV data

Often the transmitted data will be compressed to speed the transmission process over the network. The use of a network opens up the possibility of data corruption during transmission. It is tempting to think of files like the ones discussed above as mere ons and offs not to be worried about. However, we must not forget how important data is. It may well become the information that people use to take decisions, so bad data leads to bad information. Data quality is a vital issue. If your source

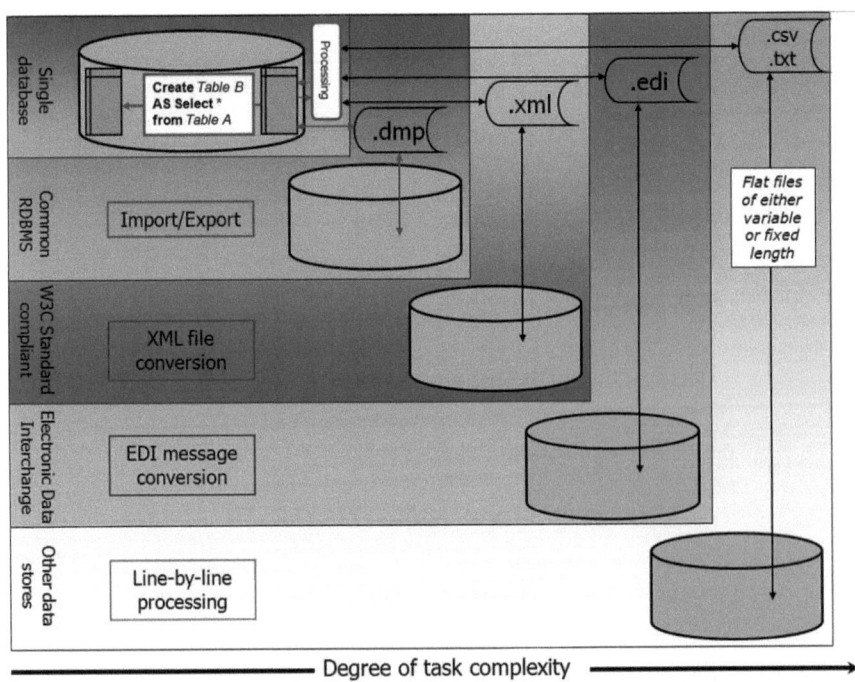

Fig. 8.6 Common alternative methods for moving data

database has a flag set to say that Patient A is allergic to penicillin and might die if he ingests any it is vital that the flag is also set in the target database once any data transfer is completed.

8.4.5 Not All Systems Are Data Intensive

This book's title includes the word Data, and data is clearly one of an organisation's most valuable assets. However, even in the era of big data there are systems that are not database focused. Networking and communication systems, for example, play a large part in any reasonably sized company's IT infrastructure. Whilst such systems may use a small database to store settings and similar data, they are not data focused. They can, however, be a major source for Big Data as they spew out log data that, if captured and analysed, can provide useful information about network use.

Communications and networking specialists are needed to provide an organisation's employees with speedy and accurate access to each other and to data. Their skills are part of the mix we discuss in Chap. 5. In the developed nations the mobile phone has become a standard business tool, but its use needs to be managed, not least for security reasons. A stolen mobile phone can contain a wealth of really useful business information. Security systems are another vital requirement that needs to take a high priority on a CIO's to-do list.

8.4.6 And There Is More to Data than Storage

However, the other phrase that is in the title is Information Systems, and that is why we have concentrated on the databases that support Information Systems. Applications for querying and analysing data are an important mix and can be accessed independently from the database software. R, for example, is an open source environment for statistical computing.

The traditional front-end to a database system is the Form and the Report. Forms often sit on top of database tables or views and allow the user to input, or read data. Many form-type applications are now written with a browser font-end, allowing access to critical information from anywhere. The design of systems which allow access to the company's information is an important part of the IS field. Clunky systems with many layers of menus may eventually present the user with the data they need, but they needlessly slow the process up. Well designed systems allow access easily and intuitively. Reports are often printed on a regular basis – perhaps monthly – and, for example, present detailed management information to help line managers run the operational aspects of the company.

Dashboard systems which present busy executives with a quick overview of the data they need to help them make decisions are becoming common. They will show data previously requested by the executive, and perhaps show alerts when other items are out of normal bounds. This idea of showing quickly only what is required has been around for a while, with such systems often being referred to as Executive Information Systems (EIS). In larger organisations one of the characteristics of an EIS is that it may well have to pull data from a variety of internal database systems which may be stovepiped, as we discussed earlier. Collecting, analysing and summarising are the key steps, and they are, as we see below, key steps in Big Data too.

8.5 Open Source

Open source software is characterised by being freely downloadable, or distributed, and usable, without charge. As well as costing an initial sum to purchase, commercial, vendor-supplied, software often comes with a licence which will be quite prescriptive and only allow a certain number of concurrent users, for example, or require regular annual payments to keep the licence active. Open Source, on the other hand, allows licensees the right to copy, modify and redistribute source code or executable programmes. These licences will often impose an obligation to share any improvements made to the source code with the community of users.

Open Source software has a long track record – The Linux Operating System, one of the most famous Open Source products, is over 20 years old. However, Open

Source has come to prominence in the last decade as it begins to be used by governments and large corporates as, in some cases, the software of choice at the exclusion of vendor supplied software. It has several benefits, not least that it is free to download and use. For organisations which have programmers available to them another advantage is that you get access to the source code and can therefore improve it, or tailor for your needs.

It is probable that one of the reasons for Open Source taking time to be seen as a genuine alternative to vendor supplied software is largely to do with its geeky image. When the Windows operating system arrived people without computing degrees found that they could actually use computers. Linux, on the other hand is largely command-line driven (although some GUI environments exist) and hides a lot less of what is going on in the computer technically than does Windows. This geekiness led purchasing decision-makers to be wary of putting their company's resources, as they saw it, in the charge of some be-sandalled undergraduate intern. Proper databases, like Oracle or DB2, for example, had professionals running them who had professional certifications to prove their competence. This perception of lower risk was further supported by the reassuring knowledge that the vendors would be someone who could be sued should their software fail, whereas Open Source has no similar form of redress.

More recently there have been products arriving in the Open Source space that the big vendors cannot (yet) compete with. One example in the era of Big Data is Apache's Hadoop (see section below). This is open source software which has become the de facto means for storing and analysing large amounts of distributed data. In less than 10 years it has come from an experimental new approach to improving Yahoo's searching technology to being the tool of choice for most Data Scientists in the world, in use at most large online service providers like Facebook, Twitter, eBay, and many more.

Unfortunately the reputation for geekiness hasn't changed. Hadoop can be a very hard product to master and at the time of writing there is a well documented shortage of appropriately skilled Data Scientists to drive it (See Chap. 5). SQL Server, and to some degree all vendor databases, specialise in making the day-to-day maintenance tasks in their databases as easy and automated as possible. Those are not characteristics you can attribute to Hadoop. The use of Open Source, therefore, continues to imply the use of technically skilled IT professionals.

8.6 Application Packages

As we have seen in the Open Source section, one of the reasons that Larry Ellison is so wealthy is that his Oracle Corporation has put immense effort into ensuring the Oracle brand stands for robustness, security and maintainability. For many a Chief Information Officer (CIO) choosing Oracle, (or SQL Server, or DB2) is a something they do not need to think about. For some the very fact that Oracle is so wealthy is an indicator of the stability and relatively risk free nature of the Oracle product.

8.6 Application Packages

In Information Systems there are several key vendors who supply off-the-shelf information solutions, often with the addition of added consultancy to tailor products for particular customers. Readers who are new to this area should take some time out to review the websites of some of these key players:

Oracle Corporation	http://www.oracle.com/index.html
SAP	http://www.sap.com/
SAS	http://www.sas.com/
Microsoft SQL Server	https://www.microsoft.com/en-us/sqlserver/default.aspx
Microsoft Dynamics	http://www.microsoft.com/en-gb/dynamics/erp.aspx
IBM DB2	http://www-01.ibm.com/software/data/db2/
Jaspersoft	http://www.jaspersoft.com/

Some differences in approaches worth noting in this list:

Some vendors specialise in a niche of Information Systems domain. SAS, for example, major on Business Intelligence (BI) - we discuss how BI and Big Data compare and what might happen to them in Chap. 12. Others, like Oracle, have a broad range of products, including OLTP database platforms, BI and "applications". This latter term needs to be treated with care. It can be used as a simile to "computer programme", but in this arena it means a suite of functions and procedures which can store, manipulate and report upon data across an enterprise. Using their immense financial clout, Oracle have acquired a number of these Applications (eg. Siebel and PeopleSoft) and offer them as fulfilling the needs of particular business sectors. SAP, on the other hand, have one product which has grown out of its Enterprise Resource Management (ERP) software, but which is has tailored to suit many types of organisations.

Some of these organisations are huge global corporations. Oracle claim that:

97% of Global Fortune 500 companies use Oracle software

and that:

Over 50,000 IT professionals per year become certified on Oracle Database (http://education.oracle.com/pls/web_prod-plq-dad/db_pages.getpage?page_id= 458&get_params=p_track_id:Datab11g, Unnamed, Oracle 2013)

CNN report that :

nearly 80% of the Fortune 500 use SAP software for processes like inventory planning, and 63% of worldwide financial transactions are processed through SAP software at one point or another

(http://tech.fortune.cnn.com/2012/03/29/sap-makeover-mcdermott-hagemann/)

All of these companies sell complex products that require skilled IT professionals to run them. A large Oracle installation may need certified Applications specialists, Certified DBAs and a team of data analysts. Certification training does not tend to be cheap, and certified professionals tend to be able to attract much higher salaries than the average, straight-from-university Java programmer. All of which means that Information Systems using these products are likely to be expensive. However, |"expensive" is a relative term - in a LinkedIn thread professionals were pointing at 3% of revenue being a reasonable spend on IT costs (http://www.linkedin.com/groups/Ideally-what-should-be-percentage-51825.S.40701712, Tewary 2013). On an annual revenue of £100 million, for example, that would mean the CIO might well have a budget in the region of £3 million.

The "one stop shop" approach offered by the likes of Oracle and SAP can be very appealing to CIOs who are looking for some sort of certainty that their £3 million spend will provide both basic IT services that we all expect these days, but also some form of Return on Investment. Big Data, for example, is being advanced as potentially providing previously unavailable information about a company's customers' likes and dislikes to enable their sales drives to be far more targeted, and therefore less costly and more rewarding.

8.6.1 Open Source vs Vendor Supplied?

Risk averseness is probably the most important factor in this decision. The high financial standing of companies like Oracle and SAP mean that they have been successful over a number of years and so their products are likely to be stable and robust. If your Information Systems are business critical you will be willing to pay for the well-engineered, high quality products.

This is most definitely not to say that Open Source produces poor quality products. Far from it. Linux is used for many mission critical systems across the globe. Oracle themselves run Linux at the Oracle On Demand data centre which services many Fortune 500 companies and contains more than 10,000 servers.

What has happened recently is that the traditional providers have tended to improve their existing product ranges, whilst the open Source community try out some new technologies, such as NoSQL and Hadoop databases. Now, it turns out, these new products are extremely useful and better at certain tasks than the traditional approaches.

So the answer to the question is not an easy one. Financial considerations will of course be important: How much will this cost to buy (capital expenditure) and run (operating expenditure)? What benefits will this bring to the organisation? But other questions will need to be asked: Do our stakeholders expect that we use a particular toolset? Can we afford to wait until this new technology is mature? Can we risk using non-commercial software solutions?

This complex mix is bound to produce different answers for different organisations. And that is before you start adding the complexity of the key stake-holder's preferences – What did the CIO use at University? What about at their previous post? What skills do our team have? How well do we know (and trust) the Oracle or IBM sales representatives?

8.7 The Cloud and Big Data

Cloud computing can be seen as pushing back the line of ownership so that most company IT costs are borne by outside expert providers who typically charge on a rental basis. There is a move from asset ownership (computing hardware) and expert wages (IT staff) to renting computing resource and services as required.

Cloud computing and Big Data have caused a large increase in the use of Open Source solutions by even the most cash-rich organisations. The Open Source community was first to latch on to the importance of using many cheap commodity servers to provide scalability at a time when the data available to organisations was expanding exponentially.

The big database vendors initially laughed off these new trends. Larry Ellison, CEO of Oracle and in 2012, the 8th richest man in the world (so he probably knows a thing or two about the industry) famously pooh-poohed Cloud whilst being interviewed, laughing at the concept and saying that there was nothing new in it.

He is quoted as saying:

> *The computer industry is the only industry that is more fashion-driven than women's fashion. Maybe I'm an idiot, but I have no idea what anyone is talking about. What is it? It's complete gibberish. It's insane. When is this idiocy going to stop?*
> http://news.cnet.com/8301-13953_3-10052188-80.html

He soon changed his mind and now Oracle is one of the biggest Cloud providers there is! But, like the other vendors, Microsoft included, they may have almost unlimited resource to throw at this but they have completely lost first-mover advantage.

As we saw in Fig. 8.2, the significant change for Cloud computing is not so much the technology, which has been around for a while, but the change in business model – a change that sees customers renting servers, information systems and even specialists on an as-needed basis, rather than actually buying the hardware and systems.

One way of thinking about this is to use the analogy of electricity supply. This is a paragraph from A History of public [electricity] supply in the UK (Biscoe 2013):

> *By the end of the 19th century, it was by no means unusual for individual companies or people to install their own supply to their factory or (large) home.*
> (http://www.engineering-timelines.com/how/electricity/electricity_07.asp)

In other words, the electricity needed to drive the machines so necessary for production had to be under local control. There was no network available to supply electricity from elsewhere at first, and when a network began to appear people would not trust it. They had mission critical tasks and could not afford to run the risk of having their supply under the control of other people.

And now? Yes, maybe companies will have stand-by generators in case of a power outage, but for the most part they would not think twice about just using grid provided electricity. Electricity has become a universal utility (at least in many wealthier nations), provided by companies who own the means of power production and then transmit the electricity to customers. Other companies own and operate facilities that distribute water and gas on a similar basis.

As we saw in Chap. 2, cloud computing allows us to think of IT as a utility. If you need a server and a database, you can use the internet to connect to them. They will be in some unknown geographical location and owned by someone like Amazon or Rackspace, and they will charge you for the amount of use you make of their system. One of the real strengths of this approach is that if you do not need that server for another 11 months, you do not pay for it during that period. If you had an in-house only IT department, you may well end up paying for an expensive server for a once-a-year job.

As we discussed in Chap. 7 the move away from Capital expenditure, especially during times of economic hardship, was a key driver to the success of the Cloud. Many organisations have now moved to the Cloud. To a large extent any processes you used to carry out on your own computing infrastructure are available for rent in the cloud. As with the Open Source v Commercial software argument earlier, different organisations will come to different decisions. The risk of having another organisation, even one as financially secure and well known as Amazon, have control of your data and data processing can be a frightening one and so the risk averse may not even consider Cloud as an alternative.

From a systems perspective the decision is more likely to be around issues like security, performance and availability. Because of the replication built into most cloud applications, the reliability of a single site become less of an issue, tending towards greater availability. Performance is a tricky one since data may have to be gathered from wide geographical sources, but the ability to simply use extra processing power for a few minutes and thus to rent your way through a performance spike can be a great advantage. The problem for cloud in terms of security is more one of perception. The technology is available now to make cloud as secure as your own system, but even with strict Service Level Agreements (SLAs) in place the very idea that you can trust someone else to look after your data as well as you do is anathema to some.

Cloud has been with us for a decade or so now. It is hard to say exactly when it started since there is a grey area between web-based systems and Cloud. For Cloud to work there needs there to be access to the internet. Salesforce.com and Amazon Web services were early providers of cloud-like systems, and are still enjoying first-mover advantage as a result. 2009 was a big year with the arrival of browser based enterprise-wide applications, such as Google Apps. In addition Microsoft brought out Azure, their cloud-based relational database.

Newer to the Information Systems arena is Big Data, although, like Cloud, there is not much new here in reality. The phrase "Information Explosion" was used in the

1960s, for example, and the Springer Journal of Very Large Databases has been in publication since 1992. The basic issue for Big Data, as the name suggests, is the scale of the data available to organisations today. We will go on to discuss what actually does make Big Data different, and how it can be used, in Chap. 9.

8.8 Hadoop and NoSQL

Of particular importance to the explosive arrival of Big Data has been availability of tools to allow the storage of huge amounts of data relatively cheaply using commodity hardware to distribute data across a number of systems (or nodes). The tool of preference at the time of writing is Hadoop. It is so popular, and so good at what it does, that even the big vendors we reviewed earlier are having to provide it for users of their software as they have yet to come up with anything better themselves.

Hadoop was born out of a need to analyse the vast amount of information search engines like Google and Yahoo had to process in order to respond to the user's search query. Relational Databases, even large powerful ones like Oracle, were unable to cope well with the workload and as a result Hadoop's creators looked for ways to share out the data and allow parallel processing to happen on a number of nodes.

Hadoop is Open Source and part of the Apache open source suite. It is freely downloadable from http://hadoop.apache.org/. The website describes it as a:

> … a framework that allows for the distributed processing of large data sets across clusters of computers using simple programming models.

The two key elements of Hadoop are the distributed file management system (HDFS) and Hadoop MapReduce. The former manages the placement of data across a number of nodes, and provides a means of accessing that data when needed. MapReduce has been around as a programming algorithm for years and simply entails a two stage process:

- First, look through all the data and extracting a key identifier and a value, and then storing that in a list.
- Using grouping to reduce the data thus listed such that you can get information like group totals, averages, minimums and the like.

We look in more detail at how this works in practice in Chap. 11 when we get some hands-on experience of using Hadoop.

Also as a consequence of some weaknesses in the relational model, people started asking if there might be an alternative approach to the ubiquitous relational database. Lake and Crowther (2013) define a NoSQL database as:

> A database which does not store data using the precepts of the relational model and which allows access to the data using query languages which do not follow the ISO 9075 standard definition of SQL.

There are now many different NoSQL databases, mostly Open Source. Column-based, for example Cassandra, allows rapid access to the data values for one particular variable. This makes the column-based approach very appealing in the write-once read-many Decision Support environment. Document-based databases, for example MongoDB, allow you to store very unstructured data very quickly. This gets around the problem that relational databases have schemas to ensure data stored also follows particular rules, thus meaning you can store any type of data, in any format.

These databases do not have schemas. That is, they do not impose rigorous tests on incoming data. Many database professionals will be uncomfortable with this. Moreover, they tend not to be ACID compliant (see earlier section on OLTP databases). This means they can't easily be used in a transactional environment. Their use, therefore, tends to be in specialist areas, but, nonetheless the big vendors have been watching, and there is now even an Oracle NoSQL solution (http://www.oracle.com/uk/products/database/nosql/overview/index.html).

The same dilemmas that we came across earlier come into play when deciding whether to use these new tools. And the same answer is also true: it will depend upon the organisation making the decision. It is risky to use new technology. The NoSQL tools are quite specialist, whereas a relational database can be made to do most jobs in the IS arena. However, if speed of insert, or speed of analysis of one variable, is really important, these tools may well find their way into the IT department's armoury.

8.9 Summary

In this chapter we discussed what types of systems support an organisation's Information Strategy. We looked at the alternative ownership options offered by cloud, and spoke about the recent trend towards needing to handle vast quantities of data. When deciding which system to use there will usually be many to chose from, from expensive, high quality complete solutions, through to open source, build your own solutions, and the decision will largely depend upon the type of organisation doing the purchasing and their risk averseness.

8.10 Review Questions

The answers to these questions can be found in the text of this chapter.

- What is PeopleSoft? Give the names of some of its competitors
- What does CRUD stand for? Why is it important in databases?
- What does ACID stand for, and which types of database need ACID compliance, and which do not?

- Give three examples of filetypes that can be used when moving data between different systems
- What are Hadoop's two key elements

8.11 Group Work Research Activities

These activities require you to research beyond the contents of the book and can be tackled individually or as a discussion group.

8.11.1 Discussion Topic 1

As the newly appointed CIO of a medium sized organisation you discover your in-house information systems are not fit for purpose. They were built by a part-time computer programmer when your company was only a small business and they clearly do not scale. You quickly need to decide what systems you might use to replace existing legacy systems. Review the risks and relative strengths and weaknesses of using a full, company-wide application solution, like SAP or Oracle, compared to rebuilding in-house using Open Source software.

8.11.2 Discussion Topic 2

"*There is nothing new in Big Data except the badge.*" Discuss this assertion and then consider where an organisation might look for data now that they could not have looked in previously.

References

Biscoe J (2013) History of public supply in the UK. [online]. Last accessed 25 Nov 2013 at: http://www.engineering-timelines.com/how/electricity/electricity_07.asp

Dunlop J (2011) 20 Websites Making The Most Money. Income Diary. [online]. Posted 2011. last accessed 25 Nov 2013 at: http://www.incomediary.com/20-websites-making-the-most-money #How_Much_Does_Amazon_Google_and_Facebook_Make

Lake P, Crowther P (2013) Concise guide to databases, Springer, London. ISBN 978-1-4471-5601-7

Tewary A (2013) Ideally what should be percentage of IT spent of an organization relative to its revenue? [online]. Last accessed Nov 2013 at: http://www.linkedin.com/groups/Ideally-what-should-be-percentage-51825.S.40701712

Unknown (2009) Deutsche börse AG triples speed of xentric order routing system with in-memory database. [online]. Last accessed 29 Nov 2013 at: http://www.oracle.com/technetwork/products/timesten/overview/deutsche-borse-db-snapshot-130682.pdf

Unnamed, Oracle (2013) Database certification: 11g certified database administrators. [online]. Last accessed 25 Nov 2013 at: http://education.oracle.com/pls/web_prod-plq-dad/db_pages.getpage?page_id=458&get_params=p_track_id:Datab11g

Sources

9

9.1 What the Reader Will Learn

- that the data in Big Data is different in a number of ways
- that there are, however, some immutable characteristics of data regardless of how it is stored
- that data can be acquired in many ways but that its quality is always its most important attribute
- that data ownership is becoming a very important aspect of information systems
- that data sources can be processed in many different ways to cope with differing requirements

9.2 Data Sources for Data – Both Big and Small

As we will see in this chapter, acquiring data to the point where it is useful, regardless of whether the data is "Big" or not, often requires three key stages:

1. Accessing the data. This may include searching for the data, pre-retrieval analysis or summary of the data, and access rights if the data does not belong to us.
2. Processing the data. This may include some data cleansing or analysis.
3. Storing the data.

In terms of actually acquiring data there are many sources now available over and beyond the traditional in-company data. Some government data in many Western nations is now publicly available, and we talk a little about the open data movement in this chapter. In the UK much of this data is available through a central URL: http://data.gov.uk/

Another new phenomenon in terms of the potential source for data is the publicly available repository of vast amounts of data, such as Infochimps: http://www.infochimps.com/company/about/ . Some data sets here are free to use, whilst others are only available for a fee. The variety of data in this site continues to grow: data from Wikipedia pages; data about airports; data about music – the list is immense. In effect Infochimps are acting as brokers and data is the commodity. They also provide paid-for expertise in the area of data science.

9.3 The Four Vs – Understanding What Makes Data Big Data

We explored what is meant by the phrase Big Data in chapter One. Whilst the fact that there is often a lot of data involved, it would be inaccurate to think that Big Data is only about large volumes of data. Indeed, if it was only about volume, this would hardly be a new topic. As Lake and Crowther (2013) remind us:

> Roger Magoulas from O'Reilly media is credited with the first usage of the term 'Big Data' in the way we have come to understand it, in 2005. But as a distinct, well defined topic, it is younger even than that. However Springer's Very Large Databases (VLDB) Journal has been in existence since 1992. Whilst early hard disk drives were relatively small, Mainframes had been dealing with large volumes of data since the 1950s.

So what other attributes does Big Data have to differentiate it from plain, old-fashioned ordinary data?

For many organisations, their critical business data is simply held in a relational database (RDBMS). Anything not in the database is not important to them, and all the data collected is owned by them. Sometimes the data is not available until the end of the month. The data collected and processed is always the same every month. This description is over-simplified but it does represent an approximation of the way standard, non-"Big" data is handled. To summarise, for comparison with Big Data, there is not a huge amount of data with which the RDBMS cannot cope; the timescales for data movement are not short; the same data is collected during every cycle; the data is of known repute since it belongs to the company (Fig. 9.1).

Now let us compare this picture with the attributes that many commentators are saying make Big Data different. People are tending to refer to the **Four Vs** model as the 4 attributes they point to are:

Volume: The obvious one! Big Data often means many gigabytes, or even terabytes of data. Whilst the professional databases, such as Oracle and SQLServer can cope with large amounts of data, there does come an upper limit to what is suitable for storage in an RDBMS. However, even if the data is suitable for storage

9.3 The Four Vs – Understanding What Makes Data Big Data

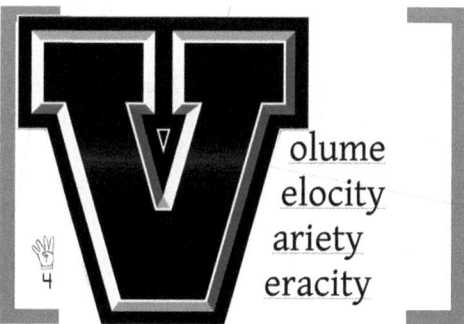

Fig. 9.1 The four Vs

in an RDBMS, its size may well make processing the data a very lengthy job. Volume is therefore something for data scientists to worry about.

Velocity: Data is available instantly from many sources these days. If you want to know what the value of certain shares are on the London Stock exchange you do not have to wait until tomorrow's Financial Times is published, you can get real time information directly from the exchange. What was a daily cycle has become instant. And this is just one of many examples of how we can often access data immediately. Creating internal systems that react to changes instantly presents the data professional with many challenges when compared with the traditional weekly or monthly cycle of data updates.

Variety: Data of all sorts is now available that never was before. For example it is now possible to mine all of Twitter to look specifically for what people are saying about your newly launched product and thus gain immediate market intelligence. As well as social media sources, governments around the world are beginning to make their data available to all through Open Data initiatives. Again, this was just not available only a few years ago. To add to the complexity of the variety attribute, the sources may present their data in one of many different formats: xml, json, csv, spreadsheets, for example.

Veracity: Because the data doesn't always belong to you care needs to be taken when using externally sourced data. One would hope that government data is factual, but there may be political reasons for some data being more available than others. And social media may be an interesting place to fish for intelligence, but it also contains a lot of useless information that needs to be sifted through. Ensuring data quality is of paramount importance for the data scientist as we see later in this chapter.

The 4 Vs do make Big Data different, but we can be sure that this observation will only be of interest for a few years since, by then, Big Data will be swallowed up by the general term Data. IS professionals are, and have always been, responsible for accessing and processing all the data an organisation needs to function.

9.4 Categories of Data

Data can be categorised in a number of ways. The two perspectives we will use are organisational purpose, and storage, with the latter encompassing issues around datatypes and serialisation techniques. We saw in Chap. 6 that data can go on to become Information and then Knowledge and you should bear this in mind when we talk about purpose. However, here we are talking about the raw material for information – data – and its sources.

9.4.1 Classification by Purpose

For many years businesses have collected and stored data relevant to areas in their business. For example the Sales department will need to collect data about the volumes of products sold, and their price. The Human Resources (HR) department will hold information about employees and contracts. The nature of this data can be very different. HR data will tend to be wordier than sales data, for example. And for over 30 years, the relational database has been the one-size-fits-all receptacle for the majority of this data.

For many years, in many organisations, the norm was for data to be collected and managed by the department concerned. Often this went further and the department would be responsible for selecting the applications and databases used to handle the data. This results in "silos" of data sitting in their own separate systems. Logically, perhaps, some of the data should be related to data in other silos, but because of the partitioned architecture gaining an understanding at the organisation-wide level can be very difficult. Managers and executives often have to make do with a suite of individual reports from each department, forcing them to make connections for themselves.

As a simple example, consider the data connected with a salesperson out on the road selling products:

The Sales Department of a company called United Transport Solutions (UTS) has a system for recording how much product was sold to which customer, when, at what price and by whom. In their system they have a Unique Identifier for each salesman. Chris is a salesman and his reference number is 0124 as he was the 124th person to join the sales team.

The HR department was responsible for recruiting and employing Chris. They have a personnel system and every employee has a Unique Identifier in that system. In this case it is S1107. The ID has the department as the lead character (S for sales) and then Chris was the 1107th person employed by the company.

Not surprisingly Chris's favourite part of working for the company is pay-day, especially if Chris had sold above quota and is entitled to a bonus. The company outsources its payroll to a third-party organisation called PayrollsRUs (PRU). In the PRU system Chris is uniquely identified as UTS0077F. Chris was the 77th employee when the UTS employees were sorted alphabetically by surname. The F indicates a full-time employee.

Obviously, without getting into deep existential philosophical arguments we can easily see that the Chris who sells products is the same Chris who gets paid at the end, despite the fact that the process identifies Chris as 0124 followed by S1107 and then UTS0077F. Unfortunately our computer systems are not as good at inference as humans and they will not know of any connection unless someone has built those connections in.

Now, in the circumstances we have outlined above, picture yourself as an executive who wants to do some research on their sales teams. Maybe they want to ask the simple question: do employees who have longer lengths of service earn more commission than newer employees?

The sales system, which is an Oracle relational database, contains information about sales by individuals. The Personnel system, which is SQLServer based will be able to give information about length of service and the payroll system will be able to return the commission earned. If all the systems had been written for the same database and the executive had authority to access the three sources, the executive might have been able to write a very complicated SELECT which joined the data from the three systems provided there was an intermediary table which mapped the various Unique Identifiers to actual people.

In reality, since the data is held in different databases, and in the case of the Payroll system, not even on-site, this question would either be declared too difficult and not asked or, typically, data from each of the three systems would be downloaded to the executive's spreadsheet where the joining process would take place. The weakness here is that it requires skills that many executives don't possess, and even if they do, the process can be very time-consuming.

This situation is not an exaggeration and many readers may recognise the silo picture for themselves. Big Data does not help when an organisation has this disjointed approach to its data – if anything it will compound the problem by adding yet more disparate data sources.

The problem can best be solved by thinking about data at an organisation-wide level rather than in silos. Of course different departments will always need to store data which is unique to them, but where data is describing the same object (as with Chris above) then, systems designers began to recognise, those objects ought to be at least connected, if not identified uniquely only once across the organisation. In the 1990s Enterprise Resource Planning systems began to be adopted, as we discussed in Chap. 3, especially in large organisations for whom silos were a significant problem. The aim was to have integrated data allowing error-free transactions and queries across all internal departments. They provided a single view of data about all the key functions within the organisation, using a single database to store that data.

Most ERP systems are modular. There may be common modules, such as for finance, which are adopted by all departments, but not all departments have to adopt ERP in one fell swoop and implementation is often targeted at one department first as a pilot. Indeed, some modules may never be adopted: there is no need for UTS, for example, to adopt the manufacturing module as they do not make anything.

ERP has a reputation for being expensive and the key providers are certainly rich organisations. Oracle and SAP are two of the biggest providers, for example, of ERP solutions. However, that expense has to be offset against the cost savings that such an approach allows, and the relative ease with which organisational key information can be acquired from the integrated system. Since we are discussing data sources here we will not say anything else about ERP systems, but there is more about them in the Structures chapter.

All of these business functions, regardless of whether their applications are part of an integrated enterprise-wide system or not, will have a variety of data sources. A retail organisation's largest flow of data may well be from its Point of Sales (POS) systems – ultimately data coming from the tills as customers purchase products. That data is likely to be largely numeric and to come in short but regular pulses, depending on how active the shop is. This is important when thinking about database design since the size of the packet of data, known as a data block, is defined when the database is created. These blocks, which contain data are what is passed around the system, usually via a network. If the block size is defined, say, as 32 kbytes, but the actual data is made up of only 2 kbytes of data then we are sending 30 kbytes of no interest in the transmission and this will have a significant impact on network's loads and database performance.

Why, then, do we not just define data block sizes as small, say 2 kbytes? Well, if the data sent is typically 6 kbytes in size we will need 3 blocks. Each block contains header information, and then the blocks need to be joined together to make a record, all of which takes time.

Typically this sort of system, often referred to as Online Transaction Processing System (OLTP) will have the data block size set at a much smaller size than a decision support type system where the data being manipulated is often much larger as the user tries to discover statistical information by reviewing a whole column or columns from a very large table. We can see that the source of the data will have fundamental impact upon the design of the systems we create.

9.4.2 Data Type Classification and Serialisation Alternatives

The data we have discussed above can be a mixture of types. In everyday life we differentiate between data-types in that we have numbers and characters. A label on a market stall may say "Basil 2.20". The data here is actually in four parts, in spite of there being only two data items: The label which describes the product, the numbers which describe the cost, and two pieces of inferred data which is that the currency is whatever the local currency is (let us assume British pound sterling) and that the cost is £2.20 per bunch. The two important data-types for normal human beings are words and numbers.

For database professionals, however, the way data is stored usually forces the adoption of many more than these two data-types. Lake and Crowther (2013) explain the building blocks of data storage thus:

9.4 Categories of Data

[…] a modern computer-based database system's primary purpose is to store and retrieve binary digits (bits). All the data in even the most highly encrypted critical systems, resolves itself into a series of 1s and 0s, or Ons and Offs. Since only simple, boolean data such as true/false or Yes/No can be stored in a bit, eight bits are connected together to form a unit called a byte which can store an unsigned integer of between 0 and 255. If the first bit is used to sign the subsequent value (+ or -), then the byte can store 0–127.

Various encoding systems have been used to allow the numbers in a byte to represent characters. Perhaps the most famous, and still in use, with western character sets, is ASCII. Text datatypes are relative simple, but even objects like audio or images can be stored in a database. Oracle, for example, has the Blob (Binary Large Object) which is a variable-length string of bits up to 2,147,483,647 characters long.

Because the data is usually made permanent using magnetic devices such as a Hard Disk Drive (HDD), and because such devices cost money, most data-types are there to minimise storage. As well as reducing the amount stored, and thus saving money, minimising the number of bytes used can also help improving database performance.

These drivers result in what ordinary humans call a number data-type being divided into several data-types such as: SmallInt, Integer, Decimal, Real, Double… the list could go on and is different in different databases. This is not a computer science chapter so we will not go into great detail here, but we should recognise that an Integer takes up less storage than does a Real.

When designing a relational database the data-type of every column needs to be defined. As well as the need to minimise data storage by defining data appropriately, this is also because RDBMSs are required to ensure the integrity of all data inserted. Every data item is checked against a schema (set of rules) to make sure that a column defined as, for example, an integer, does not have a character inserted into it. Failure to meet this rule results in record rejection.

This is not always the case with some of the newer NoSQL databases which are schema-less and allow any data types to be stored. They rely on the user, or client applications, to ensure that the data stored is valid. For those used to the rules-regulated world of relational databases this sounds dangerous. Indeed, there are dangers in this approach, as with any approach that relies on users, but the massively reduced overhead in processing an insert that result from not having to check data against a schema means that inserts can be dramatically quicker, and there are circumstances where speed of insert is needed more than guaranteeing the integrity of the data.

We have so far talked about the way data is stored in databases. Another key aspect of database systems is the way that data is captured and moved. Let us go back to our POS system. These days many supermarkets would argue that a barcode is their most valuable data. The cashier merely swipes the barcode over the reader and the system instantly knows all about the product. The barcode is actually merely a string of characters – a series of black bars and white spaces of varying widths which are printed on product labels to uniquely identify the product. A scanner will read the bars and then some software will convert those bars into a product identifier which can then be used up look up the current price from the store's database. When recorded it is usual for the translation to be stored, rather than the actual barcode, since it is not possible to write an SQL query with a barcode used as an identifier. This is the movement of data from a source to a target which involves some physical changes to the actual data being moved.

Similar data movement happens all over most data systems. Going back to our previous example, when Chris was engaged by HR they would have entered his details into their Personnel system. In order to ensure he gets paid, they will have to notify the Payroll system of his existence and pass on a few details they have captured from his acceptance form, such as his address and bank account details. For many organisations where the silos are still in place and are particularly isolated the only way to do this is through that other frequent data transport medium: paper. Personnel run a report which prints Chris's details and then they send that to Payroll, who key the data in.

Obviously a system-to-system electronic transfer would be more efficient and less error prone. Many database systems are able to output data in the form of a text file. The text file is then moved to the target system, which reads it in and uses it to create and perform an *Insert*. Two very common forms of text files are Comma Separated Values and Fixed Length. The former is a list of values which is separated by a comma (although other characters can be used) and would look something like this for our example:

Marlowe, Christopher, 03-02-1966, "10, Dog Lane, Preston", WY460799A

This would be passed to the target system as-is if the format of the rows was already agreed, or with a header which describes what the values were if not. The header might look like this:

Surname, First, DateOfBirth, Address, NICode

Similarly a Fixed Length file could have a header, but there are no separators as all the data for a particular field have to lay within the agreed position. So the same line might look like:

Marlowe   Christopher   03-02-1966   10, Dog Lane, Preston   WY460799A

In more recent times data transfer has often been accomplished using Extensible Markup Language (XML). This is a mark-up language which has rules for encoding data in a format that is both human- and machine-readable. The opening of our example could look like this:

<Surname>
  Marlowe
</Surname>
<First>
  Christopher
</First>

Notice how each data item has its descriptor in < > and the field is ended by </ >

What we have identified above is three forms of serialisation. That is, a translation has been made from some existing data such as a row, in a table, in a MySQL database so that it can be stored outside of the source database. The purpose is often so that the data can be transported to a target database which will use it to construct its own data structure.

Other forms of serialisation exist and there is a tendency for one to become the preferred technique in certain areas. JavaScript Object Notation (JSON – pronounced Jayson), is an open standard format which uses, much as does XML, human-readable text to transmit data objects. As the "J" suggests this is often preferred in the Java or JavaScript programming fraternity.

So far we have talked about data being dumped into some form of text file. Especially when the format is heavily descriptive, as with XML, file sizes can get unwieldy and entirely out of proportion with the actual volumes of data being moved. If there is no need to for the transported data to be read by a human it is possible to apply a compression algorithm to the XML file. Binary XML is such a compression of XML and its use will reduce the file size, this speeding both network transmission and parsing at the target end.

Different functional databases which are from the same vendor (perhaps they are both Oracle) can exchange data in even more efficient ways. Oracle uses its Export facility to allow rows, tables or entire databases to be moved from one instance to another. At the target end the export file is read using the Import utility.

The data we have been considering so far is what could loosely be called "traditional" data. There is nothing new for the seasoned database professional who has been dealing with data and its movement for decades. Big Data does make a difference in terms of what data sources are available and how best to deal with data which is often external.

Many Big Data projects will have Hadoop (see Chaps. 8 and 11) as the target data store and, being written in and extendible with Java it is not surprising that JSON is often the preferred serialisation medium for such projects. Many open data sources now use JSON as the standard response format for requests for data. When mining Twitter for trends (see Chap. 11) the response is likely to be JSON.

The other categorisation that could be considered as a direct result of Big Data is the data's periodicity. Whilst POS systems do have to collect data throughout the day, reporting systems tend, in traditional systems, to be based around weekly, monthly or annual cycles. If you have an automated flood warning system that is using water level monitors to send back data from rivers every second then the reporting cycle will need to be far more regular, or even in "real time" (Real time systems respond to events as they happen). Similarly, the overall sentiment in a Twitter mine can change very quickly if there is suddenly a flurry of tweets about the product, perhaps as a result of someone famous tweeting about it. Decisions made about the product's popularity can be out of date in minutes.

9.5 Data Quality

The term Data Quality describes the suitability of any given data for the particular use it is intended for; such as for decision making or use in operational systems. The most obvious characteristic of high quality data is that it is accurate, but IBM (2014) suggest other characteristics are as important:

> **Complete**: All relevant data —such as accounts, addresses and relationships for a given customer—is linked.
> **Accurate**: Common data problems like misspellings, typos, and random abbreviations have been cleaned up.
> **Available**: Required data is accessible on demand; users do not need to search manually for the information.
> **Timely**: Up-to-date information is readily available to support decisions.
> http://www-01.ibm.com/software/data/quality/

Ensuring that data is of high quality is of absolute importance. Low quality data will result in poor information and poor decisions. The significant reduction in the cost of storage media in the last decade followed by the avalanche of data that can result from Big Data, however, means that the challenge for the data scientist is more difficult because of the complexity of the incoming data.

Even thinking of one simple example – the POS scenario – there are so many places that data quality can be less than perfect. What if the barcode reader misreads the barcode? If the shopper is not observant they may end up getting charged for the wrong product. And then the data has to go down the line to the central system for recording. Such data is packaged up and sent down the network cable. Network cables are prone to a number of problems which are consequent upon the way they work. Data is turned into packets of electrons which are then fired down the wire and then, when they reach their target, they are unpacked to become data again. To send more data down the line the frequency is increased and the greater the frequency the more likely it is that problems will occur. Better quality cables is one way to lessen the risks.

On its journey the data can get lost or corrupted because of a variety of reasons. The length of the cable, for example, can be a factor because of natural attenuation – the fact that signals get weaker the further they travel. And to add to the complexity, attenuation is affected by temperature, so what is too long a cable today may be OK tomorrow! There way well be unwanted signals which are not part of the data also travelling on the cable, and this is known as noise. Noise can come from external devices such as nearby electric motors or overhead fluorescent lights. This noise can interfere with the package content and corrupt the data within. This is not a networking chapter, but suffice it to say there are, of course, mechanisms that can be put in place to lessen these problems, and flag corrupted data. However, as we can see, there are many places where things can go wrong.

So far we have seen ways that automatic processes can result in poor quality data. For many systems, however, there is an even bigger potential weakness: human interaction. Whether it is a customer filling in a webpage with information

9.5 Data Quality

about where to deliver products, or a data-entry clerk in a call centre, humans can cause errors.

As we have to accept there can be problems with the entry and movement of data, the next step is to provide some sort of quality assurance. This usually involves some form of data validation to discover inconsistencies in the data and, where necessary and possible, cleanse the data.

There are many different validation processes. In terms of checking data input, for example on an application data entry form, or a web-page equivalent, two types of check are often used to prevent the user inputting bad data:

(i) **Form Level checking**: Ensures that all mandatory data items are completed, for example. It is also possible to do consistency checking between fields: If the user has entered Female in the Gender field then the Title field should be either Mrs or Miss or Ms.
(ii) **Field Level checking**: To prevent data-type mismatches, such as a number being entered in a Name field, or no "@" character in an email field.

The user should be provided with as much assistance as possible to help avoid mistakes. A well designed form, for example, might prevent the Gender/Title problem mentioned above by adapting the drop-down list of possible titles to list only those that agree with the Gender entered on the form. This does take more programming effort and so sometimes is overlooked.

Field Level checks can include:

- **Range checking**: To make sure that the data lies within a specific range of values, such as ensuring that the Day element of a Date field is an integer between 1 and 31.
- **Special character checking**: to make sure that character like "?" or "^" are not allowed to be entered into a Name field, even though they are characters and would therefore pass the data type test.
- **Referential integrity:** Relational databases may check values against values in another table through the foreign key relationship. For example, a user may be prevented from entering Paris as the Branch they work in if Paris is not in the list of Branches held in a related table. Again, sensible design can help prevent this by populating a drop-down list from the Branches table and only allowing the user to select from that list.
- **Language checking**: If the field is text based it is possible for the input to be validated against spelling and grammar rules.
- **Uniqueness checking:** Ensures that each value is unique. This is especially relevant if the field is a Primary Key in the underlying table. Several fields together can be concatenated into a Primary Key: House Number, Street Name and Town, for example, might be the unique identifier for a record.

This sort of validation is often carried out at the client end – that is, on the web-page or form the user is entering into – rather than at the database end. Where the validation is carried out is primarily a performance driven decision. Assuming the target is a RDBMS, the database will, however, have built in integrity checks to further guard against data which does not abide by business rules.

In the era of Big Data however, we have to remember that there will be a variety of data sources being used, and not all of them will be under our control. Data coming from a Twitter trawl, for example, has had little by way of client-end validation applied to it. Furthermore, as we said at the beginning of this section, quality is not just about accuracy. Timeliness of information can be critical when accessing external data, for example. A Twitter trawl to examine what people think about Doncaster Rovers football team initiated at 3 pm, just as today's match is due to kick-off, may well generate a different picture to that generated were the trawl to be started after the match in which they won 7–0 and played superb flowing football!

Some post entry checking can be applied to standardise the data which may have not broken the validation checks but which, if left, may leave the data less usable. My fellow author is always known to me as Bob. He calls himself Bob on LinkedIn and in many other places. And yet the contract Springer has is with a certain Robert Drake. We can see that this is the same person, but a computer system would be too stupid to work out that if it had Bob's phone number it didn't need to ask for Robert's!

Fuzzy Logic techniques can be applied to data to look for this sort of anomaly. It could, for example, change all Bobs into Roberts. However, can we guarantee there are no Bobs registered as Bobs at birth? My mother was christened Betty. It wasn't an abbreviation of Elizabeth, so any global replace would actually make her record less accurate if it was changed to Elizabeth.

Which leads us on to the next question in assuring the quality of data – what do we do about data that is possibly wrong?

The most important thing for us to recognise as data professionals is that it is not our job to guess! Were you to see a patient's record with a blank in the field "Allergic to Penicillin" and you change it to a "No" you could cause the patient to die. One might think only a stupid person would do that. But what about the data entry clerk who is repeatedly hitting "N" and then "Enter" to legitimately fill in a lot of missing "N"s in the adjacent field which is "Attended Clinic". They inadvertently hit the tab key between records and end up in the "Allergic to Penicillin" field, and then continue entering potentially lethal "N"s. Now the person is less culpable and the form designer is perhaps more at fault for allowing this to happen.

We have to recognise that data is far more than just ons-and-offs on a magnetic medium. Care is needed, but so too are quality assurance techniques. When problems are discovered the answer needs to come from the data owner, not the data processor. In the penicillin case that may be a qualified medical professional, or perhaps the patients themselves. We discuss data ownership later in this chapter.

9.5.1 Extract, Transform and Load (ETL)

Data Warehousing has become an established area of study in its own right. A data warehouse is typically a central database used for reporting and data analysis. It will often consist of data from many, if not all, disparate locations of an enterprise's data stores. Because their focus is managerial rather than operational they tend to **extract** subsets of the raw data in OLTOP systems like the Sales, or Purchasing systems. Sometimes the data is **Transformed** by summarising or aggregating. Some cleansing or conversion may be needed too. Perhaps, in a multinational company, some outlets record sales of products by the Yard, whilst others use Meter. For the data to be usefully compared the warehouse needs to store data in a single unit of measure. After the data is manipulated, it is **loaded** into the warehouse.

This process can be a complex and lengthy one, requiring many passes through potentially huge operational data stores before entering the extract phase. The reason for storing the data in a separate warehouse, rather than running queries against the original data is primarily performance related. Once in the warehouse summarised data can be analysed far more efficiently. There is, however, a knock-on effect that the extract phase can impact adversely on the performance of the OLTP system. Systems with low usage rates at night will often run extracts overnight, for example.

Traditionally data warehouses have contained subsets of the organisation's own data. Big Data brings with it the probability that some important decision making information is available from elsewhere. Whatever the source, the same arguments set out early apply to data warehousing in terms of the quality of the data held in them. With data warehouses sometimes this is as simple as asking the end users if the data they see is appropriate. However, there is usually also a need to profile, cleanse, and audit the data that has been moved.

Interestingly the advent of Hadoop (see the Systems chapter) has led people to ask if we are beginning to see the end of a need for ETL since Hadoop is immensely scalable and, in theory therefore, does not need summarising.

The debate is described in this InformationWeek article (Henschen 2012):

> …historical systems were not large enough to cost-effectively store, transform, analyze and report or consume data in a single place. Times and technology change, of course, and since Hadoop came to the enterprise, we are beginning to see the end of ETL as we know it. This is not just an idea or a desire, it is really possible and the evolution is underway.
>
> With Hadoop as a data hub in an enterprise data architecture, we now have a cost-effective, extreme-performance environment to store, transform and consume data, without traditional ETL.
>
> http://www.informationweek.com/big-data/big-data-analytics/big-data-debate-end-near-for-etl/d/d-id/1107641?

9.6 Meta Data

Meta data is data about data. Traditional library card-based indexes are an example of this. Cards would contain data about the book's author, title and subject matter together with an alpha-numeric identification system which would point to the physical location of the book on the library's shelves.

With digital systems we continue to need this meta data to help guide to the information we need. The sort of data we store about data can include:

- The purpose of the data
- The time and date of creation
- The time and date of any alterations or deletions
- The physical location – a URL or a folder name perhaps
- The creator or editor of the data

As this is data the obvious place to store it is in a database, often in what is called a Meta data Repository. RDBMSs have such a repository built into them which is sometimes called the Data Dictionary. This contains the schema information which describes things like the data type a particular piece of data must be.

For all the same reasons as we gave for the need of Data Quality when talking about actual data, we also need to ensure that our meta data is accurate and useful. Meta data is becoming far more important as the open data movement gathers pace. People shopping around for data need to know what data is before maybe spending hours needlessly downloading terabytes of unwanted data. Figure 9.2 shows an example of how Meta Data is displayed on the UK government's Open Data site.

Metadata can be just as valuable as the data itself. In telling the story of the Petraeus scandal of 2012, the Guardian (Guardian US interactive team, 2013) give an example of what metadata is wrapped round something as simple as a tweet (See Fig. 9.3). As they describe, the Head of the CIA in the US took what he thought were sensible steps to prevent private messages to his mistress being intercepted on the internet by setting up an email account for them to share in which they wrote draft emails, but never sent them, allowing them to read each others messages. Unfortunately they logged in from various hotels' public Wi-Fi, and that left a trail of metadata that included times and locations which allowed the FBI to prove the connection between them.

9.6.1 Internet of Things (IoT)

Metadata is coming to the fore in the *"internet of things"*. The IoT is about connecting all objects to each other by using the ubiquitous internet to allow the objects to be remotely controlled or interrogated. Each object has information stored about what it is, where it is, and any number of other metadata items and they connect by a variety of means including radio-frequency identification (RFID) chips, Bluetooth or Wi-Fi.

9.6 Meta Data

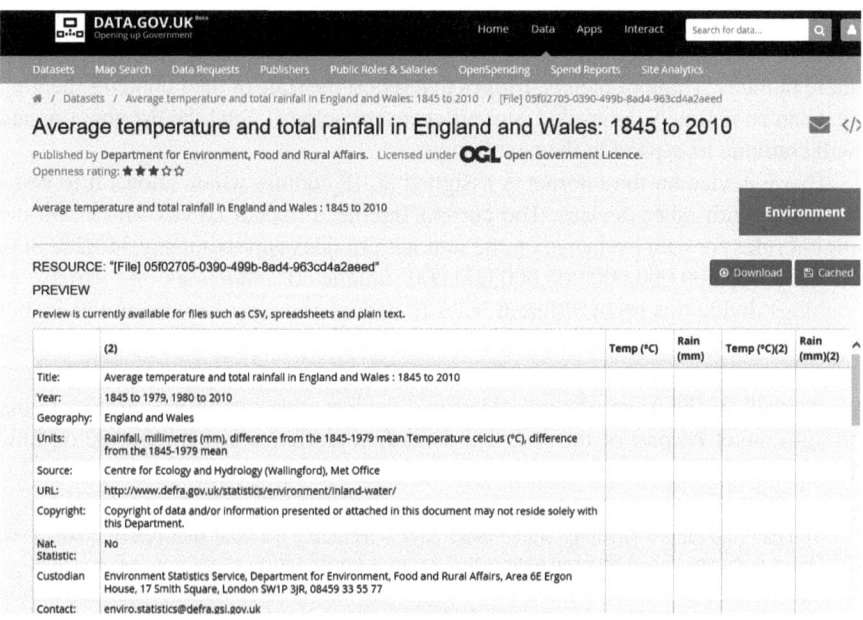

Fig. 9.2 An example of meta data as seen on the UK data.Gov site

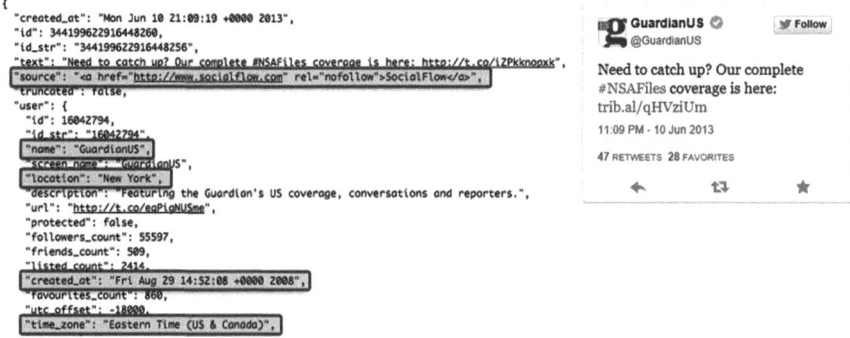

Fig. 9.3 Metadata from a tweet

This is not science fiction, and it is much more than connecting smart phones and tablets. Typical households could be generating much more internet traffic than mere humans. Think of meters, fridges that report the state of their contents, heating that can be remotely controlled, surveillance technology... and the list goes on, and will continue to expand in the next few years.

Every device on the Internet is assigned an IP address which allows it to communicate with other devices. The current Internet Protocol (IPv6) which sets the digital rules for data exchange on the internet provides approximately 340,282,366, 920,938,000,000,000,000,000,000,000,000 unique IP addresses. A variety of weblogs divide this up in different ways to demonstrate just how many this is, but suffice it to say it is several thousand addresses for each person alive today. So there is room for some extension beyond mobile telephony devices!

As well as the more obvious electronic devices, there is no reason why living things cannot be part of the IoT. The Guardian (Jefferies 2011) reported on how cows were connected:

> You can find almost anything online these days – including the vital statistics of cows. A Dutch company called Sparked has created a sensor implant that can measure a cow's vital signs, with the data transmitted to a server for access by farmers, who can instantly determine the health of the herd and respond when an animal is sick or pregnant. The animals' movements, eating habits and response to environmental factors can also be monitored.
> http://www.theguardian.com/local-government-network/2011/aug/18/internet-of-things-local-government

What a data file and cows on the internet have in common are that they need to have metadata to describe what they are to be of any use to a human. The IoT can be thought of a framework of as metadata that sits on top of the existing infrastructure. Things as disparate as cows and data files need the means of conceptual description to be very flexible. The Resource Description Framework (RDF) was designed for metadata modelling and it is fast becoming the preferred means of describing the elements of the IoT. The subject of an RDF statement is known as a uniform resource identifier (URI).

RDF uses "triples" each consisting of a subject, a predicate and an object. This can give us the ability to describe a Thing with attributes, or relate a Thing to another Thing. Here are a couple of examples which use RDF notation to describe this author's relationship with his father:

Thing Property Value
../person/A name "Peter"
../person/A name "Eric"

Thing Property Thing
../person/A hasParent ../person/B

With an agreed framework where, for example, hasParent is a Property that is in a shared dictionary and used by all, linking data between objects becomes easy. This allows exciting things to happen in the not too distant future, such as:

> Your diary notices that tomorrow is Valentine's day. It contacts your fridge to see if it contains any champagne. Seeing that it doesn't it alters your last meeting that day to finish 10 min earlier than before so that you can call in to the wine merchant's to buy a special bottle. But you are in a strange town and you need to find where the nearest merchant is, so your sat-nav in your car is programmed to go home via the merchant's. All perfectly doable and may well prevent marital fallings-out!

9.7 Data Ownership

In Chap. 10 we will look at data protection in more detail, especially from a legal perspective. However, one of the most significant pieces of metadata about data is: who owns it? This question is not really as simple as it sounds and we perhaps need to be absolutely clear about what we mean by owning data.

You might think that you own that most personal of data about yourself – your name. Even forgetting the slight complication that given names are most frequently imposed on you by parents in your youth, you can, of course change the name people call you merely by introducing yourself as Brad, instead of Bradley. Your family name, however, is not yours to change. In many western societies the only way to change that is through some legal means such as deed-poll or, in some societies, by getting married and taking your spouse's name.

Ultimately though there may be rules to abide by first, it is up to the individual to decide what their name is. In short I could, after paying money and filling in forms, become known as Mickey Mouse, but no-one in society can force me to be called that. So ownership of data is ultimately about who can change the data. However, as we have seen, data is all around us. The owners can decide to share their privileges and allow others to alter the data. They can decide whether it can be copied, or moved, read or even deleted.

Unlike an individual's name, organisational data is often not obviously owned by individuals but is a shared asset within the organisation. Some heavily departmentalised organisations might actually say that, for example, sales data "belongs" to the Sales Department, rather than the entire organisation, but in terms of ownership this is only a matter of scale. It is still a group of people who input and maintain the same data, rather than just one person. Moreover an organisation's data tends to move through the organisation, sometimes being summarised or amended on its way, sometimes being stored in different systems, and end up being reported upon in many different formats. Ownership of data in these circumstances becomes more difficult. It is clear that the technical teams, such as Database Administrators, have some responsibilities. But who is given the ultimate responsibility of ownership?

In reality there are any number of possible answers to that question. Sometimes it would be a Project Leader or a Data manager. Sometimes there will be a team based approach, but with the team leader being ultimately responsible. It is, however, very important that responsibility is clearly laid out. This is especially so when the individual employee and organisation can disagree, or when two collaborating organisations work together. Typically, for example, research data belongs to institutes not to the researchers themselves. If data is collected using public funds it is public property – hence the recent drive towards open data in western governments.

Cloud computing has caused a bit of a panic in the recent past as horror stories began to spread of service providers not deleting or returning data to their customers when the latter tried to close the contract and the worry that ownership rights could be compromised was probably a barrier to early cloud adoption. Things have moved on since those early days and although service providers' customers do need to check contracts carefully, most providers now include wording in their standard contracts such as: *all rights, title and interest, including intellectual property and proprietary rights, remain yours.*

Naturally ownership of data is important for Data Scientists in the era of Big Data. There are debates to be had about the sentiment analysis data mining against Twitter entries being carried out of the sort that we review in Chaps. 8 and 11. There is no doubt that the Terms and Conditions of joining Twitter will include the customer allowing Twitter to sell the data on to other parties, so the question is ethical rather than legal. However there may well be people who use twitter and do not know that in doing so they are providing market researchers with valuable information. And yet, walking down the high street, if I am approached by a researcher they have to identify themselves and then ask my permission to ask some questions – a far more controlled approach to data gathering.

Remembering the V for Variety in our attributes of Big Data, it is clear that the data user in this era is going to have to learn to work with metadata to allow them to find useful data. They will also have to ensure that they work with owners of the data they want to analyse if it belongs to others.

9.8 Crowdsourcing

We have thus far been talking of a person, or organisation, gathering data from many sources and processing it. What if we reverse that model and suggest that an organisation can provide data to many individuals or sub-contractors and ask them to process the data? This is called crowdsourcing. It is a relatively new concept and there are many different takes on what is actually happening when organisations, in effect, outsource to many.

In an attempt to help define this new term Estellés-Arolas and Gonzalez-Ladron-De-Guevara (2012) explored all the current literature on Crowdsourcing and identified these key attributes:

About the Crowd:
(a) who forms it;
(b) what it has to do;
(c) what it gets in return.

9.8 Crowdsourcing

About the Initiator:
(d) who it is;
(e) what it gets in return for the work of the crowd.

About the Process:
(f) the type of process it is;
(g) the type of call used;
(h) the medium used.

The same paper proposes this definition:

> Crowdsourcing is a type of participative online activity in which an individual, an institution, a non-profit organization, or company proposes to a group of individuals of varying knowledge, heterogeneity, and number, via a flexible open call, the voluntary undertaking of a task. The undertaking of the task, of variable complexity and modularity, and in which the crowd should participate bringing their work, money, knowledge and/or experience, always entails mutual benefit. The user will receive the satisfaction of a given type of need, be it economic, social recognition, self-esteem, or the development of individual skills, while the crowdsourcer will obtain and utilize to their advantage what the user has brought to the venture, whose form will depend on the type of activity undertaken.

Science has been an early adopter of crowdsourcing. It can be made to work like a giant brainstorm, using countless would-be scientists all connected by the internet. Alternatively it can be used as a way of massively distributing computing by utilising the relatively high powered PCs sitting around doing nothing in people's homes to tackle small individual computing problems which form part of a larger one. The process can be is very simple for the crowd. Often all they need to do is install a screensaver that carries out calculations when their computers are idle.

It is, for example, used to process radio signals to detect alien transmissions as part of the Search for Extraterrestrial Intelligence (SETI) project. As reported by the BBC (Wakefield 2012):

> Participants will be asked to search for signs of unusual activity. It is hoped the human brain can find things the automated system might miss. The website is the latest stage in a quest "to empower Earthlings everywhere to become active participants in the ultimate search for cosmic company".
>
> The project is being run by Dr Jillian Tarter, winner of the TED Prize in 2009 and director of the Seti Institute's Center for Seti Research.
>
> [...]
>
> "There are frequencies that our automated signal detection systems now ignore, because there are too many signals there," she said. "Most are created by Earth's communication and entertainment technologies, but buried within this noise there may be a signal from a distant technology. I'm hoping that an army of volunteers can help us deal with these crowded frequency bands that confuse our machines. By doing this in real time, we will have an opportunity to follow up immediately on what our volunteers discover."

Although science, through what are often called *citizen science projects*, has been a key player in the crowdsourcing area, it is not to say that this technique cannot be used by commercial organisations. There are already web resources available to help both crowd members and initiators get together to work on projects where the reward to the crowd is more financial than it tends to be with the science projects.

Some companies use web systems to replace the old "suggestion box" idea to allow them to collect innovative ideas from its employees and then go on to generate projects based on those ideas. BrightIdeas is one such provider: http://www.brightidea.com/. Others are using a similar extension to the "suggestion box" to engage with their customers. Starbucks coffee, for example, has its http://mystarbucksidea.force.com/ system that allows customers to provide ideas about coffee, the environment or experience.

In a similar vein systems exist to allow the crowd to vote, or undertake other tasks. Amazon's mechanical Turk (https://www.mturk.com/mturk/welcome) is one famous such site. If used to find the answer to a question this type of crowdsourcing requires the crowd to select an answer from a number of choices. Rightly or wrongly the answer given by the majority of users is considered to be correct.

9.9 Summary

In this chapter we discussed the fact that Big Data IS different in a number of ways. We saw that data can be acquired in many ways but that its quality is always its most important attribute. Metadata allows us to search for data in our data rich environment and one of the most important pieces of metadata is ownership. We went on to see that as well as a variety of sources for data, we can also have a variety of means of processing the data through cloud delivered crowdsourcing.

9.10 Review Questions

The answers to these questions can be found in the text of this chapter.

- What are the Four Vs which are the attributes of Big Data
- Name at least five datatypes as used in a typical RDBMS
- Why does data in an XML file usually take up more storage than if it were in a CSV file?
- List at least four attributes that could be used as metadata to describe a dataset
- In your own words, define Crowdsourcing

9.11 Group Work Research Activities

These activities require you to research beyond the contents of the book and can be tackled individually or as a discussion group.

9.11.1 Discussion Topic 1

Think of ways that an organisation could innovate by using crowdsourcing. Present a case for this idea by explaining the plus points and the risks.

9.11.2 Discussion Topic 2

Explore how an organisation might use an ERP system to break down the silos that exist between departmental data. Discuss issues like ownership and quality of the data and how that may be affected by any such move.

References

Estellés-Arolas E, González-Ladrón-de-Guevara F (2012) Towards an integrated crowdsourcing definition. J Inf Sci 38(2):189–200

Guardian US interactive team (2013) A guardian guide to your metadata [online]. Last accessed 02 Feb2014at:http://www.theguardian.com/technology/interactive/2013/jun/12/what-is-metadata-nsa-surveillance#meta=0000000

Henschen D (2012) Big data debate: end near for ETL? [online]. 2013 at: http://www.informationweek.com/big-data/big-data-analytics/big-data-debate-end-near-for-etl/d/d-id/1107641?

IBM (2014) What is data quality [online]. Last accessed 2 Jan 2014 at: http://www-01.ibm.com/software/data/quality/

Jefferies D (2011) How the 'internet of things' could radically change local government [online]. Last accessed 2 Feb 2014 at: http://www.theguardian.com/local-government-network/2011/aug/18/internet-of-things-local-government

Lake P, Crowther P (2013) Concise guide to databases. Springer, London

Wakefield J (2012) Seti live website to crowdsource alien life [online]. Last accessed 2 Feb 2014 at: http://www.bbc.co.uk/news/technology-17199882

IS Security 10

10.1 What the Reader Will Learn

- that IS Security is a wide ranging subject covering many aspects of an IS/IT infrastructure
- that the physical aspects of security can be as important as system-specific security
- that the human factor can be seen as the weakest element in many security systems
- that there are tools and approaches which can minimise most risks
- that there are ethical questions to be addressed when dealing with security, especially on national and international levels

10.2 What This Chapter Could Contain but Doesn't

Information System Security is one of those words that means different things to different people. Put the phrase into your library search mechanism and it will return books which focus on areas such as internet security, hacking, data protection, the CIA and other national protection agencies, and ethics. I wrote a book about databases with a colleague and we ended up accidentally addressing the same core material in two different chapters since my co-author (and many other authors) believed that Disaster Recovery (DR) belonged in a chapter about security. I wrote a chapter entitled Availability and assumed I would cover disaster recovery there! I did win that argument, and therefore I feel confident enough to exclude DR from this chapter too!

That isn't to say that it is wrong to think about DR as a security issue. But it is part of a broader definition, and would probably belong in a book about security. We only have a chapter here, so we need to be more focused. So, just to be clear, we recognise that other topics have a valid place in the security area, but here we will be thinking if Information Systems Security as:

Proactive and reactive approaches to preventing the misuse of corporate data and information, and the physical infrastructure that supports information systems.

The exception to this is that we will also quickly review ethical issues in the security arena, such as those exposed by the whistle-blower Edward Snowden just before this book was written, and such as the privacy issues raised by having data scattered around the globe. We will not explicitly talk about Big Data in terms of security since there is little by way of extra vulnerability brought about by Big Data.

10.3 Understanding the Risks

Before we begin looking in detail at security it is as well to have a broader understanding of the domain we are working in. What are the threats? And what are the possible defences we could adopt. As with many areas in IS, there is a balance to be had between the cost of making a company as secure as possible, which can be very high, and the danger of doing nothing to protect systems and data. The latter is clearly cheaper in the short term but can have some catastrophic effects on the business in the longer term.

Organisational culture will have a great impact upon the way that security is thought of. Security professionals may well have very good reasons for forcing users to change their password every 30 days, and for them to have strong passwords (see Application Access section below), but users who are used to less intense security on their home PCs may well fail to see the need and look for ways to circumvent the "nuisance" presented by security. User education, as we shall see when we review human factors in IS security, is probably one of the most important aspects of an organisation's security practice. An overview of the issues facing IS security professionals is shown in Fig. 10.1.

10.3.1 What Is the Scale of the Problem?

According to independent research by the AV-TEST Institute, they register over 200,000 new malicious programs every day. Malware is the term that is used for this sort of programme – it is a concatenation of "malicious software" and can include viruses, worms, trojan horses, key-loggers, spyware, and adware. These are examined in more detail later in this chapter. It is also clear from the graph (Fig. 10.2) that this problem is one that is continuing to grow as we see the number of pieces of malware recorded over the past 10 years.

Whilst Malware is probably the most obvious form of threat, information systems are susceptible to all sorts of other threats too. Nor does the threat have to come from a deliberately evil source. Inappropriate insider activity can be by users with legitimate access to systems who act in ways which can endanger the security of the

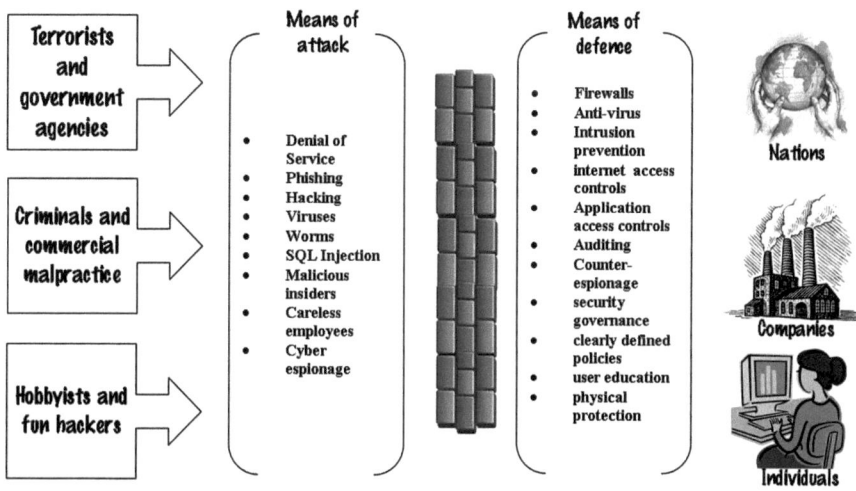

Fig. 10.1 An overview of the Security domain

Total Malware

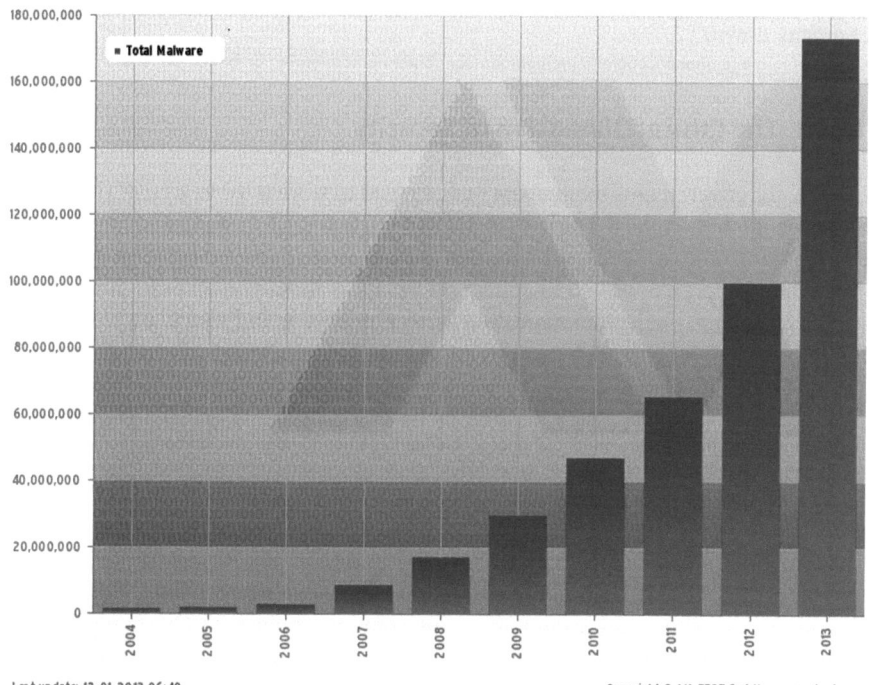

Fig. 10.2 The growth of malware over 10 year period (AV-Test 2013)

organisation's data, or even the organisation itself. Take, for example, the sales rep who downloads a list of all his company's valuable customer contacts from the secure server to his laptop. No evil intent; all he wanted to do was carry on his work over the weekend. But what if the laptop is stolen whilst the sales rep is waiting for a train? What will happen to the company if that data gets into the hands of competitors?

So this is the domain we are reviewing in this chapter. As befits a book about IS management we will begin by reviewing governance issues before looking in more detail at the risks and potential defences.

10.4 Privacy, Ethics and Governance

Governance is important at a number of levels for IS security professionals. For example, there are the rules and policies within which the professional needs to work for the organisation they are employed by, and then there are the rules set out by the nation state they work in. Both of these are important but variable since many nations have different legislation, and many companies have different attitudes to security. Another influence on the professional is that of their individual ethical position. Whilst all of these factors can be in balance, there are circumstances when one's own idea of what is right is different to one of the other norms, such as company policy, and that can cause severe mental anguish as an internal debate is had between the relative importance of personal self-esteem and letting the company down.

10.4.1 The Ethical Dimension of Security

Is it OK for governments to intercept our data and to store it for analysis? The recent Snowden affair a (collected articles available on the Guardian webpage: http://www.theguardian.com/world/edward-snowden) has demonstrated the lengths that some government agencies will go to collect information about you and me. And it isn't just governments – telecommunication service providers in Europe are required to log information for at least 6 months. As the EC's Home Affairs webpage says:

> Historical telecommunications data are highly valuable in the investigation and prosecution of crime and the protection of the public. Under EU law, telecommunications service and network providers are obliged to retain certain categories of data for a specific period of time and to make them available to law enforcement where needed.

Should we allow this to happen? We are told that this is part of the "war on terrorism" and that we have nothing to fear if we have nothing to hide. But surely I should decide who I has access about information about me? Or should I? You might be thinking that this is more to do with military security than it is to do with Information System Security, but our governments, especially if we are US or UK citizens, are storing information about all communications, and that includes inter- and intra-company communications.

Whatever your personal view, there will be people who see it as just plain wrong for the state to collect information from ordinary citizens and companies without a warrant. Those people can then be torn between the need to abide by both their county's and organisation's rules and to keep quiet about any perceived state encouraged wrong-doing, and telling the world about what they know. Snowden clearly ended up giving the upper hand to his conscience.

There seem to be two key questions involved here:

- Is what the organisation is doing wrong?
- If it is, does my moral duty to report the wrong-doing outweigh my duty to the team I am employed to work in?

It is out of the remit of this book to provide definite answers to these questions. Indeed, the reality is that the only answer that matters to you is the one you would give if you had been in Snowden's place. A simple test of your attitude is to think about the language you use to describe Snowden. Do you see him as a Whistle-blower or a Leaker, or a Traitor?

The unfortunate fact is that although leaks can undoubtedly let the public know what is going on behind their backs, some of that knowledge is dangerous if so released. In the UK, for example, government officials would expect to be able to disclose information to ministers without fear of the facts getting into the public domain. If there is doubt as to whether such secrets would remain secret, the very nature of government decision making may change for the worse. And so a leak can be both good and bad, even from the point of view of a very committed whistle-blower.

As Sagar (2013) says in his book **Secrets and Leaks: The Dilemma of State Secrecy**:

> The realization that the practice of leaking is itself prone to grave abuse puts us in a difficult position. If we prohibit the publication of leaks of classified information, we stand to lose the most effective and credible means by which we can be alerted to wrongdoing that occurs under cover of secrecy. But if we permit the publication of such leaks, then we risk contaminating our public life with conspiracy and covert warfare, as not only good men and women but also partisans and zealots take advantage of anonymity to disclose information that suits their narrow purposes.

The recent bout of leak-related stories raises interesting ethical questions since there is an argument, whether you agree or not, that allows the leaker to be seen as holding the moral high ground. Where we might assume that ethics are a little easier to grapple with is when it comes to the straightforward task of keeping out the bad guys from our own systems. But even here there are sensitive questions to be addressed. Indeed, there is a whole academic subject area named after one such issue: Ethical Hacking. An ethical hacker is someone employed expressly to attempt to penetrate networks and information systems, and in doing so to find and fix vulnerabilities.

They may be specialist consultants or, in a large enough organisation, they may be part of the IS team.

Most of the systems we rely on these days have vulnerabilities built in, usually by mistake, but just very occasionally deliberately. These vulnerabilities have increasingly been sought out by malicious hackers. One way that organisations can reduce their exposure to such hackers is to look for the vulnerabilities themselves – to pretend to be evil hackers but actually only report and fix the vulnerabilities; falling short of doing evil. However, even this process is a little murky as the very act of penetration testing can bring the researcher into contact with personal information or corporate secrets. Although the researcher will work with a "duty not to harm" there are clearly some worrying issues here. As Matwyshyn et al. (2010) say:

> During the past decade, the practice of finding and exploiting such imperfections has matured into a highly lucrative industry. To combat this escalating threat, security researchers find themselves in a perpetual race to identify and eliminate vulnerabilities before attackers can exploit them and to educate and train practitioners to test for known vulnerabilities in deployed systems. While nefarious parties operate in secrecy without fear of law, ethics, or public scrutiny, legitimate security researchers operate in the open and are subject to these constraints. Hence, researchers are sometimes hesitant to explore important information security issues owing to concern about their ethical and legal implications.

We might believe that the law of the land can help us decide what is ethically right. However, though laws are often influenced by the ethical norms prevalent at the time of enactment, they are not the same thing as ethics. If I tell you that I am a very good looking 25 year-old athlete I would be lying to you. However, I would not be breaking the law. Lying, per se, is not illegal, although lying on oath is. The other problem with relying on the law is that legislation is often decades or more behind the times, which can be really problematic in the field of Information Systems which change so rapidly.

In the US several pressure groups have joined to demand a substantial revision to the 1986 Electronic Communications Privacy Act (ECPA). As one of the groups, the ITIF, succinctly put it in a press release:

> There is no way a law enacted at the dawn of the digital age can guide law enforcement officials and protect privacy rights in an age of cloud computing and the wireless Internet, and as billions of electronic exchanges occur every hour (ITIF Press Release 2010).

As an example of how usage can quickly by-pass legislation, the ECPA allows agencies to seize emails left on a 3rd party's server after they become 180 days old, as the law deemed them to be abandoned. At the time the law was made emails were usually forwarded on to the recipients who would save them on their own email servers (hence any emails on a third party disk could be assumed to be abandoned). Now, however, email providers like Google's Gmail store the emails on the user's behalf, and allow the user access through a web-browser. Gmail is reported to have more than 400 million users, all of whom, according to the law, store their emails on a third party's premises, and are therefore available for warrant-less access by a US government agency.

Google are not the only providers of hotmail facilities, but their sheer size means they have significant influence with politicians and law makers. In the case of the 180-day rule, Google, perhaps seeing that the law is actually working unethically, have publicly stated that:

> "Google requires an ECPA search warrant for contents of Gmail and other services based on the Fourth Amendment to the Constitution, which prevents unreasonable search and seizure," Chris Gaither, a Google spokesman, said.
> (reported by Wired in 2013 http://www.wired.com/threatlevel/2013/01/google-says-get-a-warrant/)

They are, in effect, ignoring the 180-day rule of law in favour of what they perceive to be the way their clients would want the system to work. This aspect of the law may well be reformed by the time this book is published, but the principle remains true: technology generally outpaces the law, and that means that IT professionals need to be extra careful about working ethically, not merely by the letter of the law.

Professional bodies can help with this. The British Computer Society (BCS), for example has a Code of Conduct (http://www.bcs.org/upload/pdf/conduct.pdf) that members must abide by. It stipulates four duties of behaviour, and extracts of the code include:

1. **You should work in the public interest**. This should include having due regard for public health, privacy, security and well-being of others and the environment.
2. **You should maintain at all times Professional Competence and Integrity**.
3. **You should carry out your professional responsibilities with due care and diligence in accordance with the Relevant Authority's requirements**.
4. **You should accept your personal duty to uphold the reputation of the profession and not take any action which could bring the profession into disrepute**.

Not all ethical questions are matters of national concern, and as professionals we should always be aware of the ethical aspects of the work we do. As an example, Human Resources departments keep personal information about their employees and they are both morally and legally required to keep that information safe and secure. Much of this element of security is covered by data protection legislation which we review next.

10.4.2 Data Protection

Before we start this section we ought to attempt to define what we mean by data protection. This is actually no easy task, as can be seen by referring to the supposedly easy to follow "Key Definitions" web page of the UK's Information Commissioner's Office (ICO): http://www.ico.org.uk/for_organisations/data_protection/the_guide/key_definitions which is quite a lengthy page if you were hoping for a single sentence definition!

The ICO says it is: *an independent authority set up to uphold information rights in the public interest, promoting openness by public bodies and data privacy for individuals.* This helps us understand the domain we are working in – especially in terms of this Security chapter, we are primarily talking about maintaining an individual's privacy.

Let's try and simplify and summarise the key elements of the data protection arena:

Data: is information that is stored on any medium such that it can be accessed and processed at some time

Personal Data: is any information about an identifiable individual. Just storing my age, perhaps as you collect information about the average age of people in your locality, is not Personal Data, but storing my age and my name, or address, or any other identifier, is Personal Data

Data Subject: The individual about whom personal data is stored

Data Controller: The person (or group) who determines the purposes for which any stored personal data is to be used. In the UK this is a legally recognised role with responsibilities, including allowing appropriate access (within 40 calendar days of receipt) to any legitimate request to see the data about a Data Subject. Controllers are also required to ensure that appropriate technical and security measures are in place to protect personal data

The UK is also bound by the EU legislation of data protection. In 2012 The European Commission (EC) announced a comprehensive reform of the data protection rules for member countries. Information about this can be found at: http://ec.europa.eu/justice/newsroom/data-protection/news/120125_en.htm

There are, however, significant international differences in data protection law, and this has been a major stumbling block for the adoption of Cloud computing since Cloud providers tend to be multi-national and therefore personal data stored on the cloud could, in theory be stored across the globe and therefore be subject to many different legal frameworks.

As far back as in 1980 the Organisation for Economic Co-operation and Development (OECD), whose aim is to "promote policies that will improve the economic and social well-being of people around the world", began to set out their guidelines on the Protection of Privacy and Transborder Flows of Personal Data.

The principles set out are largely reflected in the EC framework proposals, but the US, for example, implements privacy legislation differently. In a recent report by the US Government Accountability Office (2013):

> No overarching federal privacy law governs the collection and sale of personal information among private-sector companies, including information resellers. Instead, laws tailored to specific purposes, situations, or entities govern the use, sharing, and protection of personal information. For example, the Fair Credit Reporting Act limits the use and distribution of personal information collected or used to help determine eligibility for such things as credit or employment, but does not apply to information used for marketing.

Data protection is another area that has changed significantly over the past decade or so as a result of the way information systems have evolved. As part of a neat summary of changes in the UK data protection area Hazel Grant (2008) suggests:

> We have seen significant changes in the law and practice of data protection between 1998 and 2008. In 1998, it is probably fair to say that data protection was seen as a mundane and administrative task: principally equating to a need to register with the Data Protection Registrar, completing a tedious form and paying for a 3-year registration certificate.

Data Protection issues have been in the news over the past few years and their prominence has doubtless helped in moving the data protection from a tedious form-filling bureaucratic exercise to an issue often raised at company board meetings or in government cabinet meetings. Citizens now expect that personal information about themselves is looked after, is secure, and will not fall into the hands of miscreants. They see privacy as a basic right. And that public perception has led to serious punishments being given out to companies which fail to look after data.

In the UK alone there are many examples. Here are just a couple:

> The Nationwide Building Society has been fined £980,000 by the City watchdog over security breaches. The fine follows the theft of a laptop from a Nationwide employee's home which contained confidential customer data. The Financial Services Authority (FSA) found security was not up to scratch after the man had put details of nearly 11 million customers on his computer.
> BBC News: http://news.bbc.co.uk/1/hi/business/6360715.stm
> July 2013 – NHS Surrey has been fined £200,000 by data regulators over the loss of sensitive information about more than 3,000 patients. Thousands of children's patient records were found on a second-hand NHS computer that was auctioned on eBay, the BBC understands. Regulators said NHS Surrey failed to check that a data destruction company had properly disposed of the records.
> BBC News: http://www.bbc.co.uk/news/technology-23286231

We can see, therefore, that data protection has become a hot topic, especially as Cloud computing begs so many questions about data flows across national boundaries. If you work in the UK you would expect that your personal data would be safe from public view and that you would have redress against any organisation that fails to look after it. But if that data is actually stored in the Philippines, which nation's law would you use to attempt to remedy any problems? And what if, though stored in the Philippines, your personal data is electronically passed to an organisation in Africa that uses it to create email lists for phishing attacks (see below for definition of phishing)? Because the technology is relatively new and legislators are slow to agree standards, the answer to these questions is less than certain as we write. In other words, if you are a data controller you should be very careful that you understand the way your particular data is stored and manipulated and ensure that contracts with any providers explicitly mention the jurisdiction to be used for any legal challenges.

10.5 Securing Systems

As we have seen already, the IS security field is a wide one. In this section we will look at some of the threats and potential solutions for systems as a whole, and in the next section we will concentrate on data.

As we saw in Fig. 10.1 there can be many different reasons for malicious attacks to occur against an organisation's systems, and there are also many different types of potential attack. All share the same starting point however – a search for weaknesses, or vulnerabilities in an organisation's security. To an extent the security professional does not care about the motive of the perpetrator of an attack. It matters not, for example, if a company's e-commerce site is out of action because it has been subject to a *denial of service* attack from passionate anti-capitalist activists or as the result of some lonely prankster sitting in their bedroom trying out their programming skills for fun. The effect is the same – the potential loss of thousands of pounds or dollars of trade for every minute the e-commerce site is out of action.

So what are the threats to systems that face organisations, and what are the potential defences?

10.5.1 Hacking

There are several dictionary definitions of the term Hacker. For the purposes of this book, in the context of IS Security we suggest a hacker is:

> *someone who, without appropriate authorisation, accesses a computer system and thereby either obtains data they are not entitled to retrieve or causes damage to the system.*

The term is therefore quite broad and covers all sorts of malicious or mischievous activities. We look at a few in more detail below. It is clear from Fig. 10.2 that the problem of the malware generated by hackers is getting much worse, and much harder to deal with as the hackers become more sophisticated. In some cases the hackers group together to pool their skills, making them potentially even more deadly.

One very prominent group of hackers, known as Anonymous, have a well documented track record of politically motivated attacks, sometimes on government institutions. They have even attempted to argue that:

> DDoS (Distributed Denial of Service – see below) attacks should be protected as a form of free speech, so that they could be used to protest.
> InformationWeek 2013: http://www.informationweek.com/security/attacks-and-breaches/9-notorious-hackers-of-2013/d/d-id/1113140

This article, entitled *9 Notorious Hackers Of 2013* goes on to describe other Hacks and goes on to demonstrate the sort of threat IS security professionals are working under.

10.5.2 Denial of Service

A *denial of service* attack occurs when attackers attempt to prevent legitimate users of a service, such as an e-commerce website, from using that service. They can do this by a number of means. One such is to flood the target system with bogus requests for a connection. On an e-commerce site, for example, the system may create a number of server-side data structures at the point at which a user makes a connection, ready for the sales process to start. The attacker requests a session, as if they were a *bona fide* customer, but fails to complete, leaving the server-side still waiting for the connection.

This is called a SYN (synchronise) attack since it utilises the normal network TCP (Transmission Control Protocol) connection, in which the client and server exchange a set of messages in order to establish the connection. This is called the three-way handshake. The malicious client sends a SYN message to the target server. The server will acknowledge with a SYN-ACK (synchronise-Acknowledgement) message. Normally the client will then complete the three-way handshake by sending an ACK (Acknowledge) and the connection will be made. In a SYN attack the attacker sends multiple SYN packet requests but never returns an ACK. This leaves the targeted host just sitting and waiting for the ACK that never comes. As the number of connections supported by the server will be finite it is possible for the attacker to generate enough bogus sessions to prevent the system from allowing genuine users to connect, thus denying them access to the service.

A denial of service attack could also be an attack on the target organisation's broadband bandwidth by attempting to consume all the available bandwidth on the target's network by generating a large number of bogus network packets directed to that network. The network becomes unable to cope and refuses access to genuine users. All devices that are attached to the network are vulnerable, not just computers. Care needs to be taken to protect items such as printers and tape drives. Disks on the target system can be caused to fill very quickly, causing a denial whilst disks are replaced. One way of doing this is to log on and then deliberately cause errors that will have to be logged (by being written to disk).

Attacks are not necessarily launched from the perpetrator's computer, or even a single computer. The flood of messages could come from an innocent organisation's PC which has been infected with malware which first looks for other vulnerable PC's it can infect and control, and which then initiates an attack by issuing the command to its slave PCs to attack the target in the way described above. This is known as a Distributed Denial of Service attack.

Denial of Service attacks can come from many sources, including, according to some US sources, state sponsored attacks. There have been several very high profile attacks which claim to have political justification. The New York Times reported on a wave of attacks against US banks, for example:

> By flooding banking sites with encryption requests, attackers can further slow or cripple sites with fewer requests. A hacker group calling itself Izz ad-Din al-Qassam Cyber Fighters has claimed in online posts that it was responsible for the attacks.

(New York Times, January 2013: http://www.nytimes.com/2013/01/09/technology/online-banking-attacks-were-work-of-iran-us-officials-say.html)

10.5.3 Denial of Service Defence Mechanisms

Organizations can suffer severe financial losses after a denial-of-service attack. If the perpetrators can be found then they can be pursued for criminal or civil charges. Police forces around the world are beginning to include specialists in this sort of cyber-crime and may well be able to help in the process of tracking down the miscreants. The sad fact is, however, that the perpetrators may never be found. The best form of defence is to attempt to ensure that this cannot happen to your organisation. As with most IS decisions, the more security layers you apply, the more it will cost, so discovering the right level of defence for the level of risk your organisation is running is vital.

Unfortunately there are many types of DoS attack – some simple, some very cunning. The biggest problem in trying to defend against the more cunning attacks is to find methods of reliably identifying which connection attempts are from valid users, and which are malicious, especially if you are allowing access to your system to anyone in the world, as well you might with an e-commerce system. This can be seen as attempting to prevent intrusions from happening. The second element of the defence is to have in place monitoring mechanisms which look for unusual activity on your network, and detect changes to important configuration information. The latter will help guard against any successful intruders, but also against insiders who have malicious intent.

Knowing what is normal in terms of your system's performance is an essential first step in looking out for suspicious activity. Baselines which measure ordinary activity in terms of disk usage, CPU usage, or network traffic are then used for comparison with current actual measurements. Unusual peaks in usage should set alarm bells ringing.

Since one target of a DoS can be the system's data storage it is sensible to enable quotas such that users can only write a certain amount of data to a disk before having their account frozen. In addition, if you can partition your data, it could be a good idea to consider partitioning your file system, separating critical operational aspects from other activity.

Redundancy is another way of ensuring that availability remains high for your systems. In effect you keep copies of your system on multiple servers. If one server becomes compromised, genuine users can still access the others. This is an expensive option, but if availability is essential for the business the cost will be easy to justify. Cloud computing opens up this sort of redundancy defence to smaller businesses who could not have afforded to run two or more parallel physical systems themselves.

There are specialist service providers who prove DoS protections services. These generally intercept traffic bound for their client's systems and use their expert skills, knowledge and tools to filter out offending traffic and only allow through clean traffic to the client. Just as with other aspects of business it can make sense to outsource to specialist consultants rather than attempt to have the skills and expensive equipment in-house. Verizon and AT&T are well known and respected names in this field and their websites will tell you more about the service.

10.5.4 Viruses and Worms and Trojan Horses (Often Collectively Referred to as Malware)

Computer viruses are so called because of their ability to spread like their infective agent namesakes in the medical arena. They are small software programs that are designed to infect a host computer and then to spread from one computer to another. They generally have some form of detrimental effect on the infected computer although viruses can also be relatively benign. These are the product of pranksters finding fun in a strange way by writing these programmes. They may do something harmless like putting a message on your screen saying "Give world peace a chance" and that ends the infection. Less benign viruses can delete or corrupt data on your system's disks. They can even cause your system to fail catastrophically. They are often self-propagating as they can access your email programme to enable it to spread to other computers.

Viruses are attached to executable files. This means that a virus can exist on a computer for years and not do any harm until the malicious program is run, at which point the computer becomes infected.

A Worm is similar to a virus. It differs in that a worm is a piece of standalone software and does not require a host program. It can make copies of itself, and it can attach itself to emails created using your contacts to ensure it gets sent to other computers, where it can again duplicate itself. Once it has replicated itself enough times it will begin to impact upon the host system's resources, such as hard drive space and bandwidth.

Trojans trick gullible users into downloading the malware onto their computer. One means of easily spreading Trojans is to attach them to some freely downloaded software that seems to the potential user to be useful. For this reason it is very important to be sure of the provenance of any software you download. Many organisations will protect their PCs by not allowing sufficient rights to users for installing new software.

Once on the target PC, or mobile device, the Trojans can perform any number of tasks depending on how malicious the creator is. Some merely act as adware and present the user with unwanted pop-up advertisements. Others do much more damage, including the destruction of data files. One more subtle result may be that the Trojan creates a "back-door". This is a new vulnerability in the host computer which allows attackers to bypass the system's authentication mechanism and gain access to the computer.

10.5.5 Spyware

Often spyware finds its way onto a target PC in the same way that Trojans do – by being bundled up with seemingly useful software that the user downloads. Sometimes however they can be deliberately installed on specific PCs through other vulnerabilities as when a target user's activities are being monitored by third parties. They differ from Trojans in that their purpose is not to cause any problems on the host PC (although they might as a by-product of their activity), but to simply record what is happening on that PC and send that information on to the perpetrator. Spyware can be made to gather all sorts of information such as stored data, including personal information and bank account data; observe browsing habits; gather login information.

10.5.6 Defences Against Malicious Attacks

The safest form of protection from infection is to avoid connecting your computer or network to the internet, as computers connected to the internet are vulnerable to outside hacking. Because it means these computers are not attached to the internet in any way, this is known as an **air gap** and is used when super-security is required, typically by national security organisations or the military. According to Security Blogger Bruce Schneier, Bin Laden remained hidden in his final hideout for so long because he used an air-gap. Schneier says:

> Holed up in his walled compound in northeast Pakistan with no phone or Internet capabilities, bin Laden would type a message on his computer without an Internet connection, then save it using a thumb-sized flash drive. He then passed the flash drive to a trusted courier, who would head for a distant Internet cafe.
> At that location, the courier would plug the memory drive into a computer, copy bin Laden's message into an email and send it. Reversing the process, the courier would copy any incoming email to the flash drive and return to the compound, where bin Laden would read his messages offline.
> https://www.schneier.com/blog/archives/2011/05/bin_laden_maint.html

Since computer users now expect instant access to the internet, and may even need access to complete their work, the weakness of this sort of defence is that it runs the danger of being circumvented by frustrated users who want to get internet access. The end of the Bin Laden story demonstrates this, as reported by NBC News:

> People in the Pakistan compound where Osama bin Laden was killed were using cell phones to communicate, creating a gaping security hole in the defenses they created to protect the al-Qaida leader, two senior U.S. officials told NBC News on Wednesday.
> http://www.nbcnews.com/id/42881728/ns/world_news-death_of_bin_laden/t/bin-laden-aides-were-using-cell-phones-officials-tell-nbc/#.Us1ygZ5_swA

It seems that even well maintained air-gaps may be fallible however. In December 2013 The Daily Telegraph reported:

> In the proof-of-concept attack from Germany's Fraunhofer Institute for Communication, Information Processing and Ergonomics, researchers were able to use the built-in speakers

and microphones of computers to transmit passwords and other data at a rate of 20 bits per second over a distance of almost 20 metres, allowing the malware to "secretly leak critical data to the outside world".

http://www.telegraph.co.uk/technology/internet-security/10490846/New-computer-virus-secretly-leaks-data-through-air.html

Of course, in this case, both sender and receiver PC need to have been compromised and have malware installed and waiting to carry out the transmission. Guaranteed clean air gap PCs would not be vulnerable, but once you add human fallibility to the equation, maybe with users bringing in pen-drives with malware on them, we can see that even a computer's sound system needs to be considered as a potential security vulnerability!

As we noted above, not connecting to the internet is an extreme and mostly impractical solution. Another sensible step often ignored, especially as many PCs come with pre-installed software bundles, is to install only the software you must have to be able to do your job. Disabling all unneeded operating system services will also reduce the vulnerability levels. The less software you install and systems services you run, the less an attacker can exploit. Again, as with an air gap, this may seem over-the-top. Indeed many ordinary users and companies do not realise these options exist, and many will not suffer as they "get away with" having a higher level of vulnerability every day that goes by and they aren't attacked. Most larger organisations, however, know how valuable their data and ICT resources are to them and will try to make life as difficult as they can for their would-be assailants – even if that means giving their own staff less flexibility on their work PC than they get on their home computers.

Patching is a very important line of defence. A patch is a piece of software designed to fix problems in general but especially security vulnerabilities. With products like Microsoft Windows these patches are often applied automatically, but it is important to ensure than patches are current since if known vulnerabilities won't get fixed, even if a fix is out there.

Perhaps the most common form of defence is for computers and servers to have **Anti-Virus (AV)** software installed. There are many products available. Names like Norton, McAfee and F-Secure have been protecting the author's computers for many years now, for example. The products all claim to have protection against viruses, worms, trojans and spyware. Most will be able to remove any malware they find on your computer.

All AV software does have a major weakness, however – they are largely reactive, dealing with existing malware. Once the footprint and modus operandi of a virus becomes known it can be guarded against. Most of the major software packages react swiftly when a new virus is found and add it to their protection routines. However, detection of a new virus hitting the internet can take weeks. This leaves a sizeable window of opportunity for malware to bypass AV software. Someone thinking of creating malware, for whatever reason, is going to try new techniques that most AV software will not identify, at least for a few days. Before being released the careful malware creator will check their new product against existing AV software to ensure that it doesn't get discovered.

This is not to say that AV software is useless. Far from it since it acts as the first line of defence against incautious users visiting untrustworthy websites and clicking on links that they should not really click. Although they do not protect against new malware, they do protect against much of the very large pool of existing malware that is out there waiting to infect unsuspecting users.

Another common form of defence is a **Firewall.** The original use of the word was literally the building of a wall to hold back the spread of a fire. In software terms a firewall's job is to act as a barrier between insecure external networks such as the public internet and the supposedly secure internal network. They can be a two way barrier since they can also prevent a computer from sending on malware should it become infected. Firewalls are now typically part of the standard operating system installation. They can be turned on or off, and their default position depends upon the operating system. Windows 7, for example, is by default on after installation. Ubuntu Linux, on the other hand, needs to be turned on after installation.

A firewall's job is to filter the data arriving at your network or computer from an external source, such as the internet. Firewalls are either entirely software based, or they can be firmware within hardware devices such as routers. Both types block specific web sites, Instant Messaging sites and other potentially dangerous content by using internal rules to compare the incoming Internet Protocol (IP) data to those in blacklists established by the firewall provider. Suspicious packets of information are either dropped or flagged and logged, although the latter is quite costly in terms of system resource usage and so tends not to be the preferred option.

AV software is not an alternative to a firewall and they should both be part of an overall security solution. Firewalls are network traffic focused and aim to detect and prevent attempts to intrude on internal systems. AV software scans specifically for malware of various types and destroys them if found.

One of the most common means of malware distribution is through e-mail. Specialist software for filtering emails recognises this. E-mail software itself has developed defences. Outlook, for example, automatically blocks attachments of certain types. Cisco has IronPort which is a security appliance which protects against SPAM (unwanted, unsolicited emails), phishing (requests for data – see below) and other email related attacks.

10.6 Securing Data

Data belonging to you or your organisation can have great value to others. Some of the most obvious examples of the misuse of personal data are the lists of credit card details that criminals make freely available for the right price. The BBC reported, in 2012, the successful culmination of a long crime fighting operation:

> Credit card numbers or bank account details of millions of unsuspecting victims were sold for as little as £2.
>
> During that period [2 years] the details of about two-and-a-half million credit cards were recovered – preventing fraud, according to industry calculations, of at least £0.5bn.

> Lee Miles, the head of Soca's cyber crime unit, told the BBC that criminals were now selling personal data on an "industrial" scale. He said: "Criminals are turning over vast volumes of these cards. We must match the criminals – it's an arms race.
> "They are industrialising their processes and likewise we have to industrialise our processes to match them."
> http://www.bbc.co.uk/news/uk-17851257

Criminals use many different ways of accessing valuable data like this. Perhaps the most obvious is for them to steal the data directly, or at least take a device with the data on it. In a response to a Freedom of Information request the UK government's Department for Business, Innovation & Skills acknowledged there had, in 2011/12, been 7 laptops and 39 mobile phones lost or stolen. There is no evidence that any of the devices contained sensitive data. However, the department had just short of 900 laptops. Seven out of nine hundred computers is a rather worrying total.

Thefts can be opportunistic, or they can be targeted, but either way information can end up in the wrong hands. The BBC reported the theft of a NASA laptop:

> Nasa said the latest incident had occurred on 31 October, when a laptop and documents were stolen from a locked vehicle of one of its employees at Nasa headquarters in Washington DC.
> As a result, Nasa has warned its workers to watch out for bogus messages.
> "All employees should be aware of any phone calls, emails, and other communications from individuals claiming to be from Nasa or other official sources that ask for personal information or verification of it," an agency-wide email
> http://www.bbc.co.uk/news/technology-20343745

The report then goes on to talk about NASA's response to this for future protection, which was to insist all data on laptops should be encrypted. Going back to our earlier observation, data on all devices can be made unreadable to would-be thieves, but at a cost. However the cost of ensuring every device has encrypted data may be insignificant compared to the cost in terms of fines and lost reputation that might happen if you lose private data that is stored unencrypted. Many organisations will now have policies that insist on laptops being encrypted as standard to protect their data and reputations.

Data encryption relies on cryptography, which is the act of making a message unintelligible to all but the intended recipient by applying an algorithm to the original message using a key. Encryption can be pre-installed and enabled from the start of a laptop's life. A windows tool, for example, is BitLocker which can encrypt the Hard Drive. Once turned on, any file you save on that drive is encrypted. If you only want to protect certain files most modern operating systems include the option to encrypt files, folders or directories. Encryption is also an important part of our day-to-day activities with the web since it happens every time we access a secure site, as when we are about to purchase something using a credit card, and the little padlock symbol appears. In effect your details get scrambled using a key value that only the recipient knows and can use to unscramble the data. This means that your data is safe as it travels around the internet.

Another way for criminals to attempt to get at data is through **phishing**. This is when a criminal pretends to be from a legitimate organisation, often in an email, and attempts to acquire valuable information such as user details and passwords, credit card or other banking details. Their success depends upon both their skill at passing themselves off as legitimate, and the recipient's level of gullibility.

Automated email protection can identify some of these emails and will put them into a safe folder so the user can identify if they are actually legitimate before opening any links in the email. But this filtering out is by no means perfect and ensuring that users are cautious about all emails, especially links and attachments, has to be the first line of defence.

SQL Injection happens when some malicious code in the form of an SQL statement is caused to run against a database and either retrieve datasets that the user is not entitled to see, or do some damage by deleting rows or dropping tables.

Databases are a key element in most modern websites, often storing information about customers, suppliers, employees and others. SQL Injection is a form of hacking technique. If the website is written with inadequate security it is possible to pass SQL commands through a web application and on to the database behind. Such injections can occur because the natural process in a database driven website is for web forms to interact with the user and then, behind the scenes, generate an SQL string which requests data from the database. The injection intercepts that normal process. Websites written using all languages, such as ASP.NET or PHP are equally susceptible if no input checking is implemented.

Here we illustrate just one of the most well known methods of forcing access to a database by SQL Injection. Many others exist.

The website authors have created some code which gathers the *username* so they can retrieve data about the user from their database where the *username* is in a column called *uname* in a table called *users*. It looks like this:

SQLStatement="SELECT * FROM users WHERE uname=' "+*username*+" ' ; "

NOTE: SQLStatement is what gets sent to the database, and *username* is a variable
  with a value of whatever is entered by the user. In normal circumstances the
  variable gets translated into a set of characters and so the result of a user called
  Tommy logging in would be that the variable SQLStatement would have a
  value of:

SELECT * FROM users WHERE uname='Tommy' ;

However, if, instead of Tommy, the malicious user set the value of *username* variable as:

' OR '1'='1

Then the SQLStatement variable would have a value of:

SELECT * FROM users WHERE uname=' ' OR '1'='1' ;

Because '1' does always equal '1' the result would be to return all rows from the table **users**.

The important thing to note is that it is only lazy coding by the website creators in the first place that allows this to happen. For the most part Injection vulnerabilities are based around the fact that the website creator has used dynamic queries that include user input. The first, and most obvious barrier then is to minimise dynamic queries. However, the application's requirements may well prevent total elimination of dynamic queries, so when the user is involved, the developer needs to check the result for injection attempts before sending the SQL to the database.

Most RDBMS packages allow for something called Stored Procedures. These can be written in Java, for example, or in the database's own language, such as PL/SQL which is Oracle's procedural language. Instead of blindly allowing a string to be passed to the SQL engine, Stored Procedures can be used to gather user input as parameters. Importantly the parameters will be type-specific. The malicious user attempting our trick above would find that the procedure will reject the attempt at passing ' **OR '1'='1** off as a valid string. Moreover, within the procedure itself the developer can write code for other validation checks to ensure that only a valid SQL statement is passed to the SQL engine.

A further sensible precaution is known as Least Privilege approach. In database terms a privilege is the right to do something. A database administrator, for example, could well have privileges to do anything to a database. At the other extreme, it is possible to create a user with privileges only to connect to the database and run *select* statements against one specific table. The safest thing is to create the application with users who have as few privileges as possible. In this way, even if you do get an intruder, they will not be able to do anything since all the nasty SQL statements (like DRP TABLE and DELETE) are unavailable to them.

10.6.1 Application Access Control

Most of us are now used to having to provide a user name and password for anything we do on the web or try to access any applications. This is, of course, a form of security, but, as we have seen, it can be vulnerable. One of the major problems is that users are, mostly, human beings, with human faults. Many of us find remembering many different passwords tedious, or impossible, so we might tend to use the same password for everything. And to help us remember, why not make the password, for example, my cat's name?

It's to be hoped the reader is beyond needing to a detailed explanation of why this is a problem! Putting it briefly, if one of your outer-ring of contacts hears you talking about your cat, they have something they can try as a password if they try to log into your email, or other application. It is also possible for the malicious developer to write code that simply tries over and over again to automatically log into an account, each time passing a slightly different password until they strike lucky. These are called brute force attacks.

One way to make guessing or brute force more difficult is to have strong passwords. Key elements of password strength are:

- Length: The longer it is the number of possible correct solutions there are, the more difficult it is to write a programme that discovers the password.
- Complexity: Straightforward words (like you cat's name) are much easier to guess than a string of mixed which combine letters, numbers, and where allowed, punctuation marks
- Unpredictability: Some code-cracking software uses dictionaries of possible passwords which can be millions of entries long. They are good at things like PURDY1997 which concatenates a cat's name and their birth-year. No dictionary is likely to have **Dnggitgn1951**. The problem with unpredictable passwords is that they tend to be far from memorable for the user! To get round that problem, the string of characters above is made up of the initial letter of one of my favourite poems: Dylan Thomas' *"Do not go gentle into that good night"*, together with its publication year.

Of course criminals will always be trying to keep ahead of the game, and as computing becomes ever more powerful it becomes ever more difficult to police. Strong passwords are a must-have, but even they may not help against this beast, as reported by Dan Goodin in 2012:

> The five-server system uses a relatively new package of virtualization software that harnesses the power of 25 AMD Radeon graphics cards. It achieves the 350 billion-guess-per-second speed when cracking password hashes generated by the NTLM cryptographic algorithm that Microsoft has included in every version of Windows since Server 2003. As a result, it can try an astounding 958 combinations in just 5.5 hours, enough to brute force every possible eight-character password containing upper- and lower-case letters, digits, and symbols. Such password policies are common in many enterprise settings.
> Ars Technica http://arstechnica.com/security/2012/12/25-gpu-cluster-cracks-every-standard-windows-password-in-6-hours/

10.6.2 Physical Security

When considering IS security we all too often forget the obvious: a computer in a locked room which has one known key-holder is much less vulnerable to being hacked than one to which the world has open access. An Oracle DBA may well have a session open on their desktop which has a connection with full privileges to the database. It is their job, so why wouldn't they? They go to get a cup of coffee from the local cafe, leaving the session open. There is now a real vulnerability. An unscrupulous passer-by with just a little knowledge could type SHUTDOWN at the appropriate place and the whole system folds.

Physical security is an important aspect throughout the organisation's infrastructure. A travelling employee who has a laptop with company data on it, especially unencrypted data as with the NASA story above, is an easy target for the opportunist thief if they leave it logged-in and unattended. As usual there are trade-offs between usability and security. You could set the laptop to go to sleep mode and require a password to restart after only one minute to make this sort of situation less likely, but then the user ends up having to enter their password countless times as they get distracted through the day.

In any case, even encrypted data is not necessarily safe in the wrong hands. All we can do is take as many sensible steps as possible to reduce the risks and to make stealing harder. Padlocked metal cases to carry the laptop, for example, or company policies saying that PCs should never be left logged-in if they are to be unattended for more than a minute.

10.6.3 Malicious Insiders and Careless Employees

For the most part we have been presuming that any threats come from the outside. Security professionals need to consider, however, that potentially a great deal of damage can be caused by people on the inside, not least because they may have valuable information such as passwords, or keys.

Imagine an employee who has just been given a written warning for bad behaviour. Perhaps they are aggrieved by the way they have been treated for what they see as a very minor offence. Every system they have access to is now vulnerable to being hacked. Management would do well to monitor all that employee's activity closely after the warning. This is one of the reasons that sacked employees are often required to leave the building immediately they are fired.

Most of the larger database installations will have auditing turned on to a fine level, which means that everything that all employees do is recorded into a log so that, at least after the event, people can discover what caused any unexpected events. Operating systems too can record who has logged on and what use they are making of CPU, RAM and hard disk space.

10.7 Does Big Data Make for More Vulnerability?

We have not talked much about Big Data in this chapter. Security is probably one of those areas where the cynics posit that "there is nothing new in Big Data" and that is almost true. However, we do have data coming from many more sources now, and the sources need to be authenticated. We are also likely to hold much more data than before, and we need to ensure that we comply with data protection regulations for this extra data.

10.8 Summary

In this chapter we discussed that IS Security is a wide ranging subject covering many aspects of an IS/IT infrastructure and that although there are tools and approaches which can minimise vulnerabilities, there are often ways round these.

We noted that there are ethical questions to be addressed when dealing with IS security. Data protection is written into much national and cross-national legislation, but the law in general is struggling to keep up with technological change.

10.9 Review Questions

The answers to these questions can be found in the text of this chapter.

- What is the difference between a Trojan, a Virus and a Worm
- Describe what is meant by Private Data and a Data Controller in the context of data protection.
- Relate the key steps in a DoS attack.
- What are the key attributes of a strong password?
- How does an Air Gap make computers safer? List other physical security practices that can help protect your systems.

10.10 Group Work Research Activities

These activities require you to research beyond the contents of the book and can be tackled individually or as a discussion group.

10.10.1 Discussion Topic 1

Is Edward Snowden a Heroic Whistle-blower or a Traitor? These coloured words can be used to describe the same event. Attempt to put together a First Proposition speech for each of these possible descriptions, as if you were opening a formal debate.

10.10.2 Discussion Topic 2

Is Ethical Hacking ethical? White hat hackers who are hired by organisations to carry out penetration testing are sometimes called "ethical hackers". Is this a good name for them? Can you think of actions that may be taken by a penetration tester that may be described as unethical. You may need to research the web to give a fuller answer.

References

Atkinson R (2010) ITIF calls for updates to privacy laws [online]. Last accessed 12 Dec 2013 at: http://www.itif.org/pressrelease/itif-calls-updates-privacy-laws

AV-Test (2013) Malware statistics [online]. Last accessed 12 Dec 2013 at: http://www.av-test.org/en/statistics/malware/

BBC News (2007) Nationwide fine for stolen laptop [online]. Last accessed 12 Dec 2013 at: http://news.bbc.co.uk/1/hi/business/6360715.stm

BBC News (2012) Credit card 'info for sale' websites closed in global raids [online]. Last accessed 12 Dec 2013 at: http://www.bbc.co.uk/news/uk-17851257

BBC News (2013) NHS surrey fined £200,000 after losing patients' records [online]. Last accessed 12 Dec 2013 at: http://www.bbc.co.uk/news/technology-23286231

Goodin D (2012) 25-GPU cluster cracks every standard windows password in <6 hours [online]. Last accessed 12 Dec 2013 at: http://arstechnica.com/security/2012/12/25-gpu-cluster-cracks-every-standard-windows-password-in-6-hours/

Grant H (2008) Data protection 1998–2008, [webpage]. Bird & Bird, London. Available at http://www.twobirds.com/en/news/articles/2008/data-protection-1998. Accessed 1 Oct 2014

ICO (2013) Key definitions of the data protection act [online]. Last accessed 12 Dec 2013 at: http://www.ico.org.uk/for_organisations/data_protection/the_guide/key_definitions

InformationWeek (2013) 9 notorious hackers of 2013 [online]. Last accessed 12 Dec 2013 at: http://www.informationweek.com/security/attacks-and-breaches/9-notorious-hackers-of-2013/d/d-id/1113140

Kravets D (2013) Google tells cops to get warrants for user E-mail, cloud data [online]. Last accessed 12 Dec 2013 at: http://www.wired.com/threatlevel/2013/01/google-says-get-a-warrant/

Matwyshyn AM et al (2010) Ethics in security vulnerability research. IEEE Secur Priv 8(2):67–72

Perlroth N, Hardy Q (2013) Bank hacking was the work of Iranians, officials say. New York Times, Technology, 8 Jan 2013

Sagar R (2013) Secrets and leaks: the dilemma of state secrecy. Princeton University Press, Princeton

Schneier B (2011) Schneier on security [online]. Last accessed 12 Dec 2013 at: https://www.schneier.com/blog/archives/2011/05/bin_laden_maint.html

Sparkes M (2013) New computer virus 'secretly leaks data' through air. The Telegraph, 3 Dec 2013

Unknown (2011) Code of conduct for BCS members [online]. Last accessed 12 Dec 2013 at: http://www.bcs.org/upload/pdf/conduct.pdf

U.S. Government Accountability Office (2013) Consumer privacy framework needs to reflect changes in technology and the marketplace. U.S. Government Accountability Office, Washington. Available at http://www.gao.gov/assets/660/658151.pdf. Accessed 1 Oct 2014

Technical Insights

11.1 What the Reader Will Learn

- How to begin to use Hadoop for Big Data
- What other tools are needed to make Hadoop useful, and how to use them
- What are the NoSQL alternatives to Hadoop and how to use some of them
- Where SQL fits in the Big Data landscape
- That the best way to understand new IS/IT concepts is to get your hands dirty with them and see for yourself what they can bring to your organisation

11.2 What You Will Need for This Chapter

You will need a PC for which you have administration rights. It should preferably be Windows 7 or later and ideally have more than 4 Gb RAM. You also need a reasonably fast internet connection.

This tutorial is aimed at giving you some early exposure to the Hadoop environment. It cannot hope to turn you into a skilled data scientist and those skills are covered in other books. In order to understand how Big Data can be used in your organisation, and be able to manage it as part of an IT infrastructure, it is sensible to attain some technical knowledge; to know what the key elements are and understand the architecture used.

You will also need some perseverance! All of the material here is new. It has not been thoroughly tested in all environments. In terms of IT Strategy one could argue that this makes using these tools less than sensible. But there is a tension with the need to keep up with the competition, and there can be little doubt that Hadoop has become the focus of much research in many organisations which seek to gain some sort of advantage from the innovative use of information.

11.3 Hands-on with Hadoop

There is often a common path in the development of database related applications. It can be seen in the history of many of today's market leaders such as the Oracle Relational Database Management System (RDBMS) and it runs something like this:

- The core is created by a group of clever, very technical people
- They provide a very basic, text-based interface for users
- Highly technical users adopt the system and persuade other users of its worth
- Some of those other users are less willing (or able) to write lots of code and in order to open the product up to more users a nice Graphical User Interface (GUI) is developed
- The GUI becomes the normal means of interfacing with the DBMS and many tools and wizards are included which mean what has always been a powerful tool is now available to many people

Hadoop is currently going through this process. It is an open source product and if you are willing, and have good Java skills you can actually join in the process of creating new functionality for Hadoop, let alone just using the end product. When the author started work on Hadoop the version had just changed to 1.2.0. In documenting the install procedure for my students I wrote three pages full of instructions, all of which required typing lengthy commands at the Linux $prompt.

In the space of 9 months we have now moved (at the time of writing) to version 2.1 of Hadoop. The system itself is a significant change architecturally and it is far more functionally rich. Perhaps the best news, however, is that the installation process has become far simpler, meaning that one of the barriers to just downloading and playing with the new technology has been removed. This is great news for you, dear reader!

11.3.1 The Sandbox

Installing what is a new piece of software on an organisation's production servers is a risk. If the new software is not fully tested in all environments, running it can cause all sorts of conflicts with existing software. A sandbox is a testing environment that isolates untested software from the production servers. Modern PCs allow quite a high level of multi-tasking and one by-product of this has been the rise of the workstation Virtual Machine. The sandbox we will encounter here is, in effect, a self-contained operating system that sits within a real PC but acts as if it is a separate computer. This allows us, for example, to run a version of Linux from within the Windows environment. This separation of the virtual machine allows us to play, safe in the knowledge that we will not damage our host system.

For the examples we give below we used a Window 8 64-bit PC with 8 Gb of RAM. We downloaded and installed VM Player, although the same can be done using VirtualBox from Oracle. We then downloaded a Sandboxed version of Hadoop which is running on Linux and is started by using VM Player. The Sandbox is provided by one of the major players in the Hadoop arena: Hortonworks. Other versions of Hadoop are available, including directly from the Apache open source site.

Another significant player in the Hadoop arena is Cloudera. They also have a "try it for free" version of Hadoop with lots of training material available. Their approach may suit readers with older operating systems since it involves browser access to a remote server running Hadoop. Both Hortonworks and Cloudera offer "getting started" training material and for the first time user there is little to distinguish them – both will do the job of opening up Hadoop to the newcomer.

Just because I attended some training given by a very able Hortonworks employee we have chosen to use their platform for this section. If you are going to try to follow this your PC does need to be a 64-bit one for this to work. If it isn't, or you don't want to install software on your PC, you should use Cloudera's version, available for free after you have registered from: http://go.cloudera.com/cloudera-live.html, and go through their training material.

To proceed with this tutorial you will need to download both the VMPlayer programme and the Hortonworks sandbox, both of which are quite sizeable and may take a long time if you have a slow connection to the internet. The steps you will need to go through are:

1. Install your chosen virtualising software. Both of these are freely downloadable:
   (a) VM Player from: https://my.vmware.com/web/vmware/free#desktop_end_user_computing/vmware_player/6_0
   OR
   (b) Oracle VirtualBox from: https://www.virtualbox.org/wiki/Downloads
2. Download the Sandbox from Hortonworks (see Fig. 11.1): http://hortonworks.com/products/hortonworks-sandbox/#install

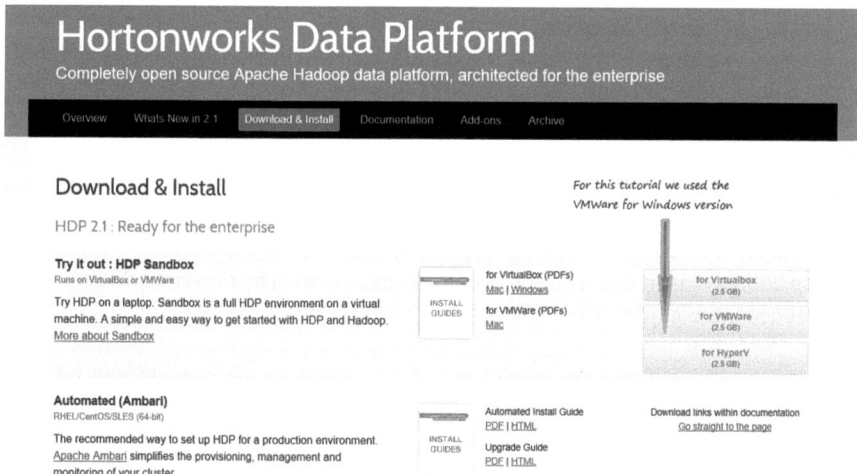

Fig. 11.1 The Hortonworks download page

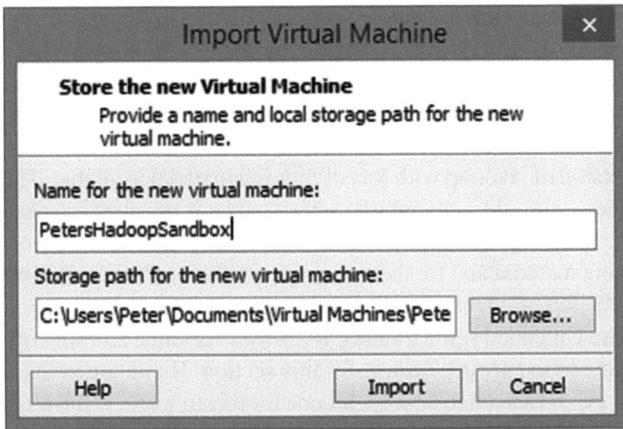

Fig. 11.2 OVA import screen

3. Start your newly installed VMPlayer
4. Import the VM you downloaded from Hortonworks by:
    (a) Click on Open a Virtual Machine from the VMPlayer menu
    (b) Locate the .OVA you downloaded in step 2 and select it by clicking on it. An OVA file is a zipped up version of an Open Virtualisation Package (OVF) which is an open standard for packaging and distributing virtual machines
    (c) Name the Virtual Machine and make sure the storage path is as you want it to be and then click on Import (see Fig. 11.2). This may take several minutes. It will unpackage the OVA file and save a virtual machine for you.
5. Once the Import is complete you will be presented with the chance to Play the Virtual Machine (VM). This is the same window you will get every time you open VMPlayer now. If you have more VMs than this Hadoop Sandbox they will be listed and you will have to select the one you want to work with and then click on *Play the Virtual Machine*.
6. Start the Sandbox VM by clicking on Play. This will start the VM, which will then begin to start Linux, which is what this Sandbox runs on. You will see several Linux start-up messages on the screen. You can ignore the messages. You will also get a hint box which you can close, and you may well be asked if you want to download updates to VM Tools to which you should answer *Remind me later*. You should eventually see a screen that looks like Fig. 11.3.
7. Use a browser to connect to the http address the sandbox provides by typing the http address given into your browser's address field. The first time through, you will need to complete the registration – but it is free!

As you will see there are many tutorials provided on the website you land on once you have registered. If you are already conversant with the fundamentals of Big Data then do feel free to use the tutorials provided. In the rest of this section we

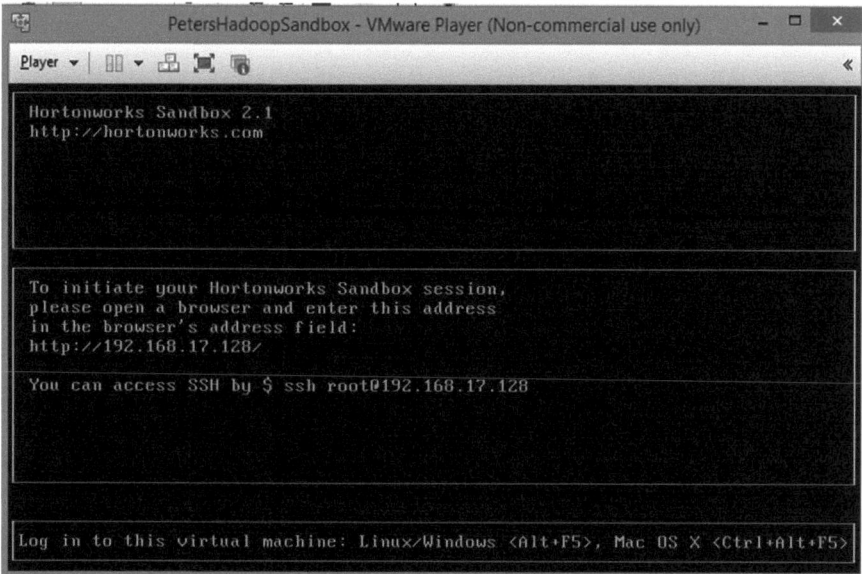

Fig. 11.3 Sandbox is started

will go through some simple processes to get a feel for Hadoop and its underlying architecture.

To start off we need to open the HUE interface to interact with the Hortonworks Data Platform (HDP). Hue provides a Web application interface for Apache Hadoop and for other tools such as Hive and Pig that we will also explore later. In your browser address add:8,000 to the address you used in step 7 above. In the case of this example that would be:

http://192.168.17.128:8000/about/

You will then have a browser-based menu to help you navigate through HDP. All of what we will do here can also be carried out on the command line using *ssh* if you are proficient in programming in that environment.

We could start by creating ourselves as a user on the system. However, in order for this to work effectively we would also need to create a user on the host Linux server so, in order to make this easy for us to get started, we will carry on using the default account **Hue (password 1111)**.

Firstly we will create a working folder to put our work into. From the menu bar click on the *File Browser*. Click on the New button on the right of the screen and then select Directory. Create a new Directory called something like Examples (see Fig. 11.4).

We are going to start off our exploration with the Hadoop equivalent of the Hello World example that many programming training sessions start their students off with. For Hadoop it isn't being able to write something like Hello World to the

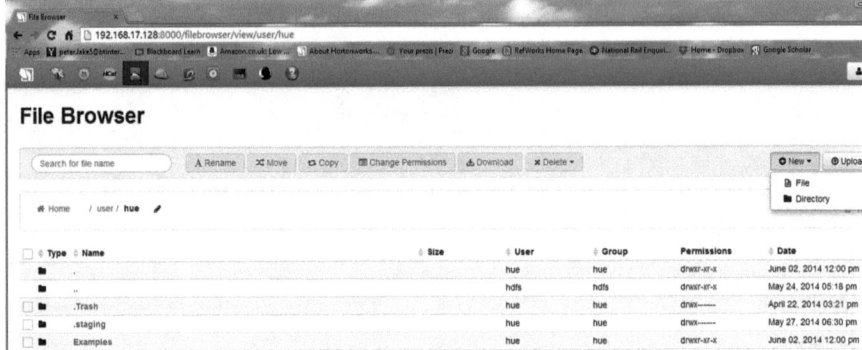

Fig. 11.4 Creating a directory

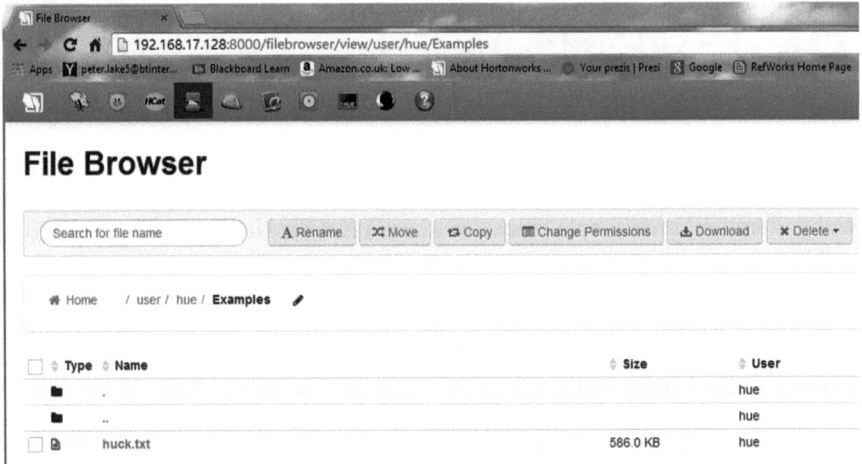

Fig. 11.5 The File Browser with Huckleberry in the Examples directory

screen which gives you the chance to say you have started using it; rather it is the ability to count words in a file.

We need to find a reasonably sized file with some words in it. Project Gutenberg (http://www.gutenberg.org/) is a good place to look. Huckleberry Finn in plain text, for example can be found here: http://www.gutenberg.org/ebooks/32325.txt.utf-8. Use a browser Download to download this to your local PC somewhere. Once you have acquired that file (and renamed it to something smaller, such as huck.txt, so that it is easier to type!) go back to the File Browser connected to the Sandbox. Click on the Examples directory. Click on Upload and select the book text you acquired from Project Gutenburg. Your screen should now look like Fig. 11.5, and you can view the content of the file by clicking on its name.

There are many tools available from Hue and this introductory tutorial will only touch on some of the important ones. We are going to start by running a word count

11.3 Hands-on with Hadoop

from within the Bash shell provided by Hue. A shell is an environment in which what you type at a command prompt is interpreted as instructions. Bash is such a command processor, which is frequently found in the Unix or Linux environments. Bash can also read a series of commands from a file, called a script file.

From the Hue menu bar, select Hue Shell, and then select Bash. At the time of writing this said it was test only – but it worked for this example! At the command prompt (the $ sign) type:

hadoop jar /usr/lib/hue/apps/jobsub/data/examples/hadoop-examples.jar wordcount /user/hue/Examples/huck.txt /user/hue/Examples/output

After a minute or so you will begin to get feedback to your screen on how the job is proceeding. Wait until you get the command prompt back before you do anything.

Right click on the File Browser icon on the menu bar and select *Open in a new tab* or the equivalent in your browser if you are not using Chrome as I am. This will allow you to switch backwards and forwards between views. Now, if you move to the viewer and click into Examples, you will see a new directory has been created called **output**. Click to open that and you will see two files. Click to open the file called **part-r-00000** and you will see the result – all the words that are in Huck.txt, together with the number of times they appear.

Just to understand what we did in the command line:

(i) hadoop jar tells hadoop to use the jar file pointed to by the next parameter, in this case: /usr/lib/hue/apps/jobsub/data/examples/hadoop-examples.jar
(ii) A jar file is a collection of Java class files. In this case it contains, amongst other things, *wordcount*, which is the next parameter.
(iii) Finally the next two parameters are the location of the source data and the location you would like the output written to. Note that the output directory must not already exist.(If it does exist you can use the File Browser to navigate to the Examples folder, then to the output subfolder, and tick the file "part-r-00000" before clicking Delete. This would allow the operation in the command line to run again.)

OK, we have got our hands dirty and actually used Hadoop to do some work for us. In this case it used the wordcount class which uses the MapReduce algorithm to summarise the number of each individual word in huck.txt. Let us now just make sure we also understand the environment we are working in:

- The software that enables the process we just went through is called Hadoop. In this case it is installed on a Linux box which is running in a Virtual Machine (VM). We know this is running when we see a screen that looks like Fig. 11.3.
- If you open a browser, such as Internet Explorer or Chrome, you can enter the URL of the Hue interface. In my case it is: http://192.168.17.128:8000/about/. The browser is using the hadoop functionality running on the VM, accessing it

through port 8000. Pointing a browser at this URL will not do anything unless the VM is running.
- Within the VM we also have the Hadoop Distributed File System (hdfs) running. This is a file system that provides data storage functionality (like a database in a way) that is designed to scale horizontally using cheap commodity servers. HDFS, MapReduce, and YARN are at the core of later versions of Hadoop, which is an Apache open source product.
- Normally used in a cluster environment, the VM allows us to mimic a working Hadoop deployment in a stand-alone setting. However, we need to be aware that hdfs is responsible for handling files for Hadoop, not the Linux operating system. This means you have to use Hadoop tools to interact with that data. The easiest way to demonstrate that is with the huck.txt file you downloaded:

(a) Go to the VM (which should look like Fig. 11.3). You may need to click on the screen somewhere to make sure it has focus. Press Alt and F5. When you need to get focus back to your host environment, away from the VM, you will need to press Ctrl+Alt.

(b) When asked, log in to Linux using **root/hadoop** for username/password. (Be aware that **root** has the highest set of OS privileges and you can break things big style if you get things wrong)!

(c) You are now logged in to the Linux box and can carry out any Linux commands you may want to. For example, try finding out which directory you are in by typing **pwd** at the $prompt.

(d) Remembering that we saved huck.txt somewhere on this VM, we should try and find it. You can see in Fig. 11.6 that it seems it is not there in the OS when we search using the Linux **find** command. In fact huck.txt is stored within Hadoop using hdfs. You therefore need to use a Hadoop command. Try and follow the example shown in Fig. 11.6 for yourself. The command we use is Hadoop fs (ie the file system) and then we can use the ls command to list the content of a directory which is **WITHIN HDFS** not in the Linux OS.

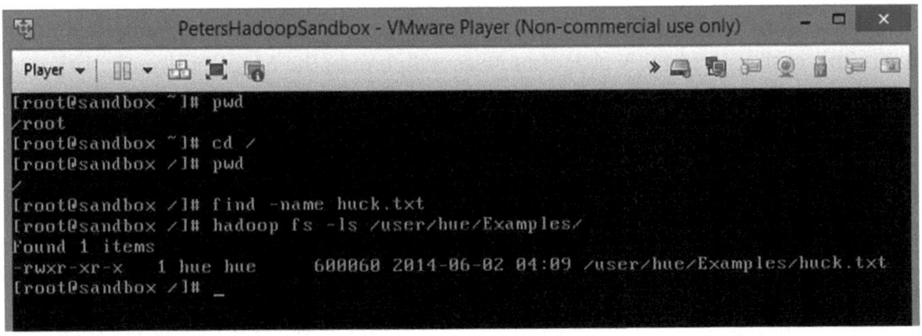

Fig. 11.6 Finding Huck.txt

(e) Tools like the Hue File Browser (Fig. 11.5) call this sort of functionality on your behalf and bring back the data to the browser to present it.

We are now going to use some of the other tools that Hue has available for us. To start with, we will need a data file for our exercises. The book example is OK for wordcounts, but there is more to data analysis than counting words! The Infochimps website has many openly available datasets we could use. Download (to your PC not the VM) from Datachimps this dataset: http://www.infochimps.com/datasets/airports-and-their-locations/downloads/253766 which contains information about airports across the world, and their location.

You then need to use unzip, or a similar tool, to extract the airport_locations.tsv file. Then you need to open your browser and connect to Hue, if you are not already connected. Use the Hue File Browser as we did earlier to move the airport_locations file into hdfs, putting it into the Examples folder.

The next thing we are going to do is make an entry in a catalogue with information about the file we have just uploaded. The catalogue is called Hcatalog. Its purpose is to store meta-data about the data held in the file and to easily make that data accessible by tools such as Hive and Pig which we will look at later. One of the key purposes is to provide some user friendly names to the dataset and its columns.

Select the Hcat (HCatalog) menu item in Hue. Then click on "create a new table from a file". Give the table a name (airports) and then you will need to create the link between this "table" and the file by using Select a File in the Input File field. Fill the other File options in as with Fig. 11.7, remembering that this is a Tab separated file. You can then move on to giving the columns names. For ease, just complete the first six columns something like:

airport_id
Lat
Lon
Name
City
Country

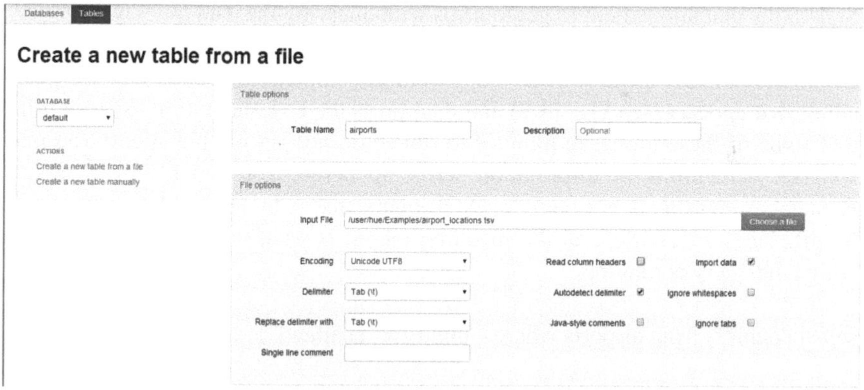

Fig. 11.7 File Options when creating an HCat table

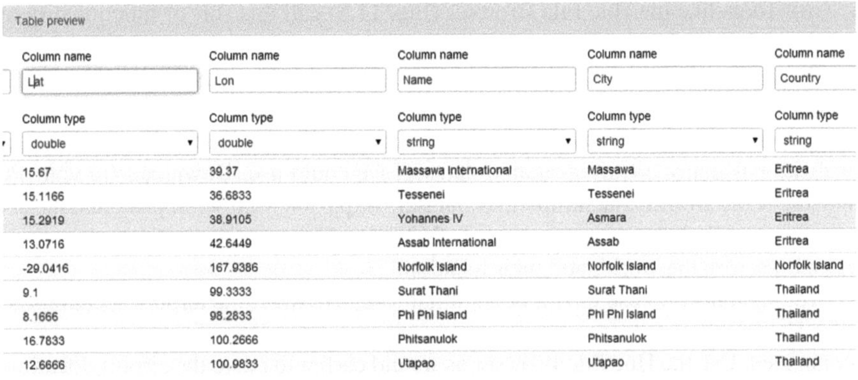

Column name	Column name	Column name	Column name	Column name
Lat	Lon	Name	City	Country
Column type	Column type	Column type	Column type	Column type
double	double	string	string	string
15.67	39.37	Massawa International	Massawa	Eritrea
15.1166	36.6833	Tessenei	Tessenei	Eritrea
15.2919	38.9105	Yohannes IV	Asmara	Eritrea
13.0716	42.6449	Assab International	Assab	Eritrea
-29.0416	167.9386	Norfolk Island	Norfolk Island	Norfolk Island
9.1	99.3333	Surat Thani	Surat Thani	Thailand
8.1666	98.2833	Phi Phi Island	Phi Phi Island	Thailand
16.7833	100.2666	Phitsanulok	Phitsanulok	Thailand
12.6666	100.9833	Utapao	Utapao	Thailand

Fig. 11.8 Column names in HCat

Click on Create Table and your table definition will appear in the list of tables. A screen shot is shown in Fig. 11.8.

Note: If you are closing down at any time (perhaps it is time for a coffee!) then in order to ensure data is saved cleanly, do not shut your PC down until you have powered down the VM. Click on the Player menu item and then select Power, and then Power Off.

11.3.2 Hive

Now we have the data available we are going to use Hive to answer the question: How many airports does Thailand have?

Hive is a powerful tool which allows the user to query the data in Hadoop using an SQL-like language called HiveQL. Naturally there is a processing overhead since, behind the scenes, a compiler translates HiveQL statements into MapReduce jobs, which are what is actually submitted to Hadoop for execution. However, newcomers to MapReduce can find it very difficult to master, but may well already have SQL skills that allow them to get to grips with querying the data quickly.

Just to see how easy it is to get started with asking questions, click on the Beeswax (HiveUI) menu in Hue. Copy the following HiveQL code into the query editor that appears (see Fig. 11.9) and then press the Execute button. Bear in mind that some of these jobs take minutes to run so do not get too impatient! You may well see screenfulls of information scroll up before you actually get a result. Remember that this is not really an SQL query that is being run, but rather some MapReduce processing, and the resulting output is what you see on your screen whilst the query is running.

select count(*) from airports where Country = "Thailand";

11.3 Hands-on with Hadoop

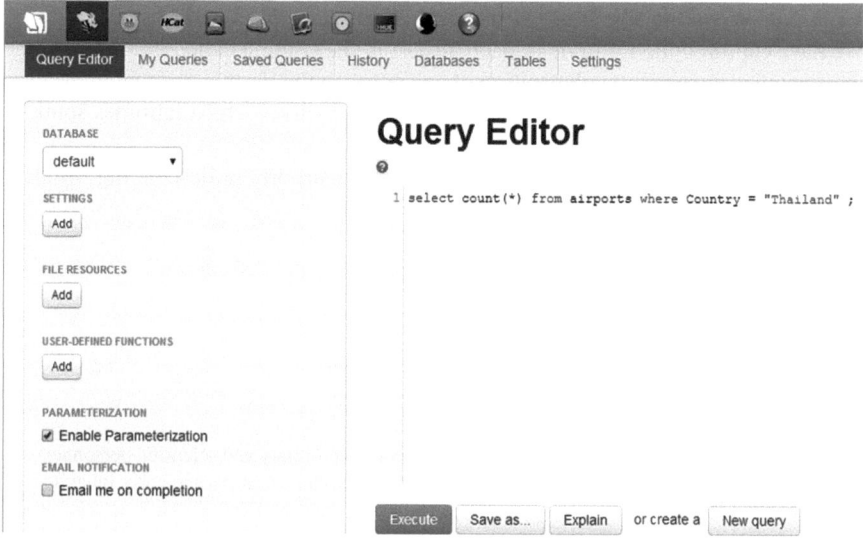

Fig. 11.9 Hive query editor

If you already have some SQL skills you could experiment at this point. Can you, for example, produce a report which lists the number of airports there are in each country? Or find out which is the most Northerly airport in the world? In short you will see that Hive makes Hadoop more approachable by providing this SQL-like interface. Don't worry if your SQL is not that good as we will work through these two questions next.

11.3.2.1 List the Number of Airports There Are in Each Country

The trick here is that we want to count the number of airports after grouping all the same country entries together. The GROUP BY SQL statement is used, together with aggregate functions (*count* in this case) to group the results by one or more columns:

SELECT country, count(airport_id) as No_of_Airports
FROM airports
Group by country;

and just to check the answers are realistic, it says Austria has 14 so let us check that:

SELECT city, name
FROM airports
Where country = 'Austria';

11.3.2.2 Which Is the Most Northerly Airport in the World?

We have captured the Latitude of each airport in the column called lat. It is latitude that specifies the north-south position of any point on the Earth's surface. In the case of our dataset, northerly latitudes are recorded as positives whilst latitudes south of the equator are stored as negative numbers.

Using the Hive query editor you could list the airports in descending order of their latitude:

SELECT name, city, country, lat from airports
ORDER by lat Desc;

> The output should look something like Fig. 11.10.
> As Wikipedia says:
>
> Alert (2011 permanent population 0,[1] but with rotating military and scientific personnel), in the Qikiqtaaluk Region, Nunavut, Canada, is the northernmost permanently inhabited place in the world,

Actually the proposed solution does not actually answer the question! As the reader of the data YOU have to decide which airport is the most northerly. The query has made this task trivial by sorting the column, but the proper answer ought really just to be one row presenting data for the most northerly airport.

In relational databases, such as Oracle, one way to do this would be:

SELECT name, city, country, lat from airports
where lat = (select max(lat) from airports);

This demonstrates the use of a nested subquery in SQL. At run-time the query *select max(lat) from airports* will return 82.5166 and that will then create a query that reads: SELECT name, city, country, lat from airports where lat = (82.5166).

Unfortunately HiveQL is not exactly like SQL and this sort of subquery in a WHERE clause is not allowed. If you copy it into your Query Editor and execute you will get an error. As is often the case there are workarounds, however. The code below is not as elegant but works in the way we want. It does so by creating a dataset called **maxdata** which contains only one row (the one with the maximum latitude in it) and joining it with an ordinary select on airports:

	name	city	country	lat
0	Alert	Alert	Canada	82.5166
1	Acadiana Regional	New Iberia	United States	80.1333
2	Roberts AAF	San Miguel	United States	80.0
3	Eureka	Eureka	Canada	79.9833
4	Svalbard	Longyearbyen	Norway	78.1916
5	Spitsberg	Svalbard	Norway	78.0

Fig. 11.10 Northerly airports

```
SELECT name, city, lat
FROM airports
JOIN (
  SELECT Max(lat) AS maxlat
  FROM airports
  ) maxdata
ON airports.lat = maxdata.maxlat;
```

11.3.3 Pig

So far we have manipulated our data manually. We copied the airports data file from the OS file system into the Hadoop file system and then manually entered the metadata definitions into HCatalog. Often, however, data professionals will need to do the same job over and over again, and some sort of script language to allow this to be automated would be a great help. This is where Pig comes in.

Pig's language is called Pig Latin and it compiles to produce a sequence of Map-Reduce jobs which allow the manipulation and analysis of large datasets.

We will start using Pig to work with the airports data we have just put into Hcatalog. Start by clicking on the Pig menu in Hue. Then paste the following into the Pig script editor:

```
allairports = LOAD 'airports' USING org.apache.hcatalog.pig.HCatLoader();
dump allairports;
```

Give the script a title (Pig1) and save it before then hitting the execute button. You can watch the blue status bar but be aware that later on some of our Pig scripts handle large amounts of data and can therefore take several minutes. If the status bar turns red you have an error somewhere. In this case it will probably be a copying mistake as there is very little else to go wrong! The screen should look something like Fig. 11.11.

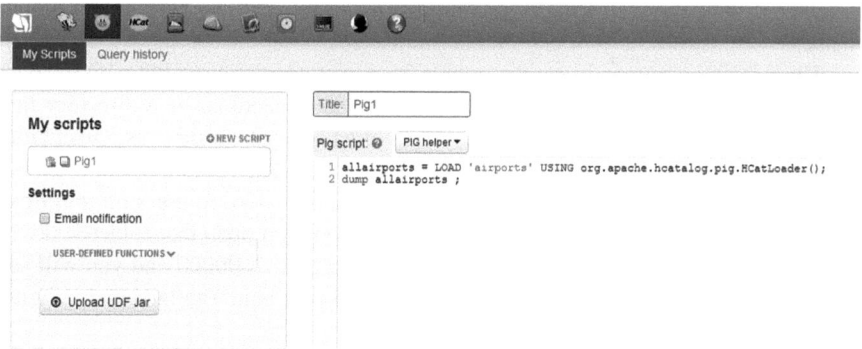

Fig. 11.11 First Pig script

Each stage in a Pig script is normally given an alias (a short-hand way of naming the dataset at any stage). In the Apache documentation these are often just a single letter, but we will use meaningful names as that tends to help others follow our logic. In this case we use the alias *allairports*. We call LOAD using the HCatLoader class to have the table schema retrieved automatically from Hcatalog. This simple script only has two steps. The second merely outputs to screen the results returned from *allairports*.

Once you have seen the output from Pig1, we will restrict the data to only airports in Thailand. Cut and paste the code below into the editor, save it as Pig2 and then Execute. Whilst you are waiting for the results you should look around the Pig editor page. You will see there is a button that allows you to Kill the current job. This can be very useful if you suddenly realise that you have set running the wrong query and it usually takes 3 h to run!

allairports=LOAD 'airports' USING org.apache.hcatalog.pig.HCatLoader();
thai=filter allairports by country == 'Thailand';
dump thai;

Note that we now have a second alias; *thai*. It takes the data from allairports and filters out all rows where the country is not exactly equal to Thailand. We then dump out to the screen again. However, this might be information that we want to use again and again, or maybe send on to someone else, so let us now save it back to the Hadoop file system as a comma separated file (CSV). In addition we will remove the unwanted columns as we do this:

allairports=LOAD 'airports' USING org.apache.hcatalog.pig.HCatLoader();
thai=filter allairports by country == 'Thailand';
wantedcols=FOREACH thai GENERATE $0 as airport_ID, $1 as lat, $2 as lon, $3 as name, $4 as city, $5 as country;
STORE wantedcols INTO '/user/hue/Examples/Thai' USING PigStorage(',');

FOREACH allows us to work on the data one row at a time. In this case we are generating a subset called wantedcols which select only the first column (column number 0) and the following five columns, using the "as" to give them column names.

The STORE command puts the output from wantedcols into a file with the data columns separated by commas. The INTO parameter needs to be a directory that does not exist and the job will fail if it does already exist. In this case **/user/hue/ Examples/Thai** is a new folder. Once the job finishes go back to the File Browser. If it has been open whilst this job was running you may need to press F5 to refresh the screen. You should see the Thai directory. If you then open that folder you will see two files. Review the content of the one called part-m-00000 and you will see we have a CSV containing only rows where the airport is in Thailand and only the columns we need.

11.3 Hands-on with Hadoop

Now let us extend our use of Pig to work on a large amount of data and to join that data to the airports data we have already generated. To do this we need to download another datafile. Luckily there are many sources of publicly accessible data these days. The US has been at the forefront of open data and sites like Infochimps that we used earlier contain a lot of US data. We will be using a dataset of more than three million US flight records from 1990 to 2009 summarised by month. Review information about the data on the Infochimps site: http://www.infochimps.com/datasets/us-domestic-flights-from-1990-to-2009. Use the Download button to bring the files down to your host operating system and then use the Hue File Browser to move the file called **flights_with_colnames.tsv** into the Examples directory.

Once in the Hadoop file system, view the content of the file. You will note two important things:

1. The first row contains not data, but column-headers
2. The airports are identified using the same three letter code as we saw in the airports file

What we are now going to do is create a report which orders the US airports according to the number of passengers leaving from them in the period covered by this datafile. It will identify the airport by its full name and the city it is in.

Our first task is to open the raw data file and remove the unwanted first row. You should now be confident enough to cut and paste these steps directly into the Pig editor and then execute the code.

```
flightdata=LOAD       '/user/hue/Examples/flights_with_colnames.tsv'     USING
    PigStorage('\t');
wantedcols=FOREACH  flightdata  GENERATE  $1  as  from_airport,$2  as
    passengers;
ranked=rank wantedcols;
noheader=Filter ranked by (rank_wantedcols>1);
removerank=FOREACH  noheader  GENERATE  $1  as  from_airport,(int)$2  as
    passengers;
dump removerank;
```

Things to note with the code above:

- We are using LOAD again, but this time our data isn't in HCatalog, but stored in a tab separated variable (tsv) file. We therefore need to use PigStorage and pass the parameter of the escape sequence that means "tab" (that is \t).
- To reduce the volume of data we are working on early the next step uses the FOREACH that we used earlier. We then use a work-around to remove the unwanted row by creating a column called rank (which will be the value of the row number) and then using Filter to only accept values in that rank column of greater than 1. We then remove the rank column before dumping the data out. Your screen should look something like Figs. 11.12 and 11.13.

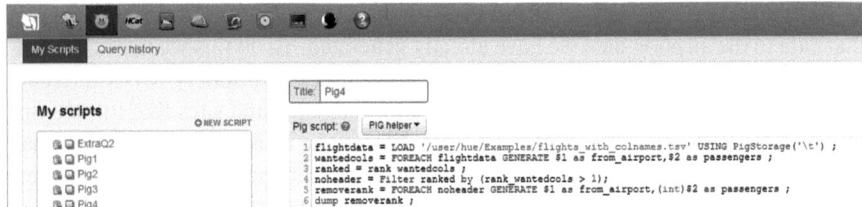

Fig. 11.12 Pig 4

```
The Job job_1403429236076_0001 has been started successfully.
You can always go back to Query History for results after the run.
(BIL,81)
(BIL,140)
(BIL,96)
(BIL,1152)
(BIL,1636)
(BIL,39)
(BIL,61)
(BIL,334)
(BIL,700)
(BIL,871)
```

Fig. 11.13 Pig4 output

- We cast the passenger count explicitly as an integer in the penultimate line. If we did not do this Pig would default to defining this column as a real number and we would have data which looked more like 81.0 as the passenger count.

And scrolling down you should see:
We will now build on this by summing the number of passengers for each airport. For this we will use the GROUP operator:

flightdata=LOAD '/user/hue/Examples/flights_with_colnames.tsv' USING PigStorage('\t');
wantedcols=FOREACH flightdata GENERATE $1 as from_airport,$2 as passengers;
ranked=rank wantedcols;
noheader=Filter ranked by (rank_wantedcols>1);
removerank=FOREACH noheader GENERATE $1 as from_airport,(int)$2 as passengers;
bydest=GROUP removerank BY to_airport;
pass_counts=FOREACH bydest GENERATE group as airport, SUM(removerank.passengers) as Pass_Count;
Dump pass_counts;

Now we will build further by joining this data with the *airports* data so that we can have rows with the airport name and city rather than code. As with relational database the joining means that the process will be to go through each of the *flight* rows that we have just created and look up the name and city values from the

11.3 Hands-on with Hadoop

airports data based upon the three letter codes being equal in both datasets. We will then sort the number of passengers in descending order so the biggest are at the top of the list and then tidy up the output a little by removing rows with zero passengers.

flightdata = LOAD '/user/hue/Examples/flights_with_colnames.tsv' USING PigStorage('\t');
wantedcols = FOREACH flightdata GENERATE $1 as from_airport,$2 as passengers;
ranked = rank wantedcols;
noheader = Filter ranked by (rank_wantedcols > 1);
removerank = FOREACH noheader GENERATE $1 as from_airport,(int)$2 as passengers;
bydest = GROUP removerank BY to_airport;
pass_counts = FOREACH bydest GENERATE group as airport, SUM(removerank.passengers) as Pass_Count;
**AirportRawData = LOAD 'airports' USING org.apache.hcatalog.pig.HCatLoader();
AirportData = FOREACH AirportRawData GENERATE $0 as airport_ID, $1 as lat, $2 as lon, $3 as name, $4 as city, $5 as country;
JoinedData = JOIN pass_counts BY (airport), AirportData BY (airport_ID);
SortedJoined = ORDER JoinedData BY Pass_Count DESC;
Nonzero = FILTER SortedJoined BY Pass_Count > 0;
Dump Nonzero;**

Now we have the data we want we could store this as a TSV and then use HCatalog to allow Hive to access the data and have SQL skilled personnel use it. We need to use tab separation since the data actually contains commas which will cause fictitious columns to be created when we import if we use a CSV format. To do this, replace the last line with:

wantedcolumns = FOREACH Nonzero GENERATE $0 as airport_ID, $1 as pass_count, $3 as lat, $4 as lon, $5 as name, $6 as city, $7 as country;
STORE wantedcolumns INTO '/user/hue/Examples/PassengerCount' USING PigStorage('\t');

You have now got a basic understanding of how powerful Pig can be in terms of cleansing and analysing data. Documentation about the Pig Latin language is to be found here:

http://pig.apache.org/docs/r0.7.0/piglatin_ref1.html
and
http://pig.apache.org/docs/r0.7.0/piglatin_ref2.html

Some more exercises using this data appear at the end of the chapter if you wish to push yourself to become more competent with these tools.

11.3.4 Sharing Your Data with the Outside World

Sometimes the Hadoop family tools may not be ideal for everything you want to do. As with many database products there is an ODBC driver available for Hortonworks Hive. ODBC stands for Open Database Connectivity and is a standard programming interface for accessing database management systems.

To open up your Hadoop data using ODBC drivers you need to follow these steps on your PC. This is not the only way to provide ODBC access, but if you want to use Tableau visualization software, you will need to follow these instructions.

1. Install Windows 32bit Hive ODBC driver (even if you are running a 64bit PC) from here: http://hortonworks.com/hdp/addons/
2. Configure the driver using the 32bit ODBC Administrator configuration tool which you will find by searching for ODBC in All programs, or using the Search in Windows 8.
3. Then select the System DSN tab and click ADD
4. Select Hortonworks Hive ODBC Driver from the list
5. Fill in the form presented so that it looks like Fig. 11.14. The Host is whatever you have been using to access the sandbox – it may not be identical to mine.
6. Enter the password for Hue (1111)
7. Click Test to ensure the connection works
8. Click OK twice to save the configuration

We now have one part of the ODBC connection set up. The next thing we need to do is grant the Hue user the privilege to run SELECT statements.

Using the file we created earlier (when we did: STORE wantedcolumns INTO '/user/hue/Examples/PassengerCount' USING PigStorage('\t');), make a Hcatalog table entry called passengercount.

We now need to allow the user Hue to write select statements against this table. Go back to the Hive editor, enter and run the following:

Grant select on table passengercount to user hue;

When complete this returns a 'no data' message since there are no rows to view. This may not seem reassuring but if you get it wrong you will get an error message instead! Now we can see if we can load this data into a spreadsheet. I am using the open source OpenOffice Calc, but you could use your own favourite spreadsheet, so long as it allows ODBC connections.

In Calc the way you make the connection is to open a blank spreadsheet and then click: File; New; Database. Your screen will look something like Fig. 11.15. Select ODBC in the Connect to an Existing Database drop down.

Click Next and then select the sandbox data source by clicking on browse.
Click Next again and enter the user name (Hue) and tick password required.
Test the connection

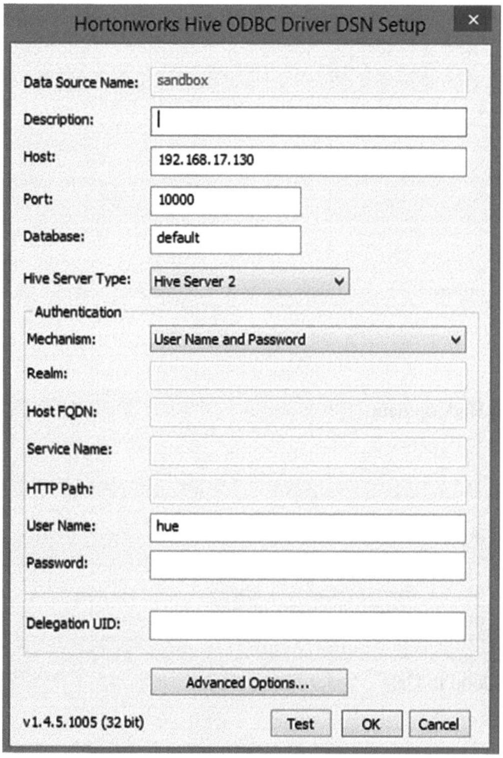

11.3 Hands-on with Hadoop

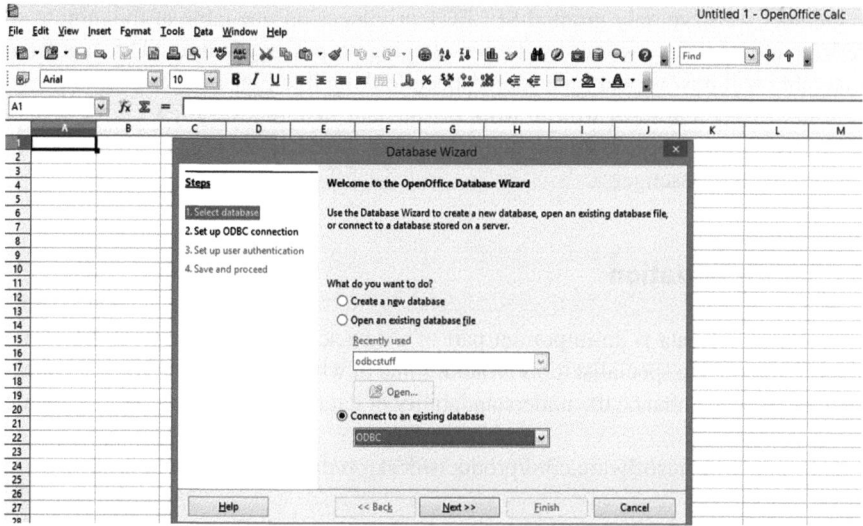

Fig. 11.14 ODBC configuration

Fig. 11.15 Setting up an ODBC connection in Calc

Fig. 11.16 Access to Hadoop data

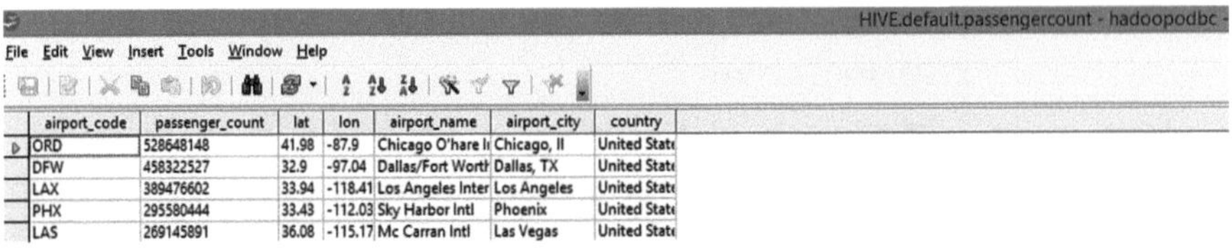

Fig. 11.17 From Hadoop to Calc

Finally, on the last screen, take the default entries and when asked, save the ODF file (which saves these settings for future use) as say, *hadoopodbc*.

You will then find yourself looking at something like Fig. 11.16.

Click on the plus sign next to "Default" to list the tables available to you. Do remember we have only granted SELECT privileges on one table at the minute so let's go ahead and view that by double-clicking on passengercount. The data from that table will now appear on a spreadsheet, looking like Fig. 11.17.

Once in a spreadsheet we can work on the data. Within a very few clicks we can even have some simple charts to help us explain the data (see Fig. 11.18 for the top 10 airports by passengers).

11.3.5 Visualization

Visualizing the data is an important part of a data scientist's role. Spreadsheets are good, but there are specialist tools around, some of which can use the ODBC connection, which can enhance the understandability of data. Try a trial version of Tableau:

http://www.tableausoftware.com/products/desktop/download?os=windows

The trial lasts only 14 days, but that should be enough for you to get a feel for how powerful this tools is, and how well it interfaces with the Big Data standard

11.3 Hands-on with Hadoop

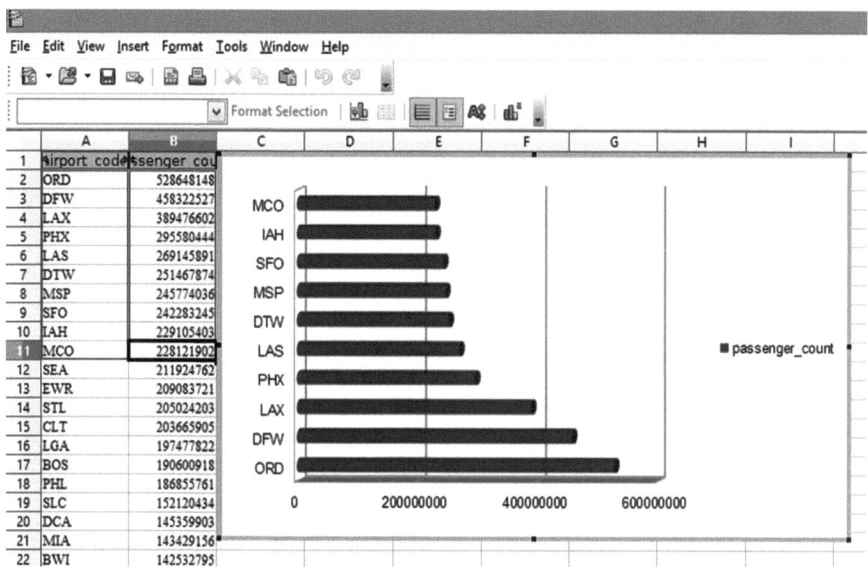

Fig. 11.18 Using the data in the spreadsheet

storage system; Hadoop. Visualization is worthy of a whole book, let alone a section in a chapter, so we are just going to do one exercise here to demonstrate the use of a visualization tool with Hadoop.

Once you have installed Tableau, and assuming you have already set up the ODBC driver (see earlier this chapter), start the Tableau programme. At the opening screen select **connect to data** by clicking on the link, or by using the Data menu item at the top. Then from the list of possible sources select **Hortonworks Hadoop Hive**. You will then get a screen to fill in similar to Fig. 11.19. Fill it in as I have, but remember that your host numbers may be different. When the form is complete, click on **Connect**.

Once connected tell Tableau that you wish to use the *default* schema by entering it in the search box as with Fig. 11.20.

Once default is in the schema list you need to click schema again and select *default*. Then select the *passengercount* table which we gave SELECT privileges to earlier.

Double-click the table and then select Update Now. It may take a minute or so but you will get back the data in that table looking like a spreadsheet. Click on **Go To Worksheet**.

Drag and drop the Airport Name to the Rows field. Wait for the data to return and then drag and drop the Passenger_Count measure to the Column field, as seen in Fig. 11.21.

As a final step to representing the passenger count data in a easy-to-understand way, click on the Packed Bubbles icon in the Show Me menu. Your output will look something like Fig. 11.22.

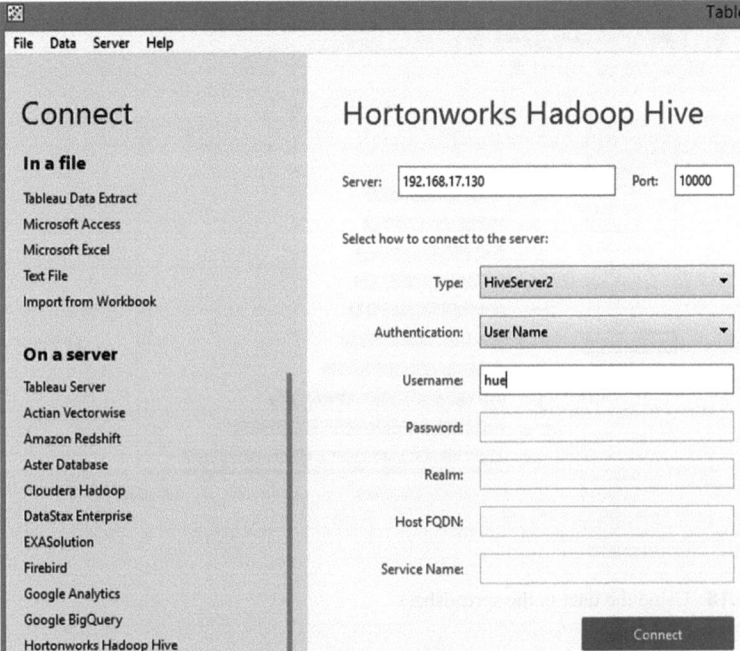

Fig. 11.19 Connecting to Hadoop using Tableau

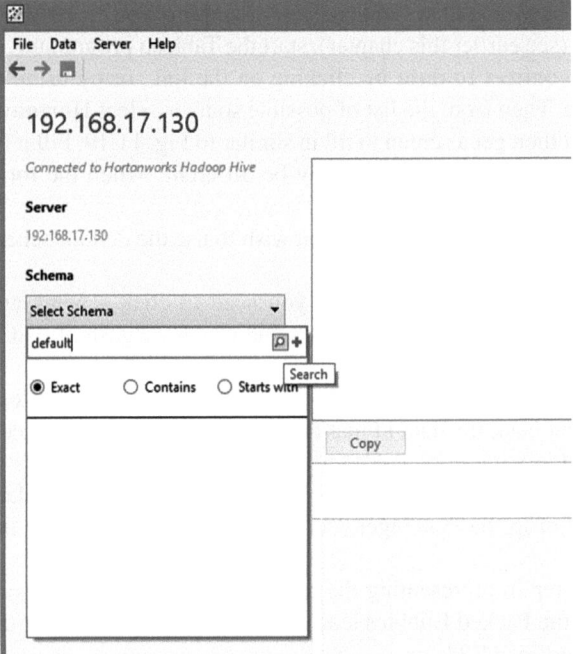

Fig. 11.20 Setting the schema

11.3 Hands-on with Hadoop

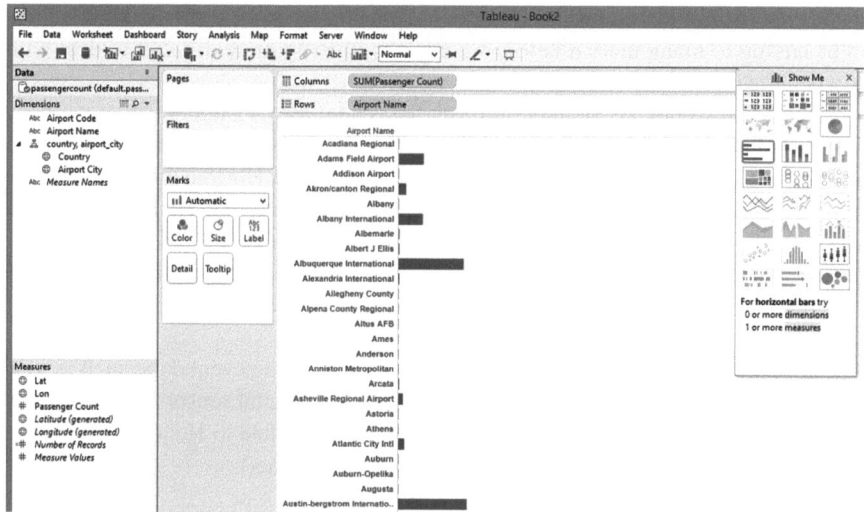

Fig. 11.21 Setting up the dimensions

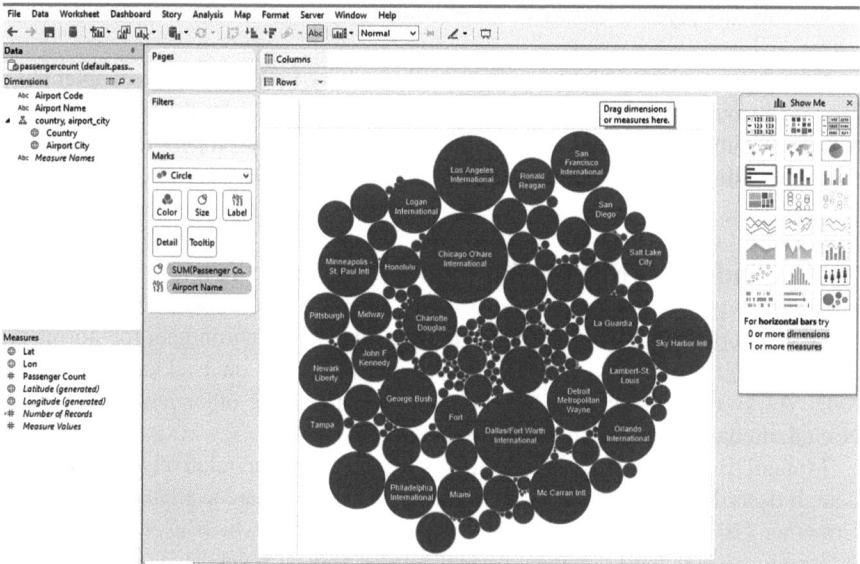

Fig. 11.22 A bubble representation of the data

11.3.6 Life Is Usually More Complicated!

What we have covered in this chapter demonstrates only a tiny fraction of what can be done in the Hadoop environment. The more observant amongst you may have spotted, for example, that the data we have used is both clean and structured. Often data is not clean (it contains errors) or is not exactly what we want; and that results in us having to manipulate it before we can use it. Even more difficult to deal with is when the data is not structured in any way.

Because this book is not about turning the reader into a Data Scientist we have not looked at these more advanced topics. Although Hadoop is relatively new there are beginning to be many tutorials out on the web, and Hortonworks themselves have many useful tutorials. If you want look at extending your Hadoop skills you could start with their tutorial for dealing with sentiment data from twitter: http://hortonworks.com/hadoop-tutorial/how-to-refine-and-visualize-sentiment-data/

Other tools you might want to examine include:

Flume: This tool is for moving large amounts of streaming event data, such as syslogs, GPS tracking data, social media updates, and digital sensors data. It allows the process of capturing event data and then writing data to Hadoop to be more easily managed. (http://hortonworks.com/hadoop/flume/)

Sqoop: transfers data between relational databases and Hadoop, and vice-a-versa. Remembering that a great deal of an organisation's existing data will be stored in some form of RDBMS this can be a very useful tool. (http://hortonworks.com/hadoop/sqoop/)

With the exception of Tableau all the tools we have looked at in this chapter have been open source. Not only does this mean you can use them freely, but, if you have the programming skills, you can get involved with the developers and contribute your own extensions and additions.

11.4 Hadoop Is Not the Only NoSQL Game in Town!

Since Hadoop is rapidly becoming the *de facto* standard environment for storing all forms of organisational data we have concentrated here on Hadoop and related tools. As you will have seen in other chapters, there are other new tools in the NoSQL arena that are worth considering.

MongoDB is becoming established as a data store for relatively unstructured data. It describes itself as a Document Store. More details are available in Lake and Crowther (2013). Chapter 5 of that book has a tutorial which uses some airport information so you will immediately feel comfortable with the data you are working with! The MongoDB website is: http://www.mongodb.org/

That book also has a tutorial covering Cassandra, which is a column-based database. The column-based approach can be much more efficient when aggregating data over many rows. Putting it very crudely, row-based can be ideal for transaction systems (OLTP) whilst column-based is ideal for decision support systems. The Cassandra website is: http://cassandra.apache.org/

Many alternatives to these two products are available. A good place to begin exploring the NoSQL domain is http://nosql-database.org/ where links to those alternatives will take you to tutorials should you wish to explore their functionality.

11.5 Summary

This chapter was largely about giving you the chance to get a feel for the Hadoop environment. We used the Sandbox to play safely and we use several tools, such as MapReduce, Hive and Pig, finishing off with an example of visualization using Tableau.

11.6 Review Questions

The answers to these questions can be found in the text of this chapter.

- What is Hue?
- Where would you store table definitions for use by Hive and Pig?
- Physically, where do files that you upload using the File Browser reside?
- Why would you need ODBC drivers to use with Hadoop?
- In the Pig environment, how are the following used:
  - LOAD
  - FOREACH
  - FILTER
  - DIMP

11.7 Extending the Tutorial Activities

These activities require you to use the tools to tackle new queries.

11.7.1 Extra Question 1

Using the techniques we outline above, put the data you stored in **/user/hue/Examples/PassengerCount/** into Hcatalog and then use Hive to display all the US Airports with a passenger count of greater than ten million that are above the 45th Parallel North. List their name, city, and passenger count.

11.7.2 Extra Question 2

Up until now we have been talking about passengers departing from airports. See if the sorted list looks any different if you add together the arrivals and the departures to give a "total passengers handled" count. There are several ways you could do this but perhaps the easiest is to produce a table in Hcatalog which uses the flights_with_colnames.tsv file.

Use Hive to write two queries against this new table: one for origin and one for destination totals and use the SAVE button to save the output from those queries. Then write another Hive query to add the passengers together.

Join with the Airports table to provide airport names to the results.

Now, with even less help:

11.7.3 Extra Question 3

To answer this question you need to know that other sources of flight information and related data are published on the web. You need to find some specific data to answer this question!

Try to find data which displays the routes flown. Bring that into the Hadoop environment and then manipulate it such that you can join it to *airports* and then answer the question: *which countries can I fly to from London?* Note: the London (UK) area, not just one airport. And watch out: there are Londons in other countries! You may need to use the Pig reference for at least one task: http://pig.apache.org/docs/r0.7.0/piglatin_ref2.html

11.8 Hints for the Extra Questions

(do not read unless you have to!)

11.9 Answer for Extra Questions

11.9.1 Question 1

Start by bringing /user/hue/Examples/PassengerCount/part-r-00000 into a table called originpassengers. Then run this query:

select origin_name, origin_city, passengers from originpassengers where Lat >45 AND passengers >10000000;

(Obviously the columns here need to match what you have called them in Hcatalog!)

11.9.2 Question 2

Generate a Hcatalog table from the flights_with_colnames.tsv file
  Use Hive to do the grouping and join with the Airports table:
  Once for origin and once for destination, saving each:

select origin_airport, sum(passengers) as Total
from flightdata
group by origin_airport
order by Total Desc;

select d.destin_airport as Airport, d.total+o.total AS FullTotal
from passengertotalsdest d, passengertotalsorigin o
where d.destin_airport=o.origin_airport;

save as totalhandled then join with airports:

select a.name as Name, a.city as City, a.lat as Lat, a.lon as Lon, t.fulltotal as FullTotal
from airports a, totalhandled t
where t.airport=a.airport_id
Order by FullTotal Desc;

Save as totalhandledwithgeoinfo

select name, city, FullTotal from totalhandledwithgeoinfo where lat <45 AND fulltotal >10000000;

11.9.3 Question 3

The data is here:

https://sourceforge.net/p/openflights/code/HEAD/tree/openflights/data/routes.dat?format=raw

  Put into Hcatalog and then use Pig, but watch out there are Londons elsewhere!

AirportRawData=LOAD 'airports' USING org.apache.hcatalog.pig.HCatLoader();
AirportData=FOREACH AirportRawData GENERATE $0 as airport_ID, $4 as city, $5 as country;
RouteData=LOAD 'routes' USING org.apache.hcatalog.pig.HCatLoader();
JoinedData=JOIN RouteData BY (sourceairport), AirportData BY (airport_ID);
wanted=FILTER JoinedData BY city == 'London' AND country == 'United Kingdom';

dest = JOIN wanted BY (destairport), AirportData BY (airport_ID);
onlycountries = FOREACH dest GENERATE $14 as destcountry;
destinationcountries = distinct onlycountries;
Dump destinationcountries;

Reference

Lake P, Crowther P (2013) Concise guide to databases. Springer, London. ISBN 978-1-4471-5601-7

The Future of IS in the Era of Big Data

12.1 What the Reader Will Learn

- that accurately predicting any future developments in Information Systems is almost impossible
- that there is a need to review new technologies for fear of being left behind by the competition, but that the review should be suitably critical
- that the pressure to keep up with technology is just one influence upon the decision-making practice of any organisation
- that Hadoop and MapReduce are likely to play a large part Information Systems design in the near-to-mid term
- that managers of Information Systems will have new tools, but also will have complex new architectures to manage

12.2 The Difficulty of Future Gazing with IT

There can be few other fields with quite so many wrong calls on what the future holds than IT has. The chances are that you will have access to some computing, either on a PC or laptop you own, or facilities offered in the library or university. Computing, in the western world at least, has become an everyday utility. How would the following experts feel now about these claims then:

- *Where a calculator like the ENIAC today is equipped with 18,000 vacuum tubes and weighs 30 tons, computers in the future may have only 1,000 vacuum tubes and perhaps weigh only 1½ tons.* (Hamilton 1949)
- *There's no chance that the iPhone is going to get any significant market share.* Steve Ballmer, USA Today, April 30, 2007."
- *There is no reason anyone would want a computer in their home.* (Ken Olson, president, chairman and founder of Digital Equipment Corp., 1977)

(All of the above are from this Wiki: http://en.wikiquote.org/wiki/Incorrect_predictions)

In Information Systems the list of failed hyped-to-the-max solutions that were expected to change the world is a very long one. Dan Tynan (2009) gives an interesting list, but it is by no means complete:

http://www.pcadvisor.co.uk/news/tech-industry/3205635/six-great-tech-ideas-that-failed-to-take-off/

With these in mind the authors will approach this chapter with some trepidation. However, as we established in earlier chapters, it is important for an IT professional to constantly appraise new development in IT to see if any might offer competitive advantage for their organisation, no matter how short-lived.

Another difficulty for predictors is that of deciding which ideas will actually enthuse customers enough to try them, let alone replace their existing systems with the new technology. And that uncertainty has nothing to do with how good the new solution is from a technical perspective. On top of that, Big Data is new. It is not a mature technology and things are moving very quickly (another familiar trait in IT developments). Far more quickly than the typical book author-publisher cycle takes, for example. So some of what we say will have already been proven (or disproved) by the time you read this!

12.3 The Doubts

Businesses have always used technology to look for ways of reducing costs, increasing efficiency, or provide a competitive advantage. The basic decision making question remains the same now as it was decades ago: *Is this technology going to present benefits to my organisation that outweigh the costs and potential implementation problems?* At the moment we have a few new factors around that have led to the use of a new buzz word: Big Data. But the question remains the same – is it worth investigating Big Data? Even mere desk research takes time. Trying some of the new solutions out will take time, and it may require new, specialist knowledge which will be expensive to acquire. A more sensible use of our limited resources may be to concentrate on getting more from our existing technology. For technophiles these may seem like questions from the stone age, but they are necessary questions if we are not to waste money on unproven technologies.

As is often the case with newer technologies, there is plenty of hype around, with vendors falling over themselves to tell you the advantages of their particular Big Data products and services. As Mandl (2013) observes:

> ... the term [Big Data] seems to get thrown around recklessly and cluelessly more often than not and, even when it's used appropriately, applied much more widely than is warranted.

One of the big worries is that the fact that we have suddenly got so much data available to us will be seen as some sort of silver bullet. Twitter analysis is a new exciting way to get virtually instantaneous customer feedback on new products; but it will not tell you how to source your raw materials for that product. Because of the newness of the approach the sales and marketing possibilities for Big Data are by far the most frequently mentioned in the press and journals. However, Pelz-Sharpe (2013) warns us:

> All data is not equal – most of it is just noise.
> http://www.channelregister.co.uk/2013/03/11/alan_pelz_sharpe_big_data/

In other words, gathering and storing data may not be the most important aspect of Big Data's evolution. It will be more around how to filter out the noise and perform analysis that generates important new information for the business, or society.

12.4 The Future of Information Systems (IS)

The discussions above have been broadly around the IT domain. What does the future hold for Information Systems in particular? The field has certainly changed over the last 20 or more years.

Teubner (2013) provides an excellent overview of the state of the art in Strategic IS(SIS). There is discussion of how practice and theory have seemingly separated over recent years, and then some discussion of how new frameworks and decision making tools are beginning to appear to lessen the gap. He also goes on to discuss Galliers' (2011) new model. The importance of this new model is that Galliers was a leading researcher in the 1990s and was proposing different models then. There is a marked change in focus between the two models. Note, especially, that there is no longer a differentiation between IT, IS and service strategies (see Fig. 12.1 (old) and Fig. 12.2 (new))

But the change of emphasis described by Galliers may not be the only issue in the field. We have known for a while that IS will not provide lasting competitive advantage. It is the nature of IS developments that they are, ultimately, copyable by anyone else, so if you do use something successfully, others will follow. Buhl et al. (2012) are even more outspoken and say:

> Put bluntly, results of SIS research do not have the potential to create competitive advantage. They lose their impact upon publication. They may at best inform managerial decision makers on SIS topics. This paradox is rooted in the characteristic differences of strategy and scientific research.

The very idea that Information Systems cannot lead to an organisation gaining competitive advantage is to challenge the worth of the domain in the first place. The paradox they allude to is a deep seated philosophical difference in approach

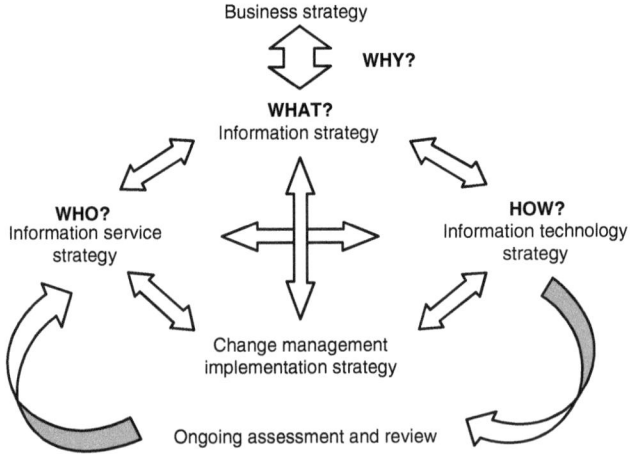

Fig. 12.1 Galliers old model

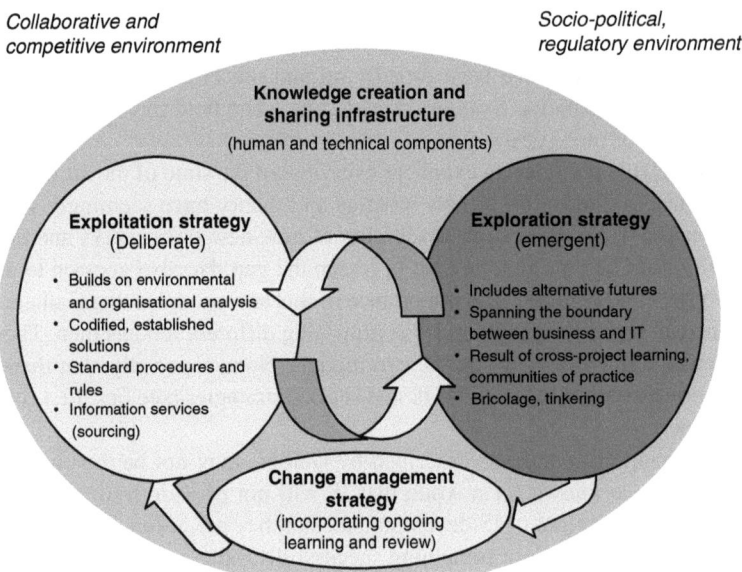

Fig. 12.2 Galliers new model

that is very difficult to manage. The excitement the IT researcher feels when they begin trying new technologies is of no consequence to an organisation. And, from the other perspective, the appropriate SIS decision for an organisation may well be the most boring, dated solution on the market.

The age old question is: *Are organisations' IS decisions driven by changes in technology or by business need?* It is possible for the two to coincide, and it is true that failure to investigate the opportunities afforded by new technology could cause

12.4 The Future of Information Systems (IS)

your organisation to fall behind the market leaders, at least temporarily. However, when future gazing, it is sensible to keep feet firmly on the ground by remembering just what it is we are actually trying to do in IS. Surely, to be of worth, we need to be exploring the use of information technologies in their widest sense in a business or social context? We should be evaluating the ways that our businesses, or society, can be improved by adopting some newer technology. Not to do so leaves us at risk of being the last sled puller just after the wheel was invented (and how many sled pullers do you know in your neighbourhood?).

12.4.1 Making Decisions About Technology

There will always be the place for the hand-crafted goods fashioned by craftsman with traditional tools. And sometimes the turnover of these companies is so small that there can be no argument whatsoever for them investing in an IT solution. However, all but these staunchly traditional companies will, at some stage, opt to change the technologies they use to help them do business. The key question is often; **When**?

There are many factors that might influence decisions about whether or not an organisation invests in new technology. Figure 12.3 depicts most of them. Some are external to the organisation but probably the biggest are those from within the organisation. Let us look at each of the factors in the figure in turn.

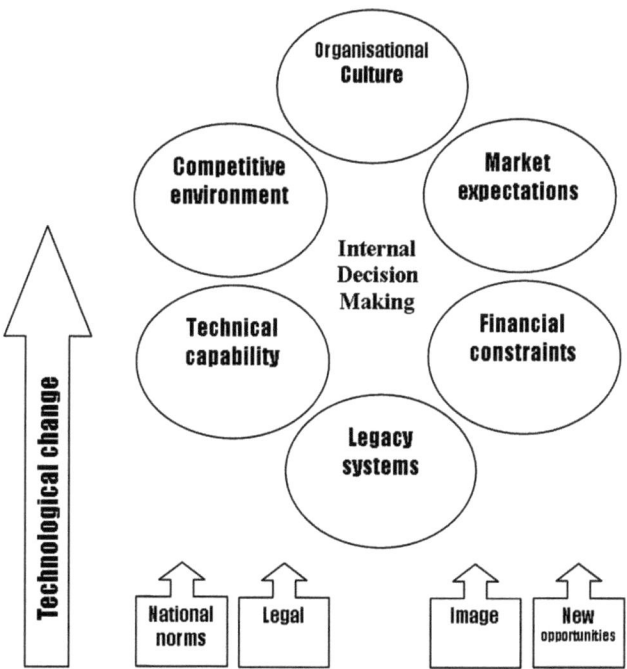

Fig. 12.3 Factors influencing decisions on IT/IS change

12.4.1.1 Organisational Culture

Some organisations are naturally conservative, whilst others may encourage change and innovation. This is not the place for detailed discussion of why and how cultures occur, but amongst the many good texts on the subject is one by Alvesson (2001) in which he suggests the following assumptions can be made about cultural phenomena:

1. they are related to history and tradition;
2. have some depth, are difficult to grasp and account for, and must be interpreted;
3. they are collective and shared by members of groups;
4. they are primarily ideational in character, having to do with meanings, understandings, beliefs, knowledge, and other intangibles;
5. they are holistic, intersubjective and emotional rather than strictly rational and analytical.

In terms of taking decisions about the use of IT/IS, the degree to which a company is naturally risk averse will clearly impact upon the value they put on keeping up-to-date. And, let's be honest, given the IT industry's track record for failures, this may be a very sensible stance to take even if you are willing to take risks elsewhere. The problem with not taking the risk, however, is the one we alluded to above – the company that plays it safe runs the risk of being the last sled-puller in the game; falling behind their competitors as a result.

As well as the general organisational culture, it is also true that the Information Systems professionals differ in attitude. Even conservative organisations can be persuaded by a proactive Chief Information Officer (CIO) with board level access – usually by citing the projected cost savings or productivity gains that would come from investing in a new technology.

Attitudes to IS itself vary too. To a large part it will depend upon whether the IS systems are viewed as a utility, or as an opportunity generator. If they are the former then keeping costs down will probably be the biggest deciding factor.

12.4.1.2 Competitive Environment

What Enterprise Systems specialist vendor SAP have done really well over the past decades is to provide their enterprise wide solutions to one leading company in a market sector, like Oil and Gas, or Retail, and then use the success story that generates to persuade others in the same sector that they need to adopt a similar solution. So what the competition themselves are doing can act as a significant driver in the decision making. Of course, there is always the argument that to use identical solutions is to lose the opportunity to excel and differentiate.

An organisation's relationship with suppliers and customers will also be an influence. Electronic Data Interchange (EDI) has been around for decades. It is where there is a standard interface for communication between companies around electronic documents like order forms. In the UK there was a time when the National Coal Board (NCB) was a very major purchaser of mining machinery. If you were a machinery manufacturer you really did want to do business with the NCB. In order to try and reduce the costs associated with running a very labour intensive manual purchasing system, the NCB declared that all purchase orders would be

12.4 The Future of Information Systems (IS)

sent by EDI. What this meant for small suppliers to the NCB was that if you wanted to keep on doing business with one of your major customers you had to invest in a computer. Powerful customers, then, can clearly influence decisions.

12.4.1.3 Market Expectations

If you are a digital native (had ICT around you all your life) then you will probably be one of the people who get cross when you ask if the large DIY superstore has something in stock and they say: "just wait there for a few minutes and I will go and look round in the storeroom." Why can't they look on an App and tell you instantly? Better still, why can't you look for yourself on your own phone before you set off to the store? Some outlets would probably lose their place in the market if they don't keep up with what their customers are expecting of them.

12.4.1.4 Technical Capabilities

If an organisation has an in-house IS department in can find itself limited by the skillsets of the people working there. In the era of Big Data, for example, it would make little sense to decide to try out Hadoop if you had no Java skilled personnel, if all your database people had only SQL skills and you had no data scientists to take advantage of the data you store.

You could take a business decision that regardless of any skills shortfall you will install and use Hadoop, in which case there would need to be a skill gap analysis undertaken and the gaps will need to be plugged by employing new staff, retraining existing staff, or temporarily buying in contract staff to fill the gap. These are of course expensive solutions, which brings us to the next factor; Finances.

12.4.1.5 Financial Constraints

Probably the biggest single influence on decisions will be financial. There is, of course, the obvious point that if the organisation is currently struggling financially a new system may just not be affordable. However, it may be that immediate cash is not available but that the investment in a new system is projected to add considerably to profitability, in which case borrowing might be a way round the problem.

In the era of rented services through the Cloud, the need for immediate injections of large amounts of capital for any new project can be removed by renting on an as-needed basis. This can be more expensive overall but has the advantage of spreading the cost over a number of years and having it show as a revenue cost rather than a capital cost. This means that proposed projects that once would have been immediately rejected may now be able to find an acceptable means of funding.

12.4.1.6 Legacy Systems

Only in start-ups and very small businesses is one ever likely to buy a brand new system that is not replacing an existing one, or at least needs to communicate with one. Legacy systems in large organisations could well be mainframe based. But even large client/server systems will have cost the company a lot of money and time to get to their current state. Those systems are likely to have specialists looking after them who know the system intimately and keep it running efficiently. If they are doing the job they were designed for it is a brave CIO indeed who recommends killing them off and replacing them with a completely new system.

There has, however, to be a tipping point – a time when the existing systems either do not do what they were designed for, or, more likely, a whole new set of requirements have arisen, probably driven by the expectations of employees who may be used to their home computers and see them running faster than the in-house computing solution. Even when this tipping point happens, though, the other factors discussed in this section can still trump it. A lack of corporate cash, for example, can make a slow reporting system seem quite low down on the list of priorities.

12.4.1.7 Technological Change

Often changes will happen gradually. As I write this Oracle is on Version 12c of its database software. The newer product is significantly different from each of Oracle 6, 7, 8i, 9i and 10g. However there will be organisations which have their business systems running on the earlier versions. Upgrading can cost extra in terms of licence fees, and there may well be significant repercussions on the viability of application code written to a particular version of the database. Many organisations, however, do upgrade to take full advantage of the additional functionality in newer releases. More cautious DBAs will wait until, for example, 11.2 before upgrading, waiting for the early adopters to find the bugs. Some, however, will need something that has been added to the new release urgently, and they will be willing to go for 11.0.

Sometimes, however, a major technology shift occurs. A very recent one is the sudden meteoric rise in the use of Hadoop in order to manage the large amount of data involved in Big Data. Here we have a new technology which is adding value to a organisation's data. Not to adopt it may be to fail to keep up – to be the sled-puller we talked about earlier. But in order to adopt it we need to be sure we can afford it, that we have the skills to use it, and the real business need to drive it through to successful implementation. As we said above, the question is: *Are organisations' IS decisions driven by changes in technology or by business need?*

12.4.1.8 Other External Factors

In the UK organisations had to suddenly worry about the PC monitors that their employees were using when the Health and Safety (Display Screen Equipment) Regulations of 1992 legislation came into force. It meant that monitors had had to meet several safety criteria and that it was the employer's responsibility to make the employer comfortable and safe. For caring organisations this was a very small issue, and new monitors would be purchased where needed, but it does demonstrate how external factors can enforce adoption of some technologies.

Other factors include the need to maintain a certain image. For many large corporates the impressively efficient computer systems they have are part of the overall perception that stakeholders have of them. At the extreme, for example, would you honestly say that you would give as much time to the salesman that turned up with a 1980s brick sized mobile as you would the one with an iPhone? Even if the answer was *yes*, companies are aware that many others would say no and do not want to run the risk of seeming out of date.

Big Data is an example of a technology which is offering new opportunities. As we see elsewhere in the book, sentiment analysis to provide companies with information about how their products are being received in near real-time is now available. If that opportunities seems potentially useful to an organisation then the technology needed to implement it will need to be acquired.

National norms also play a part. If your organisation is in the US many of its employees will be of the Digital Native generation and their expectations will be different from employees of some other nationality for whom the internet may not be anywhere near as readily available.

12.5 So What Will Happen in the Future?

With the caveats and doubts out of the way, we ought to try and establish what the future of Information Systems looks like as best we can. As we said above, we don't want to be left behind as this can lead to wasted opportunities. To start with, let us review what might happen with Big Data. We will then go on to investigate Information Systems Management in general.

12.5.1 The Future for Big Data

Only 2 years ago no-one would have been sure whether the term Big Data had any staying power. It could have been just another one of those concepts that got lots of hype but didn't get anywhere. It is now clear that it is not a fad. Big Data is here to stay – at least for the next few years. However, there are many definitions of what Big Data actually is, and this uncertain present makes predicting the future even more tricky.

We can be sure that Hadoop is here to stay for the next few years. The traditional RDBMS vendors will keep arguing about the strengths of their products and the limited use that businesses might put Hadoop to, but we need to view any such comments warily as we only have to review which of those vendors now have Hadoop embedded in their own products. Even Microsoft have a cloud-based Hadoop service for Azure users. There were industry rumours that Microsoft were developing their own equivalent to Hadoop, called Dryad, as far back as 2006, but in the end they have given up and a Microsoft blog in 2013 stated that:

> Microsoft recognizes Hadoop as a standard and is investing to ensure that it's an integral part of our enterprise offerings.
> http://blogs.technet.com/b/microsoft_blog/archive/2013/10/28/announcing-windows-azure-hdinsight-where-big-data-meets-the-cloud.aspx

With the sort of financial reserves that Oracle and Microsoft have tucked away it may be a safe bet that at least one of them will be developing an alternative to Hadoop at some point. It must be very galling for them to have to include open source software in their offering since part of their customer appeal is the robustness of their well known brand – an argument that is diminished by the use of free to use software.

When a commercial version arrives (if it hasn't already by the time this goes to press) it is likely to have a much more friendly front end to it. As organisations like Hortonworks and Cloudera have found, people are willing to pay to have some of the layers of complexity hidden from them by a nice friendly GUI front-end. As you saw in the brief technical overview of Hadoop in Chap. 11, in its natural, download-from-Apache format, Hadoop is far from friendly.

Friendly it may not be, but relatively cheap and extensible it is. Organisations which regularly deal in large amounts of data will, more and more, begin to use Hadoop as the Case Study stories on the Web increase. It may come as a surprise, but not many organisations would have considered buying a client/server database like Oracle in the early 1980s. Now products like Oracle are the backbone of nearly every major company in the world. So the precedence is there for Hadoop. It could indeed take over the IS world.

It is certainly true that Hadoop continues to improve and to grow in terms of user base. Where will this end? Is there any reason why Hadoop could not replace products like Oracle RDBMS and SQL Server, for example? Is it possible that OLTP systems might become Hadoop based? The technology is certainly not against it. And it is being worked on as we write. But is there a danger here of every problem being a nail because we have a new Hadoop hammer?

Most large organisations have already invested heavily in their RDBMS based Information Systems. If they are working well why would they change? At least in the short term, therefore, it is likely that organisations will try Hadoop solutions out on new data analytics projects, but run those projects in parallel with their current Information Systems. The availability of short term Cloud solutions, such as Amazon's EC2 to host Hadoop clusters allows this sort of trialling to happen without the need for potentially mistaken heavy capital investments.

Part of the reason for the success of Hadoop may have something to do with it being open source – especially in an era of economic hardship like that we have been going through in the last few years. Had Oracle brought this out as one of their products and charged hefty licence and support fees the go-ahead for organisations to experiment might well have been harder to justify on expense grounds. The open source project has also spawned other Hadoop-related tools like Pig, Sqoop and Hive which would doubtless have been charged-for extras if vendor supplied. Indeed open source for things other than just Linux has had a real boost as a result of the Apache projects and that, in its own right, may be a longer term issue for vendors.

On top of the advantages conferred on Hadoop by being open source, it was also lucky enough to come to prominence just after another recent technology had become accepted – Cloud computing. As we saw in the Systems chapter (Chap. 8) Cloud opens up whole new possibilities for people interested in distributed data systems. Though not essential, Cloud is an enabler, even an accelerator, for Hadoop and whilst Cloud computing continues to grow we can assume it will have the effect of leading more people to try distributed data solutions.

As well as being a distributed data management system, Hadoop also uses MapReduce to process data. MapReduce is not new, and the basic steps are unlikely to change, but we may see some extension to the original functionality. MapReduce, for example, is not very easy to use where compound records are involved, or where joins are involved. Relational databases cope with both of these complexities. Ferrera et al. (2012) talk about Tuple MapReduce, and suggest that Pangool allows tuples (records) to be processed in the same way as a key-value pair which is at the heart of traditional MapReduce function. The technocal issues are discussed in Chap. 11 and there is more about Pangool on their website: http://pangool.net/

Hive allows SQL type queries to be run over data stored in Hadoop's Distributed File System (HDFS). This is incredibly useful for organisations with SQL-skilled data analysts already in place since they do not need to look at increasing their pool of analysts in order to query all the data being collected. It is an open source solution, and there is probably room in the market for a commercial product that does something similar, although the big players have already added this sort of functionality to their product ranges.

Oracle, for example, provides an Oracle SQL Connector for Hadoop Distributed File System (http://docs.oracle.com/cd/E37231_01/doc.20/e36961/sqlch.htm) which allows analysts to use SQL to query Hadoop, and/or Hive tables.

Many new sources of data have become available in the last few years, but accessing them is not an easy task. Tools like Sqoop and Flume have been developed to help, but, much like Hadoop itself, they are far from easy to master. This is not surprising since the task itself is not trivial. The future is bound to see drag-and-drop being built into front ends of these tools, to make the mapping process between source and target easier. Again, the big vendors are there already. Oracle has its Oracle Loader for Hadoop (http://docs.oracle.com/cd/E27101_01/doc.10/e27365/olh.htm), for example.

For decades computer processing speeds have doubled roughly every 2 years, an observation now known as Moore's law. These improvements mean that the time to process a particular set of data will have been halving every 2 years. However, as we saw in earlier chapters, the datasets we are processing also growing exponentially. Many believe Moore's law has to end some time since there are physical limits to what can be built. As reported in PCWorld by Ian Paul (2013) in an article entitled *The end of Moore's Law is on the horizon, says AMD:*

> The company's [AMD] Chief Product Architect John Gustafson believes AMD's difficulties in transitioning from 28-nanometer chips to 20-nanometer silicon shows we've reached the beginning of the end.

That worry aside, advances in underlying technologies will continue to bring down the cost of hardware, meaning that we will get to the point were the question "should we save this data" is never asked since we can store it for next to no cost, just in case it is useful in the future. The hidden danger here is that we end up with swathes of unwanted data which hides the important stuff, so some form of data management will always be required.

The cost of RAM may well continue to fall too, and, together with the improved reliability of Solid State Disks (SSD), this will lead to in-memory solutions becoming more prominent. As we saw earlier, one big bottleneck in database performance is reading from and writing to Hard Disk Drives (HDD), despite the fact that HDD technology has improved their performance and reliability considerably over the past 10 years. In memory databases solve that problem. Of course they have their own problems, such as ensuring data permanency to minimise the loss during a power outage, and the fact that RAM is far more expensive per Kilobyte than is a HDD. However, if speed is vital in your application, you will put up with the extra cost.

Oracle have had an in-memory database since they acquired TimesTen in 2005. A more recent entrant to the scene, and one which is deliberately proposing the benefits of in-memory to meet the needs of Big Data, is SAP. Their in memory solution is called SAP HANA. On their website banner (http://www.saphana.com/welcome) recently they said:

> SAP HANA converges database and application platform capabilities in-memory to transform transactions, analytics, text analysis, predictive and spatial processing so businesses can operate in real-time.

That is a fair amount of sales pitch in one sentence, but this is undoubtedly an exciting product. The term Real Time Data is used a lot with products like HANA. We have already discussed the importance of the "V"s of Big Data (Chap. 9), including the most obvious one: Volume. There is, however, another important driver that doesn't begin with V, and that is Timeliness. Managers and decision makers want to use powerful technologies to speed up the analysis process so that their decisions can be taken earlier. With traditional systems key indicators may be reported on only on a monthly basis, and whilst this may originally be partially as a result of the standard monthly accounting cycles, it may well also be as a result of all the effort hat is required to gather data from disparate in-house systems and merge them together. Having a single system able to contain all the company's data and, moreover, being able to perform analytics at high speed because the processing is in-memory changes the expectations.

When you review the SAP-HANA website you will see many of the Use Cases and video clips from customers who are talking about the advantage of HANA being the speed with which information needed for decision making is made available. When you add the ability to do real time sentiment analysis, perhaps by monitoring Twitter feeds as they happen, you begin to move into an environment where the companies who have to wait for the end of the month to get key data will lose opportunities in comparison to those with a live handle on their information.

Just occasionally speeding up information flows can be detrimental. In a stock market, if the market valuation starts to go down, and that reduction can be seen in real-time it can establish rapid positive feedback and the market could collapse.

Up until now we have spoken only of data acquisition, manipulation and storage. The real area where we would expect to see an explosion in innovative new products is around analysis and presentation. Tools for these aspects are built into SAP and

12.5 So What Will Happen in the Future?

Oracle products already, although they will always be looking to improve them. However, these premium complete solutions will not be so appealing to Small-to-Middle sized companies (SMEs) who tend to spend less on Information Systems. The trend to one system for everything was begun in the 1990s with the development of Enterprise Resource Planning (ERP) systems by vendors like SAP and Oracle.

One paper's (Grabski et al. 2011) view on the current state of ERP systems is:

> ERP is now pervasive in large firms and has a quickly growing presence in small and midsized enterprises SMEs. ERP adoption in industry continues to evolve and expand. Installations are becoming increasingly complex through upgrades, expanded functionality, tighter integration with legacy systems, extensions by integrating new applications, and increased interorganizational reach. ERP systems are now available as Software as a Service SaaS....

The SaaS reference means, in effect, Cloud-based. And this availability of systems on a renta-as-needed basis will continue and will be of great interest to SMEs who had, until this era, been simply prevented by price from using anything other than a home grown ERP system.

One of the earliest players in the open source "complete solution" market was Jaspersoft. They package up some of the building blocks we have already discussed; Hadoop, Hive, Pig, Sqoop, but also provide open source Business Intelligence to sit on top of that stack. In 2012 they announced a 22 % growth in their open source community. Solutions like this may bring performance dashboard business intelligence to SMEs. Interestingly one of Jaspersoft's declared investors is SAP Ventures!

12.5.2 Ethics of Big Data

Does it matter if the owners of the sentiments being analysed in sentiment analysis on Twitter do not know they are being analysed? There are many other ethical dilemmas that are beginning to be noticed as the Big Data trend continues to expand.

There are fundamental differences in approach to handling data. Attitudes are likely to differ across generations, for example. In a paper entitled "Generational views of information privacy" Regan et al. (2013) conclude that:

> ... we see interesting patterns in these analyses that indicate that there may indeed be generational differences and patterns in some attitudes towards privacy.

Digital Natives (people born in developed nations since 1980) will know no other environment than one which is rich with ICT. When they use online applications they are far less likely to worry about the use to which information they provide might be put than someone who is older. In addition to differences in attitude based upon age and gender, organisations will have different approaches. Those dealing with national security data, like the military, are more likely to have a cautious culture than broadcasters. Other factors in attitude to data privacy include nationality and social class.

So, back to the original question: Does the author of this book have the right to know what you did last night? If I came up to you in the street and asked you, you would doubtless tell be to get lost! And yet, if you tweeted *"Lovely meal at Zinni's with George"* I could easily find out what you were doing by using the Twitter API as we demonstrated in Chap. 11. Is that you being careless? Or am I being unethical?

Another ethical issue is that some people do not have access to Big Data and that will create digital divides. This limited access could be because of broadband availability. After all, most of what we have talked about when discussing Big Data has been around moving large volumes of data around easily. No-one would expect to do Big Data with a 56 kbit Modem.

In a recent Pew Research Centre report (2013) they identified that for US adults:

> The demographic factors most correlated with home broadband adoption continue to be educational attainment, age, and household income. Almost nine in ten college graduates have high-speed internet at home, compared with just 37 % of adults who have not completed high school. Similarly, adults under age 50 are more likely than older adults to have broadband at home, and those living in households earning at least $50,000 per year are more likely to have home broadband than those at lower income levels.

So it is clear that there is a digital divide, even within one of the most advanced nations in the world. Now expand beyond the US. A recent UNESCO report *"The State of BroadBand 2013: Universalizing BroadBand"* (http://www.broadbandcommission.org/Documents/bb-annualreport2013.pdf) said that: By the end of 2013, some 2.7 billion people will be online, equivalent to a global penetration rate of 39 %.

Globally then there clearly is a big divide between those who can and can't access Big Data. This, and other ethical issues are difficult questions and they will need to begin to be addressed in the near future.

12.5.3 Big Data and Business Intelligence

Earlier in this book we have spoken about both Business Intelligence and Big Data as if they were different. Certainly BI has been around for a good many years. SAS is one of the biggest vendors in terms of BI and they have been in business since the 1970s. At the time of writing their website is distinctly less vocal about Big Data than some other vendors. It isn't that they don't think Big Data isn't important – indeed they do say that it is – but rather that it is merely a part of the business intelligence and analytic process that many organisations are already carrying out. They tell us that their tools cope with the extra data volume and speed of change that come with Big Data sources.

(See http://www.sas.com/)

This is a sensible, pragmatic view. Jaspersoft too has a similar approach. As we said before, Big Data isn't really anything new in concept. It is possible, therefore, that when the term Big Data goes out of fashion (which it will do eventually) it will merely be subsumed by the term business analytics or business intelligence.

12.5.4 The Future for Data Scientists

The future for the term "Big Data" may be unsure, but that organisations will continue to need to analyse all the data they have available to them is a certainty. The role of Data Scientist, as discussed in Chap. 5, then is set to become much more prominent. As the Harvard Business Review (2012) said in their article headline:

Data Scientist: The Sexiest Job of the 21st Century

There have been several reports (including McKinsey 2011, Her majesty's Government 2013) suggesting that there is a shortage of data scientists already, and that this shortage will get much worse in the next few years. As organisations wake up to the potential benefits of Big Data and realise they have a skills gap which prevents them from taking advantage of those benefits, demand will simply outstrip demand.

A visit to the IT Jobs watch site (http://www.itjobswatch.co.uk/jobs/london/data%20scientist.do) shows what is happening in the UK market. Figure 12.4 show a very rapid increase in the demand for Data Scientist over the year of 2013. The sorts of skills being looked for are shown in Fig. 12.5. These graphs were as at 12/12/2013.

There can be little doubt based on this evidence that Data Scientists will continue to be in especial demand over the next few years, and that the shortage of such people will also mean that their salaries will rise. For SMEs this may cause a longer term problem in that only the richer companies will be able to afford appropriately skilled specialists. This will probably lead to a market for consultant Data Scientists and for Cloud-based analytical services to fill that gap.

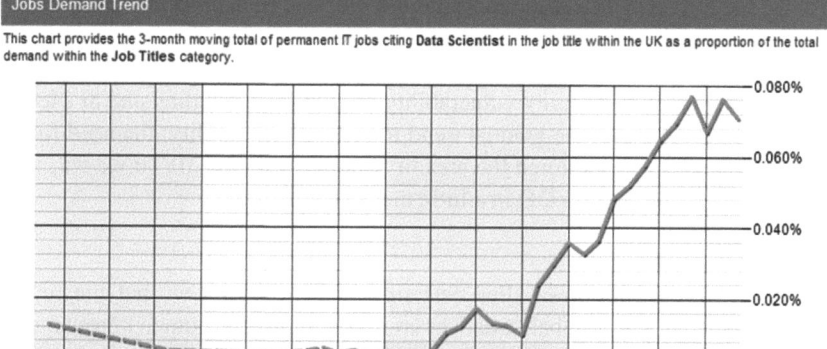

Fig. 12.4 Demand for data scientists

Data Scientist
Top 30 Related IT Skills

For the 6 months to 12 December 2013, IT jobs within the UK that cited Data Scientist in their job title mentioned the following IT skills in order of popularity. The figures indicate the number of jobs and their proportion against the total number of IT job ads sampled with Data Scientist in their job title.

#	Count (%)	Skill	#	Count (%)	Skill
1	88 (57.89%)	Statistics	16	39 (25.66%)	SPSS
2	86 (56.58%)	R	17	35 (23.03%)	Predictive Modelling
3	83 (54.61%)	Big Data	18	33 (21.71%)	Data Analysis
4	75 (49.34%)	Analytics	18	33 (21.71%)	Machine Learning
5	73 (48.03%)	Data Mining	19	31 (20.39%)	Degree
6	71 (46.71%)	Hadoop	20	29 (19.08%)	MapReduce
7	69 (45.39%)	SQL	21	27 (17.76%)	C++
8	68 (44.74%)	Mathematics	22	26 (17.11%)	Data Modelling
9	65 (42.76%)	Python	23	25 (16.45%)	Visualisation
10	50 (32.89%)	SAS	23	25 (16.45%)	Relational Database
11	48 (31.58%)	MATLAB	24	23 (15.13%)	Marketing
12	47 (30.92%)	Computer Science	24	23 (15.13%)	Statistical Analysis
13	44 (28.95%)	Java	25	22 (14.47%)	Business Intelligence
14	41 (26.97%)	PhD	25	22 (14.47%)	NoSQL
15	40 (26.32%)	Apache Hive	26	21 (13.82%)	Apache Pig

Fig. 12.5 Data scientists skills

12.5.5 The Future for IS Management

We have looked at the future for Information Systems both broadly, and with particular emphasis on Big Data. Finally we should explore the future for the processes of planning, designing, development and acquisition of systems used to provide information – how will IS management need to change?

As we see it the key IS-related technologies we need to plan for in the current to short-term future are Cloud, Big Data and Mobile computing. As always there are decision changing influences around too: the trend towards "Bring Your Own Devices"; the perceived security vulnerability of mobile computing, and to a lesser degree Cloud computing; the gradual trend towards IT as a utility; the need for IT to become Greener. We explored the area of Security in Chap. 10, so we will here explore Green issues and BYOD in a little more detail.

12.5.5.1 Green Agenda

Greener IT, also sometimes called Sustainable IT, is not new, but the recent inter-governmentally led global initiatives around reducing the human impact on the environment have helped bring it back up to the top of the agenda. The Carbonfund website (http://www.carbonfund.org/reduce) tells us that:

12.5 So What Will Happen in the Future?

With the world's growing reliance on the Internet, the office is becoming a major driver of climate change. The energy required to power all the world's computers, data storage, and communications networks is expected to double by 2020.

The Schmidt et al. (2009) paper called Sustainable Information Systems Management, explains the scale of the problem that faces IT/IS in terms of the need to be socially acceptable:

> The current discussion about "Green IT" has brought back the ecological impact of IT into the public and academic focus. IT service providers, such as Google, whose 450 000 operating servers consume approximately 800 gigawatt hours electricity per year, account for tremendous amounts of indirect CO_2 emissions (Chou 2008, p. 93). The energy consumption of all servers worldwide approximately equates to the consumption of the entire Polish economy (Koomey 2007).

IS vendors, whilst obviously committed to make IT greener for its own sake, also see that the public perception of their green credentials will be an important factor in any decision-making process. Note, for example, a Microsoft Webpage which tells of the work they have done with the Carbon Trust to lessen their carbon footprint year on year. Oracle also have Green pages on their website: http://www.oracle.com/us/solutions/green/overview/index.html on which they proudly announce that they have reduced electricity usage at their HQ by 28 % since 2000.

To a degree the obvious place to look for ways of lessening a company's IT/IS generated carbon footprint is at the big power consumers – the servers sitting in air-conditioned server-rooms. And naturally manufacturers see this as an opportunity. The recently released HP Moonshot Servers make much of their efficiencies. Part of the sales pitch on their website (http://h17007.www1.hp.com/uk/en/enterprise/servers/products/moonshot/index.aspx#.UqmjNPRdUwA) is this observation:

> If the public cloud were a country, it would rank fifth in electricity consumption. Reducing that number by even 50 % would save the equivalent of the electricity consumption of the United Kingdom.

But server power usage is only part of the problem:

- Every time you read something from a HDD you expend energy, not to mention reduce its life expectancy. Applications can often be written with inefficient SQL queries which cause the HDD to spin-up needlessly.
- A laptop is more efficient than a desktop and monitor.
- When you leave your laptop on standby instead of turning it off you waste energy

So there are many issues for the managers of IS systems to consider. In the UK the government has recently announced that companies which are quoted on the stock exchange will be required to report their annual greenhouse gas (GHG) emissions. The costs that are examined when planning for internal IT expansion of any kind will now have to be more that merely financial; decisions about whether the benefit of the new system outweighs the increase of carbon emissions will be needed.

12.5.5.2 Bring Your Own Device (BYOD) and Mobile Computing

A mere 10 years ago the idea of allowing your employees to use their own computing devices for business would have been laughed at by many a CIO. Proper, business-focused computing was something that needed IT professionals to look after. Home computing was for hobbyists or for IT geeks who liked playing with new technologies that their employers didn't allow them to have.

Yet now things are different. Many employees have a more powerful computer at home than they have at work, and many more have their own mobile computing devices such as smartphones and tablets. This computer literate generation expects to be able to use their devices for every computing need, including work-related. Reports should be available whenever, and wherever, they are, and if the report required doesn't exist they want to be able to generate it even if they are on the 8:22 train into work.

A press release about a recent Broadband Commission (part of UNESCO) report (Broadband Commission 2013) tells us:

> ...that mobile broadband subscriptions, which allow users to access the web via smartphones, tablets and WiFi-connected laptops, are growing at a rate of 30 % per year. By the end of 2013 there will be more than three times as many mobile broadband connections as there are conventional fixed broadband subscriptions.
> http://www.itu.int/net/pressoffice/press_releases/2013/36.aspx#.UqNWuPRdUwA

For the IS department planning to meet business needs has suddenly become even more complex as expectations change from an era when users were pleased with whatever computer they got, to one where users expect up-to-date computing that provides instant answers anywhere.

One solution to this problem may be the BYOD solution: rather than imposing a centralised computer purchasing policy, allow users to choose, and maybe even buy for themselves, their own devices. Help will need to be provided for those less competent users, but the IT department is relieved of a need to select and purchase products. Instead the focus becomes one of integration as the number of different devices needing to gain access to IS systems increases.

The complexity issue is underlined by the details of a US survey by Juniper Networks (Juniper Networks Company Press Release 2012) some of their findings will be rather worrying for CIOs:

> Mobile users worldwide own an average of three Internet-connected devices, while nearly one in five people (18 percent) own five or more devices.
>
> Three-quarters (76 percent) of mobile users access their banking or personal medical information while on the go, while 89 percent of respondents who use their personal devices for business purposes, say they access sensitive work information.
>
> Further, the trend toward a "bring your own device" (BYOD) enterprise is creating new concerns for IT leaders, with nearly half of all respondents using their personal device for work (41 percent) without permission from their company

It would be a mistake to think of BYOD as being a guaranteed way of cutting an IT budget. Total Cost of Ownership needs to cover all the extra support, security and networking infrastructure a company may need to spend on to support the variety of new devices the users are bringing in. On top of this an organisation-wide purchase of large volumes of one type of device will usually result in greatly reduced per-item costs, and that discount for volume advantage disappears if devices are bought individually.

Security is often seen as the biggest worry with mobile computing. As a CIO you can ensure you are meeting your data protection obligations far more easily than if people begin to store company data on their own devices. They may have to resort to local data storage if they are moving in and out of communications for example. What if that data is on an iPad that is stolen? Because it is the individual's property it is difficult to ensure that they have followed whatever security procedures and protocols you have defined. We discuss mobile security in more detail in Chap. 10.

There are also legal issues to worry a CIO. Take the simple case of the often automatic scan on company-owned equipment for illegal material such as pornography. If you are found with such material on a works PC you will almost certainly be required to be present at a disciplinary hearing, if not actually be fired. The key thing is, this is work's property so they have a right (and an obligation) to know it is being used appropriately. Do they have a similar right with your device? And what about a device, like an iPad, that may have a mix of work and private material on it? These are new areas without clear answers, and will need addressing in the near future.

Mobile computing will undoubtedly continue to expand. The constraints of a desk-bound computer will be a thing of the past, except for the specialist needing to provide server-based systems. Cloud computing can allow ubiquitous access to systems and this is fuelling the rush to mobile computing. Whether BYOD will become the norm is another matter. To a degree it will depend on the type of industry concerned.

12.5.6 Keeping Your Eye on the Game

BYOD is just an example of a recent trend in the computing arena. The all round CIO will continuously scan the technology horizon to keep abreast of these trends, seeing if any may be of use to their organisation. There will be sleepy or blinkered CIOs who fail to keep up. The blinkers are often as a result of adequate IT performance at some point in the near past. Problematic IT systems are more likely to force the examination of alternatives and change. If your users were happy last year, then there is a trap that says we just keep doing more of the same. This is a fatal trap as user, technology and business needs always change.

So how does one keep up to date? One excellent means is reading specialist articles, either online or from journals. Look to the experts to provide and overview and then point you in the right direction to get more details if the development is of interest. Gartner are world-renowned experts in IT, for example. This link points to a press release of theirs listing the Top 10 Strategic Technology Trends for 2014: http://www.gartner.com/newsroom/id/2603623#!

"Following" on social sites like facebook, twitter or LinkedIn can lead to useful information. This author follows Wired.com, for example. As a result I got to find out about Facebook engaging a Deep Learning guru. All new stuff to me. It may be of no ultimate use but the important thing is that I now know about it as a result of my practice of constantly scanning.

> With deep learning, Facebook could automatically identify faces in the photographs you upload, automatically tag them with the right names, and instantly share them with friends and family who might enjoy them too. Using similar techniques to analyze your daily activity on the site, it could automatically show you more stuff you wanna see.
> (Metz, Cade 2013) http://www.wired.com/wiredenterprise/2013/12/facebook-yann-lecun-qa/?cid=co15703974

Conferences are a good way of keeping abreast and often have the added advantage of talks from users of the products, rather than the bias you may pick up from the vendors. Even watching TV can help. The BBC has a programme called Click (http://www.bbc.co.uk/programmes/b006m9ry) which, in nice bite-sized chunk, keeps us up to date with happenings in the digital world.

The important thing to recognise is that it is part of your job as an IT Professional to keep your eyes open for new developments which might be valuable to your organisation. The beauty of being an IT professional is that the new technology may well be exciting as well, and therefore provide you with the opportunity to play whilst doing good for your employers!

12.6 Summary

In this chapter we discussed how difficult it is to predict future developments in the IT arena, but emphasised the need, nonetheless, to keep abreast of the latest trends and tools. We saw that Hadoop and MapReduce are probably here for the long run now and that the shortfall in appropriately skilled Data Scientists will impact on organisation's abilities to make the most of Big Data. This shortfall is also likely to drive the move toward more friendly interfaces for the current Big Data tools.

12.7 Review Questions

The answers to these questions can be found in the text of this chapter.

- Describe five influences upon the decision making process when a company begins to think about updating technology
- What may eventually make Moore's law incorrect?
- What is SAP Hana an example of?

- In what ways can an organisation's IT systems affect its Carbon Footprint?
- Describe some of the issues surrounding allowing your employees to use their own technology.

12.8 Group Work Research Activities

These activities require you to research beyond the contents of the book and can be tackled individually or as a discussion group.

12.8.1 Discussion Topic 1

Review the article from Gartner referenced above called "Gartner Identifies the Top 10 Strategic Technology Trends for 2014". If you are reading this after 2014, look for a similar page referring to next year.

Now pick one of the 10 trends and do some more research on it. How might it be useful for business? Is it of use to only certain types of business? Put together a Strengths and Weaknesses list for this trend from the perspective of a CIO in a large corporation.

12.8.2 Discussion Topic 2

In the text we ask: *Are organisations' IS decisions driven by changes in technology or by business need*? What are your views about which drivers are the most important? The answer will probably depend upon the sort of business you are envisaging when you think about the problem. Can you go on to discuss what differences there may be in the answer to this question for each of a Small, a Medium and a Large company?

References

Alvesson M (2001) Understanding organizational culture. Sage Publications, Thousand Oaks
Broadband Commission (2013) The state of broadband 2013: universalizing broadband. Broadband Commission, Geneva
Buhl HU et al (2012) Where's the competitive advantage in strategic information systems research? Making the case for boundary-spanning research based on the German business and information systems engineering tradition. J Strateg Inf Syst 21(2):172–178
Clarke Q (2013) Announcing windows azure HDInsight: where big data meets the cloud. [online]. Last accessed 2 Dec 2013 at: http://blogs.technet.com/b/microsoft_blog/archive/2013/10/28/announcing-windows-azure-hdinsight-where-big-data-meets-the-cloud.aspx
Ferrera P et al (2012) Tuple MapReduce: beyond classic MapReduce. In: Data Mining (ICDM), 2012 IEEE 12th international conference on, pp 260–269

Galliers RD (2011) Further developments in information systems strategizing: unpacking the concept. In: Galliers RD, Currie W (eds) The Oxford handbook of management information systems: critical perspectives and new directions. Oxford University Press, Oxford, pp 229–245

Grabski S, Leech S, Schmidt P (2011) A review of ERP research: a future agenda for accounting information systems. J Inf Syst 25(1):37–78

Hamilton A (1949) Brains that click. Popular Mechanics, March 1949, pp 162–258 Published by Hearst Magazines

Her Majesty's Government (2013) Seizing the data opportunity: a strategy for UK data capability. HM Government, London. Crown Copyright. Available at https://www.gov.uk/government/uploads/system/uploads/attachment_data/file/254136/bis-13-1250-strategy-for-uk-data-capability-v4.pdf. Accessed 1 Oct 2014

Juniper Networks Company Press Release (2012) Global survey reveals mobile technology adoption at risk if consumer trust not addressed. [online]. Last accessed 12 Dec 2013 at: http://newsroom.juniper.net/press-releases/global-survey-reveals-mobile-technology-adoption-a-nyse-jnpr-0884830

Mandl D (2013) Big data: why it's not always that big nor even that clever. [online]. Last accessed 29 Nov 2013 at: http://www.theregister.co.uk/2013/02/13/big_data_not_clever/

Manyika J et al (2011) Big data: the next frontier for innovation, competition, and productivity. McKinsey & Company, New York

Metz C (2013) Facebook's 'Deep learning' guru reveals the future of AI. [online]. Last accessed 12 Dec 2013 at: http://www.wired.com/wiredenterprise/2013/12/facebook-yann-lecun-qa/?cid=co15703974

Oracle Manual (2013a) Oracle SQL connector for hadoop distributed file system. [online]. Last accessed 06 Dec 2013 at: http://docs.oracle.com/cd/E37231_01/doc.20/e36961/sqlch.htm

Oracle Manual (2013b) Oracle loader for hadoop. [online]. Last accessed 6 Dec 2013 at: http://docs.oracle.com/cd/E27101_01/doc.10/e27365/olh.htm

Paul I (2013) The end of Moore's law is on the horizon, says AMD. [online]. Last accessed 6 Dec 2013 at: http://www.pcworld.com/article/2032913/the-end-of-moores-law-is-on-the-horizon-says-amd.html

Pelz-Sharpe A (2013) SOD big data! most of what you're keeping is digital landfill. [online]. Last accessed 2 Dec 2013 at: http://www.channelregister.co.uk/2013/03/11/alan_pelz_sharpe_big_data/

Regan PM, Fitzgerald G, Balint P (2013) Generational views of information privacy? Routledge. Innov Eur J Soc Sci Res 26(1–2):81

Schmidt N-H et al (2009) Sustainable information systems management. Bus Inf Syst Eng 1(5):400–402

Teubner R (2013) Information systems strategy. Bus Inf Syst Eng 5(4):243–257

Tynan D (2009) Six great tech ideas that failed to take off. [online]. Last accessed 3 Dec 2013 at: http://www.pcadvisor.co.uk/news/tech-industry/3205635/six-great-tech-ideas-that-failed-to-take-off/

Unknown (2013) Incorrect predictions. [online]. Last accessed 29 Nov 2013 at: http://en.wikiquote.org/wiki/Incorrect_predictions

Zickuhr K, Smith A (2013) Broadband adoption in the US. Pew Research, Pew Research Center's Internet & American Life Project, Washington, US

Index

A
A/B testing, 24
Access, 170, 177, 178, 216, 233
ACID model, 174
Acquiring data, 193
Adhocracy, 60, 63, 67
Air gap, 228, 229
Aligning IT/IS strategy, 12, 20, 47
Amazon, 65, 68, 74, 142, 179, 188, 212, 276
Anarchy, 67
Anonymous, 224
Anti-Virus, 229
Applications Portfolio Management, 48
Architectural landscape, 165
Availability, 139–141, 169, 177, 179, 215
Availability heuristic, 139, 141

B
Bias, 139
Big Bang approach, 157
Big data, 1–3, 6, 11, 12, 14, 20, 22, 24, 29, 32, 38, 54, 65, 68, 69, 74, 78, 81, 100, 103, 105, 108, 109, 120, 121, 125, 126, 135, 137, 144, 147, 149, 152, 158, 159, 164–166, 169, 182–189, 191, 193–195, 197, 201, 202, 204, 205, 210, 212, 216, 235, 239, 242, 258, 267–269, 273–275, 278–282, 286
Big data adoption, 54
Big data lifecycle, 20, 23, 25
Bring your own device (BYOD), 282, 284, 285
Business Analyst, 104, 120
Business environment, 13, 21, 23, 26, 27, 29, 38, 51, 57, 83, 89, 91
Business Intelligence (BI), 104, 120, 164, 185, 279, 280
Business processes, 10, 38, 61
Business process management, 38
Business process re-engineering, 38, 61, 99

C
Cassandra, 15, 121, 170, 190, 262
Causality, 7, 108, 125, 126, 133, 134, 136, 144
Change management, 110, 148
Chief Executive Officer (CEO), 53, 56, 64, 71, 75, 77, 97–99, 111, 112, 115, 136, 137, 161, 187
Chief Information Officer (CIO), 148, 184, 272
Citizen science projects, 211
Cloud, 4, 15, 139, 147, 158, 163–165, 169, 171, 179, 187, 188, 190, 210, 212, 220, 222, 223, 226, 273, 275, 276, 279, 281–283, 285
Cloudera, 241, 276
Cluster analysis, 24
Codify, 55, 61
Column-based databases, 176
Competitive advantage, 12, 23, 33, 36–38, 43, 48, 50, 149, 160, 163, 268, 269
Competitive environment, 272
Complex systems, 22
Computing, 150, 267
Control systems, 73, 76
Coordination, 57
Correlation, 6–8, 14, 63, 108, 125, 126, 133–136, 142, 144
Cost-benefit analysis, 160
Cost leadership, 44
Crowdsourcing, 15, 25, 40, 45, 64, 95, 210–213
CRUD, 172, 190

Cryptography, 126
"Cultural Web", 71
Culture, 20, 27, 53, 56, 69–71, 73–75, 78, 79, 81, 96, 97–99, 103, 110, 130, 148, 156, 216, 279
Customer Relationship Management, 23, 34

D
Dashboard systems, 183
Data, 1–3, 5, 7, 14, 20, 24, 25, 28–30, 36, 38, 54, 69, 74, 78, 81, 86, 90, 95, 96, 98, 103–105, 108, 109, 120–122, 126, 137, 149, 164, 165, 170, 175, 176, 179–182, 184, 189, 193–196, 198, 202, 204–206, 209, 210, 216, 221–223, 230, 231, 235, 236, 243, 259, 262, 268, 272, 275, 278, 280, 281, 286
Data analysts, 175
Database(s), 3, 4, 15, 23, 96, 110, 120, 170–173, 176, 180, 183, 184, 186, 190, 194, 196, 197, 199, 201, 203, 215, 250, 262, 277, 278
Database Administrator's (DBA), 169, 172, 177–180, 234
Database management Systems, 170
Data compression, 5
Data Controller, 236
Data Engineer, 121
Data, Information, Knowledge and Wisdom (DIKW) Hierarchy, 127, 128
Data literacy, 81, 86, 90
Data migration, 179
Data mining, 24
Data ownership, 209
Data Protection, 221, 223
Data Quality, 202, 206
Data Science team, 109
Data scientists, 14, 25, 81, 96, 104, 108, 109, 121, 164, 184, 210, 281, 286
Data Sources, 8, 33, 164, 165, 176, 193, 197, 198, 201, 204
Data storage, 3, 170
Data Subject, 222
Data-types, 198, 199
Data validation, 203
Data warehouses, 176
Data warehousing, 205
Decision-making, 81, 85, 86, 93, 94
Decision Science, 25
Decision Support Systems, 175
Denial of service attack, 224, 225

Denial of Service Defence Mechanisms, 226
Differentiation, 44
Digital divide, 280
Digital native, 273
Direct supervision, 57
Disaster recovery, 172, 215
Distributed DBMS, 171
Distributed systems, 171
Document-based databases, 176, 190
Domain knowledge, 81, 86, 91, 92, 97

E
Edward Snowden, 16, 216, 236
Electronic Communications Privacy Act (ECPA), 220, 221
Electronic Data Interchange, 180, 272
Emotional Intelligence, 132
Enterprise resource planning (ERP), 13, 23, 38, 41, 58, 59, 61–66, 78, 159, 160, 185, 197, 198, 213, 279
Environmental audit, 27
Ethical Hacking, 219, 236
Ethics, 9, 16, 215, 218–220
European Court of Justice, 9
Executive Information Systems, 183
Extensible Mark-up Language (XML), 180, 200, 201, 212
Extract, Transform and Load (ETL), 205

F
Federalism, 67, 68
Feudalism, 67, 68
Field Level checking, 203
Finance Director, 148, 149, 158
Firewall, 230
Five-force framework, 30
Focus, 44, 76, 132
Form Level checking, 203
Four Ds, 81, 83, 86, 90
Functional silos, 23, 59, 61, 63
Functions of management, 54, 57, 100
Fuzzy Logic, 204

G
Google, 6, 7, 9, 11, 17, 36, 56, 65, 68, 71, 74–79, 103, 104, 121, 142, 179, 188, 189, 220, 221, 283
Governance, 16, 218
Green agenda, 282

Index

H
Hacking, 224
Hadoop, 15, 120, 121, 159, 169, 170, 184, 186, 189, 191, 201, 205, 239–243, 245, 246, 248, 249, 251–253, 256, 259, 261–264, 267, 273–277, 279, 286
Hadoop Distributed File System (HDFS), 189, 246, 277
HANA, 177, 278
HCatalog, 247, 251, 253, 255
Heuristics, 14, 138, 140, 142, 144
Hierarchical charts, 56
Hierarchy, 36, 55–57, 59, 61, 64, 65, 67, 70, 72, 73, 84, 87, 95–99, 120, 127, 128
High-performance teams, 113, 117
Hindsight bias, 142
Hive, 243, 247–250, 255, 256, 259, 263–265, 276, 277, 279
HiveQL, 248, 250
Hortonworks, 241–243, 256, 259, 262, 276
HUE, 243
Human Resource Information System, 23
Hybrid Manager, 104
Hype Cycle, 9, 10

I
IBM, 3, 5, 6, 105, 159, 162, 166, 174, 185, 187, 202
Information politics, 53, 66
Information Systems (IS) Strategy, 148
Injection, 232
In Memory systems, 176
Insourcing, 161, 162
Internet of Things, 206

J
JavaScript Object Notation (JSON), 180, 201
Judgement, 125, 130, 138–140, 143, 144, 150, 156

K
Key-value databases, 173
Knowledge, Skills and Attitudes, 117–119
Kodak, 162

L
Leadership, 13, 44, 45, 68–70, 75, 81–83, 87, 95, 98–99, 113, 116, 142, 149, 150
Legacy Systems, 273

LinkedIn, 65, 68, 74, 91, 97, 103, 104, 109, 120, 121, 186, 204, 286
Linux, 159, 183, 184, 186, 230, 240–243, 245, 246, 276
Loaded, 176, 205

M
Machine Bureaucracy, 58, 59, 67
Machine-Learning Statistician, 121
Malware, 216, 227
Management, 13, 15, 23, 40, 51, 59, 62, 82, 84, 88, 93, 99, 110, 147, 149, 150, 153, 156, 170, 172, 185, 235, 240, 275, 282, 283
Management by Objective (MBO), 94
Management Information Systems (MIS), 23, 59
Management styles, 11, 13, 70, 82, 87, 89
Manufacturing resource planning (MRP), 61
MapReduce, 3, 121, 189, 245, 246, 248, 263, 267, 277, 286
Meta data, 206
Microsoft, 3, 6, 32, 61, 159, 174, 177, 185, 187, 188, 234, 275, 283
Mission statement, 21
Mobile computing, 282, 284, 285
Monarchy, 67, 68
MongoDB, 15, 170, 190, 262
Monte Carlo simulations, 29, 95
Moore's Law, 5, 277, 286

N
Networking, 85, 182
NoSQL, 3, 15, 120, 176, 186, 189, 190, 199, 239, 262, 263

O
ODBC driver, 256, 259
Online Transactional Processing (OLTP), 173–176, 185, 190, 198, 205, 262, 276
Open Source, 158–160, 183, 184, 186–191
Oracle, 2, 3, 6, 61, 63, 159, 160, 170, 173, 174, 177, 178, 180, 184–187, 189–191, 194, 197–199, 201, 233, 234, 240, 241, 250, 274–279, 283
Organisational culture, 13, 27, 53, 54, 56, 69, 71, 72, 74, 78, 98, 103, 272
Organisational structure, 11, 13, 53, 54, 56, 61, 64, 66, 67, 73, 75, 78, 97, 99, 117
Organisation charts, 56, 57, 69, 87

Outsourcing, 161, 162
Owner/manager, 55

P
Paradigm, 71–73, 78, 79
Patching, 229
Performance, 24, 39, 115, 169, 177, 178, 188
Performance management, 24
Personal Data, 222
PESTEL, 19, 27, 28, 51
Phishing, 223, 230, 232
Physical architectures, 170
Pig, 243, 247, 251–255, 263–265, 276, 279
Point of Sales, 198
Power structures, 72, 75
Predictive modelling, 24
Privacy, 218, 220, 222
Probabilities, 93, 95, 137, 139, 141
Probability of events, 141
Professional Bureaucracy, 59, 60, 67
Project failures, 15, 149, 150
Project managers, 158
Prototyping techniques, 152

R
Randomness, 135
Record keeping, 55
Relational Database Management System (RDBMS), 15, 169, 170, 173, 174, 176, 194, 204, 212, 233, 240, 262, 275, 276
Relational Databases, 170, 189
Requirements analysis, 147, 151
Requirements creep, 153
Resource Description Framework, 208
Right to be forgotten, 9
Risk analysis, 29
Risk hierarchy, 30
Rituals and Routines, 73, 76
Role(s), 13, 53, 55–57, 61, 66, 75, 81, 83–85, 87, 89, 93, 100, 103, 109, 111, 112, 116, 118–120, 125, 148, 154, 164
Role-holders, 56
Roll-back, 174, 175
70-20-10 rule, 76
Rules of behaviour, 114, 122
Rules, procedures and policies, 55, 59

S
SaaS, 279
Sample size, 8, 137, 141

Sandbox, 240–242, 244, 263
SAP, 3, 6, 61, 62, 160, 164, 177, 185, 186, 191, 198, 272, 278, 279, 286
SAS, 164, 185, 280
Scalability, 169, 177
Scenario planning, 29, 53
Scientific method, 17, 106–108, 121
Securing data, 230
Securing systems, 224
Security, 11, 16, 177, 183, 215, 216, 218, 222, 224, 228, 234, 235, 282, 285
Sensitivity analysis, 29
Sentiment analysis, 25, 34, 40
Service Level Agreements, 148, 163, 188
9S-framework, 1, 11, 14, 16
Six-Sigma, 38, 58
Skills gap, 162, 164, 165, 281
Small-to-Middle sized companies (SMEs), 279
Social analytics, 25
Social network, 25
Soft Systems, 151
Software development life-cycle, 152
Spyware, 228, 229
SQL, 120, 173, 175, 178, 180, 184, 185, 189, 200, 232, 233, 239, 248–250, 255, 273, 276, 277, 283
SQL Server, 173, 178, 180, 184, 185, 276
Stakeholder(s), 20, 21, 23, 26, 48, 89, 139, 150–157, 164–166, 173, 186, 274
Stakeholder Analysis, 154
Stakeholder Buy-In, 154
Statistical thinking, 14, 90, 125, 126, 131, 144
Statistics, 28, 125
Storage, 4, 172
Stories, 73, 77
Strategic analysis, 12, 20, 47
Strategic direction, 12, 19, 20, 46, 47, 164
Strategic IS, 269
Strategic objectives, 22
Strategic position, 19, 21, 23, 38
Strategy implementation, 47, 147, 148
Structured Systems Analysis and Design, 152
Styles of management, 86
Supply Chain Management, 23
Sustainable IT, 282
SWOT 'Analysis', 38
Symbols, 13, 72, 74, 127, 234
System, 1, 2, 129–133, 135–137, 140, 142–144
Systems Development Life-Cycle, 152

Index

T

Tableau, 256, 258, 259, 262, 263
Team , 6, 37, 49, 64, 67, 70–73, 75, 84, 91, 94, 97–99, 103, 109, 111–122, 137, 141, 152–155, 157, 159, 164, 165, 173, 180, 186, 187, 196, 204, 206, 209, 219, 220
Team building, 117
Technocratic utopianism, 66
Technostructure, 57–59, 66
Ten things we know to be true, 76
Textual analysis, 25
Three "Vs", 3
Total cost of ownership, 158
Total Quality Management, 38, 58, 99
Transactional data, 23, 24, 33, 34, 38
Transformed, 205
Trojan Horses, 16, 227
Tuning SQL, 178
Twitter, 4, 24, 29, 40, 74, 108, 184, 195, 201, 204, 210, 269, 278–280

U

Uncertainty, 22, 29, 89, 94, 95, 108, 131, 135, 165, 268
Undo, 174
Unified Modelling Language, 151
User, 24, 31, 33, 38, 76, 99, 152, 153, 155, 156, 158, 160, 165, 170, 174, 176, 178, 183, 189, 198, 199, 203, 210, 211, 220, 225, 227, 230–234, 241, 243, 245, 247, 248, 252–256, 263, 264, 276, 285

V

Value Chain, 19, 32, 36, 37
Value Disciplines, 45, 51
Value system, 38
Variety, 3, 12, 20, 23, 33, 164, 195, 210
Velocity, 3, 12, 20, 23, 33, 164, 195
Veracity, 164, 195
Virtual Machine, 240, 242, 245
Viruses, 227
Vision, 20, 21, 74, 83, 87, 100, 128, 147, 149, 165
Visualization, 258, 259
Volume, 3, 12, 20, 23, 33, 164, 169, 194, 278

W

Worms, 227

Y

Yahoo, 65, 70, 103, 105, 184, 189

If you have any concerns about our products,
you can contact us on
ProductSafety@springernature.com

In case Publisher is established outside the EU,
the EU authorized representative is:
**Springer Nature Customer Service Center GmbH
Europaplatz 3, 69115 Heidelberg, Germany**

Printed by Libri Plureos GmbH
in Hamburg, Germany